IMPACT OF TOXICOLOGY ON FOOD PROCESSING

ift BASIC SYMPOSIUM SERIES

Edited By
INSTITUTE OF FOOD TECHNOLOGISTS
221 N. LaSalle St.
Chicago, Illinois

Other Books in this Series

FOOD PROTEINS
Whitaker and Tannenbaum

POSTHARVEST BIOLOGY
AND BIOTECHNOLOGY
Hultin and Milner

Other IFT-AVI Books

CARBOHYDRATES AND HEALTH
Hood, Wardrip and Bollenback

EVALUATION OF
PROTEINS FOR HUMANS
Bodwell

IMPACT OF TOXICOLOGY ON FOOD PROCESSING

Edited by

John C. Ayres, Ph.D.

D. W. Brooks Professor
Food Science Department
University of Georgia

John C. Kirschman, Ph.D.

Central Research Department
General Foods Corporation
White Plains, N.Y.

avi

AVI PUBLISHING COMPANY, INC.
Westport, Connecticut

ISBN 87055-387-9

Printed in the United States of America by
The Saybrook Press, Inc.

Preface

This symposium on the Impact of Toxicology on Food Processing was the fourth in the series of basic symposia on a topic of major importance to food scientists and food technologists. The symposium, sponsored by the Institute of Food Technologists and the International Union of Food Science and Technology, was held June 6–7, 1980, immediately prior to the 40th Annual IFT Meeting. It was so planned to provide an up-to-the-minute status of food safety issues and to provide the framework for proceedings that would be of importance and of current interest to anyone involved in the development, production, packaging, and distribution of food products.

The symposium was organized into four sections, each presented in a half-day session. The first section defined terms, outlined parameters, and delineated what toxicology embraces, its impact on regulatory practices, the role that government agencies take in their function as regulators, the costs that such regulation engenders, the benefits derived, and finally some effects of food processing that result in the formation and destruction of toxic constituents in various commodities.

The second session dealt with a number of unwanted biological substances in foods, beginning with enzyme inhibitors and followed by plant produced cyanogenetic glycosides. Toxins of algal, fungal, and microbial origin were each discussed separately.

The second day was devoted to the consideration of chemical substances in foods and to factors that enhance food processing and preservation. In the morning, consumer responses such as hypersensitivity, flatus, and intolerance were evaluated, and the role of pesticides and of various condiments elucidated.

The last session was devoted to a discussion of the possible toxicity of certain vitamins, colors, processing aids, fillers, and irradiated foods, and an overview of regulatory and safety assessments that pertain to food packaging. A few summary remarks from Drs. Ayres and Kirschman concluded the program.

Planning and execution of this Basic Symposium has truly been an impressive joint effort on the part of scientists from industry, government, and academia. The important role of the Basic Symposium Committee—Dr. J.R. Whitaker, Dr. D. Ashton, Dr. G.E. Inglett, Dr. G.A. Leveille, Dr. J.M. McIntire, and Dr. O. Silberstein—is gratefully acknowledged.

The success of the fourth basic symposium was also the result of the expert assistance of Calvert L. Willey, Executive Director of IFT; John B. Klis, Director of Publications, and the IFT staff who helped provide publicity for the symposium, coordinated registration, and took care of the many details of arrangements for meeting rooms, hotel reservations, and numerous other details that go into a successful meeting.

John Klis also served as coordinator and Anna May Schenck, JFS Assistant Scientific Editor, as copy editor for publication of the manuscripts presented at the symposium and it is through their patience and persistence that this monograph has come to fruition.

Success of the Symposium is also due to the excellent cooperation of the many food companies who provided financial assistance as well as moral support. To these companies we are deeply indebted:

Archer Daniels Midland Co., Decatur, Ill.
Armour Food Co., Scottsdale, Ariz.
Beatrice Foods Co., Chicago, Ill.
Beatrice Foods Co., Special Products Div., Chicago, Ill.
Best Foods, CPC International, Englewood Cliffs, N.J.
Californian & Hawaiian Sugar Co., Crockett, Calif.
Campbell Soup Co., Camden, N.J.
Carnation Co., Van Nuys, Calif.
The Coca-Cola Co., Atlanta, Ga.
Curtice-Burns, Inc., Rochester, N.Y.
Del Monte Corp., Walnut Creek, Calif.
Durkee Foods, Cleveland, Ohio
The R. T. French Co., Rochester, N.Y.
General Foods Corp., White Plains, N.Y.
General Mills, Inc., Minneapolis, Minn.
Gerber Products Co., Fremont, Mich.
H.J. Heniz Co., Pittsburgh, Pa.
Hershey Foods Corp., Hershey, Pa.
Heublein, Inc., Hartford, Conn.
Hoffmann-LaRoche, Inc., Nutley, N.J.
Hunt-Wesson Foods, Inc., Fullteron, Calif.

ITT Continental Baking Co., Inc., Rye, N.Y.
Kraft, Inc., Glenview, Ill.
Land O'Lakes, Inc., Minneapolis, Minn.
Life Savers, Inc., New York, N.Y.
McCormick & Co., Inc., Hunt Valley, Md.
Mead Johnson, Evansville, Ind.
Nestle Enterprises Inc., White Plains, N.Y.
The Pillsbury Co., Minneapolis, Minn.
The Proctor and Gamble Co., Cincinnati, Ohio
The Quaker Oats Co., Barrington, Ill.
Roland Industries, St. Louis, Mo.
The Seven-Up Co., St. Louis, Mo.
Standard Brands, Stamford, Conn.
Stouffer Foods, Solon, Ohio
Sunkist Growers, Ontario, Calif.
Wm. Underwood Co., Westwood, Mass.
Universal Foods Corp., Milwaukee, Wisc.

Indeed, the seed of the idea of an annual basic symposium planted in the fall of 1974 has survived the winters of uncertainty and doubt and has sprung forth once again to bear fruit . . . making a worthwhile contribution to our knowledge of food science and technology.

JOHN C. AYRES
Food Science Department,
University of Georgia,
Athens, Georgia

JOHN C. KIRSCHMAN
Central Research Department,
General Foods Corporation,
White Plains, New York

December, 1980

Contributors

AYRES, JOHN C., Ph.D., D.W. Brooks Professor, Food Science Department, University of Georgia, Athens

BEEREBOOM, JOHN J., Ph.D., Manager, Food Chemicals R&D, Central Research, Pfizer Inc., Eastern Point Road, Groton, Conn.

CHICHESTER, C.O., Ph.D., Vice President, The Nutrition Foundation, Inc., 489 Fifth Avenue, New York, N.Y.

CONN, ERIC E., Ph.D., Professor, Department of Biochemistry and Biophysics, University of California, Davis

DANIEL, J.W., Ph.D., D.Sc., Life Science Research, Stock, Essex, England

DIEHL, J.F., Ph.D., Director and Professor, Federal Research Center for Nutrition, Karlsruhe, West Germany

DIENER, URBAN L., Ph.D., Professor, Department of Botany, Plant Pathology and Microbiology, Agricultural Experiment Station, Auburn University, Alabama

EMMERSON, JOHN L., Ph.D., Director, Toxicology Studies, Lilly Research Laboratories, Division of Eli Lilly & Co., Greenfield, Indiana

FOGLEMAN, R.W., D.V.M., River Road, R.D.1, Box 590-D, Upper Black Eddy, Pennsylvania

FOSTER, E.M., Ph.D., Food Research Institute, University of Wisconsin, 1925 Willow Drive, Madison

FRIEND, BEVERLY A., Ph.D., Department of Food Science and Technology, University of Nebraska, Lincoln

GRAHAM, DEE M., Ph.D., Director, Central Research, Del Monte Corporation Research Center, 205 N. Wiget Lane, Walnut Creek, California

HALL, RICHARD L., Ph.D., McCormick & Co., Inc., 11350 McCormick Road, Hunt Valley, Maryland

HAYES, K.C., D.V.M., Ph.D., Department of Nutrition, Harvard School of Public Health, 665 Huntington Avenue, Boston, Mass.

KIRSCHMAN, JOHN C., Ph.D., Central Research Department, General Foods Corporation, 250 North St., White Plains, N.Y.

KOLBYE, ALBERT C., Jr., M.D., J.D., M.P.H., Associate Bureau Director for Toxicology, Bureau of Foods, Food and Drug Administration, Washington, D.C.

LEE, TUNG-CHING, Ph.D., Professor, Department of Food Science and Technology, Nutrition and Dietetics, University of Rhode Island, Kingston

MILLER, ROBERT M., Corporate Manager, Regulatory Compliance, Medical Department, Hercules Inc., 910 Market Street, Wilmington, Delaware

NAKAYAMA, T.O.M., Ph.D., Professor, Department of Food Science, University of Georgia, Agricultural Experiment Station, Experiment, Georgia

SHAHANI, KHAM M., Ph.D., Department of Food Science and Technology, University of Nebraska, 116 H.C. Filley Hall, Lincoln, Nebraska

TRYPHONAS, HELEN, M.S., Toxicology Research Division, Health Protection Branch, Health and Welfare Canada, Tunney's Pasture, Ottawa, Ontario, Canada

WHITAKER, JOHN R., Ph.D., Professor, Department of Food Science and Technology, College of Agricultural and Environmental Sciences, 3450 Chemistry Annex, University of California, Davis

Contents

1

Definition of Toxicology and Physiological Effects

John C. Kirschman[1]

It is critical that scientists responsible for maintaining a safe and wholesome food supply understand the forces at work which now and in the future will affect the ways of assessing and assuring food safety.

As soon as one starts talking about toxicity he is shortly stumbling through the various disciplines of the biological sciences including pharmacology, physiology, anatomy, biochemistry, nutrition, cytology, and pathology. Indeed, the practice of toxicology involves all of these disciplines and then some—more recent additions are genetics, epidemiology, allergenicity and hypersensitivity, and behavior—perhaps law and public relations should be added as well. We dare not compartmentalize our thinking or research when addressing food safety issues since they all must be considered in every case.

Let's consider that the subject of concern, be it human or animal, is an operating chemical plant—which it is. Our objective is to keep it operating efficiently and economically as long as possible. In order to do so we need to know the potential limiting factors and the dynamics of their interaction. Production at the plant can be adversely affected—toxicologically—in a variety of ways. For example, it depends upon:

1. Structural adequacy	(Anatomy)
2. Availability—scarcity or over-abundance—of materials	(Nutrition)

[1] General Foods Corporation, White Plains, New York.

3. Adequate maintenance	(Physiology and Nutrition)
4. Proper plant design—work flow	(Pharmacology)
5. Equipment capacities and maintenance	(Pathology)

Since the ultimate visible impact on the plant will be the same from a variety of causes, it is important to understand the qualitative and quantitative aspects leading to the endpoint of toxic phenomena and some insight into mechanism of action must be determined and taken into account in evaluating toxicity test results for use in risk assessment. Only in this way can one properly begin to establish their relevance to safety in use for man. For example, simple reading of endpoints such as incidence of test animal deaths at a given exposure level, can yield very accurate data yet generate incorrect conclusions.

Extremely high chemical doses for prolonged chronic exposure can elicit toxicological effects by poisoning a system directly or secondarily by overloading normal functions or inducing nutritional deficiencies, conditions that would not obtain at lower ranges of exposure rates.

By preventing absorption of or using up all of available nutrients (*e.g.*, GSH, Zn) during metabolism, exceedingly high test chemical doses could cause responses not shown in the control animals where the diet is nutritionally adequate in the absence of a chemical overload. In such cases there might have been a control group in the study yet the study was not properly controlled. Thus the observed test response should be considered a secondary one resulting from an imposed nutritional deficiency rather than a specific toxic effect of the chemical. Such factors are a key part of the discussion in recent years about the use of NCI's bioassay data for making determinations of risk to man.

As we start reviewing the safety of materials already in our foods and long generally considered as safe (GRAS), and materials designed as replacements for normal components of foods, there develops an increasing need and opportunity for interdisciplinary approaches to the problem.

The toxicologist must involve the nutritionist, clinician, epidemiologist and biochemist earlier in the study planning than ever before. It has been said for test protocol design, "As with an obstetrician, the statistician should be brought in before the labor begins." As we start testing materials with nutritional value (*e.g.*, irradiated foods, modified ingredients) we must bring in the nutritionist and biochemist earlier than ever before.

Whenever one is able to acquire data on the toxicological and biochemical characteristics of a chemical *in man*, it is important to do so for help in designing and interpreting the animal studies. This should be possible more often with food ingredients already in use than with new xenobiotic (strange to biological systems) chemicals. Without such information one must presently rely solely on animal data and the conservative approach of setting an Acceptable Daily Intake (ADI), for example, by applying a 100-fold safety factor to the highest no observed effect level in the most sensitive test species. Most foods would not survive this rigid procedure.

Additional attention in the future will be focused on products of reactions between additives and nutrients or other food constituents during manufacture, storage and preparation for serving. This need will also mandate closer than ever working relationships between toxicologists and analytical chemists.

After adding to these opportunities the galloping snail of advancing toxicology (*e.g.*, genetic tox, allergenicity, hyperactivity, behavior) we have an exciting era ahead of us in the arena of Food Safety.

2

Role of Toxicity in Regulatory Practice

R. W. Fogleman[1]

Toxicology is a multi-disciplinary application of scientific knowledge to the problems of hazard assessment. Therefore, by definition, toxicology is the receiver of the input of knowledge of many scientific disciplines and applies these facts, phenomena, laws and proximate causes, gained and verified by exact observation, organized experimentation and ordered thinking to define the conditions under which a product may be used safely. The role of the toxicologist is to discover the limits within which a chemical may be used safely, *i.e.*, with minimum risk to the target organism and to all other factors of the ecosystem and environment.

While this may sound simple, there are many complicating factors which represent specific concepts of hazard or risk, specific concepts of social acceptability, personalities, power structures, and economic considerations, which impact on what should otherwise be a scientific process. This paper will examine both the technical and the nontechnical aspects of toxicology and its role in Regulatory Practice.

FACTORS ENTERING INTO A TOXICOLOGICAL PROBLEM

Many factors enter into a toxicological problem; the most important considerations are:

1. What are the exposure conditions?
2. How much?
3. What are the effects—both good and bad?
4. Benefit/Risk.
5. Public Relations.

[1] Consulting Toxicologist, Upper Black Eddy, Pennsylvania.

What Are the Exposure Conditions?

How is the chemical to be used? For example, a food additive to be used in the preparation of bread represents one set of conditions whereby a large number of humans and animals will be exposed, probably for long periods of time, and there are no limits on age, *i.e.*, small children, the infirm and aged will also be exposed. On the other hand, a drug to be administered once or at most only a few times to a defined population under close supervision of a well qualified physician represents another set of conditions. Obviously there are many shades between these two extremes, but it is essential that the proposed pattern of use be defined so that the exposure can be known.

How Much—of What?

As Paracelsus stated back in the sixteenth century, it is the dose alone that makes a thing a poison. Early in any program, the amount, or quantity of the substance entering into the exposure has a significant impact on planning. Using our example of a food additive in bread, the chemist can supply fairly accurate data on the quantity of the additive that is to be present in the finished product, and the exposure, in terms of probable daily dosage, can be estimated from these and other readily available facts. The same also is true in our drug example, provided the drug is limited to humans. Assuming that same drug is to be given to animals used for human food, other problems are immediately suggested. Residues in the food derived from the treated animal, not only of the parent compound but metabolites and degradation products as well, become important both from a qualitative and quantitative point of view.

What are the Effects?

A preliminary evaluation of the known structure, preliminary data on toxicity, and prior experience with compounds of similar structure point out problem areas and begin to give some insight to the potential risk which might be expected. For example, some structures are associated with known carcinogenic activity, others are known to affect key enzyme systems. Some act rapidly in biological systems, while others are stored for long periods of time.

Benefit/Risk

This is a very controversial subject and much has been written about it (Bazelton 1979; Comar 1979). Obviously a benefit is expected, but for every benefit there is a potential risk to health, to the environment, and to society. Many factors, many nonscientific, enter into this equation, and it is a very difficult area with which to deal. However, an early assessment is necessary on which to base a decision, and that assessment must be continually updated as the program develops.

Public Relations

This is an odd consideration for a scientific presentation, but it is one that is seriously overlooked by most toxicologists. By way of background, science generally, and toxicology specifically, has a poor reputation among the general public. We have lost credibility and our presentments are not to be trusted. The result is a public fear of "chemicals" and a public demand for their suppression and control. This public fear is being fed by those who capitalize on that fear. Unfortunately, some scientists are guilty of this practice, too. They are easily recognized, however, by the discerning observer who notes that these individuals publish their findings in such illustrious journals as *The New York Times* and are immediately funded by large private or government grants.

Another area of concern involving public relations hinges on the fact that the interpretation of toxicologic data is a "negative" science, in that we attempt to demonstrate that a given event will not occur. As a result we must deal in probabilities, not absolutes; and the public has been carefully conditioned to accept absolutes. The "buzz-words" today are "might," "could," "under some conditions," "it is possible," or "in the absence of data," coupled with the words "cancer" and "birth defects." The public has also been conditioned to accept the proposition that the resolution of all doubt is the result of a new study, more money, a new bureau, and more time.

Knowing these conditions, the toxicologist must examine his conscience and select his path. As I have already unhappily noted, some of our colleagues have opted for the short-term funding approach at the expense of the consumer, science, and their own reputations.

ROLE OF THE TOXICOLOGIST

In examining the role of toxicity, the role of the toxicologist must be carefully considered.

First of all, the toxicologist must be grounded in many disciplines, such as physiology, biochemistry, pharmacology, medicine, mathematics, genetics, immunology, and psychology, to mention a few. In addition, management experience is helpful, because he must deal with the management of money, personnel and facilities as they impact on management decisions.

Observing many organizations, I find toxicologists are being placed high on the decision tree. They serve in staff positions at the highest level, providing the input needed to plan and carry out research projects. In addition, most organizations maintain laboratory facilities, and toxicologists fill these line responsibilities, but the emphasis is on the management role, and it is here that performance is critical.

The same is true in government. Toxicologists provide staff input in the regulatory decisions to the various regulatory agencies.

USE OF TOXICOLOGY LABORATORY SERVICES

To function, the toxicologist must have data that are reliable. The source of the data may be from several types of facility. Any facility must be adequately staffed and equipped to do the job in a timely manner. It may be a part of the research function in industry, a contract toxicology laboratory, a university, or a government laboratory.

A toxicology laboratory is a capital intensive, high technology operation, undergoing constant change. It is expensive to maintain and to operate. A management decision to have a toxicology laboratory involves considerably more thought than deciding to get a few cages. Consider a typical budget for the toxicology studies necessary to evaluate a new food additive.

Typical Costs of Toxicology Studies

Acute and Subacute	$ 7,000 –	$ 50,000
90-Day Rat and Dog	70,000 –	100,000
2-Year Chronic Rat	125,000 –	450,000
18-Month Mouse	200,000 –	350,000
3-Generation Reproduction	100,000 –	150,000
Teratology	35,000 –	70,000
Mutagenicity	4,000 –	50,000
Environmental	10,000 –	150,000
Inhalation	2,000 –	200,000
Special Studies	25,000 –	250,000
	$565,000 –	$1,820,000

Consider also the disciplines required beyond the toxicologist. Essential technical support includes pathologists, biochemists, computer scientists, and other specialists, each with a full complement of technical assistants and equipment. Few, if any, laboratories in industry, government, or academia are staffed and equipped to handle all aspects of a full-blown toxicology evaluation.

My personal preference is for the in-house laboratory in industry to serve as the initial source of data and the exploratory group for defining potential problem areas. The initial toxicology studies are keys to finding what a chemical can do in a biological system. There is much more to an acute oral LD_{50} than just the LD_{50} value. A biological profile, which can be rapidly developed from acute and subacute studies, will give considerable guidance in knowing what to expect and how to design further studies.

From these preliminary inputs, protocols must be designed to define the limits of safety, by emphasizing those aspects of the scientific problem which are important, and deleting, or deemphasizing those aspects which are unproductive. From an economic point of view, the protocol must give the maximum information for the cost. The most expensive data are those bits of key information which were not gathered when the opportunity was presented. Generally, if the toxicologist has done his job, there are very few surprises in a toxicology program. There may be bad news, but no surprises.

The government regulatory agencies have prepared detailed guidelines of toxicology studies which they expect to be followed in studying a chemical. From the regulatory point of view, it provides a basis for (a) being certain all key areas of a program are examined; (b) the studies are adequate for interpretation; and (c) a comparison of data from similar compounds or similar use conditions can be compared. To the extent practical, these guidelines should be followed, but they should by no means be considered binding or absolute. To avoid conflict with the regulatory scientists and the resultant delays in the decision making process at the regulatory level, any alterations and deviations in the guideline program must be discussed in advance and documented in the records.

Once a protocol is designed, factors such as costs, time, technical competence, and reliability must be evaluated in placing the study. There is a strong tendency to conduct the work in the company's facility if it is available. I do not necessarily think this is the best approach. The capabilities may or may not be there. There is generally a problem of scheduling and priorities must be set within the entire research complex. Costs are usually high, offset by the fact that these costs are ongoing whether the facility is used or not. Some of these are management decisions while others are technical.

As an alternative, there are a number of well qualified commercial laboratories which conduct the more extensive toxicology studies, and which are well staffed in key areas to meet specific needs. For example, inhalation toxicology is a special case which is not readily available in all laboratories, and an in-house facility rarely has a sufficient volume of work to attract a top scientist in this field. Equipment costs are high and technically complex. Another example is environmental studies requiring specially designed exposure chambers for fish and marine organisms. A third example is technical competence of key support elements which may be available, such as a pathologist with a special reputation in the tissues most likely to be affected by the test compound, such as liver tumors in mice, or mammary tumors in mice and rats, where interpretation is critical, and diagnosis easily confused. Another example is analytical capability for residue or metabolic studies where special equipment for analysis, radio tracer capability, and specific scientific expertise in critical areas all may be required.

In these cases, it is usually more cost effective to identify these special needs, select a commercial laboratory on the basis of its qualifications, and closely monitor the work to its final completion.

University laboratories are another source of data but there are unique problems in fitting them into a toxicology research program. By their very nature, universities are oriented toward teaching and research, they have little or no control over schedules, and much of the work is done by students under the general supervision of a senior professor. Programs can get caught up in technical detail and the approach may be altered or diverted in the interest of pure science, and this changes the timing of the final report. An advantage is that new ground may be broken, and new techniques may be developed to help evaluate the problem.

Government facilities are primarily used to assess problems beyond the responsibility of an individual or company to undertake. Among these are the NCI Bioassay programs, the NCTR facility and its programs, the FDA and USDA laboratories at Beltsville and elsewhere. One does not expect the government to conduct toxicology studies for the benefit of a profit-making group. These laboratories are available, however, for evaluating new concepts, and their studies should be closely watched and the knowledge utilized when it is appropriate to the problem at hand.

Any toxicology study must meet the requirements of 21CFR Part 58, the Good Laboratory Practices for Non Clinical Laboratory Studies, and this requirement has helped considerably in assuring that the work is done as planned, and that schedules are met.

To briefly recapitulate, the toxicologist plays a significant role in the development of a new chemical or product by:

1. Evaluating the exposure
2. Determining the effects of the exposure
3. Interpreting the limits of safety under conditions of use.

The position is twofold in a management organization:

1. Staff to management
   (a) Planning
   (b) Costs
   (c) Advice and interpretation
2. Line responsibility
   (a) Laboratory operation
   (b) Reports.

Once the industry toxicologist has done the job of gathering and evaluating the data, the submission in the form of a petition is presented to the appropriate government agency. The toxicology data undergoes thorough review and results in an independent evaluation which may, or may not, be the same as the industrial presentation. This interface many times creates serious problems.

The first is the use of the checklist. As noted earlier, the regulatory agencies have prepared guidelines to assist petitioners in providing the necessary data in a suitable format for evaluation. Any deviation requires discussion and documentation. In the absence of a written record, the data may be rejected out of hand by the agency. It is important to consider the regulatory approach in changing from the guidelines. First is that the agencies operate with only a single philosophy—that of protecting the public health; any question will be resolved on the conservative side. They may request additional data, a rerun of the study, including two-year studies, or studies in additional species; the alternative is rejection of the petition. The regulatory agency is not required to approve the use of the chemical, it is required to protect the public health.

A second point concerns the expertise the regulatory agency toxicologist brings to bear on a problem. My philosophy is based on the fact that the industrial toxicologist knows the compound in depth. He has handled the compound, he has observed its effects first hand, and he has had the responsibility to his management for planning and executing the studies. Therefore he is best qualified to decide what studies are needed to answer the questions on safety.

The regulatory toxicologist, on the other hand, has none of this background. His only exposure is from the written words in carefully prepared reports. Therefore, he must be cautious in his approach, depending on his experience from viewing other data, his intuition on the adequacy of the laboratory facility and personnel, internal reports from others who have inspected the facility, and his interpretation of the data as he sees it. The regulatory interpretation will also take into consideration facts not available to the industry toxicologist such as proposed new use patterns, other chemicals of a similar type with unusual problems of a technical or political nature, or the extent of the overall exposure of the population to a class of chemical.

For example, bromine residues have reached levels in our food supply whereby new uses may result in a total exposure unacceptable to health standards. Or, a similarly acting cholinesterase inhibitor is widely used, and a multiple exposure may result which must be considered. Or, the laboratory conducting the study has failed a GLP review and is being closely watched, and any data from this source are suspect. Or, they have received a petition from an activist group which challenges the current policy as it relates to the particular problem or usage. Or, an article has appeared in an obscure foreign journal which raises questions about the test procedure, the interpretation, or some other aspect of the evaluation. Many additional examples can be cited by those who have gone through the process.

Finally there are the legal and political pressures which are brought to bear on the government regulatory agencies, and these are of significant impact on the role of the toxicologist, both in industry and in government. In the past, these have been serious causes of delay in the decision making process. In fact, one agency admits that up to three years is now the usual interval between filing and acceptance. I leave it to the economists to estimate the value in terms of GNP, earnings, tax dollars, and wages lost by these delays. At the same time, I challenge anyone to show that efficient handling of well put together petitions would endanger the health and safety of our people or our environment.

There are some serious problems. Some have been alluded to, and others also require your attention and thought. Of prime importance is the integrity of science, the scientist, and public opinion about the technologic advances in food, agriculture and medicine.

Back in 1973, Dr. Phillip Handler, of the National Academy of Science (NAS), spoke on this problem of scientifically defining low levels of risk coupled with near hysteria which reigns when issues of safety are discussed in the public arena. Citing the DDT hearings, it was his opinion that two-thirds of the so-called "scientific evidence" presented could not have been published in reputable journals (Handler 1974).

Walter Cronkite (1979), speaking to the Food Marketing Institute, made the following statement:

> In this complex and media-confusing world, we seem to have lost the ability to perceive a problem, to state it simply, and to think it through. We even seem to have lost the belief that there can still be some simple truths.

If his subject had been toxicology and issues of safety, he could not have stated it better.

Unfortunately, scientists are people, and some people connive, twist facts, cheat and otherwise deceive to gain their ends; so have some scientists. Some of them have been shown up, but in the public eye, they have tainted all of us. Some of our colleagues have done limited studies, rushed into print in nonreferenced journals and applied for grants, almost in the same breath. It must be a successful approach. However, one never hears how the final result came out, nor the confusion which resulted from the initial publication. To cite a case in point, several years ago two microbiologists published a letter in *Science* citing the soil microbiologic conversion of a general class of herbicides into known or suspected carcinogens. They subsequently received grants from both industry and government to continue the work and better define it. In the meantime, all registration evaluations for similar compounds were stopped and the sponsors requested to determine if this also occurred with their compounds. After 18 months, the synthesis of hundreds of possible metabolites with a C^{14} tag, and extensive laboratory work, no instance was found of such a conversion.

It was subsequently decided the original finding was an artifact, and did not exist at all.

I can cite another instance where a scientist has utilized the lay press to publicize his ideas which could be supported only by conjecture, but not by scientific fact, but which were highly popular at the regulatory level and popular politically. It was recently announced that he received a $250,000 grant to attempt to confirm his position.

In a third instance, a series of compounds were reported to be carcinogens, using a new technique. When the data were examined closely, however, it was found that the compounds had been allowed to deteriorate and were essentially unknown mixtures, and the final diagnosis was made by feeling the intact animal, not by microscopic examination of the tissue and a reliable diagnosis of the tumor. This individual became a most vocal proponent of the potential hazards of chemicals and became a consultant in high circles of government.

These instances cite university scientists as examples, but government scientists and industry scientists are not blameless. The NCI Bioassay program, which emphasized histopathology as the end point with only a token nod to the principles of toxicology is a good case in point. Much of the data we are using as a basis for evaluating carcinogenicity of older compounds was conducted by changing the dosage levels up or down as the test animals became toxic, or recovered. In numerous studies, dosage levels were reportedly changed many times over a two-year period. Today, we still see examples of the dosage being reported as the "time-weighted average." Recent notices in the Federal Register fail to state the dosage, so one must go to the report to find out what happened.

Also, considerable attention has been given to the NCTR ED_{01} study (Staffa and Mehlman 1980) in which an attempt was made to define the dose response curve for a known carcinogen by using large numbers of mice. It seems to be the overall conclusion that little was proved, but both sides, *i.e.*, those who argue there is no threshold for a carcinogen, and those who argue that there is, cite the same report for their argument.

In industry, a few scientists have reported data on two-year feeding studies when it has been shown the animals never existed. This occurred in the early 1950s and as late as the 1970s. Animals have been terminated at 18 months because the cages were needed, but the records continued to show the animals were being fed to 24 months. Animals have died and been replaced on studies without recording such a fact. Also, animals have been numbered at the end of the study, rather than at the beginning. Poor supervision has resulted in lost animals from autolysis. Reports have been altered to include data that do not exist. Unfavorable reports have been suppressed and replaced with more favorable ones. The list goes on and on.

All of these problems are the results of little people with big egos. Some of these problems can be removed by such programs as the GLP regulations. But how should society resolve the dilemma of conflicting information from supposedly qualified scientists, when society receives only the end result of power plays and publicity ploys of these same self-serving scientists? How does science clean its own house?

One solution is training and experience. Qualifications of a toxicologist are under discussion now, and the American Board of Toxicology is attempting to "certify" those it feels are "qualified" by passing an examination. But that is not enough. The demand for toxicologists far exceeds the supply. It is estimated that as many as 5,000 positions in toxicology are being filled by unqualified individuals (Anon. 1977; Fogleman 1979). Steven Jellenek of EPA summed up the situation nicely when he pointed to the serious injury which results to both the profession and to the general public by these untrained people, when he said:

> There is a very large price to pay, and that price is bad decisions on the part of government and industry. The public demands decisions on . . . health issues. These decisions will be made regardless of the level of knowledge and professional skill brought to bear on them (Anon. 1977).

There are some checks and balances which need to be brought into play. Among them is the process of peer review of technical decisions. Peer review means criticism, constructive in nature, and nonpersonal and non-self promoting. There is a trend toward this in the more recent EPA notices published in the Federal Register for pesticides, wherein the data and conclusions are summarized. However, one must see the data to offer constructive criticism, and these are only limitedly available to the toxicology community.

Another check I would like to see established is an opportunity for public evaluation of those who review data in the regulatory process. For example, the GLP regulations define closely the qualifications of key personnel involved in conducting a nonclinical laboratory study, and the agency can reject a study if it finds those individuals do not meet the requirements. It seems to me that it is equally important to the scientific community, to consumers and others interested in safety that the qualifications of the reviewers be also on display, and that they, too, can be removed for lack of qualifications.

Representative Wampler (D-Va.) has proposed that a Supreme Court of Scientists be established to resolve major differences of opinion on the interpretation of data (Wampler 1980). While there are obvious problems in the present bill, there may be something worthwhile in examining this approach. It might put an end to some of the rather ridiculous and childish petitions which have been proposed; for example, the petition by "Public Citizen Inc." which demanded that nitrites in bacon be declared "color additives," or the "Friends of the Earth" petition to essentially ban aerial applications of pesticides, by rendering scientific decisions on which sound policy could then be based.

The arena of public opinion manipulation is usually avoided by the serious scientist. It is an axiom of the press that good news rarely sells papers. Controversy, fear, doubt, and suspicion are all suitable causes for molding public opinion. Most are shortsighted attempts at gaining public attention for the moment. However, it seems to me that the responsible press must look at the ripple effects of its crusades, and anticipate the consequences of their actions. For example, one does not cry "Fire!" in a crowded theater. Although it may bring a fleeting moment of recognition, it can also lead to pandemonium. Yet, we are crying "Fire!" in the food production and processing field where the situation is analagous to the crowded theater. We are not now able to produce enough food, protect it and get it to the consumer, yet we create fear and near pandemonium among consumers by implying that the food is not safe.

It seems to me that it is exceedingly important that the consumers, somehow, be told they are being used by special interests for their own gains; and being used, the consumers are the ultimate losers—in quantity and quality of the food and medical care they are able to get, and in the areas of self-respect and self-determination of their own opinions. By being exposed to conflicting opinions, they finally lose respect for all authority. We are close to that point now—not just in the arena of public safety, but the whole realm of public decision making. I see the consumer protection effort as represented by open meetings, advisory committees, and other mechanisms, being prostituted by careful agenda selection, suppression of opposing views, and well placed public relations efforts to support policies, concepts and programs which cannot be supported by the scientific evidence. I can cite example after example of this type of situation. For instance, I know that I have been excluded from several governmental advisory committees solely on the basis that I, an independent consultant, am classed as an industry representative, while the committees have been filled with scientists from universities who depend on agency grants for support of a major portion of their graduate programs, or from government scientists who rely entirely on governmental policy decisions for their research facilities and funding. To my personal way of thinking, integrity and personal honesty is not a function of the source of the paycheck. But, if I am accused, so I accuse! I am quite sure members of advisory councils to government have the highest integrity, and bring into their deliberations only the loftiest of motives. But, if bias cannot be excluded, then, in fairness to all, bias should be balanced.

I am honored to have been elected the eighth President of the Council for Agricultural Science and Technology, or CAST, which represents a consortium of 25 scientific societies involved in agriculture and food technology. The Institute of Food Technologists is an important member of this consortium. CAST functions by establishing multi-disciplinary task forces of leading scientists to assess the known scientific facts of problems of national importance to agriculture, prepare reports in lay terms pointing out the scientific knowledge available and the areas of conflict, so that decision makers may have a basis for their decisions. CAST has been attacked because this process does gore sacred cows, and there are those who do not wish to be confused by facts. I would strongly suggest to the investigative press that they could profitably examine the motives, financial interests and goals of those pressure groups who are the most vocal advocates of restricting agricultural and food technology. I am certain they would also discover their own role in the process of being "used" to enhance and extend the purposes of these groups.

We all have a role to play in educating the general public to toxicological problems, real and assumed. First is a reestablishment of credibility of science and the scientific process to solve technical problems. When science cannot supply definitive answers, logic, not fear, must be the basis of the decision. Those who utilize fear as a mechanism to gain their own personal advantage should be strongly attacked by their peers and shown up for what they are. Each of us, when the opportunity presents itself must speak up rather than dodge the issue. In essence, we have to stop talking to ourselves and start talking to the public, the decision makers, and to the press. As Pogo, the comic strip character, several years ago observed, "I have seen the enemy—and he are us!"

The toxicologist, assigned the responsibility of developing the data on the limits of safety of a new product, entrusted with millions of dollars of research to supervise, and charged with protecting the health and safety of the present and future generations, is a unique scientist. I know of no other endeavor that is more worthwhile, challenging, or rewarding. The job requires training, experience and judgment on the part of the toxicologist, but even more, it requires support of management, colleagues, regulatory officials, and the general public. This is the role of the toxicologist in a regulatory practice.

BIBLIOGRAPHY

ANON. 1977. Training scientists for future toxic materials problems. Draft Report of Workshop sponsored by NIEHS, CIIT, Conservation Foundation, and EPA. Annapolis, Md., Sept. 8–10.

BAZELTON, D.L. 1979. Science *205*, July 20, 277–280.

COMAR, C.L. 1979. Science *203*, Editorial, Jan. 26.

CRONKITE, W. 1979. Speech before Food Marketing Institute, Washington, D.C., Oct. 10.

FOGLEMAN, R.W. 1979. Toxicology and its role in regulatory practice. *In* Toxicology and Occupational Medicine—*4*. W. Deichmann (Editor). Elsevier-North Holland, New York.

HANDLER, P. 1974. How Safe is Safe—The Decision of Policy on Drugs and Food Additives. Academy Forum, NAS, Washington, D.C., p. 1–8.

STAFFA, J.A. and MEHLMAN, M.A. (Editors). 1980. J. Environ. Path. and Tox. *3*, Special Issue.

WAMPLER, W.C. 1980. H.R. 6521—National Science Council Act of 1980, introduced Feb. 13.

3

Government and Its Influence on Toxicology

Albert C. Kolbye, Jr.[1]

The subject of this presentation concerns the role of government agencies and their influence on the field of toxicology and its sub-specialties. However, before we concentrate on agencies of the U. S. Government, its states and possessions, it might be helpful to reflect on the role of international agencies and their influence upon the field of toxicology. The European Economic Community (EEC) has been very active in attempting to elaborate principles and guidelines with respect to toxicological testing, primarily the pre-marketing clearance of chemicals within the EEC. The member countries of Western Europe joined in an eco-economic union with one purpose being to standardize safety requirements in order to minimize nontariff trade barriers.

The Organization for Economic Cooperation and Development (OECD), which involves not only Western Europe, but the North American countries, is also active in elaborating principles and guidelines for the purpose of harmonizing toxicological requirements for determining the safety of various product classifications. Last, but not least, and even on a broader scale, is the World Health Organization headquartered in Geneva which, through specialized committees and research centers is also attempting to establish principles and guidelines for promoting safety in international commerce; for example, through such committees as the Joint WHO-FAO Expert Committee on Food Additives. With regard to a particularly vexing problem, that of cancer, WHO also maintains the International Agency for Research on Cancer (LARC), based in Lyon, which coordinates a variety of activities dedicated to elucidating the potential risks of various chemicals to influence the incidence of cancer in humans.

[1] Associate Bureau Director for Toxicology, Bureau of Foods, Food and Drug Administration, Washington, D.C.

Also, on an international basis, the governments of the United Kingdom, Canada, and the United States, per the Tripartite Agreement, cooperate on matters concerning the regulation of foods and drugs.

ROLE OF THE FEDERAL GOVERNMENT

Within our own country, it would be helpful to begin our understanding of the role of government agencies in a broader context of the role of the Federal Government. As you know, there is a constitutional division of functions in the United States among the legislative, judicial, and executive branches of government. The Legislative Branch is charged with enacting laws and adopting budgets consistent with the powers and limitations accorded to the U.S. Congress by the Constitution.

The major role is played by the Legislative Branch of Government not only by the statutes enacted, but also by the Appropriations and Oversight Committees who establish the funding and directions of toxicologic research and regulatory activities. The General Accounting Office (GAO) is the investigative arm of the Legislative Branch and is used frequently to investigate the efficiency and effectiveness of the various federal agencies involved either in research or regulation of chemical safety. It is almost impossible to keep track of the many investigations mounted by GAO into the affairs of the government regulatory agencies. Each investigation requires the time and attention of the agency in question, if only for providing accurate information and attempting to educate investigators who may not have specialized expertise in the subject matter of concern.

The various federal agencies concerned with research and regulation of chemical products can and do exert profound and powerful influences on toxicology by the directions and emphasis they place on various research activities, including good laboratory practice regulations. The Federal Government is the largest financial sponsor of toxicological research conducted both intra- and extramurally.

In this country there is a strong tradition, not necessarily consistent nor always constructive, that "if there is a problem there should be a law against it." If we look back in the preceding two decades, perhaps we can gain some insight and oversight with respect to some of the sociological and political forces at play that can and frequently do have a tangible effect on toxicology. Two decades ago, analytical chemists usually measured in parts per thousand, or occasionally in parts per million; today, parts per billion and parts per trillion are our present limits of detection brought about by quantum leaps in the technology of analytical chemistry. One of the results of these advances in analytical chemistry has been to open up new universes of awareness and concern about chemicals and their potential influence on human health. One could say ignorance was a certain amount of bliss several decades ago compared to our current awareness of parts per trillion contaminants in parts per billion ingredients of various substances composed of chemicals.

Food Additives Amendment

In 1958, Congress legislated and the President signed into law the Food Additives Amendment to the Federal Food, Drug, and Cosmetic Act, particularly Section 409, which brought about two rather remarkable changes in law which influenced drastically the practice of toxicology in the United States and abroad. The first aspect dealt with a new concept of safety in that in order to gain pre-market approval for chemicals to be used as food additives, the manufacturer had to prove "safety" in that with a reasonable degree of certainty, no harm to the public health would result from particular usage of such chemicals. This change in law shifted the burden of proof from the previous situation where the Government had to prove potential danger to human health over to the manufacturer who now had to prove safety. If one reviews the definitions given for the word "safe," the only statement made in the law was with "reference to the health of man or animal." A second and very major change occurred during the same time period with the same amendments concerning potentially carcinogenic chemicals proposed for use as food additives, namely, the Delaney Clause. Essentially, the Delaney Clause says that "no additive shall be deemed to be safe if it is found to induce cancer when ingested by man or animal, or if it is found, after tests which are appropriate for the evaluation of the safety of food additives, to induce cancer in man or animal . . ." It is important to note the particular context in which the words "safe," "induce," and "appropriate" appear. Several years later, an exception was made to the Delaney Clause insofar as additives and drugs used in food-producing animals were concerned, this exception being known as the "No Residue Clause" or the "DES" clause. Up until the early 1970s, the primary regulatory agency that manufacturers and users of chemicals had to concern themselves with primarily was the Food and Drug Administration. Consequently, the adoption of the Delaney Clause and practice of the Delaney philosophy concerning chemical carcinogens were of profound importance not only to FDA, but also to other regulatory agencies that were created at a later time.

The Mrak Commission

During the late 1960s, the agricultural, environmental, and human health concerns related to pesticide registration were the subject of an

Interagency Agreement on Pesticides among the Departments of Agriculture, Health, Education, and Welfare, and the Interior. In 1969, the Mrak Commission (more formally known as the Secretary's Commission on Pesticides and Their Relationship to Environmental Health) was formed under the auspices of the then Secretary of HEW, Robert Finch. Although several previous commissions, including that of the NAS-NRC, had addressed themselves to the subject, this was the first commission with substantial political power to evaluate issues related to environmentally persistent pesticides and potential biological hazards to various life forms including human health. A very substantial effort by the Commission's subcommittees and ad hoc committees resulted in a report and recommendations that survive today as substantially valid principles for addressing the potential toxicological and environmental hazards posed by man's usage of chemicals in the environment. It is perhaps worthwhile to reflect that the Mrak Commission was keenly aware of the risk-benefit considerations and the fact that such considerations differ from country to country and culture to culture, depending upon particular factors related to environment and stage of economic development.

Soon after the Mrak Commission report was issued, new agencies of the Federal Government were created to regulate chemicals and other products with special enabling statutes and powers of jurisdiction. The Consumer Product Safety Commission was created, as was the Environmental Protection Agency, and the Occupational Safety and Health Administration was strengthened considerably in its statutory mandate. The Environmental Protection Agency has responsibilities for air and water pollution, solid waste disposal and, last but not least, pesticide registration. Even though the Interagency Pesticide Agreement had been revised in 1970 to reflect a new awareness of the human and evironmental health concerns, this interagency agreement quickly became obsolete as EPA took over the primary role for pesticides. About this time, several other factors were entering the equation. The consumer and environmentalist movements were taking shape and gaining momentum. Advocates reviewed the Innes report which concerned itself with screening various pesticides for carcinogenic potential in mice and used that report despite warnings to the contrary from the authors to advocate the proposition that very few chemicals were carcinogens. When one reviews the evaluations of the Mrak Commission concerning the carcinogenicity of pesticides, one sees that approximately 30% of those tested at that time were carcinogenic. Today one can reflect upon the fact that approximately half the chemicals being tested in the NCI bioassay program are being designated as carcinogens.

CARCINOGENS

The public's concern about chemical carcinogens became almost a cancer of fear which was expressed by the Legislative Branch of Government in a variety of ways to federal agencies concerned with research and/or regulation. Through the devices of Oversight and Appropriation Committees, the National Cancer Institute was ordered to accelerate its efforts to identify and designate chemical carcinogens. That mandate resulted in tremendous human efforts and federal monies being pumped into the NCI's bioassay program to detect carcinogens. The carcinogen of the year soon became the carcinogen of the month, only to become the carcinogen of the week, as more and more positive reports were issued as a result of such research conducted by federal and nonfederal institutes and the associated enthusiastic coverage by the press and television media. The environmentalists and consumer activists added to the clamor.

Back in the 1960s, the thalidomide scare was superimposed on the previous cranberry scare (concerning residues of aminotriazole on some cranberries), and public anxiety concerning the safety of chemicals was enhanced by coverage in the press of a variety of somewhat alarmistic statements made by various advocates who challenged the principles and practices of the Federal government in relation to determinations of safety concerning particular usages of chemicals and related potential human exposures. Also at this time, a group of experts was formed to consult and render advice concerning the use of Agent Orange and its usage as a defoliant in Vietnam. Such concern was initiated by government scientists who alleged teratologic effects in mice of 2,4,5-T. Further reflection and investigation focused attention on the chlorinated dioxins which were secondary contaminants of the industrial processes used to manufacture 2,4,5-T. Dioxins were heralded as the most potent toxic chemicals known and public anxiety increased accordingly. Concurrently, interest in the potential biological hazards posed by lead was reawakened and the methylmercury in tuna and swordfish scare occurred. Shortly thereafter, the disease Yusho became almost a household word as the public was introduced to the potential hazards associated with a large family of related isomers known collectively as the polychlorinated biphenyls (PCBs). The frequency of press coverage and consequent public anxiety began to mount as more and more chemical incidents were identified and publicized, sometimes with misleading information that purported to be factual representations.

Also coming into vogue was the tentative hypothesis being transformed to a truism that 90% of cancer was environmentally caused which was immediately interpreted and publicized by advocates that most cancer was caused by chemicals in the environment. The Surgeon General's Report on Smoking and Health (1964) and the subsequent reports issued on an annual basis since 1967 helped to reinforce that concern. Congress, as expected, responded to these concerns by enacting various laws empowering regulatory agencies to, if I may be permitted to paraphrase, "search and destroy" potentially hazardous chemicals in the environment.

In 1974, in early May, the FDA became aware that dairy feed in the State of Michigan was contaminated with polybrominated biphenyls (PBBs) and a public uproar ensued despite responsible attempts to minimize potential hazards to human health which in retrospect were substantially successful. Politically oriented individuals used the public's anxiety for secondary gain and the expectable result of near panic occurred to the point where some federal witnesses were assigned uniformed and plain clothes police body guards for their protection.

FOOD ADDITIVES

The public's level of anxiety concerning the safety of food additives was increased considerably during the late 1960s when the cyclamate situation unfolded, to be followed shortly thereafter by a Presidential mandate to review the safety of substances in food generally recognized as safe (GRAS). In the early 1970s, FDA contracted with FASEB[2] to initiate and conduct a major review of the GRAS substances in food by reviewing all available information concerning these substances in order to determine whether present or anticipated human exposures were potentially dangerous to human health. Other concerns such as with Red 2 and Violet 1 were then followed by concern over the safety of Red 40, saccharin, nitrosamines, and nitrite.

POLITICAL IMPLICATIONS

A regulatory agency primarily exerts its influence through the issuance and enforcement of regulations it is authorized to propose under enabling legislation which both empowers and limits the scope of action of each agency. Realistically speaking, any regulatory agency is influenced by the philosophy not only of the Legislative Branch, but also of the Executive and Judicial Branches of Government. Particular individuals of one Administration may come into positions of high responsibility with preconceptions and stereotypes about government in general, and how to exert regulatory influence on toxicology in specific. Changes can be ex-

---

[2] FASEB - Federation of American Societies of Experimental Biology.

pected as personalities and Administrations change. These changes involve not only emphasis, but tone. In turn, the emphasis and philosophy which regulatory agencies accord to particular perceived problems are influenced by the results of administrative hearings and judicial review of regulations and by petitions and suits initiated by consumer and environmental advocates. The regulation of chemicals in various sectors of the environment is a very complicated process. Any regulator should be aware that it is essentially a no-win profession because some powerful groups somewhere always will be alienated. The moral of this story is that you cannot please all of the people all of the time, and you can consider yourself very lucky if you can please some of the people some of the time. There are many legal strategisms and managerial techniques available to administrators and commissioners of regulatory agencies.

The interaction between science and law is itself complicated. It is not unrealistic to expect that a political philosophy will set the tone for regulatory philosophies and that the legal advisors to a governmental agency will exercise considerable influence over how and by whom scientific evidence is presented to the public. A very real danger is that lawyers in discharging their responsibilities to uphold the enforcement actions of regulatory agencies will exert an unduly selective influence on the scientific activities of such agencies. Subtle pressures can be exercised in many ways within regulatory agencies to influence the statements spoken or written by scientists and the circumstances in which such statements are publicized. My personal viewpoint of this type of situation is that a scientist should be somewhat circumspect in his or her statements while employed in a regulatory agency, but just because one is employed in a regulatory agency is no excuse for being less than fully honest to the public. Federal employees, however, do have to be somewhat selective in choosing an appropriate forum for making such statements, since they may be viewed as being outside of the "party line" and therefore heretics.

Administrative hearings are not necessarily appropriate vehicles for discussing the various facets of toxicological problems of fundamental importance. The adversarial process can result in pitting "worst case" advocates against "best case" advocates with insufficient attention being paid to the middle ground wherein the truth more generally resides. Witnesses frequently are selected for their willingness to testify and their eloquence, not always for their wisdom or integrity, although I do not wish this statement misinterpreted as a generalized attack upon scientists testifying at hearings whether the scientists are federally or privately employed. It may also be relevant at this point to note that witnesses appearing before legislative hearings are not subjectable to cross-examination. The practical result is that legislative hearings frequently involve witnesses pre-selected for their viewpoints. The opinion of responsible regulatory officials is then subjected to criticism by witnesses pre-selected to represent other viewpoints.

The political pressures upon regulatory agencies have a major and continuing influence upon the field of toxicology at large. The emphasis on detecting carcinogens has over-stressed our national resources for continuing chronic bioassays of chemicals in test animals. Consequently, pressure is mounting to adopt many of the short-term screening tests for the purposes of indicating which chemicals should receive intensive scrutiny. That in turn, if unchecked, could eventually lead to the adoption of short-term tests directly for use as decision-making procedures concerning the safety of chemicals, which will lead to additional problems.

We face some fundamental problems of semantics, logic, science, and law in relation to the operating criteria and definitions currently in vogue today concerning the designation of chemicals as carcinogens. The operative philosophy today is that a statistically significant increase in the incidence of cancer in test animals exposed to the substance in question, as compared to controls, will suffice to designate the substance being tested as a carcinogen. Insufficient attention has been paid to biomechanisms and, from my viewpoint, insufficient attention has been paid within the Federal Government to a very extensive and substantial body of scientific evidence that strongly suggests that many different substances can influence the incidence of cancer in animals or in humans by a variety of mechanisms other than direct carcinogenic action (Trosko and Chu 1975; Miller and Miller 1976; Van Duuren 1976; Berenblum 1978; Weinstein 1978; Weisburger 1978; Boyland 1980). Many of these mechanisms can operate to enhance the induction of cancer through indirect mechanisms not associated with the initiation of genotoxic damage by electrophilic carcinogens, such as decreasing biological resistance to endogenous or exogenous carcinogens (Kolbye 1979A, 1979B, 1980). More attention should be paid to reviewing and documenting the scientific evidence concerning tumor promoters and modifiers. We should be formulating testable hypotheses concerning promoters and modifiers, and testing them by relevant experiments or epidemiological observations. By no means, in my personal opinion, should these potentiators and modifiers of carcinogenesis be automatically classified as carcinogens in the sense of the Delaney philosophy (Federal Food, Drug and Cosmetic Act 1958). It is not unreasonable to conclude after extensive reviews of the problems associated with defining and determining food safety that our current legal philosophy concerning carcinogens should be re-examined and re-evaluated (Kolbye 1976, 1979C). It would also be desirable to exercise more care before we adopt short-term tests for direct regulatory decision-making, since otherwise we will likely repeat some of the same mistakes we have made in carcinogenesis and extend them into the field of mutagenesis and other areas of toxicological concern (Kolbye 1978A, 1978B, 1980B).

THE CONCEPT OF SAFETY

It is very easy to ask questions about whether or not a potential human exposure to a chemical will be "safe" because the word "safety" is subjectable to many, many interpretations. There is no such thing as absolute safety, because any chemical is potentially toxic provided critical exposures are attained. What constitutes a critical exposure to an individual depends upon the susceptibility of that individual to toxicological insults of one type or another. While we must be circumspect about evaluating potential hazards to human health, we should not permit ourselves to fall into the trap of declaring a given exposure unsafe just because some outstanding questions may presently remain unanswered. All safety is relative and perhaps now is the time for us to be conceptually aware that some practical definition of relative safety should be adopted which would permit comparisons with and greater understanding of known parameters of potential hazards to human health.

The field of risk assessment has attracted much attention in recent years, primarily because simplistic mathematical solutions are offered in lieu of the more complex and difficult to understand judgments based upon toxicological and epidemiological observations. Philosophies associated with linear extrapolations of risk for carcinogens perhaps are not fully appreciated for both the good and the bad involved with such models. With good intentions, it is one thing to state that a linear model will project X risk of cancer incidence in relation to Y exposure to a carcinogen. However, the other side of the coin is relevant also. Those who advocate linear extrapolations of risk are really saying that we cannot prevent or reduce cancer in humans unless we reduce most exposures to chemical carcinogens to near zero levels. That philosophy is not consistent with my observations and insight into the multifactorial etiology of cancer risk factors gained over the past two decades of being active in preventive toxicology.

For those interested in the phraseology of realistic perceptions of current issues in toxicology, I would recommend spending some time reviewing the Bureau of Foods' Research Plan issued this year. While it may not read like an exciting novel, it does identify in reasonably understandable English many of the current issues of considerable importance to toxicology and its sub-specialties today. No matter where we are employed, with industry, universities, or government, each of us and all of us have the obligation to use all available biomedical information constructively and to evaluate potential hazards to human health in a realistic, honest, and competent way.

COLLABORATIVE EFFORTS OF SCIENCE AND GOVERNMENT

At the present time, the various regulatory agencies and research institutions concerned with toxicology are collaborating in two related efforts. The National Toxicology Program, under the stewardship of the National Institute of Environmental Health Sciences, is attempting to bring some cohesion and coordination to the many research activities sponsored by the Federal Government that impact on toxicology. This Program now includes the Cancer Bioassay Program, formerly with NCI, and involves some of the resources at the National Center for Toxicological Research. The Interagency Regulatory Liaison Group (IRLG) is composed of regulatory scientists representing the federal agencies having regulatory responsibilities over potentially toxic chemicals in various sectors of the environment. The Interagency Group, through its committees and sub-committees, has been very actively pursuing the establishment of criteria and guidelines for conducting short and long-term toxicological testing, documenting epidemiological observations, and evaluating the potential hazards associated with the phenomena of carcinogenicity, mutagenicity, teratogenicity, and other related concerns. With the recent and increasing emphasis on immunologic and neurobehavioral phenomena, we can expect to see increased activities in these areas of toxicology. Government's influence on toxicology will continue to increase in the coming years. However, in a democratic society, it behooves all citizens concerned with sound decision-making to exercise effectively their constitutional rights to participate in such decision-making endeavors.

CONCLUSION

We spend much time, human energy, and research monies generating new information but, in my judgment, we pay insufficient attention to the broad variety of in-depth scientific information already available in the scientific literature. I believe now is the time to pause and reflect upon the past two decades which have been very exciting years for toxicology. Now is the time to ask ourselves, how can we improve our insight and perspective into the various diseases of public health importance and learn better how to prevent such diseases in keeping with a realistic attitude towards the many potential risks we face in life? We should re-examine various criteria, definitions, and premises to see if they are still valid. If modifications are scientifically appropriate, we should have the courage to modify our thinking and to make appropriate judgments concerning evaluating potential risks to public health.

BIBLIOGRAPHY

BERENBLUM, I. 1978. Established principles and unresolved problems in carcinogenesis. J. Nat. Cancer Inst. *60*, 723–726.

BOYLAND, E. 1980. Some implications of tumour promotion in carcinogenesis. IRCS Med. Sci. *8*, 1–4.

Federal Food, Drug, and Cosmetic Act as amended. 1958. Sections 409, 512 and 706, U.S. Code 348, 360b, 376.

KOLBYE, A.C., JR. 1976. Cancer in humans: Exposures and responses in a real world. Oncology *33*, 90–100.

KOLBYE, A.C., JR. 1978A. Cancer and toxic substances: Current status. *In* Actualities Toxicologiques de la Collection de Medicine Legale et de Toxicologie Medicale. III, L. Roche (Editor), Lyon (French)

KOLBYE, A.C., JR. 1978B. Regulatory considerations concerning mutagenesis. J. Soc. Cosmet. Chem. *29*, 727–732.

KOLBYE, A.C., JR. 1979A. Problems associated with evaluating food safety. *In* Developments in Toxicology and Environmental Science—4, W. Deichmann (Editor). Elsevier-North Holland, New York.

KOLBYE, A.C., JR. 1979B. Legal and scientific concerns re carcinogens in food. *In* Developments in Toxicology and Environmental Science—4, W. Deichmann (Editor). Elsevier-North Holland, New York.

KOLBYE, A.C., JR. 1979C. Decision-making issues relevant to cancer inducing substances. *In* Regulatory Aspects of Carcinogenesis and Food Additives: The Delaney Clause, F. Coulston (Editor). Academic Press, Inc., New York.

KOLBYE, A.C., JR. 1980A. A U.S. Viewpoint: Legislative and scientific aspects of cancer prevention. Preventive Medicine *9*, 267–274.

KOLBYE, A.C., JR. 1980B. Impact of short-term screening tests on regulatory action. *In* Applied Methods in Oncology—4. Elsevier Biomedical Scientific Publishing Co., Amsterdam.

MILLER, E.C. and MILLER, J.A. 1976. The metabolism of chemical carcinogens to reactive electrophiles and their possible mechanisms of action in carcinogenesis. *In* Chemical Carcinogens, ACS Monograph 173, G.E. Searle (Editor). Amer. Chem. Soc., Washington, D.C.

TROSKO, J.E. and CHU, E.H.Y. 1975. The role of DNA repair and somatic mutation in carcinogenesis. Adv. Cancer Res. *21*, 391–425.

VAN DUUREN, B.L. 1976. Tumor-promoting and co-carcinogenic agents in chemical carcinogenesis. *In* Chemical Carcinogens, ACS Monograph 173, G.E. Searle (Editor). Amer. Chem. Soc., Washington, D.C.

WEINSTEIN, I.B. 1978. Current concepts on mechanisms of chemical carcinogenesis. Bull. N.Y. Acad. Med. *54*, 366–383.

WEISBURGER, E.K. 1978. Mechanisms of chemical carcinogenesis. Ann. Rev. Pharmacol. Toxicol. *18*, 395–415.

4

Benefits And Costs of Food Additive Regulations

Dee M. Graham[1]

The transition of society in our time, from mostly rural to mostly urban, places totally new demands on the food system. The food system can only meet these new demands through the judicious use of food chemicals. Processed foods have become our mainstay. The primary aims of food processing (Table 4.1) are designed to guard the intrinsic quality, wholesomeness, and safety of the food supply. It is in meeting these primary aims that the judicious application of food chemicals is important. This increasing need for the use of food chemicals has led to a new need; that is, an effective control system to govern the proper use of food chemicals.

TABLE 4.1. PRIMARY AIMS OF FOOD PROCESSING[1]

• Freedom From Pathogens
• Maintenance of Quality (No Chemical or Microbial Decay)
• Preventing Losses From Insects
• Maintenance of Nutritional Quality

[1] World Food and Nutrition Study. 1975. BARR/NRC, p. 165–174.

The formal control system to govern the use of chemicals deliberately added to food began with a Food and Drug Administration (FDA) survey in 1958. This was the origin of the now well known Generally Regarded As Safe (GRAS) list.

[1] Del Monte Corporation, Walnut Creek, California.

Many scientists, including a few flavor chemists associated with the Flavor and Extract Manufacturers Association (FEMA), were concerned about the limited number of opinions received by FDA from the scientific community regarding the commonly used food chemicals which now comprise the GRAS list. As a result of this concern, a team of scientists began an independent study and conducted their first survey of industry in December, 1958. This led to the first publication from the FEMA Expert Panel in 1965.

During the turbulent decade of the 60s many events transpired: the publication of "Silent Spring" by Rachel Carson; the disenchantment with DDT; the 1969 White House Conference on Food, Nutrition and Human Health; and the now infamous cyclamate event of October, 1969. Cyclamate was the first major GRAS chemical to fall into disfavor. The sudden event resulted in immediate consumer rejection of products containing cyclamate. Then FDA banned cyclamate based, at best, on limited, and many believe, inadequate information. The resulting losses to the food and chemical industries exceeded $150 million (Table 4.2). Perhaps even more damaging was the immediate and continuing loss of sales in a product category which had received large investments for research and product development. The lost sales are estimated to exceed $1.3 billion. Another highly important resource invested in the cyclamate ban was at least 3.6 Person Years of scientific effort on the part of suppliers and processors.

All of this led, understandably, to a Presidential directive in 1969 for a complete reaffirmation of the safety of GRAS food additives. Much of this paper will deal with that review—its costs, its benefits, and its implications for the future.

TABLE 4.2. COST IMPACT OF THE CYCLAMATE BAN

Merchandise Written Off		
Suppliers		$ 3.20 Million
Food Processors		150 Million
Cost of Lost Sales		
Suppliers		42 Million
Processors		1,350 Million
Technical Time Expended		
Suppliers	2,000 Hours	
Processors	5,400 Hours	
	7,400 Hours = 3.6 Person Years	

THE NAS SURVEYS

In the early Fall of 1969 Drs. Richard Hall of McCormick and Company, Larry Atkin of Standard Brands, and Dale Lindsay of the Food &

Drug Administration met at the National Academy of Sciences. They discussed the possibility of a comprehensive survey on the usage of all food additives along the lines of the earlier FEMA survey. Later, Drs. Herbert Carter of the University of Illinois, L. J. Filer of the University of Iowa, Leon Golberg of the Albany Medical College, Ben Oser of Food & Drug Laboratories and I joined the group. Thus began the series of National Academy of Science (NAS) surveys on the use of chemicals in food. The scope of those surveys is shown in Table 4.3.

TABLE 4.3. SCOPE OF THE NAS SURVEYS OF INDUSTRY ON THE USE OF FOOD ADDITIVES

	Phase I (Pilot)	Phase II (GRAS)	Phase III (Direct)
Questionnaires returned	1,075	24,000[1]	7,500
Firms responding	42	550	500
Substances reported	282	2,000	1,140
Person Years[2]	8.6	32.6	19.5

[1] Includes 18,000 on flavors collected by FEMA and other groups.
[2] Total of industry response, committee and NAS staff.

The major steps in the GRAS reaffirmation process are shown in Figure 4.1. The comprehensive surveys undertaken by NAS were the necessary first steps, to be followed in turn by safety reviews, evaluation of reports, publication of proposed rulings with opportunities for public input and, ultimately, the publication of final rulings. This process has occupied a decade. The GRAS review has been completed and the reevaluation of regulated additives, not originally visualized, is now well underway.

The purposes of the NAS surveys of industry on the usage of food additives were to provide reliable information on the levels at which chemicals are used in food, the specific foods to which those chemicals are added, the extent of the consumption of those foods by individuals, and the resultant potential and average intakes of each additive by various sectors of the population.

After overcoming some initial difficulties in the Phase I and Phase II surveys, a reliable methodology for this comprehensive task has evolved and the initial purposes have been achieved (Table 4.4). The special study on saccharin directed by the Congress in November 1977 has provided data from another source which, when compared with the 1977 Phase III NAS survey, shows a remarkable agreement for such a complex endeavor. Additional study on caffeine, all of which is imported, provided a means of knowing the absolute amounts introduced into the food system. This provided another check which also confirmed the basic accuracy of the NAS Phase III survey data. Data on some substances are less accurate but in general the data for most of the chemicals included in the 1977 survey are correct within a fivefold range.

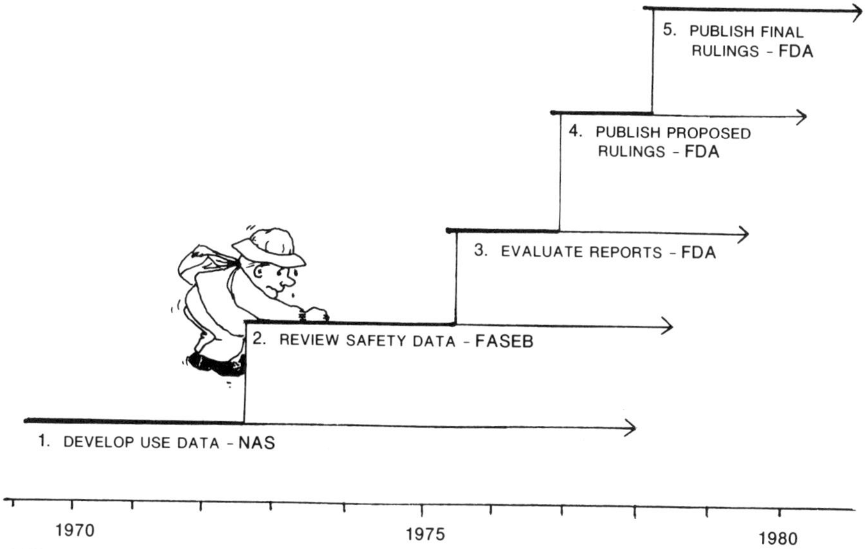

FIG. 4.1. STEPS IN THE GRAS REAFFIRMATION PROCESS, 1970–1980

TABLE 4.4. COMPARISON OF DATA FROM NAS PHASE II WITH THE SPECIAL CONGRESSIONAL REVIEW ON SACCHARIN

	Intake - mg per day	
Age Group	Congressional Study	1977 NAS Survey
2 to 5 Years	9.3	7.9
13 to 17 Years	15.7	12.0
55 to 64 Years	33.4	33.0

THE SAFETY REVIEWS

The second step in the GRAS reaffirmation process, namely, the safety review, has been conducted by the Federated American Societies of Experimental Biology (FASEB). The FASEB group has completed safety reviews on 415 GRAS substances, preparing 118 monographs. Each chemical has been rated regarding its relative safety in view of present and future uses, the need for further study, and the adequacy of evidence on which safety decisions may be based (Table 4.5). Seventy-five percent of the substances reviewed were classified safe at present and anticipated future uses. Fifteen percent were considered safe at present uses. The remainder require further study for reasoned decisions to be made.

The major results of the GRAS review process included the development of specific knowledge about chemicals previously cleared on the

TABLE 4.5. ACTION RESULTING FROM FASEB SAFETY REVIEW OF 415 GRAS SUBSTANCES

%	Status[1]
75.5	1
15.2	2
4.5	3
1.2	4
3.6	5

[1] Each compound was placed in one of these five categories:
1 = safe at present and anticipated future uses;
2 = safe as presently used;
3 = no hazard but needs further study;
4 = insufficient evidence to clear as used now;
5 = insufficient evidence to classify.

basis of general judgment, stimulated further study, particularly on teratology and mutagenicity, and fostered better management of food chemicals by the user industry. In summary, the GRAS reviews and safety reevaluations have helped to reduce unknowns about the safety of the food supply.

COST OF THE GRAS REVIEW

The cost of the GRAS review process (Table 4.6) has been approximately $24 million and has required the investment of 253 person years of technical talent. These investments have been made by the public through the Food and Drug Administration, the National Academy of Sciences, and the Federated American Societies of Experimental Biology, as well as by U.S. industry through FEMA, several related trade association, and more than 500 participating companies.

In the midst of the GRAS review process, an important regulated color additive was banned. The cost impact of the Red #2 ban, while less than that of cyclamate, was highly significant. It comprised over $2 million of merchandise written off, approximately $0.5 million in technical and legal expenditures, and an indeterminate amount of lost sales. The annual sales of Red #2 immediately preceding the ban exceeded $4 million. This action emphasized the need for a similar review of the safety of regulated additives, leading to what is now called the Cyclic Review of Regulated Food Additives (Table 4.7). This began with the Phase III NAS survey, the so-called Food and Color Additives Survey of 1977, and has involved the Food & Drug Administration, trade associations, and many sectors of the scientific community. This review is still in progress and indeed will be in progress many years to come. The dollar cost now exceeds $16 million and the investment of technical talent exceeds 80 Person Years. The demand upon the scientific community for the safety evaluations will make the cyclic review of regulated additives substan-

TABLE 4.6. COST OF THE GRAS REVIEW PROCESS, 1970 TO 1980

	Million $	Person Years
FDA	20	80
NAS - Phase I & II	—[1]	8
FASEB	—[1]	83
FEMA	1.4	32
Related Trade Associations	3.0	50
	24.4	253

[1] Cost included in FDA contract research.

TABLE 4.7. COST[1] OF THE CYCLIC REVIEW OF REGULATED ADDITIVES

	Million $	Person Years
FDA	6.1	2.25
NAS	6	19.5
Trade Associations	10.0	60.0
Safety Evaluations	30 (partial)	300 (partial)

[1]1977 to date

tially exceed any of the previous GRAS work in terms of dollar cost and scientific talent invested.

Another aspect of controlling food chemical usage is the ongoing regulatory cost. These costs involve direct expenditures by Government for enforcement as well as expenditures by industry and their related trade associations in the attempt to comply with complex government regulations. The expenditures by Government are approximately $6 million and 200 Person Years annually. My best estimate of the compliance cost by industry and trade associations is at least $17.5 million and approximately 600 Person Years per year.

UNANSWERED QUESTIONS

The type of questions which are raised about food additives (Table 4.8) emphasize the seriousness of the current investigations. Questions about the possible role of food chemicals in problems such as birth defects, cancer, and brain damage must be answered. Such questions are under intensive study and unfortunately there are no cheap and quick answers. In fact these investigations have led to the development of even more basic questions which should be addressed now. The questions about the tolerance of healthy individuals for specific carcinogens must be answered. The complicating interactions of carcinogens with diet, natural antagonists, promoters, and other carcinogens also must be addressed. Methodology, particularly the use of high dose levels to accelerate results must be validated. The philosophical question "should the margin of safety be greater for synthetic chemicals than for naturally occurring food chemicals" must be answered. The role of the natural defense

TABLE 4.8. QUESTIONS INVOLVED IN CURRENT FOOD ADDITIVE SAFETY STUDIES

- Does Caffeine Cause Birth Defects?
- Is Nitrite Carcinogenic?
- Is Saccharin Carcinogenic?
- Does MSG Cause Brain Damage?
- Is Lead Carcinogenic for Humans?

systems of the body in relation to carcinogens also is highly pertinent and must be addressed.

Such questions defy measurement on a dollar scale. Obviously they must be measured and weighed on a scale of human values which is very difficult to measure in intrinsic terms. Nonetheless, our resources are finite and reasoned decisions must be made about how those resources are used.

SUMMARY

The summary of cost (Table 4.9) related to the control of food additives from 1970 to 1980 will help us place the dollar cost and the investment of technical talent into the equation. The dollar cost exceeds $350 million and the investment of technical talent exceeds 15,000 Person Years over the past decade. This amounts to an average cost of approximately $116,000 and 5 Person Years of technical effort for each of the 3,000 food chemicals which have been studied. It is my purpose to place these costs and the questions in the public record. Decisions regarding the equity or inequity of this program must be made by others.

TABLE 4.9. SUMMARY OF COSTS[1] RELATED TO CONTROL OF FOOD ADDITIVES 1970 TO 1980

	Million $	Person Years
Government	80	2,732
Associations	40	500
Industry	161	5,698
Special Safety Evaluations	58	808
Consumer Action	11	5,390
Total	350	15,128

[1] Average cost per additive = $116,667 and 5 person years

5

Effect of Food Processing in the Formation and Destruction of Toxic Constituents of Food

C. O. Chichester[1]
T-C. Lee[2]

A large number of food processing operations impact upon the presence or absence of pseudo-toxic materials in the food. The thermal environment of food may modify the naturally occurring food materials and may leave the generation on materials which could, under some circumstances, be considered physiologically active. In order to avoid becoming encyclopedic, this paper is restricted to those materials which are naturally present in food and are not bacterial toxins, snake venoms and plant toxins.

A great number of food materials which are consumed by man or animal can, if utilized in excess, be considered toxic. Almost all animals have evolved detoxification mechanisms which allow the consumption and utilization of products which, if absorbed by the body intact, could be considered toxic. Digestion itself can be considered a detoxifying mechanism since it may reduce products such as proteins to their peptides and amino acids which can be utilized and absorbed while simultaneously destroying the toxic structure of the products.

[1] Nutrition Foundation, New York, New York.
[2] University of Rhode Island, Kingston, Rhode Island.

HEMAGGLUTININS

Of the products which occur in foods which can be considered toxic, probably the proteins are of major importance. Proteins can either be considered toxic or may act in an anti-nutritional manner (NAS 1973). Examples of these products are the hemagglutinins which have the ability to agglutinate red blood cells (Jaffe 1969). These proteins are found primarily in plants, although a similar number may also be found in the lower animals. From the standpoint of importance, however, the legume or soybean hemagglutinin is perhaps of particular importance.

The legume hemagglutinins were demonstrated many years ago in that soybeans when heated demonstrated better growth than raw soybeans in experimental animals. However, the orally ingested material was, in general, of comparatively low toxicity compared to the hemagglutinin of black beans. Black beans fed to rats will cause decreases in weight, not merely retardation in weight gain, and, in many cases, death. There is wide variation in the toxicity of legumes, in contrast to the black beans; peas and lentils are essentially nontoxic (Jaffe 1973).

The plant hemagglutinins are proteins, most of which contain a carbohydrate moiety, and plant products processed even at moderate temperature will destroy their activity. In fact, this particular property led to the discovery of their action.

Other toxic materials, such as enzyme inhibitors, are covered in Chapter 6. Those that inhibit the proteolytic enzymes are of particular importance. Trypsin inhibitors are particularly prevalent and occur in such widely differing products as egg white, soybeans, navy beans, potatoes, etc. Equivalently, chymotrypsin is also moderately widely distributed and occurs in many similar products. Other protein-based inhibitors also occur which are active against amylase, invertase, peroxidase, and catalase. As with other protein-based substances, these are rather easily inactivated by heat and thus the effect of thermal processing is to reduce or eliminate those negative factors.

ANTI-VITAMINS

Another class "of toxic materials" which occurs naturally in foods are the anti-vitamins or the vitamin antagonists. Somogyi (1973) differentiates the anti-metabolites and anti-vitamins into two groups: (1) those with structural similarities, which can be considered competitive inhibitors, and (2) those which modify the structural nutrients acting as noncompetitive inhibitors rendering them unavailable.

The existence of such compounds has been known since the early part of this century. Perhaps the most important of these are the antagonists of thiamin. Thiaminase occurs in fish, shellfish and in bacteria. The action of the compound is to destroy vitamin B-1. The compound is moderately stable and thus, under some mild conditions of food processing, is not destroyed. The other compound which acts as an antagonist and is widely distributed is avidin which forms a stable complex with biotin and renders it biologically unavailable. This compound, like many other proteins, is moderately unstable to heat and, as a consequence, the process of heating and denaturation of egg white eliminates the problem. There appears to be a number of other toxic materials associated with antagonism to various vitamins but they are of only minor importance in a diversified food supply.

EFFECTS OF THERMAL PROCESSES

In essence, the thermal processes of food are extremely beneficial. In general, increases in digestibility destroy the antagonists of vitamins and enzymes and in many instances destroy toxins which occur under normal conditions in food.

On the other hand, when foods are heated, a number of reactions take place; the most obvious casual observation is that the food materials darken. This reaction is called the Maillard or nonenzymatic browning reaction (Hodge 1953) since the change or darkening is in the direction of a brown-appearing color, due to the general absorption of blue light. The reaction is specifically between reducing carbohydrates such as aldoses and ketoses, and an amine which may be an amino acid residue of a protein or in some cases a free amino acid.

The browning reaction is fairly rapid and occurs at comparatively low temperatures. A number of food materials ranging from toasted bread to fried chicken, gravy mixes and beef stew undergo browning. In fact, it would be hard to imagine food materials which, when heated, do not undergo some browning.

In all cases, the carbohydrate-amino acid browning reaction produces literally hundreds of reaction products (Hodge 1953; Anet 1964; Reynolds 1963, 1965, 1969). Some time ago, based partially upon reaction kinetics and the vast number of products produced, it was speculated that a free radical mechanism may be operative in most cases (Mituso *et al.* 1977). Despite the fact that the Maillard reaction has been investigated for many years, we cannot as yet identify all of the reactant compounds. The first steps are, however, clearly established. The aldose or ketose reacts with amine to produce an N-substituted glycosyl amine (Fig. 5.1). This rearranges, as illustrated, to produce a 1-amino-desoxy-2-ketosyl amine. If it is blocked, the overall reaction is blocked. The key compound or compounds can then continue to react (Fig. 5.2). As can be

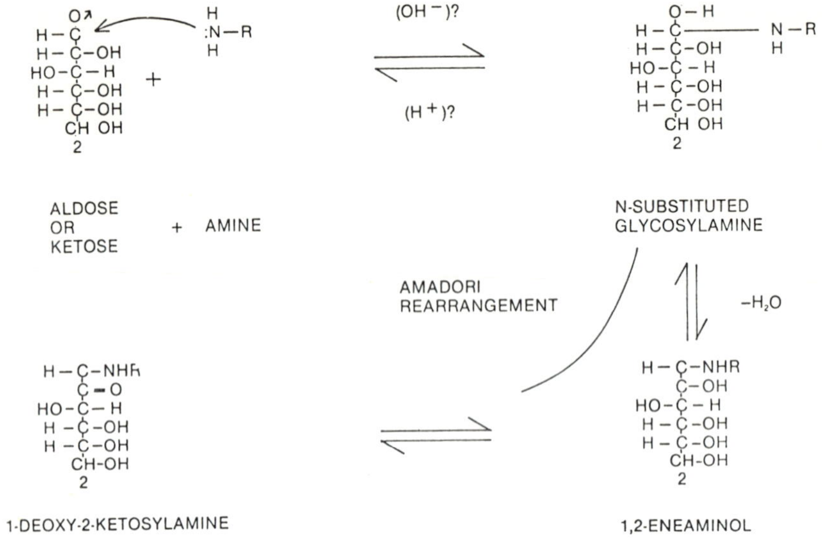

FIG. 5.1. INITIATION OF THE MAILLARD REACTION
If the keto (Amadori) compound is not formed, there is no Maillard browning.

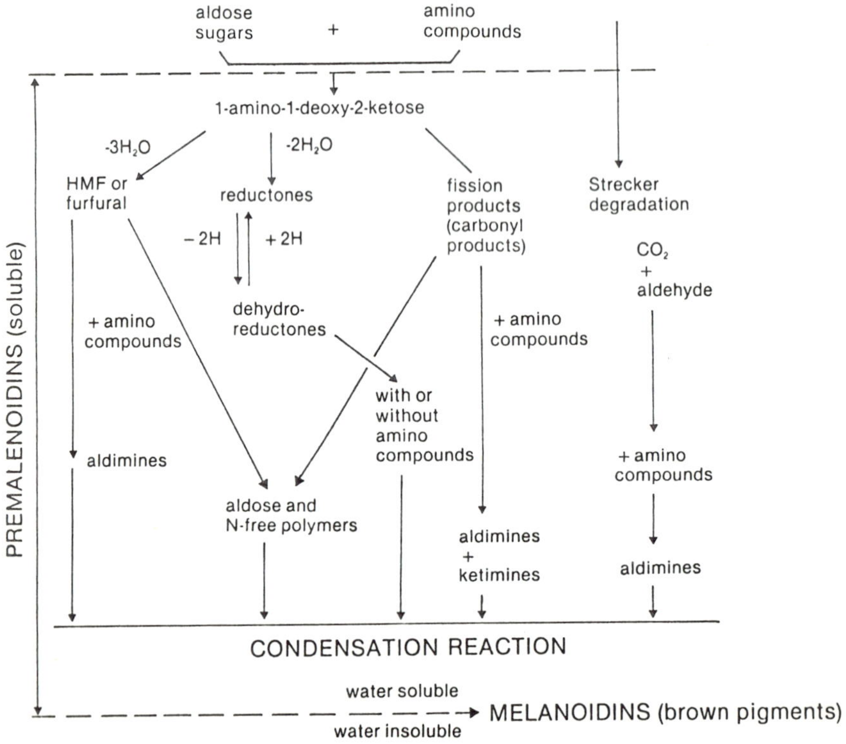

FIG. 5.2. HODGE SCHEME OF THE BROWNING REACTION

seen, the desoxy-ketose or amadori rearrangement product can dehydrate to produce furfural-like compounds or, through the loss of water, produce reductones. All of these compounds can react with one another or with other amine compounds to produce a wide variety of reaction products.

Two aspects of the reaction are particularly interesting. First, the color or the brown product is a long chain of rather unsaturated nitrogen-containing products, sometimes called melanins. Its composition is not constant but is dependent upon the extent of the reaction and the mix of reactant. It appears to be a moderately good chelating compound and thus may have some interesting characteristics from a nutritional standpoint.

Another part of the reaction which is of interest is the Strecker degradation of the amino acids which produces carbon dioxide (sometimes causing container failure), and an aldehyde which may then further condense with other compounds. These aldehydic condensation products, together with the amino acid-carbohydrate residue, are responsible for many flavors. By deliberately reacting mixtures of different amino acids, flavors of chicken, beef and pork can be reproduced. One direct application of this reaction is to induce the darkening of foods heated in a radar range. An amino acid-sugar mixture can be placed on the outside of the food which will react rapidly to produce a dark or brown surface and can, if the mixture is chosen correctly, contribute to the flavor of the food.

Table 5.1 shows the difference between heating a protein and a protein with an aldose sugar. There is a tenfold increase in light absorption of the egg albumen-glucose mixture above egg albumen when heated for 5 min in a microwave oven. An even larger difference is shown between soybean protein and soybean protein with added glucose.

TABLE 5.1. BROWN COLOR DEVELOPMENT OF PROTEIN AND PROTEIN-GLUCOSE MIXTURES DURING COOKING
(Absorbancy[1] of TCA Soluble Portion at 420 nm)

Cooking Method	Microwave Oven Time (minutes)			Conventional Oven Time (minutes)	
Samples	1	3	5	30	45
Egg Albumin	0.010	0.015	0.059	0.00	0.045
Egg Albumin-Glucose	0.001	0.135	0.506	0.246	0.788
Soybean-Protein	0.002	0.008	0.043	0.015	0.050
Soybean-Protein-Glucose	0.050	0.170	1.35	0.140	0.290
Casein-Glucose	0.007	0.102	N.D.[2]	N.D.[2]	1.744
Lactalbumin-Glucose	0.002	0.259	0.994	0.894	1.084
Zein-Glucose	0.046	0.057	0.107	0.088	0.092

[1] The absorbancy was measured against the uncooked sample.
[2] N.D.—not determined.

The loss of nutritive value when protein or protein-rich foods are heated or stored in the presence of carbohydrates has been studied by a large number of groups (Mauron *et al.* 1955; Neshim and Carpenter 1967; Adrian 1974; Sgarbieri *et al.* 1971; Tomaka *et al.* 1975A; Chichester and Lee 1979; Kimiagar *et al.* 1980). From the nutritional standpoint, Table 5.2 shows that the digestibility of proteins is decreased as well as the availability of amino acids and carbohydrates after the

TABLE 5.2. LOSS OF NUTRITIVE VALUE WHEN PROTEINS OR PROTEIN-RICH FOODS ARE HEATED IN THE PRESENCE OF CARBOHYDRATES

1. Digestibility of proteins↓
2. Availability of amino acids↓
3. Availability of carbohydrates↓
4. Biological value of proteins↓
5. Data indicate possibility of cumulative toxic effects from continuous consumption of Maillard browned foods

Maillard reaction takes place. A derivative from this is that the biological value of proteins has also decreased. For example, in Table 5.3 one can see significant decreases in amino acids of egg albumen stored at 37°C in the presence of roughly the equivalent amount of glucose. The moisture content of the mix was 15%. One can see (line 4 from the bottom) that after 10 days, there is a very significant decrease in lysine availability which continues to decrease as the browning is prolonged. At 40 days, roughly 57% of the lysine is lost (Tanaka *et al.* 1977).

TABLE 5.3. AMINO ACID COMPOSITION (g/16g N) OF BROWNED EGG ALBUMEN HYDROLYZED BY 6N HYDROCHLORIC ACID

Amino Acids	0 Days	10 Days	20 Days	30 Days	40 Days	% Loss in Protein After 40 Days
Aspartic acid	10.12	10.15	10.42	9.58	10.58	—
Threonine	3.50	3.39	4.22	3.45	3.53	—
Serine	7.26	6.40	6.57	6.88	5.72	21.2
Glutamic acid	11.01	9.78	10.24	10.01	9.44	14.3
Proline	2.39	2.82	2.50	2.41	2.40	—
Glycine	3.99	3.42	3.65	3.33	3.88	2.8
Alanine	7.52	5.51	6.50	5.84	6.82	9.3
Valine	6.53	6.24	6.77	6.37	6.49	—
½ Cystine	3.44	2.46	2.62	2.71	2.86	16.9
Methionine	3.34	3.47	3.55	3.28	3.07	9.1
Isoleucine	5.97	5.71	5.36	5.37	5.25	12.1
Leucine	8.97	9.13	8.97	8.27	7.46	16.8
Tyrosine	3.33	2.97	3.02	3.04	3.04	9.7
Phenylalanine	5.26	5.92	5.82	5.52	4.93	6.3
Lysine	7.68	5.92	4.19	4.04	3.29	57.2
Histidine	2.76	2.53	2.36	2.39	2.12	23.2
Arginine	3.68	3.26	3.01	2.22	1.78	51.6
Tryptophan[1]	1.61	1.47	1.34	1.24	1.26	21.7

[1] Tryptophan was determined after alkaline hydrolysis.

Other changes are shown in Table 5.4 (Tanaka 1974) where a number of nutritional indices are compared for the egg albumen-glucose mixture, which our group has used as a model mixture. Using the zero or nonreactive day as 100, there is a steady decrease in protein score, chemical score, etc. Particularly interesting is the protein efficiency ratio, a measurement of the ability of the diet to maintain growth, which decreases by one-third within 10 days. This is a significantly higher decrease than any of the other measurements would suggest. Thus the biological nutritive changes observed are more complicated than merely a loss in the availability of amino acids or proteins.

Our group and several others have shown that supplementing a diet which has undergone browning with those amino acids which are lost cannot completely restore its biological value (Rao *et al.* 1963; Sgarbieri *et al.* 1973A, B). This suggests the possible formation of some inhibitory or anti-nutritional compounds during the Maillard reaction. Typical growth rates of rats on a diet in which the protein was egg albumen-glucose which had been browned for 10 days versus a control set of animals over a long period of time is shown in Fig. 5.3. If at any time additional amino acids or proteins are added to the diet, there is no catch-up phenomenon and the animals on the browned diet will always be at a significant disadvantage.

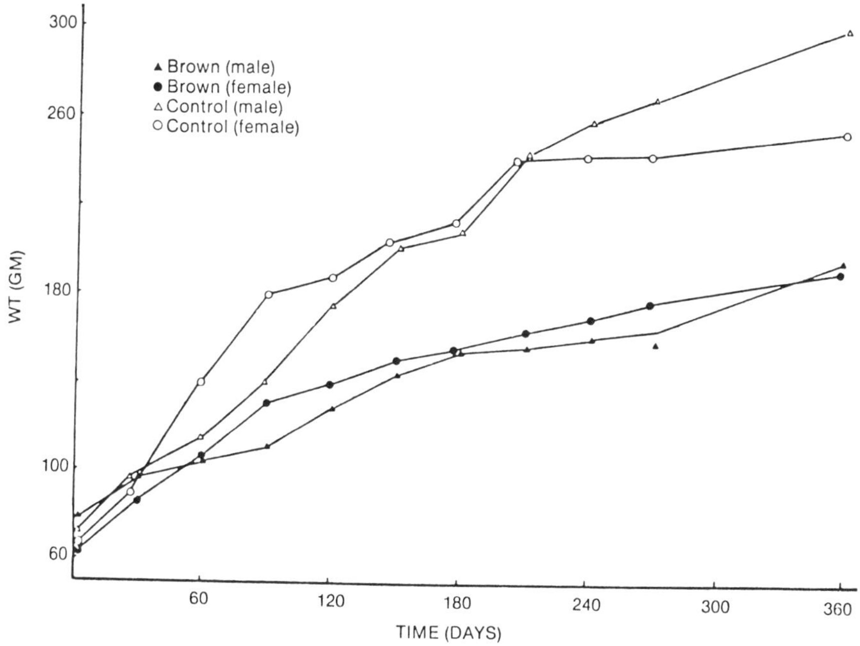

FIG. 5.3. GROWTH CURVE FOR RATS ON BROWN AND CONTROL DIETS

TABLE 5.4. CHANGES IN THE NUTRITIONAL VALUE OF EGG ALBUMEN DURING STORAGE

Methods	0 Days	10 Days	20 Days	30 Days	40 Days	Student's t Test
EAA index	100	92.6	87.3	85.6	81.1	
Protein score	100	96.5	86.5	83.2	76.7	
Chemical score	100	91.7	83.4	77.0	68.5	
PDR index	100	76.9	70.5	58.1	55.9	
PPD index	100	72.2	58.9	55.6	50.2	
Available lysine (g/16g N)	7.37	4.98	4.12	3.56	2.97	
BV(%)	90.1 ±2.0[1]	44.5 ±5.0	34.3 ±1.8	29.1 ±2.5	23.7 ±2.9	0>>10>>>20>>30>>40[2]
PER	3.62±0.25	1.32±0.29	0.72±0.16	0.47±0.15	0.193	0>>>10>>>20>>30
True digestibility (%)	95.9 ±1.4	82.8 ±4.2	80.1 ±3.1	74.8 ±3.1	74.9 ±3.3	0>>>10, 20>>30, 40

[1] Averages± SE of mean.
[2] Student's test > Difference significant at $p<0.05$; >> difference significant at $p<0.01$; >>> Difference significant at $p<0.001$.
[3] Three rats lost weight.

Even a very short period of browning at 37°C is measurable in terms of the protein-efficiency ratio (PER) using a 28-day feeding experiment. Table 5.5 illustrates that even after 1 day of browning at 37°C, there is a 30% reduction in the PER measured conventionally (Tanaka *et al.* 1977). We have standardized most of our work in utilizing the 10-day sample. The PER of this material is sufficiently high so that the animals can survive and yet sufficiently low so that the maximum physiological effect on the animals is observed.

TABLE 5.5. EFFECT OF BROWNING DURATION ON THE RAT PER VALUE

Days Browned	PER (Mean + S.D.)
0D	3.28 ± 0.17
½D	3.14 ± 0.28
1D	2.44 ± 0.37
2D	2.50 ± 0.32
3D	2.30 ± 0.24
6D	2.0 ± 0.54
10D	1.1 ± 0.10

If one observes animals on a diet with a high concentration of browned materials in it, one immediately observes that almost all of the animals have a severe diarrheal condition. It is also obvious on further examination that animals on the diet develop an enlarged cecum. Another observed effect upon the digestive system of animals is the increase in the excretion of essential and nonessential amino acids in the form of short peptides, four to six residues long, in the feces. Coupled with this, in general, the fecal-nitrogen content is 35% above the control, possibly relating to the existence of diarrhea and the increase in the rate of stomach emptying (Amaya *et al.* 1980).

Although these changes were primarily noted when diets such as egg albumen-glucose were fed, similar changes are observed when more conventional diets are fed. For instance, Tsen *et al.* (1977) observed equivalent reductions in PER when a number of breads were heated in microwave ovens, in steam, or when baked using conventional methods. Here, reductions in PER were threefold or more.

Several years ago, it was first demonstrated that when heavily browned mixtures were fed at moderate levels, several physiological changes took place in the experimental animal (Table 5.6). It will be noted (by comparing the last line to the control) that significant decreases in lactase, sucrase, and maltase activity take place (Lee *et al.* 1977B). In order to demonstrate that these were due to the brown mixture and not the reduction in PER, the browned egg albumen diet was supplemented with the amino acids which appeared to have been lost or bound (Line 2).

TABLE 5.6. DISACCHARIDASE ACTIVITIES IN THE INTESTINAL MUCOSA OF RATS FED CONTROLS, BROWN AND SUPPLEMENTED BROWN EGG ALBUMEN DIETS[1]

Dietary Group	Body Weight (g)	Activity, units/g		
		Lactase	Sucrase	Maltase
Control	338 ± 3.6	10.6 ± 1.02	35.7 ± 3.32	221 ± 16.3
Supplemented brown	300 ± 12.3a**	8.1 ± 1.31a*	30.8 ± 0.78a*	205 ± 11.3
Unsupplemented brown	278 ± 10.7a***,b*	6.0 ± 1.20a**	24.6 ± 1.24a**,b**	172 ± 13.7a**,b**

[1]Significantly different from the control: a* = $P<0.05$; a** = $P<0.01$; a*** = $P<0.001$.
Significantly different from the supplemented brown diet: b* = $P<0.05$; b** = <0.01.

Although there was some improvement under these conditions, there is still a significant decrease in some of the disaccharide activity.

In Table 5.7, if one examines the control, the brown lines, and the columns marked "terminal weight gain" and "kidney and liver," it is obvious that there is a reduction in body weight, but there is an increase in kidney and liver weight (Tanaka *et al.* 1977). Equivalently, in Table 5.8, again looking only at the lines control and brown, there are significant changes in serum glucose, blood urea/nitrogen, serum glutamate-oxylate transaminase, serum glutamate pyruvate transaminase and serum alkaline phosphatase (Tanaka *et al.* 1977). These increases in the blood enzymes can be taken as a measure of liver damage indicating that significant changes had occurred or were occurring in the liver. The obvious interpretation of these data, together with many other experimental observations, would suggest that under conditions of moderate to heavy browning in foods or in model systems, products which are physiologically active are produced.

These data and other data have been criticized on the basis that the effects were entirely nutritional and that they occurred because of food inadequacies. We have recently completed some work which would indicate that food inadequacy is not the cause of these effects (Kimiagar *et al.* 1980). In these experiments, rats were fed the usual browned egg albumen-glucose mixture for periods up to 12 months utilizing pair-feeding techniques and a control ration resembling the nutritional quality of the browned diet. Thus, food inadequacy was eliminated as a variable and the observed effects could therefore be attributed only to the existence of browned components. In these experiments, egg albumen was browned in the presence of glucose (three parts egg albumen to two parts glucose) at 37°C at 15% moisture for 10 days. The browned samples were then freeze-dried and incorporated in the diet at a 10% level. The PER of the diet was determined to be 1.1. The rats were fed the browned diet for 1, 3, 6, and 12 month periods together with two control groups. One control group was fed a 10% egg albumen diet *ad libitum*. We called this group control A. The other control group was pair-fed a 5% albumen-5% nonessential amino acid diet designed to resemble that of the browned diet from a nutritional standpoint against the animals consuming the browned diet. The differences between animals fed these two diets for 1 month are shown in Table 5.9. Note that there is no significant difference between organ weights in the liver, spleen, heart, etc. with the possible exception of the cecum in which there is a significant difference. Additionally, there is essentially no difference in the number of the enzyme parameters measured nor in the hematocrit, which would suggest that at least from a nutritional standpoint these two diets are equivalent.

TABLE 5.7. RELATIVE ORGAN WEIGHTS OF RATS FED BROWN AND CONTROL DIET FOR THREE MONTHS

Group	Terminal Wt. (GM) Avg ± S.D.		Kidneys (% Body Wt) Avg ± S.D.		Liver (% Body Wt) Avg. ± S.D.		Spleen (% Body Wt) Avg. ± S.D.		Heart (% Body Wt) Avg ± S.D.		Testes (% Body Wt) Avg. ± S.D.
	Male	Female	Male	Female	Male	Female	Male	Female	Male	Female	Male
I Control	358 ±27	296 ±10	0.61 ±0.038	0.83 ±0.04	2.41 ±0.22	3.16 ±0.12	0.137 ±0.006	0.170 ±0.021	0.31 ±0.056	0.32 ±0.018	0.95 ±0
II Brown	110[1,2,3] ±23	132[1,2,3] ±10	0.95[1,2,3] ±0.10	0.725[1] ±0.05	4.16[1,2,3] ±0.73	3.40 ±1.0	0.189 ±0.058	0.153 ±0.036	0.46 ±0.13	0.37 ±0.54	1.83 ±0.34
III 5% Protein 5% NEAA	140 ±12	182 ±12	0.80 ±0.06	0.71 ±0.03	3.08 ±0.60	3.95 ±0.26	0.154 ±0.02	0.189 ±0.004	0.43 ±0.026	0.363 ±0.023	1.50 ±0.29
IV 4.5% Protein	161 ±19	165 ±15	0.69 ±0.16	0.74 ±0.11	2.54 ±0.11	3.65 ±0.54	0.169 ±0.01	0.155 ±0.043	0.35 ±0.019	0.365 ±0.029	1.50 ±0.028

[1] Significantly different ($p < 0.05$) From Group I.
[2] Significantly different ($p < 0.05$) From Group III.
[3] Significantly different ($p < 0.05$) From Group IV.

TABLE 5.8. BLOOD CHEMISTRY OF RATS FED BROWN AND CONTROL DIET FOR THREE MONTHS

Group	Serum Glucose (mg %) Avg ± S.D.		Blood Urea Nit. - Gen. (BUN) (mg %) Avg ± S.D.		SGOT (IU) Avg ± S.D.		SGPT (IU) Avg ± S.D.		% PCV Avg ± S.D.		Serum Alkaline Phosphatase (IU) Avg ± S.D.	
	Male	Female	Male	Female	Male	Female	Male	Female	Male	Female	Male	Female
I Control	63 ±14.8	69.3 ±5.3	14.9 ±2.8	11.0 ±2.1	395 ±46	288 ±27	121 ±33	72 ±4	46.5 ±2.1	45.3 ±1.5	44.5 ±6.4	127 ±2.3
II Brown	110[1,2,3] ±28.5	64.6 ±23	19.6[2] ±5.25	11.1[3] ±3.36	513[2] ±14	340[2] ±76	210[3] ±89	87 ±21	37.7 ±3.3	45 ±1.4	259.5[1,2,3] ±75.5	178.7 ±85
III 5% Protein + 5% NEAA	74 ±13.4	84 ±3.4	12.2 ±6.3	7.8 ±2.9	379 ±55	211 ±51	118 ±11	75 ±9	44.7 ±4.5	44.0 ±2	133 ±29.7	159 ±21.7
IV 4.5% Protein	61 ±18.5	82.6 ±6.5	14.1 ±4.8	6.7 ±1.6	547 ±94	257 ±26	68 ±4	84 ±26	49.5 ±0.7	47.7 ±0.58	119 ±4.9	142.7 ±15.5

[1] Significantly different from Group I.
[2] Significantly different from Group II.
[3] Significantly different from Group IV.

TABLE 5.9. BODY WEIGHT, RELATIVE ORGAN WEIGHT AND BIOCHEMICAL VALUES IN RATS FED FOR ONE MONTH AT EQUIVALENT NUTRIENT INTAKE

	Brown Mean + S.D.	Control Mean + S.D.	Significance of Difference
Body Weight	85 ± 8	87 ± 5	NS[1]
Relative Organ Weight: Liver	4.82 ± 0.39	4.23 ± 0.74	NS
Kidneys	1.19 ± 0.11	1.24 ± 0.08	NS
Testes	1.78 ± 0.27	1.81 ± 0.13	NS
Spleen	0.201 ± 0.02	0.215 ± 0.01	NS
Heart	0.426 ± 0.03	0.463 ± 0.02	NS
Lungs	0.842 ± 0.10	0.917 ± 0.04	NS
Cecum	2.53 ± 0.58	1.99 ± 0.01	Significant
Small intestinal dipeptidase	7.5 ± 2.0	6.5 ± 2.2	NS
Small intestinal sucrase	3.62 ± 1.4	2.83 ± 1.4	NS
Liver GOT	580 ± 110	492 ± 148	NS
Liver GPT	240 ± 108	289 ± 72	NS
BUN	18.4 ± 11	8.7 ± 1.8	NS
Serum glucose	106 ± 8	72 ± 31	Significant
Serum protein	4.72 ± 0.66	5.32 ± 0.59	NS
SAP	205 ± 64	172 ± 38	NS
SGOT	23 ± 5	23 ± 4.5	NS
SGPT	26 ± 3	27 ± 3	NS
Hematocrit	38.3 ± 5.3	38.2 ± 4.3	NS

[1] NS = Not significant

Table 5.10 shows the data on body weight ratios of animals fed the two control diets and the browned diets for the periods 3, 6, and 12 months. As would be expected from previous experiments, the ceca of the rats on the browned diet were significantly heavier than either of those of the two control groups. Additionally, the livers of rats fed the browned diet were, on the average, 23% larger than the lower-efficiency control diet and 62% larger than the *ad libitum* fed rats. The kidney was also enlarged in the rats fed the browned diet. Table 5.11 shows that the specific gravity of the urine of rats after 6 months' feeding was significantly higher than for the animals on the browned diet. This increase in urine-specific gravity coupled with kidney enlargement suggests that something in the browned diet affects its function. Table 5.12 contains the hematology of rats on the two control diets and the rats on the browned diet. The first column shows that serum alkaline phosphatase in group B increased relative to group S for all feeding periods and that group C (second control) was not significantly different from group S. After one year of feeding, the serum alkaline phosphatase of group B, the browned group, was 130% of the control group. The increase in alkaline phosphatase activity and in glutamate oxylate transferase, coupled with

TABLE 5.10. ORGAN WEIGHT TO BODY WEIGHT RATIOS OF RATS FED *AD LIBITUM*, AND PAIR FED BROWNED AND CONTROL DIETS (mean ± S.D.)

Feeding Period	Diet[4]	Weight (g)	Organ Weight to Body Weight Ratio (% Body Weight)							
			Liver	Kidneys	Testes	Spleen	Heart	Lung	Cecum	Stomach
3 Months	A	321[2,3]	2.86	0.740	0.950[2,3]	0.157	-ND[5]	—	—	—
		±37	±0.42	±0.13	±0.01	±0.02	-ND[5]	—	—	—
	B	121[1,3]	3.78	0.836	1.83[1]	0.171	—	—	—	—
		±17	±0.93	±0.15	±0.34	±0.05	—	—	—	—
	C	161[1,2]	3.52	0.754	1.50[1]	0.172	—	—	—	—
		±24	±0.63	±0.06	±0.29	±0.02	—	—	—	—
6 Months	A	411[2,3]	2.48[2]	0.702[3]	0.774[2,3]	0.183	0.290[2,3]	0.421[2,3]	0.959[2,3]	—
		±126	±0.27	±0.09	±0.04	±0.05	±0.01	±0.06	±0.25	
	B	155[1,3]	4.03[1]	1.10 [1,3]	1.78[1]	0.268[3]	0.493[1,3]	0.743[1]	2.10[1]	—
		±70	±1.36	±0.36	±0.03	±0.09	±0.15	±0.19	±0.97	
	C	207	3.28	0.820[1,2]	1.58[1]	0.188[2]	0.405[1,2]	0.694[1]	1.55[1]	—
		±12	±0.50	±0.08	±0.15	±0.04	±0.04	±0.10	±0.23	
12 Months	A	479[2,3]	2.64[2]	0.695[2]	0.712[3]	0.126[2]	0.267[2,3]	0.430[2,3]	1.74[2]	0.533[2,3]
		±111	±0.28	±0.06	±0.06	±0.01	±0.02	±0.08	±0.31	±0.05
	B	196[1,3]	3.38[1,3]	0.857[1,3]	1.12	0.154[1]	0.398[1]	0.631[1,3]	2.93[1,3]	1.03[1,3]
		±80	±0.70	±0.13	±0.18	±0.02	±0.07	±0.12	±1.1	±0.27
	C	277[1,2]	2.80[2]	0.701[2]	0.958[1]	0.148	0.367[1]	0.543[1,2]	1.61[2]	0.710[1,2]
		±36	±0.33	±0.07	±0.04	±0.03	±0.4	±0.06	±0.40	±0.15

[1] Significantly different from group A: $P < 0.05$ or less.
[2] Significantly different from group B: $P < 0.05$ or less.
[3] Significantly different from group C: $P < 0.05$ or less.
[4] A—*ad libitum*; B—browned; C—control.
[5] ND—not determined.

TABLE 5.11. URINE SPECIFIC GRAVITY OF RATS FED BROWNED AND CONTROL DIETS FOR 6 MONTHS

Diet	Specific Gravity
Brown	1.0549 ± 0.0008[1]
Control	1.0310 ± 0.010

[1] Significantly different from the control group ($P<0.01$).

the enlargement of the liver, is completely indicative of liver damage in rats fed the browned diet. Additionally, histopathological examination of the liver reveals the accumulation of a black-brown pigment of an unknown nature. At 3 months of feeding, 50% of the rats developed heavy pigmentation with significant changes in the architecture of the cells. Table 5.13 summarizes these results.

After feeding for 12 months, 100% of the rats fed the browned mixture had fatty livers and pigmented and vacuolated hepatocytes (Kimiagar *et al.* 1978). Certainly the incidence compared to the equivalently fed control is indicative of a remarkable effect.

Table 5.14 illustrates the statistical analysis of the data which suggests significant changes in cecum, liver and kidney weights between browned and nutritionally equivalent control diets in the 12 month rats. Equivalently, serum glutamate oxylate transferase, alkaline phosphatase and serum glucose levels are all significantly different for these two controls. From this and previous data, it is clear that as the feeding period of browned materials increases, the adverse effects become more and more pronounced. This pattern indicates that there is a cumulative effect and it resembles, in many instances, the effect expected of a toxic compound.

Sugimura and Nagao (1979) recently suggested that some of the compounds found in overcooked foods are mutagenic when tested for mutagenicity by the Ames method. Further, Coughlin *et al.* (1979) reported that the nitrosylated Amadori rearrangement products were mutagenic when tested by the Ames method. Since Tannenbaum and others (1978) demonstrated that nitrosylation can occur in the intestine, it is possible that browning reaction products may be undergoing this reaction *in vivo*. This should not, however, be compared to the possible mutagenicity of the browned products themselves. We tested a number of our products using the Salmonella Mutagenicity Assay method of the Ames method (Pintauro *et al.* 1980). In this test a mutant strain of Salmonella which is histidine-dependent is cultivated in the presence of the test materials. This strain (which is moderately unstable and is subject to reversion, that is, it becomes nonhistidine dependent) can revert to the wild type. Any materials which increase the rate of reversion and would thus cause the growth of the organism on nonhistidine media can be said to be mutagenic.

TABLE 5.12. HEMATOLOGY DATA FROM RATS FED *AD LIBITUM*, AND PAIRS FED BROWNED AND CONTROL DIETS (mean ± S.D.)

Feeding Period	Diet[4]	Serum Alkaline Phosphatase IU	Serum GOT IU	Serum Glucose mg/100 ml	BUN mg/100 ml	Serum Protein g/100 ml	Hgb. g/100 ml	Hematocrit
3 Months	A	96[2]	32	66	12.6	8.2[2,3]	—	45.8
		±42	±4.8	±9	± 3.0	±0.48		±1.6
	B	211[1]	39	87	15.4	6.89[1]	—	41.4
		±92	±11	±33	±5.8	±0.84		±4.5
	C	146	29	79	10.1	6.25[1]	—	44.3
		±28	±10	±9	±4.9	±0.58		±3.1
6 Months	A	78[2]	62	85[3]	19.4[3]	6.60	17.9	46.7[2]
		±21	±28	±7	±2.2	±1.4	±0.4	±2.4
	B	136[1]	66[3]	97[3]	19.4[3]	5.35	15.1[3]	38.4[1,3]
		±68	±18	±21	±6.4	±1.4	±3.1	±7.7
	C	98	53[2]	71[1,2]	12.9[1,2]	5.84	18.6[2]	48.6[2]
		±30	±4	±8	±3.0	±0.40	±2.2	±4.0
12 Months	A	50[2]	39[2]	76[2]	18.4[2,3]	6.77	14.9[2]	46.9
		±23	±1	±4	±5.3	±0.49	±1.4	±4.1
	B	138[1,3]	56[1,3]	82[1,3]	13.5[1]	6.38[3]	12.7[1,3]	44.4[3]
		±81	±9	±4	±3.6	±0.58	±1.0	±3.2
	C	60[2]	40[2]	76[2]	12.1[1]	6.99[2]	14.8[2]	50.5[2]
		±43	±8	±6	±3.4	±0.38	±1.8	±3.8

[1] Significantly different from group A: $P<0.05$ or less.
[2] Significantly different from group B: $P<0.05$ or less.
[3] Significantly different from group C: $P<0.05$ or less.
[4] A—*ad libitum*; B—browned; C—control.

TABLE 5.13. HISTOPATHOLOGICAL EXAMINATION OF THE LIVER IN RATS FED BROWNED AND CONTROL DIETS (% OF THE TOTAL RATS IN THAT GROUP)

Feeding Period (Months)	Diet	Vacuolated Helpaocytes	Fatty Liver	Pigmented Hepatocytes
3	C			0
3	B	50	25	0
6	C	0	0	0
6	B	56	44	44
12	C	0	0	0
12	B	100	100	100

When egg albumen-browned proteins were tested, no significant changes were found which would indicate mutagenicity of the products (Pintauro *et al.* 1980). At least under the present test conditions, we must conclude that the materials produced under Maillard browning conditions in our tests did not possess this property.

It is obvious that significant changes in nutritive value are caused by browning. Additionally, there is a suggestion that some of the browning products possess in themselves a low level of toxicity. This toxicity is evident over long periods of time and appears to be cumulative. While we have used a model compound, it is not too far from what one would expect in food. There are many potential problems in this area in the food supply and the problem is certainly worth additional investigation.

TABLE 5.14. TEST OF DIFFERENCE (STUDENT'S t TEST) BETWEEN GROUPS FED *AD LIBIDUM*, AND PAIR FED BROWNED AND CONTROL DIETS (mean ± S.D.)

Feeding Period	Groups Compared[4]	SGOT	Ser. Glucose	SAP	Ser. Protein	BUN	Hematocrit	Hemoglobin	Body Weight	Relative Organ Weight: Stomach	Cecum	Liver	Kidneys	Testes	Spleen	Heart	Lung	Urine sp.gr.
3 Months	B vs C	NS[5]	NS	NS	NS	NS	NS	—ND[6]	[2]	—	—	NS	NS	NS	NS	—	—	—
	B vs A	NS	NS	[1]	[2]	NS	NS	—	[3]	—	—	NS	NS	[1]	NS	—	—	—
	C vs A	NS	NS	NS	NS	NS	NS	—	[3]	—	—	NS	NS	NS	NS	—	—	—
6 Months	B vs C	[1]	[2]	NS	NS	[2]	[2]	[1]	[1]	—	NS	NS	[1]	NS	[1]	[1]	NS	[2]
	B vs A	NS	NS	[1]	NS	NS	[1]	NS	[3]	—	[1]	NS	NS	[3]	NS	[1]	[2]	—
	C vs A	NS	[2]	NS	NS	[2]	NS	NS	[3]	—	[2]	[1]	[1]	[3]	NS	[3]	[2]	—
12 Months	B vs C	[3]	[1]	[2]	[2]	NS	[3]	[2]	[1]	[2]	[2]	[1]	[2]	NS	NS	NS	[1]	—
	B vs A	[2]	[2]	[1]	NS	[1]	NS	[1]	[3]	[2]	[1]	[1]	[1]	[1]	[1]	[3]	[2]	—
	C vs A	NS	NS	NS	NS	[2]	NS	NS	[3]	[1]	NS	NS	NS	[3]	NS	[3]	[3]	—

[1] Significantly different at $P<0.05$.
[2] Significantly different at $P<0.01$.
[3] Significantly different at $P<0.001$.
[4] A—*ad libitum*, 10% egg albumen diet; B—browned; C—control.
[5] NS—not significantly different ($P>0.05$).
[6] ND—not determined.

BIBLIOGRAPHY

ADRIAN, J. 1974. Nutritional and physiological consequences of the Maillard reaction. World Rev. Nutr. Diet. *19*, 71.

AMAYA, J. 1974. The Maillard reaction of proteins. Ph.D. dissertation, University of Rhode Island, Kingston, R.I.

AMAYA, J., LEE, T-C., and CHICHESTER, C.O. 1980. Unpublished data.

ANET, R.F.L.J. 1964. 3-Deoxyglycosuloses (3-Deoxyglycosones) and the degradation carbohydrates. Adv. Carbohydrate Chem. *19*, 181.

CHEN, T., LEE, T-C., and CHICHESTER, C.O. 1980. Unpublished data.

CHICHESTER, C.O. and LEE, T-C. 1979. Nutrition in food processing. *In* World Review of Nutrition and Dietetics. S. Jarger (Editor). Basel, Munchem, Paris, London and New York.

COUGHLIN, J.R., WEI, C.I., HSIEH, D.P.H., and RUSSELL, G.F. 1979. Synthesis, mutagenicity and human health implications on N-nitroso Amadori compounds from Maillard browning reactions in the presence of nitrite. Presented at Am. Chem. Soc./Chem. Soc. Japan. Chemical Congress, Honolulu, Hawaii, April 2–6.

HODGE, J.E. 1953. Dehydrated foods. Chemistry of browning reactions in model systems. J. Agric. Food Chem. *1*, 928.

JAFFE, W.G. 1969. Hemagglutinins. *In* Toxic Constituents of Plant for Foodstuffs. I.E. Liener (Editor), Academic Press, New York.

JAFFE, W.G. 1973. Toxic proteins and peptides. *In* Toxic Constituents of Plant Foodstuffs, 2nd Edition. National Academy of Science, Washington, D.C.

KIMIAGAR, M., LEE, T-C., and CHICHESTER, C.O. 1978. Chronic feeding effects of Maillard browned protein to rat. *In* FASEB Proceedings, 62nd Annual Meeting, Atlantic City, N.J.

KIMIAGAR, M., LEE, T-C., and CHICHESTER, C.O. 1980. Long-term feeding effects of browned egg albumin to rats. J. Agric. Food Chem. *28*, 150–155.

LEE, C.M., LEE, T-C., and CHICHESTER, C.O. 1977A. The effect of Maillard reaction products on the absorption of tryptophan. Comp. Biochem. Physiol. *56A*, 473.

LEE, C.M., LEE, T-C., and CHICHESTER, C.O. 1977B. The effect of Maillard reaction products on disaccharidase activities in the rat. J. Agric. Food Chem. *25*, 775.

MAURON, J., MOTTU, F., BUJARD, E., and EGLI, R.H. 1955. The availability of lysine, methionine, and tryptophan in condensed milk and milk powder in *in vivo* digestion studies. Arch. Biochem. Biopys. *59*, 433.

MITUSO, N., HAYASHI, T., and OHTA, Y. 1977. Novel free radicals formed by the amino-carbonyl reactions of sugars with amino acids, amines and proteins. *In* Protein Crosslinking. Nutritional and Medical Consequences. Plenum Press, New York.

NAS (1973). Toxicants Occurring Naturally in Foods, 2nd edition. National Academy of Sciences, Washington, D.C.

NESHEIM, M.C. and CARPENTER, K.J. 1967. The ingestion of heat-damaged protein. Br. J. Nutr. *21*, 399–411.

PINTAURO, S.J., PAGE, G.V., SOLBERG, M., LEE, T-C., and CHICHESTER, C.O. 1980. Absence of mutagenetic response from extracts of Maillard browned egg albumin. J. Food Sci. *45*, No. 5, 1442–1443. (in press)

RAO, M.N., SREENIVAS, H., SWAMINATHAN, M., CARPENTER, K.J., and MORGAN, L.B. 1963. The nutritional available lysine and methionine of heated casein-glucose mixtures. J. Sci. Food Agric. *14*, 544.

REYNOLDS, T.M. 1963. Chemistry of nonenzymatic browning. The reaction between aldoses and amines. Adv. Food Res. *12*, 1.

REYNOLDS, T.M. 1965. Chemistry of nonenzymatic browning. II. Adv. Food Res. *14*, 167.

REYNOLDS, T.M. 1969. Carbohydrates and Their Roles. *In* Nonenzymatic Browning Sulfur-Amine Interactions. AVI Publ. Co., Westport, Conn.

SGARBIERI, V.C., TANAKA, M., CHICHESTER, C.O., and AMAYA, J. 1971. Some nutritional consequences of the Maillard reaction. Proceedings of III Western Hemisphere Nutrition Congress. Futura Publishing Co., Mount Kisco, N.Y.

SGARBIERI, V.C. 1971. Nutritional consequences of the Maillard reaction. Ph.D. dissertation. Univ. of California, Davis.

SGARBIERI, V.C., AMAYA, J., TANAKA, M., and CHICHESTER, C.O. 1973A. Nutritional consequences of the Maillard reaction. Amino acid availability from fructose-leucine and fructose-tryptophan in the rat. J. Nutr. *103*, 657.

SGARBIERI, V.C., AMAYA, J., TANAKA, M., and CHICHESTER, C.O. 1973B. Response of rats to amino acid supplementation of brown egg albumin. J. Nutr. *103*, 1731.

SOMOGY, J.C. 1973. Antivitamins. *In* Toxicants Occurring Naturally in Foods, second edition. National Academy of Science, Washington, D.C.

SUGIMURA, T., and NAGAO, M. 1979. Mutagenic factors in cooked foods. CRC Critical Reviews in Toxicology. p. 189–209.

TANAKA, M. 1974. Effect of the browning reaction on quality, digestion and absorption of protein. Ph.D. dissertation. University of Rhode Island, Kingston, R.I.

TANAKA, M., LEE, T-C., and CHICHESTER, C.O. 1975A. Effect of browning on chemical properties of egg albumin. Agric. Biol. Chem. *39*, 863.

TANAKA, M., LEE, T-C., and CHICHESTER, C.O. 1975B. Nutritional consequences of the Maillard reaction. The absorption of fructose-L-tryptophan in the large intestine of the rat. J. Nutr. *105*, 989.

TANAKA, M., AMAYA, J., LEE, T-C., and CHICHESTER, C.O. 1976. Effect of the browning reaction on the quality of protein. Proc. IV Intl. Cong. Food Sci. Technol., Madrid, Spain. Vol. I, p. 631.

TANAKA, M., KIMIAGAR, M., LEE, T-C., and CHICHESTER, C.O. 1977. Effect of Maillard reaction on the nutritional quality of protein. *In* Nutritional,

Biochemical and Chemical Consequence of Protein Crosslinking. Plenum Publ. Co., New York.

TANNENBAUM, S.R., FETT, D., YOUNG, V.R., LAND, P.D., and BRUCE, W.R. 1978. Nitrite and nitrate are formed by endogenous synthesis in the human intestine. Science *200*, 1487–89.

TSEN, C.C., REDDY, P.R.K., and GEHRKE, C.W. 1977. Effects of conventional baking, microwave cooking and steaming on the nutritive value of regular and fortified bread. J. Food Sci. *42*, 402–406.

6

Naturally Occurring Peptide and Protein Inhibitors of Enzymes

John R. Whitaker[1]

Animals, plants, and microorganisms contain specific proteins able to inactivate selected enzymes by formation of stable enzyme-inhibitor complexes. Proteins which inhibit proteolytic enzymes, particularly trypsin, have been studied in great detail and the crystallographic structures of at least three enzyme-inhibitor complexes have been elucidated (Rühlmann *et al.* 1973; Sweet *et al.* 1974; Hirono *et al.* 1979). The trypsin inhibitors appear to be ubiquitous. Inhibitors of other proteases are widely distributed in animals, plants and microorganisms but have only recently received much attention. Inhibitors of nonproteolytic enzymes, found in many organisms, deserve more attention than they have received in the past.

Initial interest in the proteinase inhibitors came from nutritionists concerned with the effect of these inhibitors in feeds and foods on animal and human nutrition. The nutritional value of food materials, such as soybeans, is improved by heat treatment. Part (perhaps 40%; Kakade *et al.* 1973) of this improvement is due to destruction of the proteinase inhibitors; however, improvement is also due to the destruction of lectins (hemagglutinins), goitrogenic substances, possibly amylase inhibitors and through enhanced digestibility due to denaturation of the proteins (Kakade *et al.* 1973; Rackis 1974; Boonvisut and Whitaker 1976; Savaiano *et al.* 1977). Biochemists are interested in the protein inhibitors because

[1] Department of Food Science and Technology, University of California, Davis.

of the opportunity afforded to study the factors affecting protein-protein interaction, to study their role in control of basic metabolic reactions and to explore their possible therapeutic use in a variety of diseases. Biologists and physiologists are interested, on the other hand, in the physiological functions of these proteinase inhibitors in animals, plants, and microorganisms under normal conditions.

The discovery and elucidation of the properties of protein inhibitors, especially the protease inhibitors, have grown by leaps and bounds the last 10 years as a result of the promise for therapeutic uses of some of these inhibitors. These accomplishments are delineated in the proceedings of two major symposia (Fritz and Tschesche 1971; Fritz *et al.* 1974) and several reviews (Vogel *et al.* 1968; Feeney and Allison 1969; Liener and Kakade 1969; Kassel 1970, 1978; Laskowski and Sealock 1971; Whitaker and Feeney 1973; Ryan 1973; Means *et al.* 1974; Tschesche 1974; Lorand 1976; Richardson 1977; Laskowski *et al.* 1978). While I shall strive to list all well-characterized protein inhibitors, and some others, it would be extremely difficult to be all inclusive. Complicating any exhaustive review is the diversity of names used for some of the less well-described inhibitors and the occurrence of isoinhibitors (multimolecular forms).

PROTEINASE PROTEIN INHIBITORS FOUND IN ANIMALS AND PLANTS

Four major types of proteolytic enzymes, based on essential amino acids in the active site and/or mechanism of action, are known. These are the serine proteinases (e.g. trypsin, chymotrypsin, elastase, thrombin, plasmin, subtilisin), the sulfhydryl proteinases (e.g. papain, ficin, bromelain, streptococcal proteinase, cathepsin B), the metalloproteinases (e.g. carboxypeptidases A and B, aminopeptidases) and the acidic (carboxyl) proteinases (e.g. pepsin, rennin, penicillopepsin, *Endothia parasitica* protease, *Mucor pusillus* protease). Protein inhibitors of each of these types of proteinases are known. In some cases, only one proteinase within a type is inhibited; in other cases the inhibitor appears to be type-specific; and in still other cases the inhibitor may be effective against more than one type of proteinase. Laskowski *et al.* (1978) have recently expressed reservations as to the validity of cross reactivity between two or more types of proteases.

The diversity of types of inhibitors is illustrated by the glycoprotein inhibitors found in egg whites, the ovomucoids and ovoinhibitor (Table 6.1). Chicken and quail egg white ovomucoids inhibit trypsin, tinamou ovomucoid inhibits chymotrypsin and subtilisin, and turkey ovomucoid inhibits trypsin, chymotrypsin, and subtilisin. The papain inhibitor of

TABLE 6.1. PROTEINASE INHIBITORS IN ANIMAL TISSUES

Source	Type	Molecular Weight (daltons)	Sub-Units	pI	Specificity	Comments	References
Human plasma	α_1-Trypsin inhibitor (α_1-antitrypsin)	54,000			Trypsin, chymotrypsin, elastase, plasmin	Contains one disulfide bond; 15.9% carbohydrate; accounts for at least 70% of inhibitory activity of human plasma	Kress and Laskowski (1974); Travis *et al.* (1974); Hodges *et al.* (1979)
	α_2-Macroglobulin	725,000	4	5.4	Very broad	Glycoprotein; binds with all classes of proteases; complex retains activity for small substrates	von Schönenberger *et al.* (1958); Frénoy *et al.* (1972); Jones *et al.* (1972); Barrett and Starkey (1973); Roberts *et al.* (1974); Harpel (1976A)
	Antithrombin-heparin cofactor	62,000–67,000		5.1	Thrombin, other serine proteases of blood clotting sequence	Heparin strongly modulates activity	Rosenberg and Damus (1973); Damus and Rosenberg (1976)
	$C\bar{1}$ inactivator	104,000	1	2.7–2.8	$C\bar{1}$ protease, plasmin, kallikrein, others	Identical to α_2-neuraminoglycoprotein	Schultze *et al.* (1962); Haupt *et al.* (1970); Harpel and Cooper (1975); Harpel (1976B)
	Inter-α-trypsin inhibitor	160,000	1		Trypsin, chymotrypsin; to lesser extent plasmin	Identical with protein π; glycoprotein	Steinbuch and Loeb (1961); Heimburger *et al.* (1971); Steinbuch (1976); Dietl *et al.* (1979)
	α_1-Antichymotrypsin				Chymotrypsin; not trypsin, plasmin, thrombin	Identical with α_1X-glycoprotein	Heimburger *et al.* (1971)
	Thiol proteinase inhibitor	90,000			Ficin and papain; cathepsin B and bromelain less		Sasaki *et al.* (1977); Ryley (1979)
	Cathepsins B and H inhibitors				Cathepsins B and H	Not clear whether different from one or more of the above inhibitors	Lenney *et al.* (1979)
Human respiratory tract	BSI-I BSI-II	20,000 14,000			Trypsin, chymotrypsin, pronase, elastase	Double-headed inhibiting trypsin and chymotrypsin independently; protects mucous membranes from leucocyte proteases; glycoprotein	Hochstrasser (1976)

TABLE 6.1.(*Continued*

Source	Type	Molecular Weight (daltons)	Sub-Units	pI	Specificity	Comments	References
Seminal fluid							
Human	(a) HUSI-I	10,500			Trypsin, chymotrypsin	Neither inhibitor contains carbohydrate; human seminal plasma also contains two serum inhibitors, α-anti-trypsin and α-antichymotrypsin	Zaneveld *et al.* (1974); Schiessler *et al.* (1976)
	(b) HUSI-II	6,217			Trypsin, acrosin		
Boar		11,000–12,000	1		Acrosin, trypsin, plasmin	Contains ~35% carbohydrate. Amino acid sequence is known for A_1. Isoinhibitors A, A_1 and B reported	Tschesche *et al.* (1974, 1975B); Fritz *et al.* (1976)
Guinea pig	(a) Trypsin inhibitor (TI)	6,600–6,800	1		Trypsin, acrosin	TI contains arginine in active site;	Fink and Fritz (1976)
	(b) Trypsin-plasmin inhibitor (TPI)	6,600–6,800	1		Trypsin, acrosin, plasmin	TPI contains lysine, no carbohydrate	
Human pancreas	Pancreatic secretory trypsin inhibitor	6,300		4.7–8.7	Trypsin	Does not inhibit chymotrypsin or kallikrein unlike the trypsin-kallikrein inhibitor (Kunitz inhibitor); amino acid sequence known for human, porcine I, bovine and ovine inhibitors. pI depends on the isoinhibitor	Kunitz and Northrop (1936); Kalser and Grossman (1955); Greene *et al.* (1968); Feinstein *et al.* (1974); Pubols *et al.* (1974); Greene *et al.* (1976)
Muscle							
Skeletal	Ca^{++}-activated neutral protease	270,000 (bovine cardiac) 67,000 (chicken skeletal)	4		Ca^{++}-activated neutral protease	In bovine cardiac muscle a second inhibitor of 70,000 with activity also on trypsin and chymotrypsin	Ishiura *et al.* (1977); Waxman and Krebs (1978); Waxman (1978); Toyo-oka *et al.* (1978)
Rat liver	Ca^{++}-activated neutral protease	~300,000			Ca^{++}-activated neutral protease	Relatively acid and heat stable; inactivated by trypsin; similar inhibitor in rat brain	Nishiura *et al.* (1978); Nishirua *et al.* (1979)

TABLE 6.1. *(Continued)*

Source	Type	Molecular Weight (daltons)	Sub-Units	pI	Specificity	Comments	References
All tissues rat, human	Cathepsins B and H inhibitors	~14,000 (rat lung) ~11,000 (hog kidney)			Cathepsins B and H	Also found in hog, protozoa, tuna fish, chicken and toad; appear to be intracellular in origin	Lenney *et al.* (1979)
Cartilage and aorta	Collagenase inhibitor	~11,000 ~30,000 (rabbit bone)		~11	Collagenase, trypsin; rabbit bone inhibitor acts on other neutral metalloproteinases	May control collagen turnover in bone	Kuettner *et al.* (1976); Sellers *et al.* (1979)
Cow colostrum	Trypsin inhibitor	11,000		4.2	Trypsin, chymotrypsin, plasmin, acrosin	Glycoprotein with >30% carbohydrate. Has appreciable homology with basic pancreatic polyvalent inhibitor (Kunitz), trypsin inhibitor from *Helix pomatia* and snake toxins. Several forms found.	Laskowski *et al.* (1952); Tschesche *et al.* (1975A); Čechová (1976)
Dog submandibular glands	Elastase inhibitor	A_2, 12,000	1		Elastase, subtilisin, other trypsin- and chymotrypsin-like enzymes	Double-headed inhibiting elastase and subtilisin independently; homology with pancreatic secretory trypsin inhibitors (Kazel type); forms I*, A_2, II* and C isolated	Werle *et al.* (1968); Fritz *et al.* (1971); Fritz and Hochstrasser (1976)
Egg white, chicken	Ovomucoid[1-3]	28,000		3.8–4.4	Trypsin	Contains approx. 20% carbohydrate	Fredericq and Deutsch (1949); Bier *et al.* (1953); Deutsch and Morton (1961)
	Ovoinhibitor	46,500			Trypsin, chymotrypsin, subtilisin, *A. oryzae* protease	Trypsin and chymotrypsin bind at separate sites independently, chymotrypsin and subtilisin compete	Tomimatsu *et al.* (1966); Liu *et al.* (1971)
	Papain inhibitor	12,700			Papain, ficin	Papain and ficin compete	Fossum and Whitaker (1968); Sen and Whitaker (1973)

TABLE 6.1.*(Continued)*

Source	Type	Molecular Weight (daltons)	Sub-Units	pI	Specificity	Comments	References
Tinamou	Ovomucoid	28,000		4–5	Chymotrypsin, subtilisin	—	Osuga and Feeney (1968)
Turkey	Ovomucoid	28,000		4–5	Trypsin, chymotrypsin, subtilisin	Trypsin and chymotrypsin bind independently	Rhodes *et al.* (1960); Kato (1976)
Penguin	Ovomucoid	28,000		4–5	Trypsin, chymotrypsin, subtilisin	Subtilisin strongly inhibited	Osuga *et al.* (1974)
Quail (Japanese)	Ovomucoid	28,000		4–5	Trypsin	Human trypsin inhibited	Feeney *et al.* (1969)
Cuttlefish *(Loligo vulgaris)*	Trypsin-kallikrein inhibitors	A, 6,630; B, 6,686; E, 6,925	1		Trypsin, chymotrypsin, kallikrein and plasmin	Isoinhibitor E has lysine in active site; isoinhibitor L has arginine	Tschesche and Rücker (1973); Tschesche (1976)
Leeches	Bdellins	A-2,3, 6,339; B-3, 4,830	1		Plasmin, trypsin, acrosin	Bdellin B-3 homologous to pancreatic secretory trypsin inhibitor (Kazal type) and seminal acrosin inhibitor	Fritz and Krejci (1976)
	Hirudin	<10,000	1	4.0	Thrombin		de la Llosa *et al.* (1964); Markwardt (1955, 1970); Gráf *et al* (1973); Bagdy *et al.* (1976)
Snake venom	Russell's viper inhibitors	I and II, ~7200	1		Kallikreins, trypsin, chymotrypsin, plasmin	Has 50–60% sequence homology with bovine pancreatic trypsin inhibitor and snail isoinhibitor k	Iwanaga *et al.* (1976)
Brazilian snake (Bothrops jararaca)	[Gln-Lys-Trp-Ala-Pro	608	1		Carboxydipeptidase		Greene (1974)
Brazilian snake (*Bothrops jararaca*)	[Gln-Trp-Pro-Arg-Pro-Gln-Ile-Pro-Pro	1,100	1		Carboxydipeptidase		Greene (1974)

TABLE 6.1.*(Continued)*

Source	Type	Molecular Weight (daltons)	Sub-Units	pI	Specificity	Comments	References
Anemonia sulcata	Sea Anemone inhibitors	5,500–7,000	1		Trypsin, chymotrypsin, plasmin, kallikreins	Homology with basic pancreatic trypsin inhibitor, snail inhibitors and viper inhibitors expected; there are some 10 inhibitors in anemones	Wunderer *et al.* (1976)
Snail epidermis	Trypsin-kallikrein inhibitors	B, 6,463; E, 6,431; G, 6,591; H, 6,575; K, 6,463	1		Trypsin, trypsin-like enzymes; chymotrypsin, chymotrypsin-like enzymes	Related in structure and properties to bovine trypsin-kallikrein inhibitor (Kunitz); cow colostrum inhibitor; Russell's viper venom inhibitor; toxins I and K from black mamba venom	Čechová-Pospísilová *et al.* (1969); Strydom (1973); Takahashi *et al* (1974); Dietl and Tschesche (1975); Tschesche and Dietl (1975, 1976)
albumin gland	Trypsin-kallikrein inhibitors	74,000			Bovine trypsin and plasmin, porcine plasmin	Glycoprotein	Dietl and Tschesche (1976A, B)
Ascaris lumbricodes	Inhibitor I Inhibitor II Inhibitor III Inhibitor IV	17,515 15,584 16,124 31,719			Pepsin (porcine) Pepsin (porcine) Pepsin (procine) Pepsin (porcine)	Ascaris also contains two different trypsin inhibitors, chymotrypsin-elastase inhibitors and carboxypeptidase A inhibitor	Kucich and Peanasky (1970); Peanasky *et al.* (1974)
Bee venom	Trypsin inhibitor	8,000			Trypsin		Pudles *et al.* (1967)
		9,000			Trypsin	Trypsin only proteinase tested	Shkenderov, (1973)
Silk worm hemolymph	Chymotrypsin inhibitors (3 inhibitors)	7,000			Chymotrypsin	One inhibitor has weak activity on trypsin; MW's identical but pI's of 4.0, 9.4 and 9.6	Sasaki (1978)

chicken egg white inhibits papain, ficin, and cathepsin B and the ovoinhibitor inhibits a variety of proteinases. In some cases the enzymes compete for the same binding site on the inhibitor (papain inhibitor) while in others there are separate binding sites for the different enzymes. A molecule of chicken egg white ovoinhibitor will complex with two trypsin and two chymotrypsin molecules simultaneously and independently; one molecule of turkey ovomucoid will complex with one molecule of trypsin and one molecule of chymotrypsin simultaneously; and one molecule of duck ovomucoid will complex with two molecules of trypsin and one molecule of chymotrypsin independently and simultaneously (Rhodes *et al.* 1960; Tomimatsu *et al.* 1966). These latter types of inhibitors are called "double headed" or "polyvalent" inhibitors (Rhodes *et al.* 1960; Stevens *et al.* 1974). Laskowski *et al.* (1978) have shown that there are three separate tandem domains in the ovomucoids and that one, two or all three domains may be expressed depending on the specific ovomucoid. α_2-Macroglobulin can combine (competitively) with proteinases of each of the four types (Heimburger 1974).

Many tissues contain a large number of different types of protein inhibitors. For example, human plasma contains at least nine different types (α_1-antitrypsin inhibitor, α_1-antichymotrypsin inhibitor, inter-α-trypsin inhibitor, antithrombin III inhibitor, $C\bar{1}$ inactivator, α_2-macroglobulin, a β-lipoprotein neutralizing thrombin, an inhibitor of plasminogen activation and a thiol proteinase inhibitor; Table 6.1) (Heimburger 1974). Potato tubers contain at least six different types of proteinase inhibitors (chymotrypsin inhibitor I, proteinase inhibitors IIa and IIb, kallikrein inhibitors, carboxypeptidases A and B inhibitor, and a papain inhibitor, Table 6.2).

The proteinase inhibitors are relatively heat stable, especially those of lower molecular weight. The molecular weights of characterized proteinase inhibitors range from 3100 daltons for the potato tuber carboxypeptidase inhibitor (Table 6.2; ignoring the polypeptide inhibitors from the actinomycetes and snake venoms) to 725,000 daltons for the α_2-macroglobulin of human plasma (Table 6.1). Some are glycoproteins, others are not. Heat and pH stabilities of a number of the proteinase inhibitors are a result of small size, single polypeptide chain and extensive disulfide bonds. For example, the Bowman-Birk inhibitor from soybeans of 8000 daltons has seven disulfide bonds (Ikenaka *et al.* 1974).

The proteinase inhibitors very frequently occur in multiple molecular forms, complicating the study, description, and uniformity of nomenclature. For example, chymotrypsin inhibitor I has been resolved into at least ten isoinhibitors based on different isoelectric points (Richardson *et al.* 1976). There are at least seven forms of the acidic cysteine protease inhibitors from pineapple (Table 6.2) and four to six forms of the lima

TABLE 6.2 PROTEINASE INHIBITORS IN PLANT TISSUES

Source	Type	Molecular Weight (daltons)	Sub-Units	pI	Specificity	Comments	References
Soybean	Kunitz	21,700	1	4.5	Trypsin	Has tryptophan; primary sequence of 181 amino acids known	Wu and Scheraga (1962); Frattali and Steiner (1968); Feeney and Allison (1969); Birk (1976B)
	Bowman-Birk	8,000	1		Trypsin, chymotrypsin	Combines at separate, non overlapping sites with trypsin and chymotrypsin; contains 7 disulfide bonds	Odani and Ikenaka (1973A); Ikenaka *et al.* (1974)
	Elastase				Elastase, also trypsin and chymotrypsin	Five chromatographic fractions from crude soybean trypsin inhibitor (Kunitz) had elastase activity; one was much more active	Bieth and Frechin (1974)
	Components I–IV	7,000–8,000		6.2–4.2	Trypsin	Immunologically distinct from Bowman-Birk inhibitor	Hwang *et al.* (1977)
Lima bean		9,000	1	3.6	Trypsin, chymotrypsin	There are at least 4, and possibly 6 isoinhibitors; trypsin and chymotrypsin combine at separate, independent, non overlapping sites	Jones *et al.* (1963); Stevens (1971); Stevens *et al.* (1974)
Garden bean (Great Northern variety)		I, 8,086; II, 8,371; IIIb, 8,884	1		Trypsin; chymotrypsin weakly by I and II, chymotrypsin strongly inhibited by IIIb	Isoinhibitor IIIb has independent binding sites for trypsin and chymotrypsin	Wilson and Laskowski (1973); Birk (1976C)
Navy bean		23,000; 7,900			Trypsin, chymotrypsin	Possibly four isoinhibitors	Wagner and Riehm (1967); Whitley and Bowman (1975)

TABLE 6.2 *(Continued)*

Source	Type	Molecular Weight (daltons)	Sub-Units	pI	Specificity	Comments	References
Mung beans (*Phaseolus aureus*, Roxb)		12,000			Trypsin, endopeptidase of mung beans	Another inhibitor of ~2,000 daltons was also reported	Baumgartner and Chrispeels (1976)
Pinto bean (*Phaseolus vulgaris* cultivar Pinto)		19,000			Trypsin, chymotrypsin	Two isoinhibitors present; probably different binding site for trypsin and chymotrypsin	Wang (1975)
Broad bean (*Vica faba*)		11,000		BBPI-1, 8.5; BBPI-2, 7.5	Trypsin, chymotrypsin, thrombin, pronase, papain (slightly)	Possibly four isoinhibitors present	Warsy *et al.* (1974)
Chick peas (*Cicer arietinum*)		10,000		4.96–8.6	Chymotrypsin, trypsin	Does not contain carbohydrate; independent binding sites for trypsin and chymotrypsin; probably two isoinhibitors with 4 more found as result of proteolysis	Belew *et al.* (1975); Belew (1977); Smirnoff *et al.* (1979)
Black-eyed peas	Chymotrypsin and trypsin inhibitor	~8,000		5.1	Trypsin, chymotrypsin	Independent binding sites for trypsin and chymotrypsin	Gennis and Cantor (1976)
	Trypsin inhibitor	~8,000		6.5	Trypsin	Binds with two molecules trypsin simultaneously	Gennis and Cantor (1976)
Potato	Chymotrypsin inhibitor I	39,000	4		Chymotrypsin	Binds four moles of chymotrypsin	Melville and Ryan (1972)
	Proteinase inhibitor IIa				Chymotrypsin, nagarse, trypsin		Iwasaki *et al.* (1974A, B)
	Proteinase inhibitor IIb				Chymotrypsin, nagarse		Iwasaki *et al.* (1974B, 1975)

TABLE 6.2 *(Continued)*

Source	Type	Molecular Weight (daltons)	Sub-Units	pI	Specificity	Comments	References
	pKI-56, pKI-64				Kallikrein		Hojima *et al.* (1973)
	Carboxypeptidases A and B inhibitor	3,100	1		Carboxypeptidases A and B	No activity on trypsin or chymotrypsin	Ryan *et al.* (1974)
	Papain inhibitor	80,000			Papain, chymopapain	Glycoprotein. There are eight binding sites four of which can bind either papain or chymopapain, the remaining four bind only chymopapain	Rodis (1974)
Sweet potato	Inhibitor II	23,000		4.24	Trypsin, plasmin, kallikrein	Also inhibitor I present	Sugiura *et al.* (1973)
	Inhibitor III	24,000		4.39	Trypsin, plasmin, kallikrein	Both Inhibitors II and III are arginine-type	Sugiura *et al.* (1973)
Tomato leaves	Inhibitor I				Both inhibit trypsin and trypsin-like enzymes; chymotrypsin and chymotrypsin-like enzymes	Only inhibits proteinases from animals, not plants	Simmons-Walker and Ryan (1977)
	Inhibitor II						Simmons-Walker and Ryan (1977)
Corn		12,500; 6,500	1		Trypsin	Chymotrypsin not inhibited	Hochstrasser *et al.* (1970); Swartz *et al.* (1977)
Sorghum grain		15,000; <6,000			Trypsin	No other enzymes tested; the <6,000 MW component may be tannins	Filho (1974)

TABLE 6.2 *(Continued)*

Source	Type	Molecular Weight (daltons)	Sub-Units	pI	Specificity	Comments	References
Barley		25,000			Alkaline proteinases of *Aspergillus oryzae, Streptomyces griseus, Alternaria tenuissima, Bacillus subtilis*, chymotrypsin	Contains 4–5 compounds with inhibitory activity	Mikola and Suolinna (1971)
		14,200		7.51	Trypsin	Arginine-type inhibitor	Ogiso *et al.* (1975)
Eggplant (*Solanum melongena* L)		~6,000			Trypsin, chymotrypsin weakly	No carbohydrate	Kanamori *et al.* (1976)
Pineapple stem	Acidic cysteine protease inhibitors	~5,600	2	4.5–4.9	Papain and ficin	There are at least seven isoinhibitors	Heinrikson and Kézdy (1976)
Groundnuts		7,450–7,700	1	8–9	Trypsin, chymotrypsin	Sites for trypsin and chymotrypsin separate but overlapping	Tur-Sinai *et al.* (1972); Birk (1976D)
Scopolia japonica cells		4,000–6,000			Trypsin, chymotrypsin, plasmin, kallikrein, pepsin	Five components with inhibitory activity reported	Sakato *et al.* (1975)

bean trypsin inhibitor (Table 6.2). Heterogeneity arises from single amino acid replacements, varying amounts of carbohydrate (the ovomucoids for example), different amide contents, polymerization, and proteolytic digestion during isolation. The last is especially critical when an affinity column of a specific proteinase is used in the isolation.

As a result of the large number of proteinase inhibitors and the multiple molecular forms, the literature on these inhibitors can be quite confusing. Fortunately, substantial progress is being made in determining the amino acid sequences of the proteinase inhibitors (Fritz *et al.* 1974), in part because of the small size of many of the inhibitors. Common homology is observed among many of the inhibitors. For example, there is remarkable homology among the trypsin inhibitors of soybeans (the Bowman-Birk inhibitor, Table 6.2), lima bean inhibitor IV and garden bean inhibitor II (Birk 1976A). Ovoinhibitor from Japanese quail and chicken egg whites contains six tandem domains (potentially or actually active against specific proteases) and homologous to the Kazal pancreatic secretory inhibitor and to the ovomucoids (Laskowski *et al.* 1978). Recently, it has been shown that human inter-α-trypsin inhibitor contains two domains with great similarity to the domains of the Kunitz-type inhibitors (Hochstrasser and Wachter 1979; Wachter *et al.* 1979; Wachter and Hochstrasser 1979; Dietl *et al.* 1979). There also appears to be sequence homology between the pineapple stem bromelain inhibitors and some of the small molecular weight inhibitors from leguminosae (Szilagyi and Szilagyi 1979). The complete amino acid sequences are known for several of the proteinase inhibitors including the lima bean inhibitor (Tan and Stevens 1971A, B), the Bowman-Birk soybean inhibitor (Ikenaka *et al.* 1974), the chymotrypsin inhibitor from potatoes (Richardson 1974; Richardson and Cossins 1974, 1975), the carboxypeptidase inhibitor from potatoes (Hass *et al* 1975), the garden bean inhibitor (Wilson and Laskowski 1975), the bromelain inhibitor from pineapples (Reddy *et al.* 1975) and ovomucoids from several birds (Laskowski *et al.* 1978).

Progress has also been made in determining elements of the recognition site between the proteinase inhibitor and enzyme. For the trypsin inhibitors, a peptide bond of Lys-X or Arg-X located within a loop of the protein closed by a disulfide bond appears to be essential (Ozawa and Laskowski 1966; Laskowski and Sealock 1971). In lima bean inhibitor, Leu_{55}-Ser_{56} appears to be a recognition site for chymotrypsin (Krahn and Stevens 1970). These sites were readily determined because of the sensitivity of the proteinase inhibitor to hydrolysis of the peptide bond at these positions as a result of complex formation between inhibitor and enzyme. Remarkable similarity has been found in the amino acid sequence at the recognition site for trypsin in several "lysine-type" inhibitors from legumes (Table 6.3). Note the apparent invariant occur-

TABLE 6.3. HOMOLOGY AMONG SOME OF THE TRYPSIN AND CHYMOTRYPSIN INHIBITORS FROM LEGUMINOSAE[1]

Inhibitor	Amino Acid Sequence: Trypsin Site ↓[2]	Amino Acid Sequence: Chymotrypsin Site ↓[2]
Lima Bean	··· Cys–Thr–**Lys**$_{26}$—**Ser**–Ile—Pro ····	···· Ile–Cys–Thr–**Leu**$_{55}$—**Ser**–Ile–Pro ···
Bowman-Birk (soybean)	··· Cys–Thr–**Lys**$_{16}$—**Ser**–Asn–Pro ····	···· Ile–Cys–Thr–**Leu**$_{45}$—**Ser**–Ile–Pro
Runner Bean	··· Ile–Tyr–**Lys**—**Ser**–Gln–(Pro?) ···	···· Asp–Val–Ala–**Leu**—**Ser**–(Pro?)
Garden Bean (Great Northern)[3]	··· Cys–Thr–**Arg**$_{53}$—**Ser**–Met–Pro ···	
Soybean Trypsin Inhibitor[3]	··· Ser–Tyr–**Arg**$_{63}$—**Ile**–Arg–Phe ···	
Ergnut[3]	··· Glx–Cys–**Arg**$_{22}$—**Ala**–Pro–Pro ···	

[1] Adapted from Hory and Weder (1976).
[2] The arrow indicates the specific recognition point involving P_1 and P_1' residues.
[3] Only inhibits trypsin.

rence of the sequence ··· Cys-Thr-Lys-Ser—Pro ··· except in PCI 3 from runner beans *(Phaseolus coccineus L.)*. The recognition site for chymotrypsin in the three "double headed" inhibitors resembles that of the trypsin recognition site, especially in the lima bean inhibitor where only the Lys_{26} is replaced with Leu_{55}. Note also the invariant Ser residue in both types of recognition sites. The more limited data on the "arginine-type" inhibitors show more sequence variability. Laskowski *et al.* (1978) have recently shown that the ovoinhibitor of Japanese quail and chicken egg whites consists of six tandem domains with remarkable homology around the protease recognition sites (Table 6.4). Domains I, II and III with Arg are potentially trypsin inhibitory sites while domains IV, V and VI with Tyr and Met are potentially chymotrypsin-elastase inhibitory sites. As noted above, these domains have remarkable homology with the Kazal pancreatic secretory inhibitor and with the ovomucoids.

While there has been much discussion of the mechanism of combination of inhibitor and enzyme, it is not essential that peptide bond cleavage occur since complex formation of equal strength can be formed with inactive derivatives of trypsin (Feinstein and Feeney 1966; Ako *et al.* 1974), chymotrypsin (Feinstein and Feeney 1966; Ako *et al.* 1974), subtilisin and papain (Fossum and Whitaker 1968). X-Ray crystallographic data indicate in certain cases the complex between inhibitor and enzyme is probably an adduct with a tetrahedral intermediate state approaching a covalent bond (Sweet *et al.* 1974; Tschesche 1974).

It has been possible to cleave some "double-headed" inhibitors into two smaller "single-headed" fragments by chemical and enzymatic means. For example, the Bowman-Birk soybean inhibitor has been cleaved with cyanogen bromide and pepsin to give two fragments of 38 and 29 residues (Odani and Ikenaka 1973B). The 38 residue fragment retained 84% of the trypsin inhibitory activity while the 29 residue fragment retained 16% of the chymotrypsin activity. Similar results of active fragments have been achieved with potato inhibitor IIa (Iwasaki *et al.* 1974A) and potato inhibitor IIb (Iwasaki *et al.* 1975). Laskowski *et al.* (1978) have reported that a number of the different avian ovomucoids contain three domains for binding proteases. In chicken ovomucoid, which inhibits only trypsin, two of the domains are silent, in turkey ovomucoid two of the domains are expressed while in duck ovomucoid all three domains are expressed. More recently Dietl *et al.* (1979) have cleaved the human inter-α-trypsin inhibitor into several fragments two of which have great similarity to the Kunitz-type inhibitors.

The better described proteinase inhibitors of animals and plants are shown in Tables 6.1 and 6.2. The main sources of animal proteinase inhibitors have been the pancreas, colostrum, blood plasma, and avian egg whites while in plants the inhibitors from soybeans, beans, peas, and

TABLE 6.4. AMINO ACID SEQUENCES CONTAINING THE REACTIVE SITES OF THE SIX DOMAINS OF JAPANESE QUAIL OVOINHIBITOR[1]

Domain	Amino acid sequence (↓[2] at Arg–Asn)	Enzyme potentially inhibited
I	··· Val –Ala–Cys–Pro –Arg –Asn–Leu –Lys–Pro–Val–Cys ···	Trypsin
II	··· Val –Ala–Cys–Pro –Arg –Asn–Met–Lys–Pro–Val–Cys ···	Trypsin
III	··· Val –Ala–Cys–Pro –Arg –Asn–Leu –Lys–Pro–Val–Cys ···	Trypsin
IV	··· Ala –Ala–Cys–Pro –Tyr–Ile –Leu –His –Glu–Ile –Cys ···	Chymotrypsin-elastase
V	··· Met–Ala–Cys–Thr–Met–Ile—Tyr –Asp–Pro–Val–Cys ···	Chymotrypsin-elastase
VI	··· Pro –Val–Cys–Thr–Met–Glu –Tyr –Ile –Pro–His–Cys ···	Chymotrypsin-elastase

[1] Adapted from Laskowski *et al.* (1978).
[2] The arrow indicates the specific recognition point involving P_1 and P'_1 residues.

potatoes have received much attention. Because of historical reasons and interest, more trypsin inhibitors have been studied than all other types of inhibitors combined. More recently there have been detailed studies on proteinase inhibitors showing primary specificity for subtilisin, elastase, plasmin, kallikrein, and papain (see Tables 6.1 and 6.2).

MICROBIAL PROTEINASE INHIBITORS

In 1962 Höyem and Skulberg reported the presence of trypsin inhibitors in the supernatant liquid from *Clostridium botulinum* (Höyem and Skulberg 1962). Several other reports of proteinase inhibitors in microorganisms appeared over the next seven years (Yamamoto and Hayashi 1962; Shimada and Matsushima 1968; Brecher and Pugatch 1969; Fossum 1970). In 1969, Umezawa and coworkers showed that a number of actinomycetes produced low molecular weight peptide derivatives which are inhibitory of many proteinases (Aoyagi *et al.* 1969B). These low molecular weight inhibitors, leupeptins, antipain, chymostatins, elastatinal and pepstatins will be described below.

A few higher molecular weight proteinase inhibitors have also been reported in microorganisms. A subtilisin inhibitor has been crystallized from *Streptomyces albogriseolus* extracts (Murao and Sato 1972). The inhibitor, with a molecular weight of 23,000 and an isoelectric point of 4.3, has activity only on microbial alkaline proteinases (Ikenaka 1974). The inhibitor appears to bind two molecules of subtilisin BPN′ (Ikenaka 1974). Baker's yeast contains several protein inhibitors of proteinases A, B and C of yeast (Lenney 1975). There are two isoinhibitors, I_2^A and I_3^A, with activity on the acidic proteinase A. The molecular weights are near 6100 daltons with isoelectric points of 5.7 and 6.3 for I_2^A and I_3^A, respectively (Saheki *et al.* 1974). There also appear to be two isoinhibitors of proteinase B. These inhibitors, I_1^B and I_2^B, have molecular weights of about 9000 daltons and isoelectric points of 8.0 and 7.0, respectively (Bünning and Holzer 1977; Maier *et al.* 1979). *Saccharomyces carlbergensis* has only inhibitor I_1^B while *Saccharomyces cerevisiae* has only inhibitor I_2^B (Bünning and Holzer 1977). Proteinase C is a carboxypeptidase (Lenney 1975). *Neurospora crassa* is reported to contain two protein inhibitors of the two endogenous aminopeptidases (Kaehn and Kula 1977). *Rhodotorula glutinis* is reported to contain an intracellular inhibitor of carboxypeptidase R produced by the same yeast (Hernández-Jodra and Gancedo 1979).

The low molecular weight polypeptide proteinase inhibitors of microorganisms will now be described.

Leupeptins (Aoyagi *et al.* 1969A; Kondo *et al.* 1969; Kawamura *et al.* 1969).—The leupeptins are produced by several species of *Streptomyces* including *S. roseus, S. roseochromogenes, S. chartreusis, S. albireticuli, S. thioluteus, S. lavendulae,* and *S. noboritoensis.* Structurally, they are propionyl- or acetyl-L-leucyl-L-leucyl-L-argininal or their analogs in which each leucine is replaced by L-isoleucine or L-valine. In solution, the compound is largely in the forms II and III (Structure 1). The leupeptins inhibit plasmin, trypsin, papain and cathepsin B at the 10–50 μg/ml level. Leupeptins have also been shown to decrease protein degradation in normal and diseased muscles (Libby and Goldberg 1978).

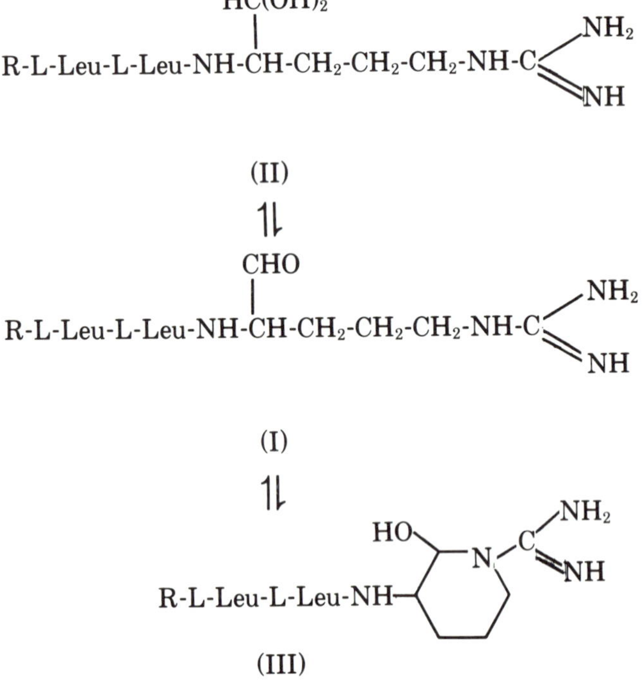

STRUCTURE 1. LEUPEPTINS (R = CH_3CO- or CH_3CH_2CO-).

Antipain (Suda *et al.* 1972; Umezawa *et al.* 1972A).—Antipain, produced by *Streptomyces michigaensis, S. yokosukaensis,* and other species of actinomycetes, is [(S)-1-carboxy-2-phenylethyl]carbamoyl-L-arginyl-L-valyl-L-argininal as shown in Structure 2. Antipain inhibits papain, trypsin, and cathepsins A and B at the μg/ml level.

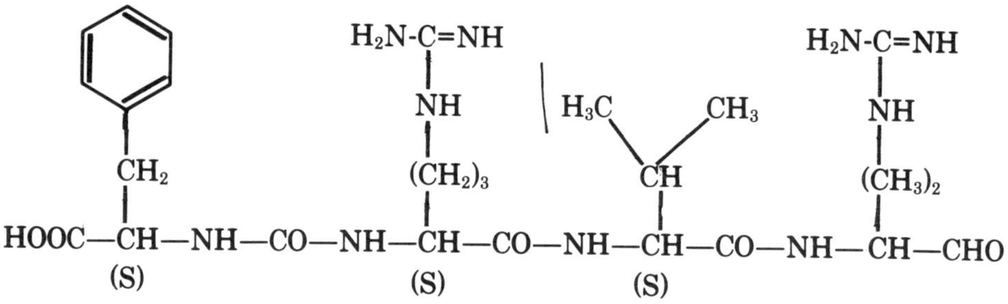

STRUCTURE 2. ANTIPAIN

Chymostatins (Umezawa *et al.* 1970A; Tatsuta *et al.* 1973).—The chymostatins are produced by *Streptomyces hydroscopicus, S. lavendulae* and other species of actinomycetes. Chymostatin A is N-{[(S)-1-carboxy-2-phenylethyl]carbamoyl}-α-[2-iminohexahydro-4(S)-pyrimidyl]-L-glycyl-L-leucyl-L-phenylalaninal (Structure 3). In chymostatins B and C, L-leucine is replaced

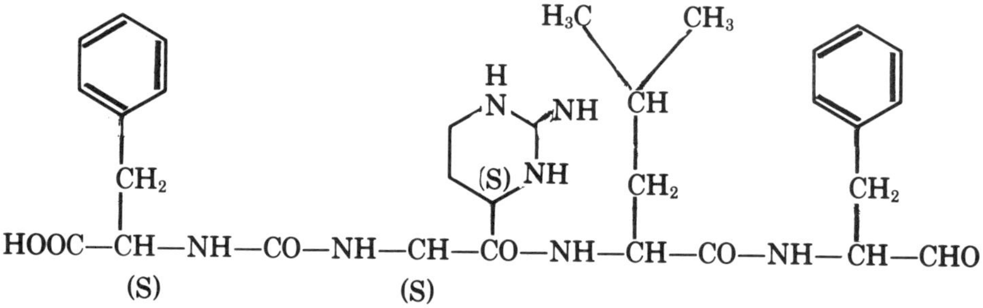

STRUCTURE 3. CHYMOSTATIN A.

by L-valine and L-isoleucine, respectively. Chymostatin inhibits chymotrypsin at the submicrogram level (ID_{50}= 0.15 μg/ml) and papain at the 7.5 μg/ml level.

Elastatinal (Umezawa *et al.* 1973; Okura *et al.* 1975).—Elastatinal, found in several species of actinomycetes, is N-[(S)-1-carboxyisopentyl] carbamoyl-α-[2-iminohexahydro-4(S)-pyrimidyl]-(S)-glycyl-(S)-glutaminyl-(S)-alaninal (Structure 4). Elastatinal inhibits elastase but not other proteases. Recently, the structure of elasnin (Structure 5), a novel elastase inhibitor, has been described (Ömura *et al.* 1979).

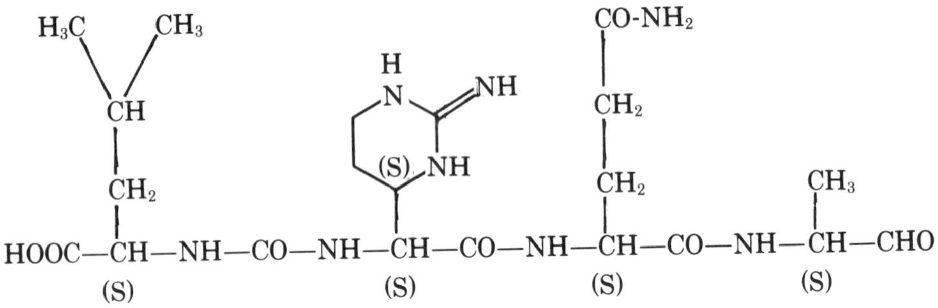

STRUCTURE 4. ELASTATINAL.

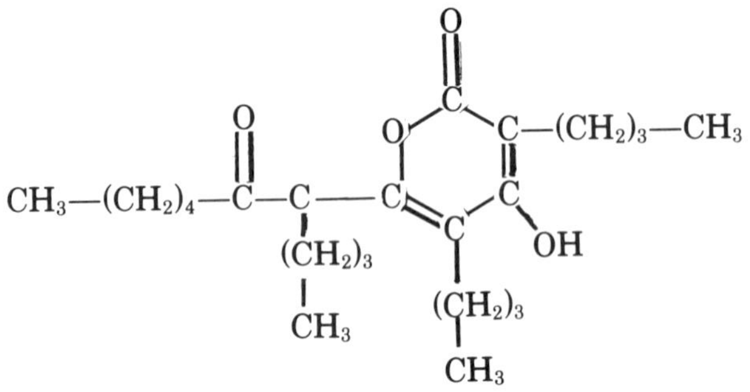

STRUCTURE 5. ELASNIN.

Pepstatins (Umezawa *et al.* 1970B; Morishima *et al.* 1972).—Pepstatin, produced by various species of actinomycetes including *Streptomyces testaceus* n.sp. and *S. argenteolus* var. *toyokaensis*, is isovaleryl-L-valyl-L-valyl-[(3S,4S)-4-amino-3-hydroxy-6-methyl]heptanoyl-L-alanyl-[(3S, 4S)-4-amino-3-hydroxy-6-methyl]heptanoic acid (Structure 6). Isoinhibitors in which the isovaleryl group is replaced with an acetyl, butyl, pro-

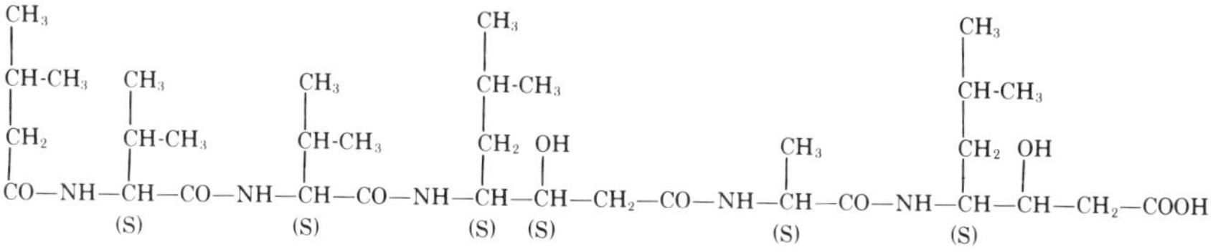

STRUCTURE 6. PEPSTATIN.

pionyl, *n*-caproyl or isocaproyl group, in which the terminal (3S,4S)-4-amino-3-hydroxy-6-methyl-heptanoic acid is replaced with 3-amino-5-methylhexanone-2 or in which L-alanine is replaced with L-serine are also produced by various strains of actinomycetes. Pepstatin has activity against pepsin, proctase B, cathepsin D and several other acid proteases.

Phosphoramidon (Umezawa *et al.* 1972B).—Phosphoramidon, produced by *Streptomyces tanashiensis* and several other species of actinomycetes, is N-(α-L-rhamnopyranosyloxyhydroxyphosphinyl)-L-leucyl-L-tryptophan (Structure 7). Removal of the α-L-rhamnopyranosyl group

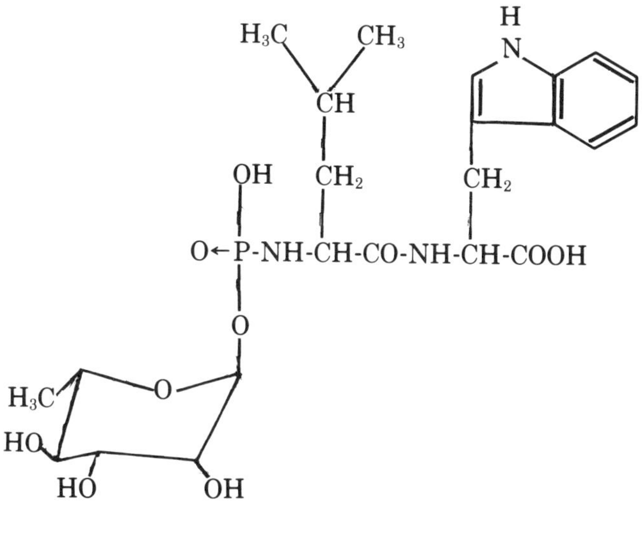

STRUCTURE 7. PHOSPHORAMIDON.

gives even a more active compound. Phosphoramidon is rather specific for thermolysin, inhibiting it at nM levels.

NONPROTEOLYTIC ENZYME PROTEIN INHIBITORS

While the great majority of protein enzyme inhibitors discovered have activity against one or more of the proteinases, several protein inhibitors have been found with activity directed against various non-proteolytic enzymes. The predominance of proteinase inhibitors may be, in part, historical in that they were discovered first and workers have searched more diligently for them. It is more likely however, that because of the potentially damaging effects of the proteinases, more protection against them has evolved.

Table 6.5 lists the majority of the nonproteolytic enzyme protein inhibitors reported in the literature. In some cases, such as the pectinase inhibitor of pears (Weurman 1954) and the peroxidase and catalase inhibitors of mangos (Mattoo and Modi 1970) confirmation is needed. The inhibitors can be grouped as (1) those directed toward enzymes which modify proteins (enzymes) post-translational (protein methylase II inhibitor, protein phosphatase inhibitor, protein kinase inhibitor); (2) those directed toward the carbohydrases (amylase inhibitor, invertase inhibitor, β-glucuronidase inhibitor); (3) those directed toward enzymes which modify the nucleic acids or derivatives (DNase I inhibitor, acid DNase inhibitor, ribonuclease inhibitor, adenylate cyclase inhibitor); (4) those directed toward esterases (phospholipase A) and (5) those directed against oxidative enzymes (hydroxy-vitamin D_3-1-hydroxylase inhibitor, peroxidase and catalase inhibitors). One must be impressed that, with a few exceptions, all the protein inhibitors are directed against the hydrolysis or modification of the large polymeric molecules—the proteins, carbohydrates and nucleic acids.

The best studied of the nonproteolytic enzyme protein inhibitors are the amylase inhibitors. These inhibitors have been found in many of the cereals (wheat, barley, oats, maize, millet, rye, and rice), legumes, mangos, taro roots, and acorns (Kneen and Sandstedt 1946; Stankovic and Markovic 1960–61; Narayana Rao *et al.* 1967, 1970; Mattoo and Modi 1970; Jaffé *et al.* 1973; Marshall 1975, 1977; Blanco, 1980) and microorganisms (Murao *et al.* 1979; Namiki *et al.* 1979; Ueda *et al.* 1979; Frommer *et al.* 1979). The amylase inhibitors are relatively heat stable and generally are found to have activity only against animal and insect α-amylases (Powers and Whitaker 1977A, B). Recently, however, Blanco (1980) has purified three amylase inhibitors from maize which inhibit the α-amylase of maize. This is the first indication of any possible physiological role of these inhibitors in the possible regulation of starch metabolism in plants.

Rate of complex formation between amylase inhibitor and enzyme is very slow, often requiring from 1–2 hr to form; however, once formed it is very tight as indicated by the red kidney bean α-amylase inhibitor-

TABLE 6.5. SOME NONPROTEOLYTIC ENZYME PROTEIN INHIBITORS

Source	Type	Molecular Weight (daltons)	pI	Specificity	Comments	References
Liver, rat	Protein methylase II inhibitor			Protein methylase II	Microsomal fraction of cell has highest amount	Kim and Paik (1971)
Muscle, rabbit	Protein phosphatase inhibitors					
	Inhibitor I	26,000		Phosphorylase phosphatase	Protein kinase-dependent in that only phosphorylated inhibitor is active. Inhibitor also found in rat liver, rat skeletal muscle, beef heart and beef adrenal cortex	Huang and Glinsmann (1976); Hwang *et al.* (1977)
	Inhibitor II	33,000		Phosphorylase phosphatase	Protein kinase-independent in that activity not dependent on phosphorylation of inhibitor. Inhibitor also found in other tissues. MW's of 33,000 to 65,000 have been reported.	Huang and Glinsmann (1976); Cohen *et al.* (1977)
	Protein kinase inhibitor					
	Type I	11,300	4.74	cAMP-dependent protein kinases	Inhibitor binds to free catalytic subunit of protein kinase, MW's of 11,300 to 26,000 reported	Walsh *et al.* (1971); DeMaille *et al.* (1977, 1979); Ferraz *et al.* (1979)
	Type II	~15,000		Nucleotide-independent protein kinases	Competes with substrate for binding to enzyme	DeMaille *et al.* (1977); Szmigielski *et al.* (1977)
Placenta, human	Urokinase inhibitor	43,000 (major) 75,000 (minor)	4.8–4.9	Urokinase, weak activity on trypsin, no activity on plasmin		Kawano *et al.* (1970)

TABLE 6.5. *(Continued)*

Source	Type	Molecular Weight (daltons)	pI	Specificity	Comments	References
Mitochondria	ATPase inhibitor	~10,500		Mitochondrial oligomyosin-insensitive ATPase	Has no activity on myosin ATPase	Brooks and Senior (1971); Ebner and Mair (1977)
Bean, Red and White Kidney	Amylase inhibitor	49,000	4.65 (major), 4.5 (minor)	Inhibitory of porcine pancreatic, human salivary and *Tenebrio molitor* larval midgut α-amylases; no activity on microbial or plant α-amylases	Contains 8.6% carbohydrate; probably 4 subunits; the amylase inhibitor of the white kidney bean is similar	Marshall and Lauda (1975); Powers and Whitaker (1977A, B)
Wheat	Amylase inhibitors	"0.28" family 11,000–14,000; "0.19" family 24,000; "0.55" family 30,000		Generally as described for the bean amylase inhibitor	Thought not to contain carbohydrate; may be six inhibitors in some varieties	Shainkin and Birk (1970); Bedetti *et al.* (1974); Granum and Whitaker (1977)
Streptomyces	Amylase inhibitors	lower molecular weight				Murao *et al.* (1979); Namiki *et al.* (1979); Ueda *et al.* (1979)
Potato White	Invertase inhibitor	17,000		Acid invertases from several sources including potato	Acid invertase inhibitors also found in artichoke tubers and carrots	Pressey (1967); Bradshaw *et al.* (1970)
Sweet	Invertase inhibitor	~20,000		Acid invertases from sweet potato	Did not inhibit alkaline invertase from sweet potato, yeast invertase	Matsushita and Uritani (1976)
Sublingual gland, porcine	β-Glucuronidase inhibitor	~340,000		β-Glucuronidase	Contains 17.5% protein, 83.5% carbohydrate	Fishman (1967); Sakamoto *et al.* (1973)

TABLE 6.5. *(Continued)*

Source	Type	Molecular Weight (daltons)	pI	Specificity	Comments	References
Beans, red kidney	Polygalacturonase inhibitor			Polygalacturonase; no activity on cellulase, xylanase, α-galactosidase, α-galacturonosidase	Properties similar to the lectins, may protect against plant pathogens	Albersheim and Anderson (1971)
Pears	Pectinase inhibitor			Pectinase		Weurman (1954)
Cucumber hypocotyls	Pectinase inhibitor			Pectinase of *Cladosporium cucumerinum*	Evidence presumptive	Skare *et al.* (1975)
Lymphocytes	Ectosialyltransferase inhibitor			Ectosialyltransferase		Cacan *et al.* (1977)
Thymus, calf	DNase I inhibitor	45,000–50,000		Deoxyribonuclease I	Inactive against DNase II	Lindberg (1964); Lindberg and Skoog (1970)
Liver, beef	Acid DNase inhibitor	~21,500		Acid DNases	Inactive on pancreatic DNase I and *E. coli* endonuclease	Lesca (1976)
Uterus tissue	Ribonuclease inhibitor	50,000–60,000		RNase	May be same as β-estradiol receptor protein	Zan-Kowalczewska and Roth (1975)
Liver, rat	Adenylate cyclase inhibitor	~1,000		Adenylate cyclase and guanylate cyclase; cyclic GMP-phosphodiesterases stimulated	Heat stable, acid stable, alkali labile; destroyed by trypsin, aminopeptidase, elastase; an activator of this enzyme from *Bordetalla pertussis* has been reported	Levey *et al.* (1975); Lehotay *et al.* (1977); Hewlett *et al.* (1979)
Pear	Guanylate cyclase inhibitor	5,000–50,000		Guanylate cyclase; no activity on adenylate cyclate	Inhibitor prevents activation of guanylate cyclase by nitroso compounds	Vesely *et al.* (1977)

porcine pancreatic α-amylase complex ($K_d = 3.5 \times 10^{-11}$ *M*) (Powers and Whitaker 1977b). The mechanism of recognition between the inhibitor and α-amylase isn't known. It is tempting to speculate that the α-amylase is recognizing a carbohydrate unit of a glycoprotein. The red kidney bean amylase inhibitor is a glycoprotein; however, the wheat amylase inhibitors appear not to be glycoproteins. Of importance, mechanistically, the complex between porcine pancreatic α-amylase and red kidney bean amylase inhibitor can still bind to Sephadex and maltose although it has no activity on starch (Powers and Whitaker 1977B). The complex also binds strongly to starch and is eluted only by 0.5*M* maltose (Wilcox and Whitaker 1980). Furthermore, Granum (1979) has observed that rye amylase inhibitor activates some bacterial α-amylases. All these results indicate that combination of enzyme and inhibitor does not involve the binding site of the α-amylase. The most reasonable tentative explanation is that a rapid binding of inhibitor with a site on α-amylase distinct from the active site occurs followed by a much slower conformational change in α-amylase that leads to loss of catalytic activity, but not substrate binding ability.

Potatoes contain an invertase inhibitor of 17,000 daltons which inhibits potato invertase and a number of other plant invertases but not yeast, *Neurospora*, weeping willow, tulip and sunflower invertases (Pressey 1967). The level of the invertase inhibitor in stored potatoes is temperature dependent (Schwimmer *et al.* 1961; Pressey and Shaw 1966). The *in vivo* function of the inhibitor is thought to be a regulation of invertase activity in potato.

The protein phosphatase inhibitors and protein kinase inhibitors are of special interest because of an apparent clear understanding of the *in vivo* role of these inhibitors. Phosphorylase and glycogen synthase are the key regulatory enzymes involved in the breakdown and synthesis of glycogen in animal tissues, respectively. The role of the protein phosphatase inhibitors and protein kinase inhibitors appears to be to regulate the amount of phosphorylase *a* present as will be described in the section on physiological functions of the inhibitors.

NUTRITIONAL AND MEDICAL SIGNIFICANCE OF PROTEIN ENZYME INHIBITORS

It is well known that feeds containing raw soybean flour inhibit growth in rats, chicks and some other monogastric animals (Rackis 1974). The conclusion drawn has been that the soybean proteolytic enzyme inhibitors are responsible for this effect. It is known that soybean trypsin inhibitor enhances the formation of a humoral pancreozymic-like substance that markedly stimulates external secretion by the pancreas

(Khayambashi and Lyman 1969). Lyman and coworkers (Green and Lyman 1972; Lyman *et al.* 1974; Schneeman and Lyman 1975) have shown that the presence of proteolytic enzyme inhibitors in the small intestine increases the secretion of proteolytic enzymes, presumably to compensate for the loss by complexation. The pancreas also becomes larger as a result of hyperplasia of some of the pancreatic cells. However, there is not a clear cause and effect relationship since the older work did not take into account the other inhibitory substances found in soybean (hemagglutinins, chymotrypsin inhibitors, amylase inhibitors, estrogens, phytic acid, etc.). Rackis has suggested that the soybean trypsin inhibitor appears to account for 30–50% of the growth inhibitory effect in raw meal and nearly all of the pancreatic hypertropic response. Some investigators believe the effect, at the level of growth retardation, is more one of limitation of essential amino acids, especially cystine. It has been suggested that the nutritional deficiency of navy beans is a result of the disproportionately large amount of cystine in the trypsin inhibitor which cannot be readily digested (Kakade *et al.* 1969). Much of the earlier work on a correlative role between bovine trypsin inhibitory activity of the feed and growth retardation effects needs reexamination in light of the findings that there is great variability in inhibitory activity with enzymes from different species, including the human (Feeney *et al.* 1969). Heat processing leads to the loss of most, but generally not all, inhibitors in human foods.

The nutritional importance of the amylase inhibitors is not clear. It was suggested that the wheat amylase inhibitor would affect only the digestion of starch by salivary α-amylase and not pancreatic α-amylase since the inhibitor is destroyed by pepsin *in vitro* (Kneen and Sandstedt 1946). However, feeding purified amylase inhibitor from wheat has been shown to result in a reduction of the rate of appearance of glucose in the blood of dog, rats and humans (Puls and Keup 1973). It has been suggested that the amylase inhibitors might be used to control hyperglycemia and hyperinsulinema in humans (Puls and Keup 1973). Feeding of massive doses of purified red kidney bean amylase inhibitor free of all detectable trypsin inhibitor and hemagglutinin activity had no effect on growth of rats (Savaiano *et al.* 1977). Other workers have reported fecal starch from rats fed raw white kidney beans (Jaffé and Vega Lette 1968) and purified wheat inhibitors (Lang *et al.* 1974).

Results of effect of inhibitors on nutrition must be interpreted carefully and in terms of purity of the inhibitor preparation fed. Obviously, the question of the nutritional role of the inhibitors is complicated and needs more definitive work.

The tremendous acceleration in investigations on proteinase inhibitors is primarily a result of the potential medical implications. Possible therapeutical applications have led Bayer to underwrite the cost of two extensive scientific symposia on these inhibitors (Fritz and Tschesche 1971; Fritz *et al.* 1974). The medical literature is filled with papers on investigation of potential use of these inhibitors in a wide range of medical problems. Of major interest is the α_1-antitrypsin inhibitor. It has been repeatedly proposed that proteolytic enzymes from the granulocytes and macrophages digest essential constituents of the lung tissue in α_1-antitrypsin inhibitor deficient patients (Eriksson 1965; Kueppers and Bearn 1966). Experiments in which animals were treated with an aerosol containing proteinases led to emphysema-like lesions in the lung (Kimbel *et al.* 1972; Mass *et al.* 1972). There is also the possibility that irritants in the air (smog) may lead to increased proteinase activity in normal humans which cannot be controlled by levels of α_1-antitrypsin inhibitor normally present. Lowered levels of α_1-antitrypsin inhibitor may also be associated with hepatic cirrhosis in infancy, adult liver disease and respiratory distress syndromes (Evans *et al.* 1970; Sharp and Freier 1972; Berg and Eriksson 1972).

Depressed levels of inhibitors associated with the blood clotting mechanism lead to disruptions in the normal levels of control of intravascular clotting and fibrinolysis (Steinbuch and Andran 1974). Low levels of $C\bar{1}$ inactivator in plasma appears to be correlated with hereditary angioneurotic edema (Rosen *et al.* 1965). α_2-Macroglobulin appears to be present in an inactive form in patients with various joint diseases (Shtacher *et al.* 1973). The role of the acrosin inhibitors of semen in the process of "capacitation" and for possible use as contraceptives are receiving a lot of attention (Zaneveld *et al.* 1974). A role for proteinase inhibitors in tumors and transformed cells in relation to neoplasia has been suggested (Schnebli 1974). Several of the low molecular weight proteinase inhibitors of microbial origin have been suggested for use in the treatment of pancreatitis and burns, stomach ulcers, cartilage disorders such as osteoarthritis, hypertension, and as contraceptive agents (Wingender 1974). A recent excellent review is available on use and potential use of proteinase inhibitors in medicine; unfortunately it is in Polish (Zbytniewski and Kanclerz 1977).

PHYSIOLOGICAL ROLE OF PROTEIN ENZYME INHIBITORS

In some cases, the physiological role of the protein enzyme inhibitors appears quite clear. The pancreatic inhibitors, the basic pancreatic inhibitor (Kunitz) and the acidic inhibitors (Kazal), play the important physiological function of protecting the pancreatic tissue against premature activation of the proteolytic enzyme zymogens which might lead to destruction of the pancreas. Those inhibitors associated with blood clotting are there to prevent the premature activation of zymogens normally found in the blood and as a mechanism of regulation between coagulation and fibrinolysis. The plasma inhibitors may also be a protective mechanism against the liberation of pancreatic proteinases in such diseases as pancreatitis. The proteinase inhibitors in the respiratory tract would appear to be a protective mechanism against proteinases liberated by the granulocytes and macrophages brought in as a result of irritation and/or diseased conditions of the respiratory tract or through inhalation of microorganisms.

The apparent physiological role of the protein phosphatase inhibitors and protein kinase inhibitors of animal tissues is a fascinating one in pointing out the delicately poised control mechanisms of living systems. Phosphorylase and glycogen synthase are key enzymes controlling the breakdown and synthesis of glycogen, respectively. Activity of phosphorylase is controlled by phosphorylation and dephosphorylation with only phosphorylase *a* being active. The two overall reactions are shown in the following equations

$$\underset{\text{(active)}}{\text{Phosphorylase } a} \xrightarrow[\text{phosphatase}]{\text{phosphorylase}} \underset{\text{(inactive)}}{2 \text{ Phosphorylase } b} + 4\, H_3PO_4$$

$$2 \text{ Phosphorylase } b + 4 \text{ ATP} \xrightarrow[\text{kinase}]{\text{phosphorylase } b} \text{Phosphorylase } a + 4 \text{ ADP}$$

Phosphorylase phosphatase activity is modulated by two key inhibitors, protein phosphatase inhibitors I and II (Table 6.5) (Huang and Glinsmann 1976; Hwang *et al.* 1977; Cohen *et al.* 1977). Inhibitor I activity in turn is controlled by the extent of phosphorylation by a specific protein kinase. Two inhibitors of phosphorylase *b* kinase have also been described (Table 6.5) (Walsh *et al.* 1971; DeMaille *et al.* 1977; Szmigielski *et al.* 1977). Type I protein kinase inhibitor can only inhibit cAMP-dependent protein kinases while Type II protein kinase inhibitor has activity toward nucleotide-independent protein kinases. A fascinating story indeed!

The physiological role of protein enzyme inhibitors in higher plants and microorganisms is less well understood in spite of the inhibitors often being present as 5–10% of the total protein (Richardson 1977). It is well-known that the level of inhibitors varies with different stages of growth suggesting that the inhibitors may be physiologically important to the organisms (Richardson 1977). It has also been suggested that the inhibitors have developed as defense mechanisms against invasion by insects and microorganisms (Ryan 1973; Richardson 1977). Infestation of potatoes with Colorado potato beetle larva leads to markedly increased levels of protease Inhibitor-I in the leaves (Green and Ryan 1972). Recently, it has been shown that all insect α-amylases examined are inhibited by the amylase inhibitor from red kidney beans (Powers 1979). Yetter *et al.* (1979) have also suggested that the wheat α-amylase inhibitors may be active against attack of the wheat by insects during storage. On the other hand, the amylase inhibitor does not have any activity against higher plant or microbial amylases tested (Powers and Whitaker 1977A). Blanco (1980) has found that the three amylase inhibitors of maize inhibit maize α-amylase, indicating a possible physiological role for these inhibitors in maize. The thiol protease inhibitors of the pineapple fruit have activity against the major proteolytic enzymes, papain and chymopapain, present in the fruit (Heinrikson and Kézdy 1976). Control of invertase activity of the potato is considered to be the role of the invertase inhibitor since its activity can be markedly affected by temperature, conditions which also affect starch-glucose interconversion (Schwimmer *et al.* 1961; Pressey and Shaw 1966). The yeast proteinase inhibitors A, B and C have strong inhibitory activity against specific proteinases A, B and C of the same yeast (Saheki *et al.* 1974; Lenny 1975; Bünning and Holzer 1977). The inhibitors appear to be stored in the vacuoles but must be important in the protein metabolism of the cell.

SUMMARY

It is clear that research on the protein enzyme inhibitors is increasing at an ever accelerating rate and that many new inhibitors are being discovered. Remarkable progress is being made in the elucidation of the primary structure of many of the proteinase inhibitors with striking homology being found among inhibitors from widely different sources (cow colostrum, snails and snake venoms among others; see Table 6.1). Some progress has been made in understanding the mechanisms of action of the trypsin inhibitors but very little progress has been made with respect to other inhibitors. Specific effect of these inhibitors on the nutritional quality of feeds and foods is complicated by the presence of a great variety of inhibitors in biological materials. While the physiological roles of many of the animal proteinase inhibitors are fairly well understood, much remains to be done in this area particularly with respect to the inhibitors in plants and microorganisms. The presence of a variety of protein inhibitors directed against nonproteolytic enzymes raises the interesting question of just how widespread are protein enzyme inhibitors and whether they evolved as a protective mechanism against pests much as the specific γ-globulins in animals are produced in response to antigens. The therapeutic use of protein enzyme inhibitors is only in its infancy but provides the impetus for continued concentrated effort on the inhibitors.

BIBLIOGRAPHY

AKO, H., FOSTER, R.J., and RYAN, C.A. 1974. Mechanism of action of naturally occurring proteinase inhibitors. Studies with anhydrotrypsin and anhydrochymotrypsin purified by affinity chromatography. Biochem. *13*, 132–139.

ALBERSHEIM, P. and ANDERSON, A.J. 1971. Proteins from plant cell walls inhibit polygalacturonases secreted by plant pathogens. Proc. Natl. Acad. Sci. (USA) *68*, 1815–1819.

ANONYMOUS. 1976. Protein inhibitor of kidney hydroxy-vitamin D_3-1-hydroxylase. Nutr. Reviews *34*, 284–286.

AOYAGI, T., MIYATA, S., NANBO, M., KOJIMA, F., MATSUZAKI, M., ISHIZUKA, M., TAKEUCHI, T., and UMEZAWA, H. 1969A. Biological activities of leupeptins. J. Antibiot. *22*, 558–568.

AOYAGI, M., TAKEUCHI, A., MATSUZAKI, A., KAWAMURA, K., KONDO, S., HAMADA, M., MAEDA, K., and UMEZAWA, H. 1969B. Leupeptins, new protease inhibitors from actinomycetes. J. Antibiot. (Tokyo) *22*, 283–286.

BAGDY, D., BARABÁS, É., GRÁF, L., PETERSEN, T.E., and MAGNUSSON, S. 1976. Hirudin, Methods Enzymol. *56B*, 669–678.

BARRETT, A.J. and STARKEY, P.M. 1973. The interaction of α_2-macroglobulin with proteinases. Characteristics and specificity of the reaction, and a hypothesis concerning its molecular mechanism. Biochem. J. *133*, 709–724.

BAUMGARTNER, B. and CHRISPEELS, M.J. 1976. Partial characterization of a protease inhibitor which inhibits the major endopeptidase present in the cotyledons of mung beans. Plant Physiol. *58*, 1–6.

BEALE, E.G., DEDMAN, J.R., and MEANS, A.R. 1977. Isolation and characterization of a protein from rat testis which inhibits cyclic AMP-dependent protein kinase and phosphodiesterase. J. Biol. Chem. *252*, 6322–6327.

BEDETTI, C., BOZZINI, A., SILANO, V., and VITTOZZI, L. 1974. Amylase protein inhibitors and the role of Aegilops species in polyploid wheat speciation. Biochim. Biophys. Acta *362*, 299–307.

BELEW, M. 1977. The trypsin and chymotrypsin inhibitors in chick peas (*Cicer arietinum* L.). The relationships among the six isoinhibitors. Eur. J. Biochem. *73*, 411–420.

BELEW, M., PORATH, J., and SUNDBERG, L. 1975. The trypsin and chymotrypsin inhibitors in chick peas (*Cicer arietinum* L.). Purification and properties of the inhibitors. Eur. J. Biochem. *60*, 247–258.

BERG, N.O. and ERIKSSON, S. 1972. Liver disease in adults with alpha_1-antitrypsin deficiency. New Engl. J. Med. *287*, 1264–1267.

BIER, M., TERMINIELLO, L., DUKE, J.A., GIBBS, R.J., and NORD, F.F. 1953. Investigations on proteins and polymers. X. Composition and fractionation of ovomucoid. Arch. Biochem. Biophys. *47*, 465–473.

BIETH, J. and FRECHIN, J.C. 1974. Elastase inhibitors as impurities in commercial preparations of soybean trypsin inhibitor (Kunitz). *In* Proteinase Inhibitors, Proc. Int. Res. Conf., 2nd (Bayer Symp. V). H. Fritz, H. Tschesche, L.J. Greene, and E. Truscheit (Editors). Springer-Verlag, Berlin and New York.

BIRK, Y. 1976A. Proteinase inhibitors of legumes seeds. Methods Enzymol. *45B*, 697–700.

BIRK, Y. 1976B. Trypsin and chymotrypsin inhibitors from soybeans. Methods Enzymol. *45B*, 700–707.

BIRK, Y. 1976C. Trypsin isoinhibitors from garden beans *(Phaseolus vulgaris)*. Methods Enzymol. *45B*, 710–716.

BIRK, Y. 1976D. A trypsin and chymotrypsin inhibitor from groundnuts *(Arachis hypogaea)*. Methods Enzymol. *45B*, 716–722.

BLANCO, A. 1980. Personal communication. Depto. de Bioquimica, Universidad Nacional Autonoma Mexico, Mexico City.

BOONVISUT, S. and WHITAKER, J.R. 1976. Effect of heat, amylase, and disulfide bond cleavage on the *in vitro* digestibility of soybean proteins. J. Agr. Food Chem. *24*, 1130–1135.

BRADSHAW, M.J., CHAPMAN, J.M., and EDELMAN, J. 1970. Enzyme formation in higher plant tissues. A protein inhibitor of invertase synthesis secreted by tissue slices of plant storage organs. Planta *90*, 323–332.

BRAGANCA, B.M., SAMBRAY, Y.M., and SAMBRAY, R.M. 1970. Isolation of a polypeptide inhibitor of phospholipase A from cobra venom. Eur. J. Biochem. *13*, 410–415.

BRECHER, A.S. and PUGATCH, R.D. 1969. A non-dialyzable inhibitor of proteolytic activity in soluble extracts of *Escherichia coli*. Experientia *25*, 251–252.

BROOKS, J.C. and SENIOR, A.E. 1971. Studies on the mitochondrial oligomycin-insensitive ATPase. II. The relationship of the specific protein inhibitor to the ATPase. Arch. Biochem. Biophys. *147*, 467–470.

BÜNNING, P. and HOLZER, H. 1977. Natural occurrence and chemical modification of proteinase B inhibitors from yeast. J. Biol. Chem. *252*, 5316–5323.

CACAN, R., VERBERT, A., HOFLACK, B. and MONTREUIL, J. 1977. Occurrence of an intracellular inhibitor of ectosialyltransferase in lymphocytes. FEBS Lett. *81*, 53–56.

ČECHOVÁ, D. 1976. Trypsin inhibitor from cow colostrum. Methods Enzymol. *45B*, 806–813.

ČECHOVÁ-POSPÍSILOVÁ, D., SVESTOKOVÁ, V., and SŎRM, F. 1969. Similarities in primary structures of cow colostrum trypsin inhibitor and bovine basic pancreatic trypsin inhibitor. FEBS Lett. *4*, 155–156.

COHEN, P., NIMMO, G.A., and ANTONIW, J.F. 1977. Specificity of a protein phosphatase inhibitor from rabbit skeletal muscle. Biochem. J. *162*, 435–444.

DAMUS, P.S. and ROSENBERG, R.D. 1976. Antithrombin-heparin cofactor. Methods Enzymol. *45B*, 653–669.

De La LLOSA, P., TERTRIN, C., and JUSTISZ, M. 1964. The C terminal chain of hirudin. Biochim. Biophys. Acta *93*, 40–44.

DeMAILLE, J.G., FERRAZ, C., and FISCHER, E.H. 1979. The protein inhibitor of adenosine 3′,5′-monophosphate-dependent protein kinases. The amino-terminal portion of the peptide chain contains the inhibitory site. Biochim. Biophys. Acta *586*, 374–383.

DeMAILLE, J.G., PETERS, K.A., and FISCHER, E.N. 1977. Isolation and properties of the rabbit skeletal muscle protein inhibitor of adenosine 3′,5′-monophosphate dependent protein kinases. Biochem. *16*, 3080–3086.

DEUTSCH, H.F. and MORTON, J.I. 1961. Physical-chemical studies of some modified ovomucoids. Arch. Biochem. Biophys. *93*, 654–665.

DIETL, T., DOBRINSKI, W., and HOCHSTRASSER, K. 1979. Human inter-α-trypsin inhibitor. Limited proteolysis by trypsin, plasmin, kallikrein and granulocytic elastase and inhibitory properties of the cleavage products. Hoppe-Seyler's Z. Physiol. Chem. *360*, 1313–1318.

DIETL, T. and TSCHESCHE, H. 1975. Trypsin-kallikrein isoinhibitor K (type Kunitz) from snails *(Helix pomatia)*. Eur. J. Biochem. *58*, 453–560.

DIETL, T. and TSCHESCHE, H. 1976A. Albumin gland inhibitor from snails *(Helix pomatia)*. Methods Enzymol. *45B*. 785–799.

DIETL, T. and TSCHESCHE, H. 1976B. Characterization and inhibitory properties of snail secretory proteinase inhibitors. *In* Protides Biol. Fluids Proc. Colloq. *23*, 271–278.

EBNER, E. and MAIR, K.L. 1977. A protein inhibitor of mitochondrial adenosine triphosphatase (F_1) from *Saccharomyces cerevisiae*. J. Biol. Chem. *252*, 671–676.

ERIKSSON, S. 1965. Studies in α_1-antitrypsin deficiency. Acta Med. Scand. *177*, Suppl. 175.

EVANS, H.E., LEVI, M., and MANDL, I. 1970. Serum enzyme inhibitor concentrations in respiratory distress syndrome. Amer. Rev. Resp. Dis. *101*, 359–363.

FEENEY, R.E. and ALLISON, R.G. 1969. Evolutionary Biochemistry of Proteins. Homologous and Analogous Proteins from Avian Egg Whites, Blood Sera, Milk and Other Substances. John Wiley and Sons, New York.

FEENEY, R.E. MEANS, G.E., and BIGLER, J.C. 1969. Inhibition of human trypsin, plasmin, and thrombin by naturally occurring inhibitors of proteolytic enzymes. J. Biol. Chem. *244*, 1957–1960.

FEINSTEIN, G. and FEENEY, R.E. 1966. Interaction of inactive derivatives of chymotrypsin and trypsin with protein inhibitors. J. Biol. Chem. *241*, 5183–5189.

FEINSTEIN, G., HOFFSTEIN, R., and SOKOLOVSKY, M. 1974. Isolation of human pancreatic inhibitor and the study of its interaction with mammalian and human proteases. *In* Proteinase Inhibitors, Proc. Int. Res. Conf., 2nd (Bayer Symp. V). H. Fritz, H. Tschesche, L.J. Greene, and E. Truscheit (Editors). Springer-Verlag, Berlin and New York.

FERRAZ, C., DeMAILLE, J.G., and FISCHER, E.H. 1979. The protein inhibitor of adenosine 3′,5′-monophosphate-dependent protein kinases. Isolation and characterization of three isoinhibitors. Biochemie *61*, 645–651.

FILHO, J.X. 1974. Trypsin inhibitors in sorghum grain. J. Food Sci. *39*, 422–423.

FINK, E. and FRITZ, H. 1976. Proteinase inhibitors from guinea pig seminal vesicles. Methods Enzymol. *45B*, 825–833.

FISHMAN, W.H. 1967. Determination of β-glucuronidases. Methods Biochem. Anal. *15*, 77–145.

FOSSUM, K. 1970. Proteolytic enzymes and biological inhibitors. Acta Path. Microbiol. Scand., Sect. B *78*, 755–759.

FOSSUM, K. and WHITAKER, J.R. 1968. Ficin and papain inhibitor from chicken egg white. Arch. Biochem. Biophys. *125*, 367–375.

FRATTALI, V. and STEINER, R.F. 1968. Soybean inhibitors. I. Separation and some properties of three inhibitors in commercial crude soybean trypsin inhibitor. Biochem. *7*, 521–530.

FREDERICQ, E. and DEUTSCH, H.F. 1949. Studies on ovomucoid. J. Biol. Chem. *181*, 499–510.

FRÉNOY, J.-P., RAZAFIMAHALEO, E., and BOURRILLON, R. 1972. Investigation of the structure of human α_2-macroglobulin. III. Isolation and characterization of one subunit. Biochim. Biophys. Acta *257*, 111–121.

FRITZ, H. and HOCHSTRASSER, K. 1976. Proteinase (elastase) inhibitors from dog submandibular glands. Methods Enzymol. *45B*, 860–869.

FRITZ, H., JAUMANN, E., MEISTER, R., PASQUAY, P., HOCHSTRASSER, K., and FINK, E. 1971. Proteinase inhibitors from dog submandibular glands—isolation, amino acid composition, inhibition spectrum. *In* Proteinase Inhibitors, Proc. Int. Res. Conf., 1st. H. Fritz and H. Tschesche (Editors). Walter de Gruyter, Berlin.

FRITZ, H. and KREJCI, K. 1976. Trypsin-plasmin inhibitors (Bdellins) from leeches. Methods Enzymol. *45B*, 797–806.

FRITZ, H. and TSCHESCHE, H. 1971. Proceedings of the 1st International Research Conference on Proteinase Inhibitors. Walter de Gruyter, Berlin.

FRITZ, H., TSCHESCHE, H., and FINK, E. 1976. Proteinase inhibitors from boar seminal plasma. Methods Enzymol. *45B*, 834–847.

FRITZ, H., TSCHESCHE, H., GREENE, L.J., and TRUSCHEIT, E. 1974. Proteinase Inhibitors, Proc. Int. Res. Conf., 2nd (Bayer Symp. V). Springer-Verlag, Berlin and New York.

FROMMER, W., JUNGE, B., MÜLLER, L., SCHMIDT, D., and TRUSCHEIT, E. 1979. Neue enzyminhibitoren aus Mikroorganismen. Planta Medica *35*, 195–217. Abstract in English.

GENNIS, L.S. and CANTOR, C.R. 1976. Double-headed protease inhibitors from black-eyed peas. 1. Purification of the two new protease inhibitors and the endogenous protease by affinity chromatography. J. Biol. Chem. *251*, 734–740.

GRÁF, L., PATTHY, A., BARABÁS, É., and BAGDY, D. 1973. On the NH_2-terminal residue of hirudin. Biochim. Biophys. Acta *310*, 416–417.

GRANUM, P.E. 1978. Purification and characterization of an α-amylase inhibitor from rye *(Secale cereale)* flour. J. Food Biochem. *2*, 103–120.

GRANUM, P.E. 1979. Personal communication. Ås, Norway.

GRANUM, P.E. and WHITAKER, J.R. 1977. Purification and characterization of α-amylase inhibitors in wheat (*Triticum aestivum* var. *Anza*). J. Food Biochem. *1*, 385–401.

GREEN, G.M. and LYMAN, R.L. 1972. Feed back regulation of pancreatic enzyme secretion as a mechanism for trypsin inhibitor-induced hypersection in rats. Proc. Soc. Expt'l. Biol. Med. *140*, 6–12.

GREEN, T.R. and RYAN, C.A. 1972. Wound induced proteinase inhibitor in plant leaves: A possible defense mechanisms against insects. Science *175*, 776–777.

GREENE, L.J. 1974. Low molecular weight carboxydipeptidase inhibitors from *Bothrops jararaca* venom. *In* Proteinase Inhibitors, Proc. Int. Res. Conf. 2nd (Bayer Symp. V). H. Fritz, H. Tschesche, L.J. Greene, and L. Truscheit (Editors). Springer-Verlag, Berlin and New York.

GREENE, L.J., DICARLO, J.J., SUSSMAN, A.J., and BARTELT, D.C. 1968. Two trypsin inhibitors from porcine pancreatic juice. J. Biol. Chem. *243*, 1804–1815.

GREENE, L.J., PUBOLS, M.H., and BARTELT, D.C. 1976. Human pancreatic secretory trypsin inhibitor. Methods Enzymol. *45B*, 813–825.

HARPEL, P.C. 1976A. Human α_2-macroglobulin. Methods Enzymol. *45B*, 639–652.

HARPEL, P.C. 1976B. C$\bar{1}$ inactivator. Methods Enzymol. *45B*, 751–760.

HARPEL, P.C. and COOPER, N.R. 1975. Studies on human plasma C$\bar{1}$ inactivator-enzyme interactions. 1. Mechanisms of interaction with C$\bar{1}$, plasmin, and trypsin. J. Clin. Invest. *55*, 593.

HASS, G.M., NAU, H., BIEMANN, K., GRAHN, D.T., ERICSSON, L.H., and NEURATH, H. 1975. The amino acid sequence of a carboxypeptidase inhibitor from potatoes. Biochemistry *14*, 1334–1342.

HAUPT, H., HEIMBURGER, N., KRANTZ, T., and SCHWICK, H.G. 1970. A method for the isolation and characterization of C$\bar{1}$ inactivators of human plasma. Eur. J. Biochem. *17*, 254–261.

HEIMBURGER, N. 1974. Biochemistry of proteinase inhibitors from human plasma: a review of recent development. *In* Proteinase Inhibitors, Proc. Int. Res. Conf., 2nd (Bayer Symp. V). H. Fritz, H. Tschesche, L.J. Greene, and E. Truscheit (Editors). Springer-Verlag, Berlin and New York.

HEIMBURGER, N. and HAUPT, H. 1965. Characterization of α_1X-glycoprotein as a chymotrypsin inhibitor of human plasma. Clin. Chim. Acta *12*, 116–118.

HEIMBURGER, N., HAUPT, H., and SCHWICK, H.G. 1971. Proteinase inhibitors of human plasma. *In* Proteinase Inhibitors, Proc. Int. Res. Conf., 1st. H. Fritz, and H. Tschesche (Editors). Walter de Gruyter, Berlin.

HEINRIKSON, R.L. and KÉZDY, F.J. 1976. Acidic cysteine protease inhibitors from pineapple stem. Methods Enzymol. *45B*, 740–751.

HERNÀNDEZ-JODRA, M. and GANCEDO, C. 1979. Characterization of an intracellular inhibitor of the carboxypeptidase R from *Rhodotorula glutinis*. Hoppe-Seyler's Z. Physiol. Chem. *360*, 913–917.

HEWLETT, E.L., UNDERHILL, L.H., COOK, G.H., MANCLARK, C.R., and WOLFF, J. 1979. A protein activator for the adenylate cyclase of *Bordetella pertussis*. J. Biol. Chem. *254*, 5602–5605.

HIRONO, S., NAKAMURA, K.T., IITAKA, Y., and MITSUI, Y. 1979. Crystal structure of the complex of subtilisin BPN′ with its protein inhibitor streptomyces subtilisin inhibitor. The structure at 4.3 Å resolution. J. Mol. Biol. *131*, 855–869.

HOCHSTRASSER, K. 1976. Proteinase (elastase) inhibitors from the ciliated membranes of the human respiratory tract. Methods Enzymol. *45B*, 869–874.

HOCHSTRASSER, K., ILLCHMANN, K., and WERLE, E. 1970. Plant protease inhibitors. VII. Amino acid sequence of specific trypsin inhibitors from maize, characteristics of the polymer. Z. Physiol. Chem. *351*, 721–728.

HOCHSTRASSER, K. and WACHTER, E. 1979. Kunitz-type proteinase inhibitors derived by limited proteolysis of the inter-α-trypsin inhibitor. I. Determination of the amino acid sequence of the antitrypsin domain by solid phase Edman degradation. Hoppe-Seyler's Z. Physiol. Chem. *360*, 1285–1296.

HODGES, L.C., LAINE, R., and CHAN, S.K. 1979. Structure of the oligosaccharide chains in human α_1-protease inhibitor. J. Biol. Chem. *254*, 8208–8212.

HOJIMA, Y., MORIWAKI, C., and MORIYA, H. 1973. Studies on kallikrein inhibitors from potatoes. V. Characterization of two isolated inhibitors. J. Biochem. (Tokyo) *73*, 933–943.

HORY, H.-D. and WEDER, J.K.P. 1976. Trypsin and chymotrypsin inhibitors in leguminosae. VII. Partial amino acid sequence of the trypsin and chymotrypsin inhibitor PCI 3 from *Phaseolus coccineus*. Z. Lebensm. Unters.-Forsch. *162*, 349–356.

HÖYEM, T. and SKULBERG, A. 1962. Trypsin inhibitors produced by *Clostridium botulinum* cultures. Nature (London) *195*, 922–923.

HUANG, F.L. and GLINSMANN, W.H. 1976. Separation and characterization of two phosphorylase phosphatase inhibitors from rabbit skeletal muscle. Eur. J. Biochem. *70*, 419–426.

HUANG, F.L., TAO, S.-H., and GLINSMANN, W.H. 1977. Multiple forms of protein phosphatase inhibitors in mammalian tissues. Biochem. Biophys. Res. Commun. *78*, 615–623.

HWANG, D.L.-R., DAVIS, LIN, K.-T., YANG, W.-K., and FOARD, D.E. 1977. Purification, partial characterization and immunological relationships of multiple low molecular weight protease inhibitors of soybean. Biochim. Biophys. Acta *495*, 369–382.

IKENAKA, T. 1974. A new alkaline proteinase inhibitor from *Streptomyces albogriseolus*. *In* Proteinase Inhibitors, Proc. Int. Res. Conf. 2nd (Bayer Symp. V). M. Fritz, H. Tschesche, L.J. Greene, and E. Truscheit (Editors). Springer-Verlag, Berlin and New York.

IKENAKA, T., ODANI, S., and KOIDE, T. 1974. Chemical structure and inhibitory activities of soybean proteinase inhibitors. *In* Proteinase Inhibitors, Proc. Int. Res. Conf., 2nd (Bayer Symp. V). H. Fritz, H. Tschesche, L.J. Greene, and E. Truscheit (Editors). Springer-Verlag, Berlin and New York.

ISHIURA, S., MUROFUSHI, H., SUZUKI, K., and IMAHORI, K. 1977. Studies of a calcium activated neutral protease from chicken skeletal muscle. I. Purification and characterization. J. Biochem. (Tokyo) *84*, 225–230.

ISHIURA, S., SUGITA, H., SUZUKI, I., and IMAHORI, K. 1979. Studies of a calcium-activated neutral protease from chicken skeletal muscle. II. Substrate specificity. J. Biochem. (Tokyo) *86*, 579–581.

IWANAGA, S., TAKAHASHI, H., and SUZUKI, T. 1976. Proteinase inhibitors from the venom of Russell's viper. Methods Enzymol. *45B*, 874–881.

IWASAKI, T., IGUCHI, I., KIYOHARA, T., and YOSHIKAWA, M. 1974A. Digestibility of the active fragment of potato proteinase inhibitor IIa by bovine chymotrypsin and a bacterial proteinase. J. Biochem. (Tokyo) *75*, 1387–1390.

IWASAKI, T., KIYOHARA, T., and YOSHIKAWA, M. 1974B. Preparation of an active fragment of potato proteinase inhibitor IIa and its properties. J. Biochem. (Tokyo) *75*, 843–851.

IWASAKI, T., WADA, J., KIYOHARA, T., and YOSHIKAWA, M. 1975. Isolation of a low molecular weight active fragment of potato proteinase inhibitor IIb. J. Biochem. (Tokyo) *78*, 1267–1275.

JAFFÉ, W.G., MORENO, R., and WALLIS, V. 1973. Amylase inhibitor in legume seeds. Nutr. Rep. Int. *7*, 169–174.

JAFFÉ, W.G. and VEGA LETTE, C.L. 1968. Heat-labile growth-inhibiting factors in beans *(Phaseolus vulgaris)*. J. Nutr. *94*, 203–210.

JONES, G., MOORE, S., and STEIN, W.H. 1963. Properties of chromatographically purified trypsin inhibitors from lima beans. Biochemistry *2*, 66–71.

JONES, J.M., CREETH, J.M., and KEKWICK, R.A. 1972. Thiol reduction of human α_2-macroglobulin. The subunit structure. Biochem. J. *127*, 187–197.

KAEHN, K. and KULA, M.-R. 1977. Demonstration of specific aminopeptidase inhibitors in *Neurospora crassa*. FEBS Lett. *79*, 85–90.

KAKADE, M.L., ARNOLD, R.L., LIENER, I.E., and WAIBEL, P.E. 1969. Unavailability of cystine from trypsin inhibitors as a factor contributing to the poor nutritive value of navy beans. J. Nutr. *99*, 34–42.

KAKADE, M.L., HOFFA, D.E., and LIENER, I.E. 1973. Contribution of trypsin inhibitors to the deleterious effects of unheated soybeans fed to rats. J. Nutr. *103*, 1772–1778.

KALSER, M.H. and GROSSMAN, M. 1955. Secretion of trypsin inhibitor in pancreatic juice. Gastroenterology *29*, 35–45.

KANAMORI, M., IBUKI, F., TASHIRO, M., YAMADA, M., and MIYOSHI, M. 1976. Purification and partial characterization of a protein proteinase inhibitor isolated from eggplant exocarp. Biochim. Biophys. Acta *439*, 398–405.

KASSEL, B. 1970. Inhibitors of proteolytic enzymes. Methods Enzymol. *19*, 839–906.

KASSEL, B. 1978. Protein inhibitors of non proteolytic enzymes. *In* Chemistry and Biochemistry of Amino Acids, Peptides and Proteins, Vol. 5. B. Winstein (Editor). Marcel Dekker, New York.

KATO, I. 1976. Amino acid sequences of third domains of turkey, chicken and Japanese quail ovomucoids. Fed. Proc. *35*, Abst. 1333.

KAWAMURA, K., KONDO, S., MAEDA, K., and UMEZAWA, H. 1969. Structures and syntheses of leupeptins Pr-LL and Ac-LL. Chem. Pharm. Bull. *17*, 1902–1909.

KAWANO, T., MORIMOTO, K., and UEMURA, Y. 1970. Partial purification and properties of urokinase inhibitor from human placenta. J. Biochem. (Tokyo) *67*, 333–342.

KHAYAMBASHI, H. and LYMAN, R.L. 1969. Secretion of rat pancreas perfused with plasma from rats fed soybean trypsin inhibitor. Am. J. Physiol. *217*, 646–651.

KIHARA, H. 1976. Studies on phospholipase A in *Trimeresurus flavovirdis* venom III. Purification and some properties of phospholipase A inhibitor in Habu serum. J. Biochem. (Tokyo) *80*, 341–349.

KIM, S. and PAIK, W.K. 1971. Natural inhibitor of protein methylase II. Biochim. Biophys. Acta *252*, 526–532.

KIMBEL, B., MASS, B., IKEDA, T., and WEINBAUM, G. 1972. Emphysema in dogs induced by leukocyte contents. *In* Pulmonary Emphysema and Proteolysis. C. Mittman (Editor). Academic Press, New York.

KNEEN, E. and SANDSTEDT, R.M. 1946. Distribution and general properties of an amylase inhibitor in cereals. Arch. Biochem. Biophys. *9*, 235–249.

KONDO, S., KAWAMURA, K., IWANAGA, J., HAMADA, M., AOYAGI, T., MAEDA, K., TAKEUCHI, T., and UMEZAWA, W. 1969. Isolation and characterization of leupeptins produced by actinomycetes. Chem. Pharm. Bull. *17*, 1896–1901.

KRAHN, J. and STEVENS, F.C. 1970. Lima bean trypsin inhibitor. Limited proteolysis by trypsin and chymotrypsin. Biochemistry *9*, 2646–2652.

KRESS, L.F. and LASKOWSKI, M., SR. 1974. Purification, properties, and composition of α_1-trypsin inhibitor from human plasma. *In* Proteinase Inhibitors, Proc. Int. Res. Conf., 2nd (Bayer Symp. V). H. Fritz, H. Tschesche, L.J. Greene, and E. Truscheit (Editors). Springer-Verlag, Berlin and New York.

KUCICH, U. and PEANASKY, R.J. 1970. Trypsin inhibitors from *Ascaris lumbricoides* var. *suis*. Biochim. Biophys. Acta *200*, 47–57.

KUEPPERS, F. and BEARN, A.G. 1966. A possible experimental approach to the association of hereditary α_1-antitrypsin deficiency and pulmonary emphysema. Proc. Soc. Exptl. Biol. and Med. *121*, 1207–1209.

KUETTNER, K.E., HITI, J., EISENSTEIN, R., and HARPER, E. 1976. Collagenase inhibition by cationic proteins derived from cartilage and aorta. Biochem. Biophys. Res. Commun. *72*, 40–46.

KUNITZ, M. and NORTHROP, J.H. 1936. Isolation from beef pancreas of crystalline trypsinogen, trypsin, a trypsin inhibitor, and an inhibitor-trypsin compound. J. Gen. Physiol. *19*, 991–1007.

LANG, J.A., CHANG-HUM, L.E., REYES, P.S., and BRIGGS, G.M. 1974. Interference of starch metabolism by α-amylase inhibitors. Fed. Proc. *33*, 718.

LASKOWSKI, M., JR., KATO, I., and KOHR, W.J. 1978. Protein inhibitors of serine proteinases; convergent evolution, multiple domains and hypervariability of reactive sites. *In* Versatility of Proteins. C.H. Li (Editor). Academic Press, New York.

LASKOWSKI, M., JR., MARS, P.H., and LASKOWSKI, M., SR. 1952. Comparison of trypsin inhibitor from colostrum with other crystalline trypsin inhibitors. J. Biol. Chem. *198*, 745–752.

LASKOWSKI, M., JR. and SEALOCK, R.W. 1971. Protein proteinase inhibitors-molecular aspects. *In* The Enzymes, Vol. 3, 3rd Edition. P.D. Boyer (Editor). Academic Press, New York.

LEHOTAY, D.C., LEVEY, G.S., VESELY, D.L., BORNET, E.P., RAY, M.V., ENTMAN, M.L., and SCHWARTZ, A. 1977. The effect of adenylate cyclase inhibitor (ACI) on guanylate cyclase, phosphodiesterase and other enzymes in heart. J. Cyclic Nucleotide Res. *3*, 55–65.

LENNEY, J.F. 1975. Three yeast proteins that specifically inhibit yeast proteases A, B and C. J. Bacteriol. *122*, 1265–1273.

LENNEY, J.F., TOLAN, J.R., SUGAI, W.J., and LEE, A.G. 1979. Thermostable endogenous inhibitors of cathepsins B and H. Eur. J. Biochem. *101*, 153–161.

LESCA, P. 1976. Protein inhibitor of acid deoxyribonucleases. Improved purification procedure and properties. J. Biol. Chem. *251*, 116–123.

LEVEY, G.S., LEHOTAY, D.C., CANTERBURY, J.M., BRICKER, L.A., and MELTZ, G.J. 1975. Isolation of a unique peptide inhibitor of hormone-responsive adenylate cyclase. J. Biol. Chem. *250*, 5730–5733.

LIBBY, P. and GOLDBERG, A.L. 1978. Leupeptin, a protease inhibitor, decreases protein degradation in normal and diseased muscles. Science *199*, 534–536.

LIENER, I.E. and KAKADE, M.L. 1969. Protease inhibitors. *In* Toxic Constituents of Plant Foodstuffs. I.E. Liener (Editor). Academic Press, New York.

LINDBERG, M.U. 1964. Purification of an inhibitor of pancreatic deoxyribonuclease from calf spleen. Biochim. Biophys. Acta *82*, 237–248.

LINDBERG, M.U. and SKOOG, L. 1970. Purification from calf thymus of an inhibitor of deoxyribonuclease I. Eur. J. Biochem. *13*, 326–335.

LIU, W.H., MEANS, G.E., and FEENEY, R.E. 1971. The inhibitory properties of avian-ovoinhibitors against proteolytic enzymes. Biochim. Biophys. Acta *229*, 176–185.

LORAND, L. (Editor). 1976. Proteolytic enzymes. Methods Enzymol. *45B*, 639–888.

LYMAN, R.L., OLDS, B.A., and GREEN, G.M. 1974. Chymotrypsinogen in the intestine of rats fed soybean trypsin inhibitor and its inability to suppress pancreatic enzyme secretions. J. Nutr. *104*, 105–110.

MAGNI, G., SANTARELLI, I., NATALINI, P., RUGGIERI, S., and VITA, A. 1977. Catabolite inactivation of bakers yeast uridine nucleosidase. Isolation and partial purification of a specific proteolytic inactivase. Eur. J. Biochem. *75*, 77–82.

MAIER, K., MULLER, H., and HOLZER, H. 1979. Purification and characterization of two inhibitors of yeast proteinase B. J. Biol. Chem. *254*, 8491–8497.

MARKWARDT, F. 1955. Investigations on hirudin. Naturwissenschaften *42*, 537–538.

MARKWARDT, F. 1970. Hirudin as an inhibitor of thrombin. Methods Enzymol. *19*, 924–932.

MARSHALL, J.J. 1975. α-Amylase inhibitors from plants. ACS Symposium Series *16*, 244–266.

MARSHALL, J.J. 1977. Pancreatic α-amylase inhibitors in cereals. Carbohydr. Res. *57*, C27–C30.

MARSHALL, J.J. and LAUDA, C.M. 1975. Purification and properties of phaseolamin, an inhibitor of α-amylase from the kidney bean *Phaseolus vulgaris*. J. Biol. Chem. *250*, 8030–8037.

MASS, B., IKEDA, T., MERANZE, D.R., WEINBAUM, G., and KIMBEL, P. 1972. Introduction of experimental emphysema. Cellular and specificity. Amer. Rev. Resp. Dis. *106*, 384–391.

MATSUSHITA, K. and URITANI, I. 1976. Isolation and characterization of acid invertase inhibitor in sweet potato. J. Biochem. (Tokyo) *79*, 633–639.

MATTOO, A.K. and MODI, V.V. 1970. Partial purification and properties of enzyme inhibitors from ripe mangos. Enzymol. *39*, 237–247.

MEANS, G.E., RYAN, D.S., and FEENEY, R.E. 1974. Protein inhibitors of proteolytic enzymes. Accounts Chem. Res. *7*, 315–320.

MELVILLE, J.C. and RYAN, C.A. 1972. Chymotrypsin inhibitor I from potatoes. Large scale preparation and characterization of its subunit components. J. Biol. Chem. *247*, 3445–3453.

MIKOLA, J. and SUOLINNA, E.-M. 1971. Purification and properties of an inhibitor of microbial alkaline proteinases from barley. Arch. Biochem. Biophys. *144*, 566–575.

MORISHIMA, H., TAKITA, T., and UMEZAWA, H. 1972. The chemical synthesis of pepstatin A. J. Antibiot. *25*, 551–552.

MURAO, S., OHYAMA, K., MURAI, H., GOTOO, A., MATSUI, Y., FUKUHARA, K., MIYATA, S., SUMIDA, M., and ARAI, M. 1979. Amylase inhibitors from *Streptomyces* species. J. Jpn. Soc. Starch Sci. *26*, 157–164.

MURAO, S. and SATO, S. 1972. S-SI, a new alkaline protease inhibitor from *Streptomyces albogriseolus* S-3253. Agr. Biol. Chem. *36*, 160–163.

NAMIKI, S., KANGOURI, K., NAGATE, T., SUGITA, K., HARA, H., MORI, E., OHMURA, S., and OHZEHI, M. 1979. Studies on the amylase inhibitors from *Streptomyces calvus* TM-521 and their physiological activities. J. Jpn. Soc. Starch Sci. *26*, 134–144.

NARAYANA RAO, M., SHURPALEKAR, K.S., and SUNDARAVALLI, O.E. 1967. An amylase inhibitor in *Colocasia esculenta*. Indian J. Biochem. *4*, 185.

NARAYANA RAO, M., SHURPALEKAR, K.S., and SUNDARAVALLI, O.E. 1970. Purification and properties of an amylase inhibitor from colocasia *(Colocasia esculenta)* tubers. Indian J. Biochem. 7, 241–243.

NISHIURA, I., TAKANA, K., and MURACHI, T. 1979. High molecular weight inhibitor of calcium-dependent neutral protease in brain. Experientia *35*, 1006–1007.

NISHIURA, I., TAKANA, K., YAMATO, S., and MURACHI, T. 1978. The occurrence of an inhibitor of calcium-dependent neutral protease in rat liver. J. Biochem. (Tokyo) *84*, 1657–1659.

ODANI, S. and IKENAKA, T. 1973A. Studies on soybean trypsin inhibitors. VIII. Disulfide bridges in soybean Bowman-Birk proteinase inhibitor. J. Biochem. (Tokyo) *74*, 697–715.

ODANI, S. and IKENAKA, T. 1973B. Scission of soybean Bowman-Birk proteinase inhibitor into two small fragments having either trypsin or chymotrypsin inhibitory activity. J. Biochem. (Tokyo) *74*, 857–860.

OGISO, T., NODA, T., SAKO, Y., KATO, Y., and AOYAMA, M. 1975. Studies on trypsin inhibitor in barley. I. Purification and some properties. J. Biochem. (Tokyo) *78*, 9–17.

OKURA, A., MORISHIMA, H., TAKITA, T., AOYAGI, T., TAKEUCHI, T., and UMEZAWA, H. 1975. The structure of elastatinal, an elastase inhibitor of microbial origin. J. Antibiot. *28*, 337–339.

ÖMURA, S., NAKAGAWA, A., and OHNO, H. 1979. Structure of elasnin, a novel elastase inhibitor. J. Amer. Chem. Soc. *101*, 4386–4387.

OSUGA, D.T., BIGLER, J.C., UY, R.L., SJÖBERG, L., and FEENEY, R.E. 1974. Comparative biochemistry of penguin egg-white proteins. 1. Ovomucoids: Composition and inhibitory activities for trypsin, α-chymotrypsin and subtilisin. Comp. Biochem. Physiol. *48B*, 519–533.

OSUGA, D.T. and FEENEY, R.E. 1968. Biochemistry of the egg-white proteins of the ratite group. Arch. Biochem. Biophys. *124*, 560–574.

OZAWA, K. and LASKOWSKI, M., JR. 1966. The reactive site of trypsin inhibitors. J. Biol. Chem. *241*, 3955–3961.

PEANASKY, R.J., ABU-ERREISH, G.M., GAUSH, C.R., HOMANDBERG, G.A., O'HEERON, D., LINKENHEIL, R.K., KUCICH, U., and BABIN, D.R. 1974. Proteinase inhibitors from *Ascaris lumbricodes*: properties and their physiological role. *In* Proteinase Inhibitors, Proc. Int. Res. Conf., 2nd (Bayer Symp. V). H. Fritz, H. Tschesche, L.J. Greene, and E. Truscheit (Editors). Springer-Verlag, Berlin and New York.

POWERS, J.R. and WHITAKER, J.R. 1977A. Purification and some physical and chemical properties of red kidney bean *(Phaseolus vulgaris)* α-amylase inhibitor. J. Food Biochem. *1*, 217–238.

POWERS, J.R. and WHITAKER, J.R. 1977B. Effect of several experimental parameters on combination of red kidney bean *(Phaseolus vulgaris)* α-amylase inhibitor with porcine pancreatic α-amylase. J. Food Biochem. *1*, 239–260.

POWERS, J.R. 1979. Personal communication. Prosser, Wash.

PRESSEY, R. 1967. Invertase inhibitor from potatoes: Purification, characterization and reactivity with plant invertases. Plant Physiol. *42*, 1780–1786.

PRESSEY, R. and SHAW, R. 1966. Effect of temperature on invertase, invertase inhibitor and sugars in potato tubers. Plant Physiol. *41*, 1657–1661.

PUBOLS, M.H., BARTELT, D.C., and GREENE, L.J. 1974. Trypsin inhibitor from human pancreas and pancreatic juice. J. Biol. Chem. *249*, 2235–2242.

PUDLES, J., ROLA, F.H., and MATIDA, A.K. 1967. Studies on the proteolytic inhibitors from *Ascaris lumbricodes* var. *suum*. II. Purification, properties and chemical modification of trypsin inhibitor. Arch. Biochem. Biophys. *120*, 594–601.

PULS, W. and KEUP, U. 1973. Influence of an α-amylase inhibitor (BAYd 7791) on blood glucose, serum insulin and NEFA (nonesterified fatty acids) in starch loading tests in rats, dogs and man. Diabetologia *9*, 97–101.

RACKIS, J.J. 1965. Physiological properties of soybean trypsin inhibitors and their relationship to pancreatic hypertrophy and growth inhibition of rats. Fed. Proc. *24*, 1488–1493.

RACKIS, J.J. 1974. Biological and physiological factors in soybeans. J. Am. Oil Chemists' Soc. *51*, 161A–174A.

REDDY, M.N., KEIM, P.S., HEINRICKSON, R.L., and KÉZDY, F.J. 1975. Primary structural analysis of sulfhydryl protease inhibitors from pineapple stem. J. Biol. Chem. *250*, 1741–1750.

RHODES, M.B., BENNETT, N., and FEENEY, R.E. 1960. The trypsin and chymotrypsin inhibitor from avian egg whites. J. Biol. Chem. *235*, 1686–1693.

RICHARDSON, M. 1974. Chymotryptic inhibitor I from potatoes. The amino acid sequence of subunit A. Biochem. J. *137*, 101–112.

RICHARDSON, M. 1977. The proteinase inhibitors of plants and microorganisms. Phytochemistry *16*, 159–169.

RICHARDSON, M. and COSSINS, L. 1974. Chymotryptic inhibitor I from potatoes: The amino acid sequences of subunits B, C and D. FEBS Lett. *45*, 11–13.

RICHARDSON, M. and COSSINS, L. 1975. Corrigendum. Chymotryptic inhibitor I from potatoes: The amino acid sequences of subunits B, C and D. FEBS Lett. *52*, 161.

RICHARDSON, M., McMILLAN, R.T., and BAKER, R.D. 1976. The protomer isoinhibitors of chymotryptic inhibitor I from potatoes. Biochem. Soc. Trans. *4*, 1107–1108.

ROBERTS, R.C., RIESEN, W.A., and HALL, P.K. 1974. Studies on the quaternary structure of human serum α_2-macroglobulin. *In* Proteinase Inhibitors, Proc. Int. Res. Conf., 2nd (Bayer Symp. V). H. Fritz, H. Tschesche, L.J. Greene, and E. Truscheit (Editors). Springer-Verlag, Berlin and New York.

RODIS, P. 1974. Nature and function of cubical protein crystals in *Solanum tuberosum*. Ph.D. Thesis. Purdue Univ., Lafayette.

ROSEN, F.S., CHARACHE, P., PENSKY, J., and DONALDSON, V. 1965. Hereditary angioneurotic edema: Two genetic variants. Science *148*, 957–958.

ROSENBERG, R.D. and DAMUS, P.S. 1973. The purification and mechanism of action of human antithrombin-heparin cofactor. J. Biol. Chem. *248*, 6490–6505.

RÜHLMANN, A., KUKLA, D., SCHWAGER, P., BARTELS, K., and HUBER,

R. 1973. Structure of the complex formed by bovine trypsin and bovine pancreatic trypsin. J. Molec. Biol. *77*, 417–436.

RYAN, C.A. 1973. Proteolytic enzymes and their inhibitors in plants. Ann. Rev. Plant Physiol. *24*, 173–196.

RYAN, C.A., HASS, G.M., and KUHN, R.W. 1974. Purification and properties of a carboxypeptidase inhibitor from potatoes. J. Biol. Chem. *249*, 5495–5499.

RYLEY, H.C. 1979. Isolation and partial characterization of a thiol proteinase inhibitor from human plasma. Biochem. Biophys. Res. Commun. *89*, 871–878.

SAHEKI, T., MATSUDA, Y., and HOLZER, H. 1974. Purification and characterization of macromolecular inhibitors of proteinase A from yeast. Eur. J. Biochem. *47*, 325–332.

SAKAMOTO, W., NISHIKAZE, O., and SAKAKIBARA, E. 1973. Isolation of an inhibitor of β-glucuronidase from porcine sublingual gland. Biochim. Biophys. Acta *329*, 72–80.

SAKATO, K., TANAKA, H., and MISAWA, M. 1975. Broad-specificity proteinase inhibitors in *Scopolia japonica* (Solanoceae) cultured cells. Eur. J. Biochem. *55*, 211–219.

SASAKI, M., MINAKATA, K., YAMAMOTO, H., NIWA, M., KATO, T., and ITO, N. 1977. A new serum component which specifically inhibits thiol proteinases. Biochem. Biophys. Res. Commun. *76*, 917–924.

SASAKI, T. 1978. Chymotrypsin inhibitors from hemolymph of the silkworm, *Bombyx mori*. J. Biochem. (Tokyo) *84*, 267–274.

SAVAIANO, D.A., POWERS, J.R., COSTELLO, M.J., WHITAKER, J.R., and CLIFFORD, A.J. 1977. The effect of an α-amylase inhibitor on the growth rate of weanling rats. Nutr. Reports Int. *15*, 443–449.

SCHIESSLER, H., FINK, E., and FRITZ, H. 1976. Acid-stable proteinase inhibitors from human seminal plasma. Methods Enzymol. *45B*, 847–859.

SCHNEBLI, H.P. 1974. Protease and protease inhibitors in neoplasia. *In* Proteinase Inhibitors, Proc. Int. Res. Conf., 2nd (Bayer Symp. V). H. Fritz, H. Tschesche, L.J. Greene, and E. Truscheit, (Editors). Springer-Verlag, Berlin and New York.

SCHNEEMAN, B.O. and LYMAN, R.L. 1975. Factors involved in the intestinal feedback regulation of pancreatic secretion in the rat. Proc. Soc. Expt'l. Biol. Med. *148*, 897–903.

SCHULTZE, H.E., HEIDE, K., and HAUPT, H. 1962. A new α_1-glycoprotein in human serum. Naturwissenschaften *49*, 133–134.

SCHWIMMER, S., MAKOWER, R.U., and ROREM, E.S. 1961. Invertase and invertase inhibitor in potato. Plant Physiol. *36*, 313–322.

SELLERS, A., MURPHY, G., MEIKLE, M.C., and REYNOLDS, J.J. 1979. Rabbit bone collagenase inhibitor blocks the activity of other neutral metalloproteinases. Biochem. Biophys. Res. Commun. *87*, 581–587.

SEN, L.C. and WHITAKER, J.R. 1973. Some properties of a ficin-papain inhibitor from avian egg white. Arch. Biochem. Biophys. *158*, 623–632.

SHAINKIN, R. and BIRK, Y. 1970. α-Amylase inhibitors from wheat. Isolation and characterization. Biochim. Biophys. Acta *221*, 502–513.

SHARP, N.L. and FREIER, E.F. 1972. Familial cirrhosis. *In* Pulmonary Emphysema and Proteolysis. C. Mittman (Editor). Academic Press, New York.

SHIMADA, K. and MATSUSHIMA, K. 1968. Studies on the production of protease inhibitor by molds—Examination of the ability of molds to produce protease inhibitor. J. Agric. Chem. Soc. Japan. *42*, 325–329.

SHKENDEROV, S. 1973. A protease inhibitor in bee venom. Identification, partial purification and some properties. FEBS Lett. *33*, 343–347.

SHTACHER, G., MAAYAN, R., and FEINSTEIN, G. 1973. Proteinase inhibitors in human synovial fluid. Biochim. Biophys. Acta *303*, 138–147.

SIMMONS-WALKER, M. and RYAN, C.A. 1977. Immunological identification of proteinase inhibitors I and II isolated from tomato vacuoles. Plant Physiol. *60*, 61–63.

SKARE, N.H., PAUS, F., and RAA, J. 1975. Production of pectinase and cellulase by *Cladosporium cucumerinum* with dissolved carbohydrates and isolated cell walls of cucumber as carbon sources. Physiol. Plant. *33*, 229–233.

SMIRNOFF, P., KHALET, S., BIRK, Y., and APPLEBAUM, S.W. 1979. Trypsin and chymotrypsin inhibitor from chick peas. Selective chemical modification of the inhibitor and isolation of two isoinhibitors. Int. J. Pept. Prot. Res. *14*, 186–192.

STANKOVIC, S.C. and MARKOVIC, N.D. 1960–61. A study of amylase inhibitors in the acorn. Glasnik Hem. Drustva, Beogard *25–26*, 519–525; Chem. Abstr. *59*, 3084d, 1963.

STEINBUCH, M. 1976. The inter-α-trypsin inhibitor. Methods Enzymol. *45B*, 760–772.

STEINBUCH, M. and ANDRAN, R. 1974. Biology and pathology of plasma proteinase inhibitors. *In* Proteinase Inhibitors, Proc. Int. Res. Conf., 2nd (Bayer Symp. V). H. Fritz, H. Tschesche, L.J. Greene, and E. Truscheit (Editors). Springer-Verlag, Berlin and New York.

STEINBUCH, M. and LOEB, J. 1961. Haematology. Isolation of an α_2-globulin from human plasma. Nature (London) *192*, 1196.

STEVENS, F.C. 1971. Lima bean protease inhibitor: Amino acid sequence and active sites against trypsin and chymotrypsin. *In* Proc. Int. Res. Conf. Proteinase Inhibitors, 1st. H. Fritz, and H. Tschesche (Editors). Walter de Gruyter, Berlin and New York.

STEVENS, F.C., WUERZ, S., and KRAHN, J. 1974. Structure-function relationships in lima bean protease inhibitor. *In* Proteinase Inhibitors, Proc. Int. Res. Conf., 2nd (Bayer Symp. V). H. Fritz, H. Tschesche, L.J. Greene, and E. Truscheit (Editors). Springer-Verlag, Berlin and New York.

STRYDOM, D.J. 1973. Protease inhibitors as snake venom toxins. Nature (London) New Biol. *243*, 88.

SUDA, H., AOYAGI, T., HAMADA, M., TAKEUCHI, T., and UMEZAWA, H. 1972. Antipain, a new protease inhibitor isolated from actinomycetes. J. Antibiot. *25*, 263–266.

SUGIURA, H., OGISO, T., TAKEUTI, K., TAMURA, S., and ITO, A. 1973. Studies on trypsin inhibitors in sweet potato. I. Purification and some properties. Biochim. Biophys. Acta *328*, 407–417.

SWARTZ, M.J., MITCHELL, H.L., COX, D.J., and REECK, G.R. 1977. Isolation and characterization of trypsin inhibitor from opaque-2 corn seeds. J. Biol. Chem. *252*, 8105–8107.

SWEET, R.M., WRIGHT, H.T., JANIN, J., CHOTHIA, C.H., and BLOW, D. M. 1974. Crystal structure of the complex of porcine trypsin with soybean trypsin inhibitor (Kunitz) at 2.6-Å resolution. Biochemistry *13*, 4212–4228.

SZILAGYI, S. and SZILAGYI, E. 1979. Amino acid sequence homology among small molecular weight, cystine rich protease inhibitors from leguminous plants. Acta Biochim. Biophys. *13*, 165–169.

SZMIGIELSKI, A., GUIDOTTI, A., and COSTA, E. 1977. Endogenous protein kinase inhibitors. Purification, characterization and distribution in different tissues. J. Biol. Chem. *252*, 3848–3853.

TAKAHASHI, H., IWANAGA, S., KITAGAWA, T., HOKAMA, Y., and SUZUKI, T. 1974. Novel proteinase inhibitors in snake venoms: distribution, isolation, and amino acid sequence. *In* Proteinase Inhibitors, Proc. Int. Res. Conf., 2nd (Bayer Symp. V). H. Fritz, H. Tschesche, L.J. Greene, and E. Truscheit (Editors). Springer-Verlag, Berlin and New York.

TAN, C.G.L. and STEVENS, F.C. 1971A. Amino acid sequence of lima bean protease inhibitor component IV. 1. Isolation and sequence determination of the tryptic peptides. Eur. J. Biochem. *18*, 503–514.

TAN, C.G.L.and STEVENS, F.C. 1971B. Amino acid sequence of lime bean inhibitor component IV. 2. Isolation and sequence determination of the chymotryptic peptides and the complete amino acid sequence. Eur. J. Biochem. *18*, 515–523.

TATSUTA, K., MIKAMI, N., FUJIMOTO, K., UMEZAWA, S., UMEZAWA, H., and AOYAGI, T. 1973. The structure of chymostatin, a chymotrypsin inhibitor. J. Antibiot. *26*, 625–646.

TOMIMATSU, Y., CLARY, J.J., and BARTULOVICH, J.J. 1966. Physical characterization of ovoinhibitor, a trypsin and chymotrypsin inhibitor from chicken egg white. Arch. Biochem. Biophys. *115*, 536–544.

TOYO-OKA, T., SHIMIZU, T., and MASAKI, T. 1978. Inhibition of proteolytic activity of calcium activated neutral protease by leupeptin and antipain. Biochem. Biophys. Res. Commun. *82*, 484–491.

TRAVIS, J., JOHNSON, D., and PANNELL, R. 1974. Properties of human α_1-antitrypsin. *In* Proteinase Inhibitors, Proc. Int. Res. Conf., 2nd (Bayer Symp. V). H. Fritz, H. Tschesche, L.J. Greene, and E. Truscheit (Editors). Springer-Verlag, Berlin and New York.

TSCHESCHE, H. 1974. Biochemistry of natural proteinase inhibitors. Angew. Chem. Internat. Edit. *13*, 10–28.

TSCHESCHE, H. 1976. Trypsin-kallikrein inhibitors from Cuttlefish *(Loligo vulgaris)*. Methods Enzymol. *45B*, 792–797.

TSCHESCHE, H. and DIETL, T. 1975. The amino-acid sequence of isoinhibitor K from snails *(Helix pomatia)*. Eur. J. Biochem. *58*, 439–451.

TSCHESCHE, H. and DIETL, T. 1976. Trypsin-kallikrein-inhibitors from snails *(Helix pomatia)*. Methods Enzymol. *45B*, 772–785.

TSCHESCHE, H., KLAUSER, R., ČECHOVÁ, D., and JONÁKOVÁ, V. 1975A. On the carbohydrate composition of bovine colostrum trypsin inhibitor. Hoppe-Seyler's Z. Physiol. Chem. *356*, 1759–1764.

TSCHESCHE, H., KUPFER, S., KLAUSER, R., FINK, E., and FRITZ, H. 1975B. Structure, biochemistry and comparative aspects of mammalian seminal plasma acrosin inhibitors. *In* Protides of the Biological Fluids *23*. H. Peters (Editor). Pergamon, Oxford and New York.

TSCHESCHE, H., KUPFER, S., LENGEL, O., and KLAUSER, R. 1974. Purification, characterization, and structural studies of proteinase inhibitors from boar seminal plasma and boar spermatoza. *In* Proteinase Inhibitors, Proc. Int. Res. Conf., 2nd (Bayer Symp. V). H. Fritz, H. Tschesche, L.J. Greene, and E. Truscheit (Editors). Springer-Verlag, Berlin and New York.

TSCHESCHE, H. and RÜCKER, A.V. 1973. Proteinase-isoinhibitor with a broad specificity for trypsin, chymotrypsin, plasmin and kallikrein from Cuttlefish *(Loligo vulgaris)*. Hoppe-Seyler's Z. Physiol. Chem. *354*, 1447–1461.

TUR-SINAI, A., BIRK, Y., GERTLER, A., and RIGBI, M. 1972. A basic trypsin- and chymotrypsin-inhibitor from ground nuts *(Arachis hypogaea)*. Biochim. Biophys. Acta *263*, 666–672.

UEDA, S., KOBA, Y., and CHAEN, H. 1979. Amylase inhibitor produced by *Streptomyces* sp. no. 280. J. Jpn. Soc. Starch Sci. *26*, 145–156.

UMEZAWA, H., AOYAGI, T., MORISHIMA, H., KUNIMOTO, S., MATSUZAKI, M., HAMADA, M., and TAKEUCHI, T. 1970A. Chymostatin, a new chymotrypsin inhibitor produced by actinomycetes. J. Antibiot. *23*, 425–427.

UMEZAWA, H., AOYAGI, T., MORISHIMA, H., MATSUZAKI, M., HAMADA, M., and TAKEUCHI, T. 1970B. Pepstatin, a new pepsin inhibitor produced by actinomycetes. J. Antibiot. *23*, 259–262.

UMEZAWA, H., AOYAGI, T., OKURA, A., MORISHIMA, H., TAKEUCHI, T., and OKAMI, Y. 1973. Elastatinal, a new elastase inhibitor produced by actinomycetes. J. Antibiot. *26*, 787–789.

UMEZAWA, S., TATSUTA, K., FUJIMOTO, K., TSUCHIYA, T., UMEZAWA, H., and NAGANAWA, H. 1972A. Structure of antipain, a new Sakaguchi-positive product of streptomyces. J. Antibiot. *25*, 267–270.

UMEZAWA, S., TATSUTA, K., IZAWA, O., TSUCHIYA, T., and UMEZAWA, H. 1972B. A new microbial metabolite phosphoramidon (isolation and structure). Tetrahedron Lett. *1*, 97–100.

VESELY, D.L., GRAVES, W.R., LO, T.M., FLETCHER, M.A., and LEVEY, G.S. 1977. Isolation of a guanylate cyclase inhibitor from the balsam pear *(Momordica charantia abreviata)*. Biochem. Biophys. Res. Commun. *77*, 1294–1299.

VOGEL, R., TRAUTSCHOLD, I., and WERLE, E. 1968. Natural Proteinase Inhibitors. Academic Press, New York.

VON SCHÖNENBERGER, M., SCHMIDTBERGER, R., and SCHULTZE, H. E. 1958. α_2-Macroglobulin. Z. Naturforsch. Teil B *13*, 761–772.

WACHTER, E. and HOCHSTRASSER, K. 1979. Kunitz-type proteinase inhibitors derived by limited proteolysis of the inter-α-trypsin inhibitor. III. Sequence of the two Kunitz-type domains inside the native inter-α-trypsin inhibitor: its biological aspects and also its cleavage products. Hoppe-Seyler's Z. Physiol. Chem. *360*, 1305–1311.

WACHTER, E., HOCHSTRASSER, K., BRETZEL, G., and HEINDL, S. 1979. Kunitz-type proteinase inhibitors derived by limited proteolysis of the inter-α-trypsin inhibitor. II. Characterization of a second inhibitory inactive domain by amino acid sequence determination. Hoppe-Seyler's Z. Physiol. Chem. *360*, 1297–1303.

WAGNER, L.P. and RIEHM, J.P. 1967. Purification and partial characterization of a trypsin inhibitor isolated from navy bean. Arch. Biochem. Biophys. *121*, 672–677.

WALSH, D.A., ASHBY, C.D., GONZALEZ, C., CALKINS, D., FISCHER, E.H., and KREBS, E.G. 1971. Purification and characterization of a protein inhibitor of adnosine 3′,5′-monophosphate-dependent protein kinases. J. Biol. Chem. *246*, 1977–1985.

WANG, D. 1975. A crystalline protein-proteinase inhibitor from pinto bean seeds. Biochim. Biophys. Acta *393*, 583–596.

WARSY, A.S., NORTON, G., and STEIN, M. 1974. Protease inhibitors from broad bean; isolation and purification. Phytochemistry *13*, 2481–2486.

WAXMAN, L. 1978. Characterization of two unique protease inhibitors and a calcium-activated protease from bovine cardiac muscle. *In* Protein Turnover and Lysosome Function. H.L. Segal and D.J. Doyle (Editors). Academic Press, New York.

WAXMAN, L. and KREBS, E.G. 1978. Identification of two protease inhibitors from bovine cardiac muscle. J. Biol. Chem. *253*, 5888–5891.

WERLE, E., TRAUTSCHOLD, I., HAENDLE, H., AND FRITZ, H. 1968. Physiologic, pharmacologic and clinical aspects of proteinase inhibitors. Ann. N.Y. Acad. Sci. *146*, 464–478.

WEURMAN, C. 1954. Pectinase in pears. Acta Botan. Neerl. *3*, 108–113.

WHITAKER, J.R. and FEENEY, R.E. 1973. Enzyme inhibitors in foods. *In* Toxicants Occurring Naturally in Foods, 2nd Ed. F.M. Strong (Editor). National Academy of Sciences, Washington, D.C.

WHITLEY, E.J., JR. and BOWMAN, D.E. 1975. Isolation and properties of navy bean proteinase component I. Arch. Biochem. Biophys. *169*, 42–50.

WILCOX, E. and WHITAKER, J.R. 1980. Unpublished data. Univ. of California - Davis.

WILSON, K.A. and LASKOWSKI, M., SR. 1973. Isolation of three isoinhibitors of trypsin from garden bean, *Phaseolus vulgaris*, having either lysine or arginine at the reactive site. J. Biol. Chem. *248*, 756–762.

WILSON, K.A. and LASKOWSKI, M., SR. 1975. The partial amino acid sequence of trypsin inhibitor II from garden bean, *Phaseolus vulgaris*, with location to the trypsin and elastase-reactive sites. J. Biol. Chem. *250*, 4261–4267.

WINGENDER, W. 1974. Proteinase inhibitors of microbial origin. A review. *In* Proteinase Inhibitors, Proc. Int. Res. Conf., 2nd (Bayer Symp. V). H. Fritz, H. Tschesche, L.J. Greene, and E. Truscheit (Editors). Springer-Verlag, Berlin and New York.

WU, Y.V. and SCHERAGA, H.A. 1962. Studies on soybean trypsin inhibitor. I. Physicochemical properties. Biochemistry *1*, 698–705.

WUNDERER, G., BÉRESS, L., MACHLEIDT, W., and FRITZ, H. 1976. Broad-specificity inhibitors from sea anemones. Methods Enzymol. *45B*, 881–888.

YAMAMOTO, K. and HAYASHI, K. 1962. Protease inhibitor in cell free extract of *Aspergillus soya* and its inactivation. Symp. Enzyme Chem. *18*, 21–29.

YETTER, M.A., SAUNDERS, R.M., and BOLES, H.P. 1979. α-Amylase inhibitors from wheat kernels as factors in the resistance to postharvest insects. Cereal Chem. *56*, 243–244.

ZANEVELD, L.J.D., SCHUMACHER, G.F.B., TAUBER, P.F., and PROPPING, D. 1974. Proteinase inhibitors and proteinases of human semen. *In* Proteinase Inhibitors, Proc. Int. Res. Conf., 2nd (Bayer Symp. V). H. Fritz, H. Tschesche, L.J. Greene, and E. Truscheit (Editors). Springer-Verlag, Berlin and New York.

ZAN-KOWALCZEWSKA, M. and ROTH, J.S. 1975. On the similarity between ribonuclease inhibitor and β-estradiol receptor protein. Biochem. Biophys. Res. Commun. *65*, 833–837.

ZBYTNIEWSKI, Z. and KANCLERZ, A. 1977. Proteinase inhibitors in medicine, Postepy Hig. Med. Dosw. *31*, 393–407; Chem. Abstr. *87*, 198384r, 1977.

7

Unwanted Biological Substances in Foods: Cyanogenic Glycosides

Eric E. Conn[1]

INTRODUCTION

Among the 2,000 (approximate) species of higher plants known to produce hydrogen cyanide (HCN), there are several species extensively utilized by man or his animals for food. The root crop known as cassava or tapioca (*Manihot esculenta* Crantz) is the main source of carbohydrate for 300 million people in the tropics; it has been estimated that cassava alone meets 8–10% of the daily global caloric needs of man (Cock 1973). *Sorghum bicolor* is the third largest cereal food grain of the world; sorghum seed is used in the form of flour as a human food in much of Africa and India. While humans consume nearly 75% of the world sorghum crop, both seed and foliage are used in animal feed. Lima beans, bamboo shoots, and the nuts of the almond and macadamia trees are other plant tissues produced by cyanogenic plants which are consumed by man. *Trifolium repens* L. (white clover) is an important cyanogenic cover crop used in many parts of the world because of its ability to fix nitrogen and thereby increase the nitrogen content of soils. While accidental poisonings occur all too frequently in connection with these plants, man has learned how to cope with their potential toxicity and thereby keep such events at a minimum. It is the purpose of this paper to review briefly the means whereby such toxicity can be avoided. The

[1] Department of Biochemistry and Biophysics, University of California, Davis.

principles involved in avoiding poisoning by cyanogenic plants require an understanding of the chemical nature of cyanogenic glycosides and an appreciation of the phenomenon of cyanogenesis.

CHEMICAL NATURE OF CYANOGENIC GLYCOSIDES IN FOOD PLANTS

Cyanogenic glycosides are the source of the HCN produced by the food plants just described. These compounds are β-D-glucopyranosides of α-hydroxynitriles, and their chemistry (Conn 1969; Eyjolfsson 1970; Seigler 1977), biosynthesis (Conn 1973A, 1979B) and toxicology (Conn 1973B, 1979A) have been the subject of recent reviews. Amygdalin (Fig. 7.1), the best known of the cyanogenic glycosides, is found in bitter

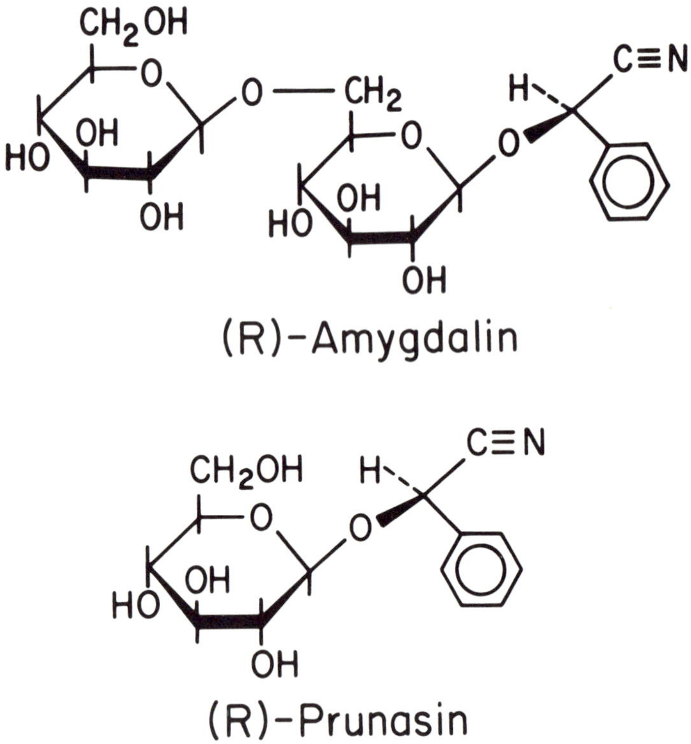

FIG. 7.1. STRUCTURES OF (*R*)-AMYGDALIN AND (*R*)-PRUNASIN

almonds and the seeds of other stone fruits such as apricot, peach, nectarine, and cherry; the leaves of these Rosaceous species contain prunasin (Fig. 7.1) which is a monoglucoside closely related in structure, having the same aglycone *(R)*-mandelonitrile as amygdalin. Linamarin and lotaustralin (Fig. 7.2) are the cyanogenic glucosides found in cassava, white clover and lima beans; the aglycones in these compounds are the cyanohydrins of acetone and 2-butanone. The cyanogenic glucoside in

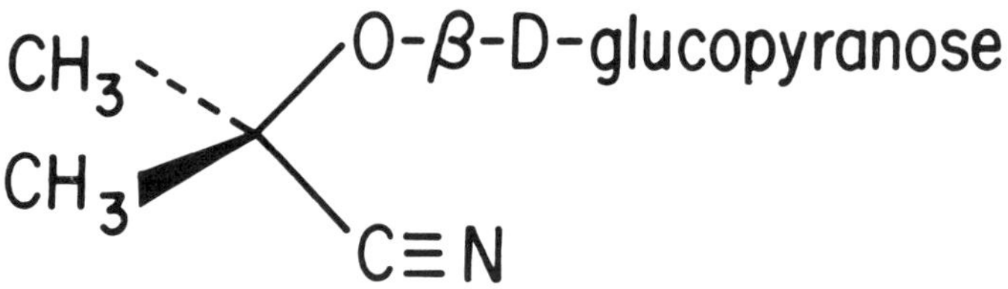

Linamarin

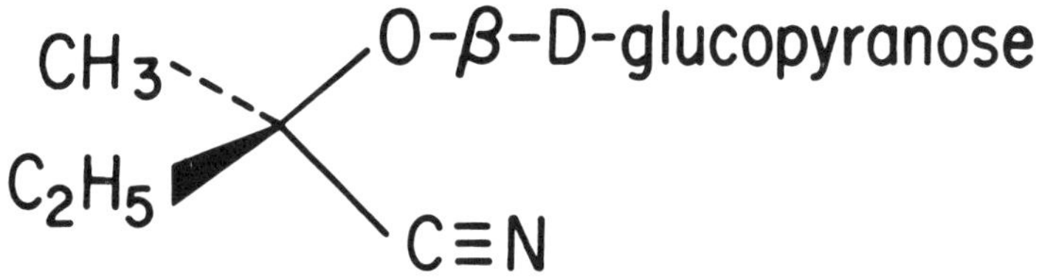

(R)-Lotaustralin

FIG. 7.2. STRUCTURES OF LINAMARIN AND (*R*)-LOTAUSTRALIN

sorghum is dhurrin (Fig. 7.3); its epimer taxiphyllin occurs in bamboo. The macadamia tree contains dhurrin and the structurally related compound proteacin (Fig. 7.4).

Table 7.1 lists typical amounts of HCN which can be released from various plant tissues (Conn 1979A). Since the lethal dose of HCN for an adult human male is in the range 30–250 mg (Montgomery 1969) when taken at one time, it is clear that consumption of 100g of several of the plant tissues listed in Table 7.1 could produce serious if not fatal poisoning. It can also be seen that different tissues of the same plant vary greatly in their capacity to produce HCN. In the specific case of sorghum it will be noted that the seed, which is the part used in making flour, is not cyanogenic. Similarly the cyanide content of cassava is lowest in the inner tuber and this again is the tissue usually used for human food after appropriate processing.

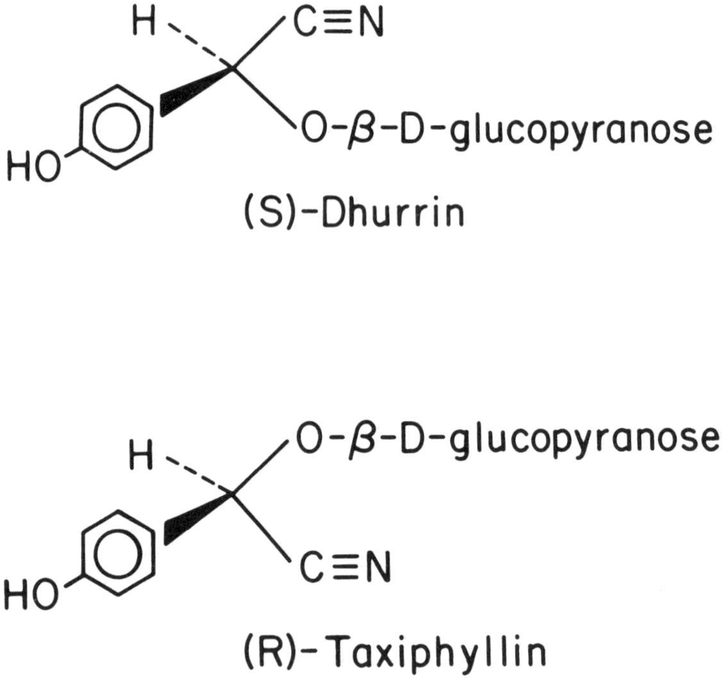

FIG. 7.3. STRUCTURES OF (*S*)-DHURRIN AND (*R*)-TAXIPHYLLIN

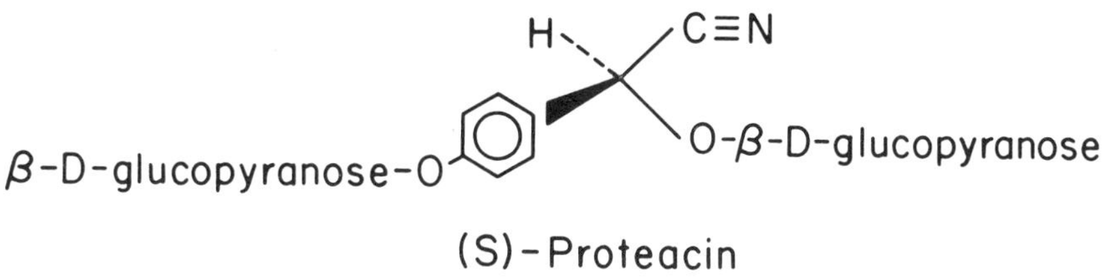

FIG. 7.4. STRUCTURE OF (*S*)-PROTEACIN

TABLE 7.1. HCN RELEASED FROM VARIOUS PLANT TISSUES[1]

Plant	HCN yield (mg/100g)
Sorghum	
mature seed	0
etiolated shoot tips	240
young green leaves	60
Almond	
bitter seed	290
young leaves	20
Apricot, seed	60
Peach	
leaves	125
seed	160
Wild cherry, leaves	90–360
Lima bean, mature seed	
Puerto Rico, small black	400
Puerto Rico, black	300
Arizona, colored	17
America, white	10
Linen flax	
seedlings tops	910
linseed cake	50
White clover, young leaves	3–352
Cassava	
less toxic clones	
bark of tuber	69
inner part of tuber	7
leaves	77
very toxic clones	
bark of tuber	84
inner part of tuber	33
leaves	104

[1] Reprinted with permission from Conn 1979A.

TOXICOLOGY OF CYANOGENIC PLANTS — THEORETICAL ASPECTS

The Enzymatic Release of HCN from Cyanogenic Glycosides

The cyanogenic glycosides are relatively stable chemical compounds at neutral pH. They can be hydrolyzed to their component parts (an aldehyde or ketone, sugar, and HCN) by acid at elevated temperatures (e.g. 0.1N HCl at 100°C for 1 hr) but are stable in dilute acid at room temperature (Conn 1979A). Dhurrin and taxiphyllin are decomposed to the same components in dilute alkali (0.1N NaOH) at room temperature, and taxiphyllin is heat labile (Schwarzmaier 1976).

HCN is usually released from these cyanogenic compounds as the result of enzymatic action. This process is known as cyanogenesis and the reactions involved are illustrated for the compounds amygdalin and prunasin in Fig. 7.5. The process involves the stepwise removal of glucose by the action of two separate specific plant enzymes known as β-glucosidases, and the subsequent action of a hydroxynitrile lyase which catalyzes the dissociation of the α-hydroxynitrile (cyanohydrin). Since the cyanogenic glycosides accumulate in significant quantities in plant tissues which also contain these enzymes it has always been proposed that

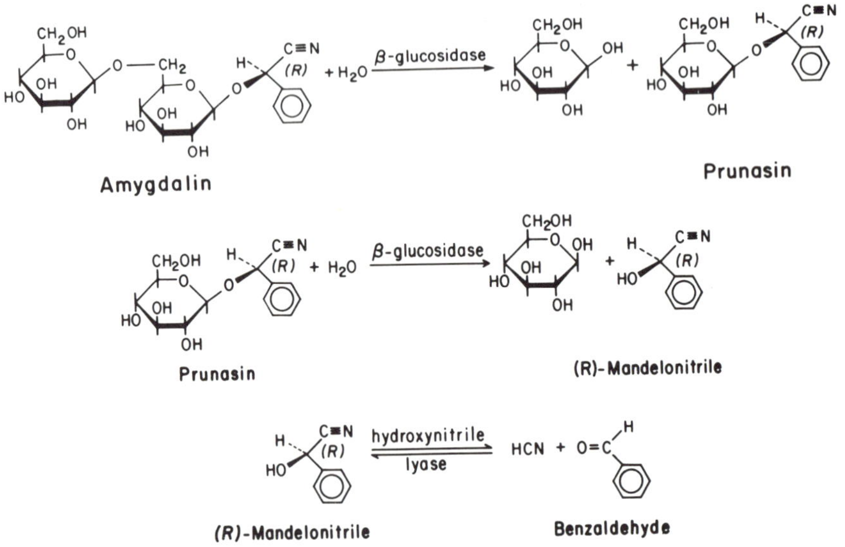

From Conn 1979A

FIG. 7.5. STEPWISE HYDROLYSIS OF AMYGDALIN FORMING PRUNASIN, (*R*)-MANDELONITRILE, BENZALDEHYDE AND HCN the substrates are sequestered separately from their catabolic enzymes in one part of the plant cell or even in separate tissues (Conn 1979C). Recently, this explanation was confirmed for sorghum leaves when dhurrin was shown to be located exclusively in the vacuoles of epidermal cells and the degradative enzymes were found only in mesophyll tissue (Kojima *et al.* 1979).

Cyanogenesis most frequently occurs when a cyanogenic plant tissue is crushed or otherwise disrupted (Conn 1979A, C). This may occur during the processing (grinding, drying, pounding) of the plant tissue during food preparation and obviously takes place when the plant tissue is ingested directly and chewed by an animal. The β-glucosidases and hydroxynitrile lyases involved in cyanogenesis exhibit optimum activity in the pH range 5–6 and this will be the pH of many plant tissues after homogenization. To the extent that the catabolic enzymes could be removed or inhibited in their action, or to the degree that the substrates could be removed or destroyed without release of HCN, the cyanogenic phenomenon could be reduced in intensity or even avoided. As will be discussed these are the guiding principles of importance in reducing the toxicity of cyanogenic food plants.

Factors Determining Toxicity

Toxicity of HCN.—Cyanide is a moderately toxic chemical that is rapidly absorbed from the digestive tract as HCN or NaCN. It is toxic because it combines with heme-proteins, particularly cytochrome oxidase and thereby inhibits cellular respiration. Death results from a generalized anoxia, the central nervous system being an especially sensitive tissue (Conn 1979A).

The lethal dose of HCN for humans is 0.5–3.5 mg/kg body weight when taken orally as a single dose (Montgomery 1969; Towill *et al.* 1978). The heart, brain, and nervous system are rapidly affected and death can occur within a few minutes if the dose is excessive. Although there are established procedures for treating acute cyanide poisoning, the condition must be quickly diagnosed and treatment rapidly initiated (Towill *et al.* 1978).

We are exposed to low levels of HCN continually in tobacco smoke, in polluted atmospheres, and in our diet (Towill *et al.* 1978). These small quantities of HCN do not accumulate but instead are detoxified by the action of the enzyme rhodanese (see below) and excreted as thiocyanate. To a major extent, one's exposure to environmental HCN can be monitored by following the thiocyanate content of urine. However, thiocyanate is also produced during the metabolism of mustard oil glycosides (glucosinolates) which occur in the Cruciferеae. Therefore, cabbage, watercress, and brussel sprouts are a dietary source of thiocyanate.

HCN is an industrial chemical and workers in certain industries may be exposed to HCN levels above those encountered by the general population. Such individuals have been monitored to determine whether or not they suffer from chronic cyanide poisoning and there is disagreement as to whether there is such a clinical entity (Montgomery 1969; Towill *et al.* 1978). While characteristic symptoms of headache, vertigo, nausea, vomiting and tremors occur, these are temporary and exposure to fresh air causes their disappearance. Such individuals may also be exposed on a continuing basis to levels of HCN sufficiently low that no obvious symptoms are exhibited. Whether there are irreversible changes in such persons due to their chronic exposure is not established.

Detoxification of HCN.—As noted above HCN is detoxified in animals by the enzyme rhodanese (thiosulfate sulfur transferase, EC 2.8.1.1). This enzyme, which is especially abundant in liver, catalyzes the following reaction:

$$CN^- + S_2O_3^{2-} \rightarrow SCN^- + SO_3^{2-}$$

and requires a supply of $Na_2S_2O_3$. Animal tissues can also catalyze transfer of the sulfur atom of cysteine to cyanide to form thiocyanate. The immediate sulfur donor is mercaptopyruvate, the keto acid of cysteine, and this is an equally important if not more significant source of sulfur atoms for detoxification.

Some cyanogenic plants have been reported to contain rhodanese, but a much more important plant enzyme for detoxifying HCN is the enzyme β-cyanoalanine synthase (E.C. 4.4.1.9) which is widespread in plants. Its concentration is roughly correlated with the level of cyanogenic glycoside which the plant contains but non-cyanogenic species also contain low levels of enzyme (Miller and Conn 1980).

The reaction catalyzed by β-cyanoalanine synthase is:

$$HCN + \text{cysteine} \rightarrow \beta\text{-cyanoalanine} + H_2S$$

Studies have established this reaction as being of major significance in detoxifying HCN administered in low levels to intact plants. While this enzyme also occurs in bacteria and fungi, there are no reports of its occurrence in animal tissues.

Genetic Factors Influencing Cyanogenesis.—Any discussion of cyanogenesis must stress that the phenomenon is polymorphic in many species (Hegnauer 1977; Jones 1972). This polymorphism is indicated by the fact that both cyanogenic and noncyanogenic individuals will exist in any population of a single species (Jones 1972). The phenomenon has been most thoroughly studied in *Trifolium repens* and *Lotus corniculatus* (birdsfoot trefoil), and clearly documented in *S. bicolor, Prunus amygdalus* (almond), *M. esculenta* and *Macadamia ternifolia* (macadamia) (Jones 1972). The genetic relationship in *T. repens* is shown in Fig. 7.6.

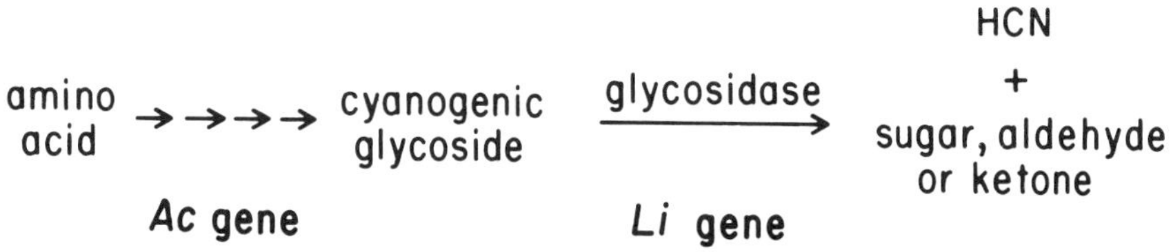

FIG. 7.6. GENETICS OF CYANOGENESIS IN *TRIFOLIUM REPENS*

This diagram specifies that in white clover alleles of the *Ac* gene determine the presence of the cyanogenic glucosides linamarin and lotaustralin (Corkill 1942); they are formed from their amino acid precursors valine and isoleucine, respectively (Conn 1979B). On the other hand, the release of HCN is determined by alleles of another, independently inherited, gene *Li* which is known, in the specific case of *T. repens*, to control the presence of the β-glucosidase (Corkill 1942). Only plants that possess at least one dominant allele of both genes will be cyanogenic. This is to say that only those plants that contain the cyanogenic glycoside(s) and the catabolic enzymes will be capable of cyanogenesis.

This genetic information has been used by plant breeders to produce strains of sweet clover which have little or no cyanogenic potential and these are the varieties favored commercially. Sweet almonds of low cyanide content have been obtained by selective breeding and these are the nuts of commercial importance. Bitter almonds are only grown as a source of bitter almond oil used as a flavoring agent. Trees that produce bitter macadamia nuts are removed from commercial orchards to prevent their cross-pollinating with trees which produce the desired sweet nut (Dedolph and Hamilton, 1959). The white butter (lima) bean of commerce is the result of breeding out undesirable qualities in the small, black, highly toxic lima bean that is native to much of Central America. Extensive genetic selection had already been accomplished in this important food crop by the time the Spanish reached North America.

These genetic factors, together with knowledge of which parts of a cyanogenic plant are safe for animal consumption, have made it possible to utilize cyanogenic species for food and are described in the next section.

TOXICOLOGY OF CYANOGENIC PLANTS—PRACTICAL CONSIDERATIONS

The poisonous potential of a cyanogenic plant would seem to depend primarily on its ability to produce a level of HCN which is toxic to the animal being exposed. However, little attention has been paid to the other products which are simultaneously released during cyanogenesis. These would be acetone and 2-butanone in the case of linamarin and lotaustralin, and benzaldehyde or 4-hydroxybenzaldehyde in the case of amygdalin, prunasin, dhurrin and taxiphyllin. The aliphatic ketones are probably of little concern, but the aromatic aldehydes might well be injurious.

Other factors determining if a given plant would be poisonous will include the size and kind of animal being exposed, the rate of ingestion, the nature of other food consumed at the same time, the possibility of the catabolic enzymes remaining active in the animal, the possibility of intracellular enzymes in the animal being able to hydrolyze any unhydrolyzed cyanogenic glycosides that are absorbed into the body, and the ability of the animal to detoxify any HCN that is produced (Conn 1979A, C). Unfortunately, there are few detailed studies on any of these points, and one can only identify certain relationships that might be relevant to the poisoning process.

PHYSIOLOGICAL FACTORS INFLUENCING CYANOGENSIS

Careful examination of the original literature on cyanogenic plants usually discloses the plant part which was found to be cyanogenic, either by qualitative or quantitative tests. Such examination also soon convinces the reader that the physiological age and state of the plant, its nutritional history and its genetic makeup are important factors in determining how strongly cyanogenic a plant specimen may be. Examples of some of these factors will become obvious as some general observations about several cyanogenic species are described.

The cyanogenic glycosides linamarin and lotaustralin are found in all parts of the mature cassava plant, but the concentration varies greatly between varieties and also with the climate and cultural conditions (DeBruijn 1973). In an individual plant, the concentration in the leaves is similar to that of the bark of the tuber but, as shown in Table 7.1, the tuber bark is higher than its interior. These facts alone would suggest that the tuber should be peeled before eating, and that the aerial portion of discarded plants should not be fed to livestock without some processing.

Cassava plants or varieties are frequently described as *bitter* or *sweet* and there is the general impression that the bitter kind is more toxic than the sweet (Coursey 1973). While chemical analysis indicates that the bitter varieties do have a higher content of cyanogenic glucosides, the sweet is not devoid of these compounds. When one also discovers that some people prefer the bitter varieties over the sweet because they have more flavor, the situation becomes more complicated!

Coursey (1973) has classified numerous ways in which different people in different parts of the world process cassava tubers before eating. These vary from being eaten raw or being processed simply (by boiling, roasting, frying, sun-drying) to being sliced, ground or pounded and then being soaked in water or being fermented in the presence of microorganisms. When the tuber tissue is disrupted by grinding, cyanogenesis will obviously occur and subsequent soaking will leech out much of the unhydrolyzed cyanogenic glycoside and also allow HCN to escape. If heat treatment is applied initially, this will tend to inactivate the catabolic enzymes and tend to yield a product still containing significant amounts of cyanogenic glycoside. Sun-drying might well represent a combination of these two processes in that some cellular disruption and enzyme inactivation might occur, but it is doubtful that all of the cyanogenic glycosides or catabolic enzymes would be destroyed during the drying. One can only conclude that these various methods yield food preparations which are variable in their content both of cyanogenic glycosides and catabolic enzymes, but also sufficiently reduced so that acute poisoning later is avoided by the consumer. In communities where the tuber is eaten raw, apparently without toxicity, one can only assume that such tubers must be relatively low in cyanogenic glycosides.

The genus *Sorghum* has long been recognized as being cyanogenic and dhurrin was first isolated and characterized from green leaves of the Egyptian "great millet" (Dunstan and Henry 1902). The impetus for this early study was the fact that animals used in military transport services had been killed by eating the plants growing naturally in the Upper Nile Valley. On the other hand, this plant has been grown for at least 6,000 years for its dry, starch-rich seed which is used in the making of flour. Careful analysis (Table 7.1) of the seed has shown that it contains no detectable cyanogenic glucoside and therefore may be eaten with impunity by man and other animals.

Sorghum seedlings grown in the dark have been used extensively in studies on the biosynthesis of dhurrin because there is a dramatic formation of this cyanogenic glucoside when the seed is soaked in H_2O, sprouted and allowed to germinate. Young dark grown seedlings will contain 5% dhurrin (d.wt.) and most of the glucoside is found in the seedling tops, the first leaf and coleoptile sheath where the concentration may approach 20% dhurrin (d.wt.). Dry seed which has been soaked for 16 hr in H_2O and allowed to sprout contains 80 mg HCN/100g tissue. While a soaking process is not obviously involved during the milling of seed to make flour, there are references to alcoholic beverages being made from soaked sorghum sprouts. It may therefore be predicted that such sprouts should contain a significant level of cyanogenic glycoside.

The edible stone fruits (peach, plum, apricot, cherry) as well as apple and pear are members of the Rosaceace, a strongly cyanogenic plant family. The fruits of these plants have been enjoyed by mankind for centuries and they are not cyanogenic. On the other hand the seeds found within the fruit are cyanogenic and accounts of poisoning have been recorded. The foliage of all of these species is also variably cyanogenic and domestic animals should not have access to the leaves. There are reports of the poisoning of livestock in the Eastern U.S. by wild cherry and plum (Kingsbury 1964).

The almond *(Prunus amygdalus)* is an excellent example of a Rosaceous species that has been selectively bred to yield an edible nut of commercial importance (Heppner 1926). In this case, the polymorphism of cyanogenesis has been specifically utilized to yield a desired product. The genetic relationship in the case of the almond can not be simple as in the case of *T. repens*, but this apparently has been no great disadvantage to the plant breeder as he has obviously obtained a desirable product (Heppner 1926). The genetics of cyanogenesis in *Sorghum* is also not straightforward, (Nass 1974) but high and low strains of *S. bicolor* are known which have been used in producing commercial hybrids.

Viehoever (1940) carried out a thorough study of the botanical and chemical characteristics of lima beans collected from around the world. His study, and others reviewed elsewhere (Montgomery 1965, 1969), establish the following points regarding this most important edible legume. The seed of the small black wild lima bean, native to most of Central America, will produce 190–380 mg HCN/100g of seeds, due to its content of linamarin. The large white lima beans (butter beans) favored by American and European housewives contain only 1–2% of the linamarin found in the wild type. Beans which are intermediate in size and color and are found in public markets around the world generally have an intermediate level of linamarin. All parts of the growing plant, including the seed pod, can be cyanogenic.

Since colored lima beans also contain linamarase which can degrade the linamarin they contain, it is probably unsafe simply to soak such beans in water without taking steps to remove the HCN which is produced in soaking. Direct boiling of dry beans should inactivate the linamarase and decrease the released of HCN from its precursor. However, people have been poisoned by colored lima beans after boiling and draining (Montgomery 1969; Rathenasinkam 1947).

From the examples cited, it can be seen that two general procedures have been followed in preparing edible foods from potentially toxic cyanogenic plant tissues. One of these is processing in an appropriate way to lower or remove the toxic HCN or its cyanogenic precursor from the tissue. The other is treating the tissue with heat to inactivate enzymes which bring about the release of HCN from the cyanogenic glycoside.

In more general terms, these procedures reduce to (a) the removal of undesirable components, and (b) heat treatment to preserve quality, neither of which are new principles or procedures to the food processing industry. A third approach, namely selective breeding to reduce cyanogenic potential, is a form of "genetic engineering" to yield a more desirable product, and this too is not a new principle in food production. Perhaps of more significance, these techniques and principles could be applied, if they haven't already, to food plants which contain other undesirable chemicals in the form of glycosides. Examples which immediately come to mind are the glucosinolate compounds (mustard oil glycosides) and phenolic acids, alkaloids, and flavonoids which exist in the plant as glycosides.

POTENTIAL TOXICITY FROM CYANOGENIC PLANTS LACKING CATABOLIC ENZYMES

It is informative to consider the consequence of ingesting a plant which, due to its genetic character, contains the cyanogenic glycosides but not the catabolic enzymes. Certainly, there will be little or no release of HCN from its precursors as the result of cellular disruption of the cyanogenic plant during either processing or ingestion by an animal. If however, other plants which are noncyanogenic but possess β-glucosidase activity were ingested simultaneously, there could be release of HCN. Little is known about the β-glucosidase activity of noncyanogenic plants or the ability of such enzymes to act on cyanogenic glycosides. Cooking procedures also would not destroy the cyanogenic compounds since, with the apparent exception of taxiphyllin, they are not thermolabile. Such a situation raises the question of the occurrence in animals of other enzymes or conditions that might hydrolyze cyanogenic glycosides and on this point there is some information.

There are several possibilities which have been considered for hydrolysis of cyanogenic glycosides that have been taken intact into an animal. For example, the acid content of the monogastric stomach might hydrolyze the β-glucosidic bond. However, incubation of amygdalin and linamarin at 37°C for 18 hr in 1N H_2SO_4 does not release any HCN from these compounds (Dunn and Conn, unpublished).

It has also been suggested that the digestive juices of the mammalian digestive tract might hydrolyze cyanogenic glycosides. However, the carbohydrases of the digestive tract are α-glycosidases and, in theory, would not be expected to hydrolyze the β-linkage found in cyanogenic glycosides. It was recently observed that direct incubation of human stomach acidic contents with amygdalin fails to release HCN (Newton *et al.* 1980).

A third possible source of enzyme would be the bacteria of the lower digestive tract. On this point the older literature is not clear in that there are conflicting reports regarding the ability of coliform bacteria to hydrolyze amygdalin (Winkler 1951; Jansz *et al.* 1974). Rumen flora apparently can degrade amygdalin (Coop and Blakley 1949).

Newton *et al.* (1980) have carried out studies which clearly indicate that intestinal bacteria are partially responsible for the rather extensive hydrolysis of amygdalin that occurs when administered orally to rats. These workers, who used earlier studies by Barrett *et al.* (1977) as a model, monitored the hydrolysis of amygdalin by following the thiocyanate excreted in the urine. Urinary thiocyanate levels rose immediately following the administration of amygdalin by stomach tube to control rats. When amygdalin was orally administered to experimental rats which had been treated with antibiotics to reduce the bacterial content of their digestive tract, there was much less thiocyanate excreted. It was also observed that significant hydrolysis of amygdalin occurred when this compound was injected intravenously into rats indicating that these cyanogenic glycosides can be hydrolyzed by intracellular enzymes. Intracellular β-glycosidases are known in mammalian tissues, but their activity against amygdalin or other cyanogenic glycosides has not been tested (Conn 1979A).

The studies of Newton *et al.* (1980) on the hydrolysis of amygdalin in animals were performed to acquire information on the possibility of acute or chronic cyanide poisoning of persons who ingest amygdalin. This cyanogenic glycoside is the main constituent of Laetrile which is actively promoted in the United States as a treatment for cancer without scientific basis for such claims (Lewis 1977). The studies of Barrett *et al.* (1977) were performed to assess the potential for chronic poisoning of persons who consume large amounts of certain foods prepared from cassava. There is a body of information suggesting that certain health problems are associated with the consumption of certain cassava-based foods under some conditions (see Conn 1979A for review). Since cassava has a very great potential for increased food production in developing countries in the tropics, any information related to reducing its potential toxicity is welcome.

SUMMARY

Cyanogenic glycosides which occur in such plants as cassava, sorghum, almonds and white clover are a potential source of hydrogen cyanide (HCN) that can poison animals, including man, which consume these plants. Man has learned to cope with the potential toxicity of these plants not only by identifying the conditions under which cyanogenic compounds accumulate but also by studying the manner in which the glycosides are degraded and release HCN. Such information in turn has led to processing procedures based on the following principles: (a) plant tissues with little or no cyanogenic compounds are selected for food; (b) tissues with significant levels of cyanogens are processed to remove the toxic cyanogen and its decomposition products; or (c) tissues containing cyanogens are heated to destroy the catabolic enzymes but leave the cyanogen more or less intact. In actual practice one or more of these procedures have been selected to allow man to safely use cyanogenic plants. In theory, these procedures should be applicable to plants which contain other toxic substances in the form of glycosides.

BIBLIOGRAPHY

BARRETT, M.D., HILL, D.C., ALEXANDER, J.C., and ZITNAK, A. 1977. Fate of orally dosed linamarin in the rat. Can. J. Physiol. Pharmacol. *55*, 134–136.

COCK, J.H. 1973. Cyanide toxicity in relation to the cassava research program of CIAT in Colombia. *In* Chronic Cassava Toxicity. B. Nestel and R. MacIntyre (Editors). Int. Devel. Res. Centre, Ottawa, Canada. Publication IDRC-010e.

CONN, E.E. 1969. Cyanogenic glycosides. Ag. and Food Chem. *17*, 519–526.

CONN, E.E. 1973A. Biosynthesis of cyanogenic glycosides. Biochem. Soc. Symp. *38*, 277–302.

CONN, E.E. 1973B. Cyanogenic glycosides. *In* Toxicants Naturally Occurring in Foods, 2nd Edition. I.E. Liener (Editor). Committee on Food Protection, NRC, Washington, D.C.

CONN, E.E. 1979A. Cyanogenic glycosides. Intl. Rev. Biochem. *27*, 21–43.

CONN, E.E. 1979B. Biosynthesis of cyanogenic glycosides. Naturwiss. *66*, 28–34.

CONN, E.E. 1979C. Cyanide and cyanogenic glycosides. *In* Herbivores: Their Interaction with Secondary Plant Metabolites. G.A. Rosenthal and D.H. Janzen (Editors). Academic Press, New York.

COOP, I.E. and BLAKLEY, R.L. 1949. The metabolism and toxicity of cyanides and cyanogenetic glucosides in sheep. 1. Activity in the rumen. N.Z. J. Sci. Tech. (Ser. A) *30*, 277–291.

CORKILL, L. 1942. Cyanogenesis in white clover. V. The inheritance of cyanogenesis. N.Z. J. Sci. Tech. (Ser. B) *23*, 178–193.

COURSEY, D.G. 1973. Cassava as a food: Toxicity and toxicology. *In* Chronic Cassava Toxicity. B. Nestel and R. MacIntyre (Editors). Intl. Devel. Res. Centre, Ottawa, Canada. Publication IDRC-010e.

deBRUIJN, G.H. 1973. The cyanogenic character of cassava. *In* Chronic Cassava Toxicity. B. Nestel and R. MacIntyre (Editors). Intl. Devel. Res. Centre, Ottawa, Canada. Publication IDRC-010e.

DEDOLPH, R.R. and HAMILTON, R.A. 1959. The bitterness problem in some seedling macadamias. Hawaii Farm Sci. *8*, 7–8.

DUNSTAN, W.R. and HENRY, T.A. 1902. Cyanogenesis in plants, Part II. The great millet. Phil. Trans. Roy. Soc. Lond. Ser. A. *199*, 399–410.

EYJOLFSSON, R. 1970. Recent advances in the chemistry of cyanogenic glycosides. Fortschr. Chem. Org. Naturst. *28*, 74–108.

HEGNAUER, R. 1977. Cyanogenic compounds as systematic markers in *Tracheophyta*. Plant Syst. Evol. Suppl. *1*, 191–209.

HEPPNER, M.J. 1926. Further evidence on the factor for bitterness in the sweet almond. Genetics *11*, 605–606.

JANSZ, E.R., JEYARAJ, E.E., PIERIS, N., and ABEYRATNE, D.J. 1974. Cyanide liberation from linamarin. J. Natl. Sci. Coun. Sri. Lanka *2*, 57–65.

JONES, D.A. 1972. Cyanogenic glycosides and their function. *In* Phytochemical Ecology. J.B. Harborne (Editor). Academic Press, London.

KINGSBURY, J.M. 1964. Poisonous plants of the U.S. and Canada. Prentice Hall, Inc., Englewood Cliffs, N.J.

KOJIMA, M., POULTON, J.E., THAYER, S.S., and CONN, E.E. 1979. Tissue distributions of dhurrin and enzymes involved in its metabolism in leaves of *Sorghum bicolor*. Plant Physiol. *63*, 1022–1028.

LEWIS, J.P. 1977. Laetrile. West. J. Med. *127*, 55–62.

MILLER, J.M. and CONN, E.E. 1980. The metabolism of hydrogen cyanide by higher plants. Plant Physiol. *65*, 1199–1202.

MONTGOMERY, R.D. 1965. The medical signficance of cyanogen in plant foodstuffs. Amer. J. Clin. Nutr. *17*, 103–113.

MONTGOMERY, R.D. 1969. Cyanogens. *In* Toxic Constituents of Plant Foodstuffs. I.E. Liener (Editor). Academic Press, New York.

NASS. H.G. 1972. Cyanogenesis: Its inheritance in *Sorghum bicolor, Sorghum sudanense, Lotus,* and *Trifolium repens*—A review. Crop Sci. *12*, 503–506.

NEWTON, G.W., SCHMIDT, E.S., LEWIS, J.P., CONN, E.E., and LAWRENCE, R. 1980. Amygdalin toxicity studies in rats predict chronic cyanide poisoning in man. Western J. Med. In press.

RATHENASINKAM, E. 1947. Poisoning by cyanogenic glycosides. J. Proc. Inst. Chem. (India) *19*, 59–60.

SCHWARZMAIER, U. 1976. Uber die cyanogenese von *Bambusa vulgaris* und *B. guadua*. Chem. Ber. *109*, 3379–3389.

SIEGLER, D.S. 1977. The naturally occurring cyanogenic glycosides. *In* Progress in Phytochemistry. L. Reinhold, J.B. Harborne, and T. Swain (Editors). *4*, 83–120.

TOWILL, L.E., DRURY, J.S., WHITFIELD, B.L., LEWIS, E.B., GALYAN, E.L., and HAMMONS, A.S. 1978. Review of the environmental effects of pollutants: V. Cyanide. U.S. Environmental Protection Agency, Document EPA-600/1-78-027, 191 pp.

VIEHOEVER, A. 1940. Edible and poisonous beans of the lima type. (*Phaseolus lunatus* L.) Thai Science Bull. *2*, 1–99.

WINKLER, W.O. 1958. Report on methods for glucosidal HCN in lima beans. J. Assoc. Off. Anal. Chem. *41*, 282–287.

8

Unwanted Biological Substances in Foods: Aflatoxins

Urban L. Diener[1]

Certain fungi (molds) synthesize chemicals that are poisonous and produce symptoms of toxicity when food or feed containing them is eaten by humans and animals. These chemicals are called mycotoxins, which is derived from the Greek words "myces" meaning fungus and "toxikon" meaning poison. Animal diseases caused by mycotoxins are referred to as mycotoxicoses. Several recent books review the mycology, chemistry, and biological effects of mycotoxins (Rodricks 1976; Rodricks *et al.* 1977; Uraguchi and Yamazaki 1978; Wyllie and Morehouse 1977, 1978A, 1978B). The significance of mycotoxins in food safety and human health has been extensively reviewed by Bullerman, particularly in relation to animal products and processed foods (Bullerman 1979).

Since the author's experience is in field contamination and laboratory research with aflatoxin and other mycotoxins in peanuts, corn, and cottonseed, this paper will be oriented in that direction.

AFLATOXIN IN PEANUTS

Aspergillus flavus and *A. parasiticus*, the two fungi that produce aflatoxin, are closely related taxonomically (Diener and Davis 1969). Many

[1] Professor, Botany, Plant Pathology, and Microbiology, Auburn University, Agricultural Experiment Station, Auburn, Alabama.

research papers have not distinguished between the two, but have referred to them simply as *A. flavus* or the *A. flavus* group. At this time, *A. parasiticus* is the species most frequently associated with peanuts and *A. flavus* is the species most frequently associated with corn and cottonseed. This view is supported by the fact that *A. parasiticus* produces the aflatoxins B_1, B_2, G_1, and G_2 and chemical analyses of contaminated peanuts usually reveal the presence of all four of these toxins. On the other hand, corn and cottonseed contaminated with *A. flavus* usually only contain aflatoxins B_1 and B_2. Although only *A. flavus* will be used in this discussion, references to *A. flavus* in peanuts will probably be *A. parasiticus*, whereas in corn and cottonseed the identification is probably correct.

Occurrence

The structure and chemistry of the aflatoxins have been studied extensively and at least 18 aflatoxins have been reported in the literature, although only 13 are considered to occur in nature as secondary metabolites produced by *A. flavus* and *A. parasiticus* or as derivatives resulting from animal metabolism of aflatoxin-contaminated foods and feeds (Diener and Davis 1976). The chemical structures of aflatoxins B_1, G_1, and M_1 are shown in Fig. 8.1.

Aspergillus flavus is a facultative parasite that appears to be unable to penetrate the immature peanut pod in the soil unless the pod has been damaged by cultivation, nematodes, insects, pathogenic fungi, or physiologically altered by environmental stress (Diener 1973). The fungus is able to invade maturing and overmature peanut pods and kernels in the soil near digging time. After digging, sound, unblemished peanut pods may be invaded by *A. flavus* if environmental conditions during the curing process are unfavorable for rapid drying of peanut pods and kernels in the windrow. During curing the fungus may aggressively invade pods that are damaged by digging even in an environment favorable for rapid drying. After curing for several days, some damage occurs during picking (threshing) of the partially dried pods from the vines, and if rapid drying by mechanical means to 9–10% kernel moisture content (KMC) is not accomplished, growth of *A. flavus* and subsequent aflatoxin production are favored.

Aspergillus flavus and *A. parasiticus* are prominent components of the soil mycoflora in peanut fields of Israel, Nigeria, and India as well as the U.S.A. *A. flavus* proliferates in the geocarposphere (pod area) as the fruit develops, and it can be isolated from undamaged pods about 30 days before maturity (harvest). Data on the mycoflora associated with immature and mature pods, at time of digging, and after curing have been reviewed (Diener 1973).

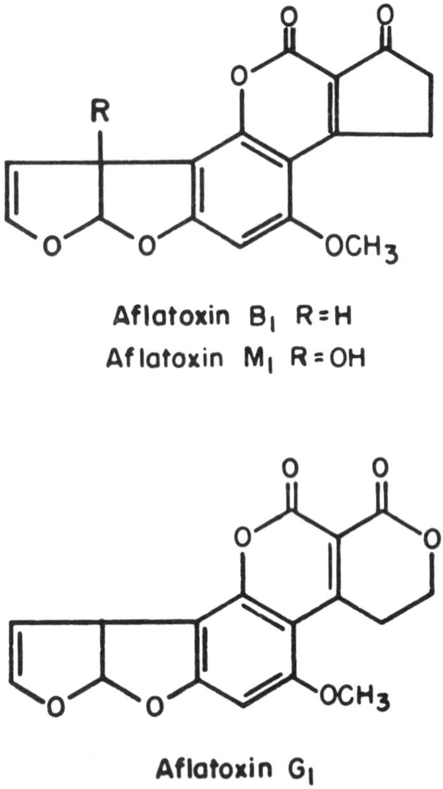

FIG. 8.1. STRUCTURES OF AFLATOXIN B_1, G_1, AND M_1

Factors Affecting Fungus Growth

Besides being a soilborne fungus in the field, *A. flavus* is also a storage fungus. This refers to species of saprophytic and weakly parasitic fungi that continue to grow at low kernel moistures after field fungi have died (Diener 1973). Invasion of peanut pods and kernels are influenced by kernel moisture dependent on relative humidity (RH), temperature, time, and gaseous composition of the microclimate. High mycofloral counts have been associated with peanuts of high initial moisture contents going into storage (Diener 1960). Experimentally, in pure culture *A. flavus* grows vigorously on peanuts at high KMC or at a RH as low as 86–88% and over a broad range of temperatures from 20–35°C (Diener and Davis 1967).

Oxygen, Carbon Dioxide.—Storage fungi are highly aerobic organisms and their development depends on the presence of oxygen (O_2) in the air. Experimentally, *A. flavus* growth, sporulation, and free fatty acid (FFA) formation were reduced when O_2 concentrations were lowered from 5% to 1% in combination with 0, 20, and 80% at 30°C (Landers *et al.* 1967). Fungus growth and sporulation were reduced with each 20% increase in CO_2 from 40 to 80% at 30°C. No growth occurred in 100% CO_2. Other experiments evaluated the combination of RH and temperature in reducing fungal growth with CO_2 (Sanders *et al.* 1968). Visible growth and FFA formation by *A. flavus* were inhibited at 86% RH and 17°C by 20% CO_2 and at 25°C by 40 and 60% CO_2. Levels of FFA decreased as RH decreased from 99% to 86%.

Factors Affecting Aflatoxin Formation

Relative Humidity.—Limiting factors affecting aflatoxin production by *A. flavus* were investigated under precisely controlled conditions in the laboratory (Diener and Davis 1967, 1968, 1970). The limiting RH, for aflatoxin production in heat-killed and freshly-dug Early Runner peanuts after 21 days at 30°C, was 85 ± 1%. Low levels of aflatoxin were formed at 84% RH in 84 days at 30°C in immature and broken mature (loose shelled, damaged) kernels, but none was formed in sound mature and unshelled, stored, nonsterile living peanuts. No aflatoxin formed at 83% RH in any treatment. Less precise laboratory studies of other workers (Austwick and Ayerst 1963) indicate a lower limit on growth at 80% RH with slow growth at 80–85% RH.

Moisture.—In the field, invasion of peanut pods and kernels by *A. flavus* before digging is usually associated with drought stress, physical or biological damage to the pod, or overmaturity. However, Norton *et al.* (1956) reported that preharvest invasion of 1,004 pods of unblemished Spanish peanuts by *A. flavus* was common. Platings of 100 kernels from unblemished pods each week for 5 weeks revealed 111 kernels contaminated by fungi with 79.3% containing *A. flavus*. Joffe and Borut (1966) in Israel reported similar results, which they attributed to (1) peanut monoculture, (2) advanced maturity of the crop at harvest, (3) 3-week period from digging of pods until their examination, and (4) use of a high nutrient laboratory medium and a long (3-week) incubation period for isolation.

Drought Stress—Preharvest.—McDonald (1969) found at Mokwa, Nigeria that aflatoxin was not a problem where the 1963 peanut crop matured and was dug well before the rains ended. However, at Kano where the rains ceased before harvest, toxicity increased as the moisture content of the kernel at digging decreased. This decreased KMC has been associated with drought, overmaturity, and with a high level of pod invasion by *A. flavus* in the soil. Also, low vigor of the plant and reduced physiological activity in the kernel coincided with the drop in KMC and overmaturity. All of these factors resulted in increased susceptibility of pod and kernel to *A. flavus* invasion and aflatoxin formation (McDonald and Harkness 1964, 1967). Pods collected from dead plants at Kano, Nigeria contained aflatoxin-contaminated kernels of 5–14% KMC, whereas living plants at harvest had no toxic kernels and 24–34% KMC (McDonald 1969). Pettit *et al.* (1971) found that peanuts grown under dryland, drought-stressed conditions accumulated more aflatoxin before digging than did irrigated peanuts.

Drying Rate, Post Harvest.—*A. flavus* appears to develop most rapidly in peanuts at KMC of 14–30% during drying in the windrow or stack (Dickens and Pattee 1966; McDonald and Harkness 1964; McDonald *et al.* 1964). Apparently *A. flavus* does not become established readily in peanuts of moisture contents higher or lower than this range (Austwick and Ayerst 1963; McDonald and Harkness 1964, 1965). Whether this is a moisture-based response or whether it is due to the fact that moisture levels of peanuts 2 days after lifting are usually in this range, which is also the time required for spore deposition, germination, penetration, and development of the fungus, is a matter of conjecture. McDonald and Harkness (1964) suggested that the drop in moisture content to a more susceptible state was associated with the physiological change from active growth to one of a low metabolic state.

McDonald *et al.* (1964) found little or no aflatoxin in peanut samples from inverted windrows dried to 15% KMC at 32°C and 50% RH, whereas samples dried at 32°C and 85% RH contained aflatoxin B_1 in quantities of 6–960 ppb. It was also demonstrated that when moisture percentage decreased rapidly in inverted windrows lower *A. flavus* and mycofloral invasion occurred (Dickens and Pattee 1966; Page 1964; Porter and Garren 1970; Porter and Wright 1971).

When curing peanuts are in the general range of 14–24% KMC, interruption and retardation of field drying by rain or overcast, humid weather, or a regain in moisture after picking and storage, usually result in aflatoxin formation by *A. flavus* (Austwick and Ayerst 1963; Bampton 1963). If peanuts have not dried to 10% KMC or less by 5–6 days after lifting, aflatoxin contamination by *A. flavus* has usually occurred (McDonald and A'Brook 1963, McDonald and Harkness 1964).

Temperature.—Experimentally, it was determined that 12 and 41°C were limiting temperatures for the formation of aflatoxin by *A. flavus* in heat-treated, in freshly dug, and in stored, unsterile, living Early Runner peanuts held 21 days at 98% ± 1% RH (Diener and Davis 1967, 1968, 1970). These data agree with earlier findings of Burrell *et al.* (1964), who noted that a constant temperature of 45°C inhibited growth of *A. flavus* in peanuts and an exposure of 2–4 hr at 50°C checked growth for about 24 hr. Dickens and Pattee (1966) found that in 10 days aflatoxin had developed in peanut samples of 15–30% moisture held at 32°C, but had developed in relatively few samples held at 21°C. In their investigation, the minimum time for aflatoxin production was 2½ days after inoculation.

In controlled environment studies with living cured peanuts, Diener and Davis (1970) found that for sound and broken mature kernels, immature kernels, and kernels of unshelled peanuts, the upper limiting temperature for growth and aflatoxin production by *A. flavus* was 40.5 ± 0.5°C at 99% RH in 21 days. The lower limiting temperature was 13 ± 1°C for sound and broken mature kernels incubated up to 84 days at 99% RH. In immature kernels some aflatoxin developed at 15°C in 21 days, although none was found at 14°C in 42 and 84 days. A negligible amount of aflatoxin developed in 21 days in kernels from intact pods at 20°C. In 42 days a large amount of aflatoxin developed at 18°C, but none occurred at 16°C. These data paralleled results with freshly-dug, living Early Runner peanuts (Diener and Davis 1968) in that some aflatoxin was found at 20°C, but none at 15°C in 21 days. Thus, living peanut kernels stored in intact pods were much less susceptible to invasion and aflatoxin formation by *A. flavus*.

Time.—Research on the relation of time to the formation of aflatoxin in peanuts after digging has given varying results. Under tropical conditions in Africa, peanuts that were free of toxin at digging time contained detectable toxin 48 hr later (McDonald and A'Brook 1963). Also, kernels with testae damaged during shelling showed sporulating *A. flavus* in 4 days. McDonald and A'Brook (1963) found that artificial drying after 4–6 days in the field gave toxin-free kernels, but samples dried for 8–12 days or those that were sun-dried for 10–16 days gave low to medium toxin yields (25–500 μg/kg). McDonald and Harkness (1964) found that contamination of kernels with *A. flavus* and aflatoxin did not occur until at least 5–6 days after lifting. They also found more *A. flavus* and other fungi in kernels from slowly-dried pods (attached to plant) than from rapidly-dried pods (McDonald and Harkness 1965). Jackson (1967) found high levels of aflatoxin as well as high percentages of kernel invasion by *A. flavus* in slowly dried as opposed to rapidly dried pods.

Oxygen, Carbon Dioxide.—Aflatoxin production by *A. flavus* in peanuts was reduced with successive 20% increases in CO_2 from 20 to 80% with none occurring in 100% CO_2 at 30°C (Landers *et al.* 1967). At lower RH and temperature, aflatoxin production was inhibited by 20% CO_2 at 17°C and 86–92% RH (Sanders *et al.* 1968). At 25°C aflatoxin production was inhibited by 60% CO_2 at 86 and 92% RH and by 40% CO_2 at

86% RH. Decreases in O_2 concentration decreased aflatoxin production with the most sizeable decreases occurring when O_2 was reduced from 5 to 1% in combination with 0, 20, and 80% CO_2. No aflatoxin was formed in peanuts stored 6 weeks at 15°C under 40% CO_2 and 5% O_2. However, aflatoxin production occurred in 1% O_2:99% N_2 and in 1% O_2:79% N_2: 20% CO_2. Thus, *A. flavus* showed a tolerance for low oxygen and high carbon dioxide that is typical of soil organisms (Stotzky and Goos 1965).

Damage.—Rapid invasion of peanut pods by *A. flavus* in the field has been associated primarily with physical and biological damage to shell and kernels (Diener 1973). Growth cracks, pathogenic fungus contamination, mechanically damaged pods, and termite and corn borer injury result in preharvest development of aflatoxin in the field. Damage to the shell and injury to the testa of the kernel during picking are major factors in *A. flavus* invasion and aflatoxin formation in the kernel during drying.

Overmaturity.—It was discovered that peanuts left in the ground 4 weeks after maturity contained aflatoxin (Bampton 1963). Also, late planted peanuts in a semi-arid region showed aflatoxin, although the plants had been in the ground for only the normal length of time. Several workers (Diener *et al.* 1965; McDonald and Harkness 1964, 1967; McDonald *et al.* 1964) have demonstrated that overmature pods are more rapidly invaded by *A. flavus* than freshly dug immature and mature pods and kernels. Decreased physiological activity associated with maturity or from low moisture in the soil environment (drought) appears to favor invasion and aflatoxin production in kernels and pods by *A. flavus*.

Mycoflora.—Microbial interactions and antagonism as well as competition for nutrients by the fungi making up the mycoflora frequently determine the degree of *A. flavus* invasion and subsequent aflatoxin production (Diener 1973). At temperatures and RHs other than those optimum for *A. flavus*, microbial competition may restrict growth and sporulation of the fungus and significantly reduce the amount of aflatoxin formed.

AFLATOXIN IN CORN

Occurrence, Storage

The status of the aflatoxin problem in corn and possible solutions have been reviewed by several investigators (Shotwell 1977A, 1977B; Lillehoj and Hesseltine 1977; Lillehoj and Zuber 1975; Zuber and Lillehoj 1979). Early work associated aflatoxin in corn with improper storage. Early surveys for aflatoxin in the 1964 and 1965 corn crops in midwestern U.S. revealed that 30 out of 1,311 samples (2.3%) contained toxin (Shotwell *et al.* 1969). A similar study of the 1967 crop showed 6 out of 283 corn samples (2.1%) contained the toxin (Shotwell *et al.* 1970). These data indicated both a low incidence and low levels of aflatoxin (3–37 ppb), primarily in the poorest grades of corn. In 1965 aflatoxin B_1 analyses of official grain inspection samples, taken from 230 box or hopper railroad cars purchased for delivery to six wet-milling plants, showed that only four contained 3–5 ppb of aflatoxin (Watson and Yahl 1971). In the same study, corn in three processing plants was sampled daily for a year and composited into 142 weekly samples. Six of these samples contained aflatoxin B_1 (3–5 ppb). Persons in the corn wet-milling industry concluded that corn arriving at major markets was largely free of aflatoxin at the time sampled. However, aflatoxin B_1 was found in spot samples from 8 of 500 carloads of high moisture corn visually inspected by corn wet-millers. All of the eight carloads had visible mold damage and two had already been rejected on that basis (Watson and Yahl 1971). Thus, the potential for aflatoxin contamination does exist in improperly handled corn.

A survey of export corn of all grades, except U.S. No. 1., collected from ten ports in 1968 and 1969 showed an aflatoxin incidence of 2.7% and levels of 6–25 ppb, but most of the samples were taken from the better grades (Shotwell *et al.* 1971). In 1969 and 1970, 60 samples of corn (49 yellow) from Alabama, North Carolina, South Carolina, Tennessee, and Virginia were analyzed for aflatoxin (Shotwell *et al.* 1973). The 21 positive samples ranged from 4–308 ppb of aflatoxin B_1 with 12 samples exceeding the administrative guideline of 20 ppb. This small number of samples from the South showed much higher incidences and levels of aflatoxin than had been recorded in earlier surveys.

In 1972, 1283 truckloads (200–400 bu) of 1971 white corn stored 1 year under 77 Commodity Credit Corporation loans in 7 counties of southeastern Missouri were sampled on delivery to an elevator (Shotwell *et al.* 1975). Aflatoxin levels were below 20 ppb in 17.8% of the truckloads and above 20 ppb in 12.8% of the truckloads with 2.3% exceeding 100 ppb. Despite the widespread contamination of this white corn, either preharvest or during storage, no aflatoxin was detected in 889 truckloads (69.3%) nor in any corn from 20 of the farm loans. Thus, corn was grown, harvested, and stored without aflatoxin contamination in an area where conditions were favorable for its formation.

Occurrence, Preharvest

As pointed out by Shotwell (1977B), surveys for aflatoxin before 1971 were made on corn moving in commercial channels. Thus, the time at which the fungus invaded the grain and produced the toxin was not known. It was generally viewed as having occurred in storage. However, Taubenhaus (1920) had reported that *A. flavus* was capable of invading developing corn ears during the milk stage in the field. He also associated these infections with the presence of corn earworm and other insects. Lillehoj and coworkers demonstrated preharvest development of aflatoxin in the 1972 crop of corn in Missouri and Illinois (Lillehoj *et al.* 1975A; Fennel *et al.* 1975), in the 1973 corn crop in South Carolina (Lillehoj *et al.* 1976B, 1976A, 1976C; Hesseltine *et al.* 1976), in 1974 corn grown in South Carolina and Florida (Lillehoj *et al.* 1976B, and 1975 corn in Iowa (Lillehoj *et al.* 1976A, 1977), in 1976 corn grown in eight of eleven southern and Corn Belt states (Lillehoj *et al.* 1978A), and in 1977 corn grown in Georgia, Missouri, and Iowa (Fennell *et al.* 1978). Another study of preharvest development of aflatoxin B_1 was made with plantings of the same corn selections in 17 states (mostly in the South, but including California, Indiana, and Illinois) during the period 1972–1974; aflatoxin was observed in at least 1 of the 3 years in 15 of the 17 states and in all 3 years in Georgia and Texas (Zuber *et al.* 1976).

Time of Kernel Invasion

Taubenhaus noted in 1920 that *A. flavus*, termed yellow mold, could only invade the ear during the milky stage of kernel development after it had been injured by corn earworm. These conclusions were supported by data from experiments conducted 55 years later in South Carolina (LaPrade and Manwiller 1976) that showed maximal fungus infection occurred during midseason when ears were inoculated in the late milk to early dough stage, but only when the inoculum was forcefully injected into the developing kernels. In experiments involving two planting dates, samples from the first planting date provided distinctly higher toxin levels in mature corn from Missouri and Georgia (Fennell *et al.* 1978), indicating that time and crop maturity are important in the critical insect-fungus invasion of the kernel.

Insect Damage

The role of insects in aflatoxin contamination of corn, cotton, and peanuts was recently reviewed (Widstrom 1979). In 1972 corn in Missouri and Illinois, aflatoxin was detected in significantly more earworm damaged samples than in those with no insect damage (Lillehoj *et al.* 1975A). *A. flavus* was isolated from 15% of the 195 insects collected from freshly harvested ears (Fennell *et al.* 1975); it was associated with a significantly higher proportion of earworms (37%) than corn borers (14%). The presence of *A. flavus* was associated with insect activity (rice weevil) in 1973 corn in South Carolina (Hesseltine *et al.* 1976). In 1974, corn in South Carolina and Florida was sprayed with an insecticide

(Sevin) that reduced, but did not eliminate, insect damage and aflatoxin in field corn (Lillehoj *et al.* 1976B). When test ears were hand-infected with corn borers, earworms, and fall army worms, data at maturity showed the ears infected with corn earworm had the greatest damage, but the levels of aflatoxin was lightest in seed from ears infested with corn borers (Widstrom *et al.* 1975). Infection of 1975 corn in Iowa by *A. flavus* with subsequent production of aflatoxin before harvest was attributed exclusively to injury resulting from the feeding of larvae of second generation European corn borer (Lillehoj *et al.* 1976A).

Varietal Differences

In 1976, two hybrids grown in the South and two adapted to the Corn Belt were grown in 11 southern and Corn Belt states. The distribution of insects infested with *A. flavus* was relatively uniform between test locations; 3.3% of the 1,621 insect larvae collected were contaminated (Lillehoj *et al.* 1978A). Data indicated that visual assessment of insect damage on southern corn could be used as an indicator of possible aflatoxin contamination. Two hybrids of varying husk types were planted in six states, three in the Corn Belt and three in the South (Fennell *et al.* 1977); presence of *A. flavus* in a broad range of insects on corn ears before harvest suggested that dissemination of fungus inoculum was not related to a specific insect. Research (Fennell *et al.* 1978) in 1977 in Georgia, Iowa, and Missouri evaluated the role of environment in the association of *A. flavus* and insect larvae (corn borer and earworm). Results provided additional evidence for the role of corn insects in transferring *A. flavus* spores from the silk region of the ear to the area of developing kernels and the subsequent formation of aflatoxin in the seed. The extent of the fungus-insect association and toxin production was influenced by regional factors with the highest *A. flavus* occurrence and aflatoxin levels in mature corn in samples from the South, intermediate levels in the southern Corn Belt (MO), and lowest incidence in Corn Belt samples.

Drought Stress

The possible relationship of drought stress in predisposing developing ears of Iowa corn to attack by either insects and *A. flavus*, or other plant pathogens and *A. flavus* , or *A. flavus* directly was proposed by Lillehoj *et al.* (1977). Data from the plantings of two hybrids in five southern and four Corn Belt states showed a correlation of high aflatoxin occurrence in Florida with July and August drought stress (Lillehoj *et al.* 1978B). In addition, the highest incidences of bright greenish-yellow (BGY) fluorescence were generally found in corn from areas with stressed growing conditions such as dense plant populations per acre or low fertilization (Anderson *et al.* 1975). Drought stress and insect damage were considered to be the most significant factors in the aflatoxin outbreak of 1977 in Georgia (McMillian *et al.* 1978; Wilson *et al.* 1979).

Temperature Effects

There may be a correlation between temperature, *A. flavus*, and aflatoxin production, since no aflatoxin occurred in samples from states with a 3-month mean temperature of 22.5°C or lower for June, July, and August and one or more aflatoxin-positive samples occurred in states with mean temperatures exceeding 23.5°C for the 3 months (Lillehoj *et al.* 1978B).

Regional Effects

Regional conditions that determine the extent of insect damage in preharvest corn ears are decisive in subsequent aflatoxin formation in the kernels (Fennell *et al.* 1978). Aflatoxin incidence in the Corn Belt has been found to be 2–3% with few lots containing more than 20 ppb, whereas 13–32% of analyzed samples from the South contained >20 ppb. Multilocation plantings of the same varieties of corn invariably demonstrated the higher natural occurrence of aflatoxin in southern states in inoculated or noninoculated experimental plots (Lillehoj *et al.* 1975C, 1978A; Zuber *et al.* 1976; Fennell *et al.* 1978). The incidence of the *A. flavus*-insect association in producing toxin in the ears was higher in Georgia, intermediate in Missouri, and low in Iowa (Fennell *et al.* 1978). Similarly, inoculation of kernels during silking resulted in more contaminated ears and higher levels of toxin in southern states (Lillehoj *et al.* 1975C; Anderson *et al.* 1975).

The performance of adapted varieties and other varietal differences are also regionally related. Aflatoxin occurred commonly on corn grown in the South, but higher levels of toxin were produced on the Corn Belt-adapted hybrids (Lillehoj *et al.* 1976B, 1978A; Fennell *et al.* 1977). Inoculated ears of a regionally nonadapted variety exhibited higher aflatoxin levels than did corn of adapted varieties (Anderson *et al.* 1975; Lillehoj *et al.* 1976B, 1978A, 1978B). A widely grown single cross hybrid supported production of higher levels of aflatoxin in four southern states than a double cross adapted to the South (Lillehoj *et al.* 1975C). No significant difference in aflatoxin incidence was noted between normal and opaque-2 endosperm types, although the latter had been reported to support lower toxin production in India (Lillehoj *et al.* 1975C).

The presence of *A. flavus* on corn insects and subsequent toxin production is influenced by the stage of maturity of the corn, by the time between the initial contact of the fungus and insect, as well as the insect activity on the ear (Fennell *et al.* 1978). Yellow and white dent corn was inoculated with *A. flavus* and ears inoculated at late milk and early dough stages were more susceptible to infection than ears inoculated at the silking and early milk stages (Rambo *et al.* 1974; LaPrade and Manwiller 1976). Research also demonstrated that damage to developing corn kernels was essential for *A. flavus* infection. Data in 1972 (Anderson *et al.* 1975) showed that aflatoxin contamination of the kernel is most likely to occur during the period from about 2 weeks after silking until the kernel has matured about 6–8 weeks later; inoculations performed 2, 3, and 4 weeks after silking produced the highest levels of aflatoxins in injected kernels. Another study demonstrated that aflatoxin was not present in kernels 20 days after flowering, but was routinely found in samples collected 40 days after flowering (Lillehoj *et al.* 1978A). *A. flavus* was found more frequently on silks from mature ears than on those from immature ears collected at silking in corn planted in six states of the South and Midwest (Fennell *et al.* 1977).

Insect damage has been identified as the critical component for preharvest *A. flavus* infections of corn (Anderson *et al.* 1975; Lillehoj *et al.* 1975A; Taubenhaus 1920). Damage caused by larvae of European corn borer, corn earworm, fall army worm, and rice weevil has been associated with the natural occurrence of *A. flavus* and/or aflatoxin in most of these investigations. However, the role of drought in increasing the severity of insect depredation is not clear, since they are frequently associated as in 1977. Experimentally, control of insects with insecticides has shown little promise as a practical mechanism for eliminating aflatoxin from preharvest corn (Anderson *et al.* 1975; Lillehoj *et al.* 1976B; Widstrom *et al.* 1976). Several studies (Rambo *et al.* 1974, LaPrade and Manwiller 1976; Lillehoj *et al.* 1975C, 1976B, 1978B) have simulated insect injury by various methods of causing mechanical damage to the developing kernels of corn followed by *A. flavus* inoculation with varying degrees of success.

Thus, (1) *A. flavus* invasion and aflatoxin contamination of corn have been widely correlated with damage caused by corn borer, corn earworms, fall army worms, and rice weevil. Insecticide applications reduced worm damage but had little effect on aflatoxin occurrence. The extent of the fungus-insect association was influenced by regional factors. (2) The most susceptible period of the developing corn kernel to invasion by *A. flavus* and subsequent aflatoxin formation is about 2 weeks after flowering until the corn has matured and dried to about 20–25% KMC; a period correlated with milk to early dough stage. (3) Highest incidences of toxin occurrence were correlated with stressed growing conditions (drought, dense plant populations, low fertilization) that may predispose the corn plant to insect and/or fungus invasion. (4) Breaks in the coat of the corn kernel have been correlated with 90% of the samples containing aflatoxin. (5) Regional conditions that determine the extent of insect damage in preharvest ears of corn are decisive in subsequent aflatoxin contamination of the kernels.

AFLATOXIN IN COTTONSEED

Aspergillus flavus is abundant in the hot and humid areas of southeastern U.S., but aflatoxin contamination of cottonseed has not been a serious problem. In the United States, aflatoxin contamination is largely limited to the low altitude (desert) regions of Arizona, the Imperial Valley in southern California; and part of New Mexico, Oklahoma, and Texas (Hamsa and Ayres, 1977; Russell *et al.* 1976). Fibers and seeds of unopened cotton bolls are protected from infection by *A. flavus* by the carpel wall, which the fungus cannot penetrate. Bolls opened 1–3 mm are prone to infection, whereas bolls opened 10 mm or more escaped infection, due to inadequate moisture in exposed fibers (Ashworth *et al.* 1969B). Invasion of the boll, and ultimately the seed, by *A. flavus* generally occurs before the boll is fully opened and is maximal over a temperature range 30–35°C (Ashworth *et al.* 1969C). Aflatoxin production, however, was maximal at 25–30°C. Aflatoxins were essentially absent from infected, unopened bolls and bolls opened no more than 1–3 mm, 14 days after inoculation (Ashworth *et al.* 1969C). Regardless of incubation temperature or degree of seed infection, aflatoxin formation did not occur probably due to inadequate aeration of seed. Once bolls are 90% open, seeds are essentially air dry and moisture levels are too low for toxin formation in infected seed (Ashworth *et al.* 1969B). Thus, the more rapidly cotton bolls open and seeds dry, under temperature conditions otherwise optimal for aflatoxin elaboration, the lower the potential for aflatoxin contamination (Russell *et al.* 1976). In 1967, seed infection by *A. flavus* and the accumulation of aflatoxins in cottonseed were 50 times greater before harvest in southern California than in the previous 2 years. The increase was due to increased development of *A. flavus* in seed rewet during a preharvest rain. However, aflatoxin concentrations in seed did not continue to increase in storage (Ashworth *et al.* 1971A).

Insects playing a major role in disseminating and facilitating boll penetration by *A. flavus* are the pink boll worm, *Lygus*, boll weevil, and stink bug (Ashworth *et al.* 1971B; Hamsa and Ayres 1977; Stephenson and Russell 1974). Exit holes made by mature pink bollworm larvae are the major portal by which the fungus enters the boll (Ashworth *et al.* 1971B). Experiments in 1973 showed a direct correlation between low levels of pink bollworm infestation and low levels of aflatoxin in cottonseed (Russell *et al.* 1976). Injury to boll locules by insects reduces the rate of boll opening and may prevent the boll from opening completely. This tends to maintain high levels of moisture in seeds for prolonged periods, favoring *A. flavus* growth and aflatoxin formation (Russell *et al.* 1976). The significance of moisture is also noted in the reduced level of aflatoxin accumulation in Deltapine 16 cottonseed when irrigation was terminated in late July 1971 and early August 1972 in field experiments (Russell *et al.* 1976).

Invasion of cottonseed by *A. flavus* was predominant at 28, 30, and 37°C, while at 15 and 20°C other fungi dominated the surface and interior of cottonseed (Hamsa and Ayres 1977). *A. flavus* invades the cottonseed embryo through the chalazal region, the micropylar region, or cracks developed in the seedcoat during ginning. Retardation of the elaboration of aflatoxin by *A. flavus* in cottonseed has been associated with seedcoat impermeability (Mayne *et al.* 1969).

In 1977 high field contamination of cottonseed with aflatoxin in Arizona was correlated with daily mean temperatures of 34°C or above that appear to be related to chronic field contamination of seed by aflatoxin (T.E. Russell, personal communication). Aflatoxin levels also increased in open storage situations. High temperatures in August and September and relatively high rainfall for Arizona during late summer and fall were the major contributing factors. During and after harvest, seed cotton modules (open bins) were wet intermittently by fall and winter rains, which probably increased aflatoxin elaboration by *A. flavus* in already heavily contaminated seed, resulting in aflatoxin levels ranging from 0.1–100 ppm. In 1978, whole contaminated cottonseed from the 1977 Arizona crop was fed to dairy cows, and aflatoxin M_1 was found in milk in amounts exceeding the 0.5 ppb action guideline set by the Food and Drug Administration for interstate commerce (CAST 1979).

BIOLOGICAL EFFECTS

The broad range of biological effects of the aflatoxins probably relates to their reaction with cell nucleoproteins and nucleic acids and the ultimate effect of these reactions on protein synthesis and cellular integrity (CAST 1979). Of 18 generally recognized aflatoxins, mold-derived metabolites and animal metabolites, the biological activity of aflatoxin B_1 appears to be the greatest in terms of both toxicity and carcinogenicity, followed closely by aflatoxin M_1. Biological effects of aflatoxin B_1 in animals are related to the level in the feed and susceptibility of the species. Most laboratory animals respond to the toxic and carcinogenic effects of aflatoxin B_1. The rainbow trout is the most sensitive animal known; less than 1 ppb in the diet will produce a significant incidence of liver cancer within 12 to 20 months. The Fischer strain of rat is probably the most sensitive mammal, with *ca.* 1 ppb in the diet required to elicit a carcinogenic response. Susceptibility varies with the species, age, and strain; among individuals within a group; and with the effect of various factors on the liver enzyme system. Young animals are notably more susceptible to aflatoxin B_1 than are mature animals. Species susceptibility to aflatoxin B_1 in terms of lethal effect varies among domesticated animals, with the single oral dose LD_{50} in mg/kg of body weight being 0.3 in rabbits, 0.34 in ducklings, 0.62 in pigs, 1.0 in dogs, 1.4 in turkeys, 2.0 in sheep, 2.0 in foals, and 6.5 in chickens.

Depending on the amount of toxin consumed and the animal's susceptibility to aflatoxin B_1, the biological effects may occur as: (a) acute and clinically obvious disease, (b) chronic, less clinically apparent, impairment of health and productivity, and (c) impairment of resistance and immune responsiveness that becomes clinically apparent as an infectious disease that the diagnostician would not readily associate with aflatoxin consumption. The effects of acute aflatoxin poisoning are dramatically characterized by severe clinical disease and mortality as observed in the 1960 outbreaks in turkeys, cattle, and swine. Reductions in growth rate, feed efficiency, carcass quality, disease resistance, and failure of immunologic response caused by lower levels of toxin intake are less dramatic, but are probably more significant economically, since these are the responses caused by the amounts of toxin usually found in contaminated animal feeds (CAST 1979).

As noted in both domesticated and laboratory animals, the principal target organ in aflatoxicosis is the liver. In addition, necrosis of the kidney tubules occurs with high doses, and the lymphoid organs of chickens, including the thymus and Bursa of Fabricius, are affected. In subacute aflatoxicosis resulting from low levels of aflatoxin intake, affected animals usually exhibit reduced weight gains, lowered productivity (milk or eggs), and in chickens reduced carcass quality due to inadequate pigmentation and increased bruising. Liver damage in the more frequently observed subacute aflatoxicosis consists of fatty change, proliferation of biliary duct epithelium, and cell necrosis. Impaired liver function results in deficiencies in complement factors and proteins associated with blood coagulation (CAST 1979). The most common biological effect of aflatoxin in animals is a reduced growth rate. This effect occurs with levels of toxin below those required to elicit a recognizable clinical disease. This subtle effect probably represents the most important, seldom diagnosed, economic loss due to aflatoxin consumption. Other effects from low level aflatoxin consumption include impairment of both native resistance and immunogenesis. In both, aflatoxin is seldom recognized as the predisposing agent. Carcinogenesis has not been recognized or reported as a common consequence of aflatoxin consumption in livestock and poultry.

The most significant question is whether aflatoxin is a hazard to human health. Epidemiological evidence has accumulated to the point that we can now give only an affirmative answer. An impressive reminder of this fact is the aflatoxin-related episode, in which acute poisoning of 400 people occurred in India in 1974 resulting in 106 deaths (Van Rensburg 1977). The circumstances were typical of those highly conducive to excessive mycotoxin exposure, *i.e.*, a poor, rural subsistence economy where the people were virtually totally dependent on a single food crop (corn) they produced themselves, and conditions favorable for aflatoxin formation resulted from rains that drenched the crop at harvest in the warm climate of the area. Only corn-eating ethnic groups were affected. No new cases occurred after the locally grown corn was exhausted. Several members of some rural households were affected and dogs eating the same food suffered a similar fate. Medical features of the syndrome were consistent with experimental data on aflatoxicosis. Aflatoxin-contaminated corn was consumed in affected households but not in unaffected households. Aflatoxin concentrations in affected samples ranged from 0.25–15.6 ppm, which is relatively high.

In subtropical parts of the world, aflatoxin B_1 has been found in many important foods and feeds (Table 8.1). The evidence of the relationship between the ingestion of aflatoxin-contaminated food in such areas and the incidence of human liver disorders has been reviewed (Campbell and Stoloff 1974; Van Rensburg 1977; Shank 1978; Wilson 1978). In Uganda, where the incidence of human liver cancer is particularly high, aflatoxin B_1 has been found in 30% of 480 food samples. Areas of high

TABLE 8.1. AFLATOXIN B_1 CONTAMINATION OF SELECTED FOODS

Country	Commodity	Samples Contaminated	AFB_1 in Positives Average $\mu g/kg$
South Africa	Peanuts	5/67	2 over > 1000
	Corn	2/52	> 1000
Uganda	Beans	15/64	500
	Peanuts	29/150	363
	Corn	19/48	133
	Sorghum	16/69	152
Thailand	Peanuts	116/216	872
	Corn	22/62	265
	Beans, general	10/322	106
Philippines	Peanuts	80/100	98
	Peanut butter	145/149	213
	Peanut candies	47/60	38
	Corn	95/98	110
	Corn products	22/32	32

Source: Campbell and Stoloff (1974).

aflatoxin B_1 contamination tend to have a high incidence of primary liver cancer. In Swaziland, liver cancer has been a serious problem particularly in males, and it was clearly demonstrated that the incidence of liver cancer increased with the amount of aflatoxin consumed. The Inhambane district of Mozambique has the highest known incidence of hepatoma (liver cancer) in the world (Van Rensburg *et al.* 1974). The mean aflatoxin B_1 intake is relatively high, averaging 15.6 micrograms per adult per day. Studies in Southeast Asia, India, Taiwan, Kenya, and the Philippines (Campbell and Stoloff 1974) have also associated liver cancer and liver cirrhosis with consumption of aflatoxin B_1. A condition known as Reye's Syndrome has been recognized as a possible cause of infant mortality. In Thailand, 129 apparent cases of Reye's Syndrome were noted in 1969 and 80% of those hospitalized died. Aflatoxin B_1 was found in 22 of 23 of the children. Since that time, a number of other cases have implicated aflatoxin B_1 as a possible causal agent (Harwig *et al.* 1975). People the world over have consumed and are consuming aflatoxins in their food.

An excellent discussion of the health risk assessment now underway in the Food and Drug Administration and other epidemiological information can be found in the CAST report (CAST 1979). To quote a few lines, "To date, evidence is lacking that contamination of foods (peanuts, corn) with aflatoxin represents a liver cancer hazard of significance in either the Southeast or the U.S.A. as a whole, although there is evidence that it has been harmful to humans in other countries. Nonetheless, aflatoxin is present continuously in the U.S. food supply and under some conditions its concentration is high enough in peanuts and corn to be hazardous to humans and livestock. Continuous caution is needed. Significant protection to the U.S. human population against an excess of aflatoxin in a batch of a given food from a given source is provided by the access of all segments of our population to a number of food products from a variety of sources. Thus, any intake by an individual of aflatoxin from one food source would be greatly diluted by the variety of other foods taken in at the same meal and in the same day."

ECONOMICS OF AFLATOXIN CONTAMINATION

Economic losses from aflatoxin contamination in peanuts, corn, and cottonseed are difficult to assess because of insufficient data. The CAST report (CAST 1979) indicated a loss of $20 million in the value of peanuts rejected for human consumption, but it was not possible to determine the amount recovered when the peanuts were sold for oil or salvage. Losses to Georgia growers, shellers, processors, and the taxpayer from aflatoxin contamination over a 7-year period were estimated by one authority at

$10–12 million. Losses from the aflatoxin epidemic in corn in the Southeast in 1977 were estimated at $32 million for North Carolina. Losses in Georgia were probably in the $28 million range in 1977 and about $20 million in 1978. Losses due to decreases in feed efficiency and weight gains of animals cannot be estimated. Losses from aflatoxin in cottonseed in Arizona in 1978 were estimated at $9 million from the drop in price for their cottonseed as compared to that for the Southeast (CAST 1979).

CONTROL

Contamination of agricultural commodities by fungi and mycotoxins was once considered a post harvest problem, and as such, focused on the control of environmental conditions during handling and storage. Although aflatoxin can develop in storage, preharvest field contamination may be unavoidable in peanuts, corn, cottonseed, and tree nuts, especially under stress conditions. With cotton, aflatoxin contamination is primarily a field problem confined mainly to Arizona and southern California. As with all field problems, prevention of contamination of the crop by fungus and/or toxin is the cheapest and most effective method of control. Similarly, the problem areas boil down to (a) infection and toxin production before harvest, (b) infection during harvest and toxin production prior to adequate drying, and (c) environmental control during storage and handling.

Management Practices

Many production practices, with slight modification based on knowledge of the fungus, can contribute extensively to the prevention of contamination. Control of insects, which may vector or transmit the spores of *A. flavus*, serves to reduce, but does not eliminate, injury and toxin contamination in peanuts, corn, and cottonseed production. Harvesting at maturity is important, particularly in peanuts, for maximum yield as well as for reducing susceptibility to *A. flavus* associated with overmaturity. Appropriate care in harvesting and transporting are essential to minimize mechanical damage to seed. Cultural practices that reduce stress such as weed control, density of plantings, and adequate fertilization are helpful (Lillehoj and Zuber 1975; Zuber and Lillehoj 1979). Proper utilization of irrigation to alleviate stress of drought is important. Prompt drying to a safe storage moisture content is recommended. Proper storage aeration will prevent hot-spots. Elimination of the blending of fungus-contaminated seed with high quality seed is important. The selection of regionally and locally adapted hybrids in corn is suggested because nonadapted lines are not likely to endure stress as well as adapted ones. Skip-row plantings and chemically-induced defoliation of the lowermost part of cotton plants to reduce moisture accumulation and improve aeration tend to reduce infection of cotton by *A. flavus* (Ashworth *et al.* 1969A).

Genetic Approaches

The development of varieties that resist invasion of *A. flavus* or inhibit aflatoxin synthesis is being investigated for both peanut and corn. Laboratory and field studies have shown varietal differences in corn and peanut but progress appears to be slow (Zuber *et al.* 1978; Bartz *et al.* 1978). However, evaluation and selection will probably be more difficult for plant resistance to infection by *A. flavus* (a saprophyte) and aflatoxin production than it has been for resistance to a disease-producing pathogen (Widstrom *et al.* 1978).

Antifungus Agents

The use of antifungus agents to control fungus invasion and toxin production is promising, especially with the large-scale applications of propionic and other organic acids being utilized to preserve high-moisture corn without reducing its value as an animal feed. However, they do not inactivate or alter mycotoxins that have been formed before treatment. Both ammonia and propionic acid (1%) significantly reduce mold growth and subsequent formation of aflatoxin and ochratoxin (another mycotoxin) in stored corn (CAST 1979). The use of intermittent applications of small amounts of gaseous ammonia in air permitted ambient temperature drying of high-moisture corn and preservation for 6 months with no sign of physical or microbial deterioration (Nofsinger *et al.* 1977).

Diversion

Diversion of contaminated seeds may prevent pollution of high-quality material. Methods for rapid detection of *A. flavus* mold in damaged peanut kernels separated during grading have allowed the peanut industry to divert contaminated lots of farmers' stock peanuts. Bright greenish-yellow fluorescence can often be observed when cottonseed and corn contaminated by *A. flavus* are examined by ultraviolet (black light) illumination. BGY fluorescence is not a specific test for aflatoxin; a positive test requires confirmation by chemical analysis.

Detoxification

In the absence of effective prevention techniques for aflatoxin contamination of peanuts, corn, and cottonseed, techniques have been developed for the detoxification of aflatoxin-contaminated commodities.

Physical Separation.—Aflatoxin in lots of contaminated peanuts is usually confined to a relatively small number of kernels, providing an opportunity for electronic sorting to reduce the aflatoxin content effectively and economically by mechanical removal of the few infected seeds (Goldblatt 1970). Physical separation methods have not been found effective for corn, except by dry milling. The aflatoxin content is lowest in the grits fraction and does not exceed 10% of the level present before dry milling (Brekke *et al.* 1975). Aflatoxin content is highest in the germ, hull, and degermer fines that go into feed. Wet milling yields starch that contains about 1% of the aflatoxin originally present, while the feed products contain more than 97% of the aflatoxin (Bennett and Anderson 1978). Ground-recovered cottonseed contains higher levels of aflatoxin than does spindle-picked seed. Segregation of the highly contaminated seed will be expensive, but offers a major means of reducing the overall levels in a given year (CAST 1979).

Extraction.—Current processing of oilseeds releases into the oil a small portion of the aflatoxin originally present in the seed. Most of the residual aflatoxin in the oil accumulates in the soap-stock obtained when the crude oil is refined with alkali, a process now used universally for edible oil production in the United States. The aflatoxin is altered chemically during refining (Goldblatt 1971). Solvents effective for extracting aflatoxins include 95% ethanol, 90% aqueous acetone, 80% isopropyl alcohol, hexane-ethanol, and hexane-methanol. These solvent systems remove essentially all of the aflatoxin from oilseed meal with little likelihood of forming toxic by-products and without appreciably reducing the protein content or nutritional quality of the meal. These methods are cumbersome, expensive, and not totally satisfactory. Solvent extraction of aflatoxin from oilseed meals has recently been reviewed (Rayner *et al.* 1977).

Physical Inactivation.—Although aflatoxins are stable up to their melting points *ca.* 268°C, partial degradation does occur when contaminated products are heated. Up to 80% of the aflatoxin is destroyed by heating moist cottonseed meal at 100°C for 2 hr (CAST 1979). Cooking, even at high moisture content, does not reduce the aflatoxin content of cottonseed or peanut meals to levels considered acceptable in the United States. Prolonged heating may adversely affect the quality of the protein. Roasting artificially contaminated peanuts under conditions simulating commercial oil- and dry-roasting techniques resulted in a reduction of 45–83% in aflatoxin content. Similar results have been obtained with pickout peanuts on a pilot plant scale under conditions corresponding to those of plant processing for preparation of peanut butter (Goldblatt and Dollear 1977). Reductions of 50–80% in aflatoxin content of artificially contaminated pecans have been obtained with pecan meals roasted under similar conditions. The level of aflatoxin in contaminated corn was reduced by 40–48% when corn with an aflatoxin content of 133–877 ppb was roasted in an electric cooker at 145°C and by 58–66% at 165°C (Conway *et al.* 1978). An 81% reduction in aflatoxin was achieved in a gas-fired roaster at 150°C with corn containing 270 ppb of aflatoxin. All roasted products were dark colored.

Chemical Inactivation.—Chemical inactivation affords a promising means of increasing the safety and availability of feeds (CAST 1979). Of more than 60 chemicals tested for inactivating aflatoxin in peanut and cottonseed meals, ammonia, methylamine, sodium hydroxide, and formaldehyde were effective without leaving deleterious residues or affecting nutritional value. A combination of ammonia and heat treatment has reduced the aflatoxin content of corn from 270 to 28 ppb by adding diluted aqueous ammonia to give 20% moisture and 0.5% NH_3 on a dry basis, holding the corn for 3 hr, and passing it through a gas-fired roaster at 145°C. Repeating the treatment reduced the aflatoxin from 28 to 3 ppb for a total decrease of 99% (Conway *et al.* 1978).

Treatment with ammonia appears to be the most promising means for inactivating aflatoxin in oilseed meals and corn. The aflatoxin content of cottonseed meal has been reduced from 500 ppb to less than 5 ppb in ton lots treated with ammonia at 48 psi for 30 min at 118°C. This meal was fed to rats as 20% of the diet in a 2-year feeding test, which indicated that ammoniation effectively detoxified the meal. Recently, the aflatoxin content of cottonseed meal has been reduced from 425 ppb to less than 1 ppb by treatment with 4% NH_3 at a moisture level of 10%, a peak temperature of 82°C, and a pressure of 30 psi for 30 min (Koltun *et al.* 1979). Aflatoxin in peanut meal was reduced to nondetectable levels by ammoniation for 30 min under 30 psi at 65°C.

Aflatoxin-contaminated cottonseed in Arizona was treated with ammonium hydroxide at 1½% and water at 12% of the dry matter content and was bagged in polyethylene in direct sunlight (Lough *et al.* 1979). Levels of aflatoxin were reduced from 1915 ppb to 78 ppb and 53 ppb in 6 and 21 days, respectively, at ambient temperatures. Dairy cattle fed cottonseed similarly treated with ammonia on a large-scale produced milk containing aflatoxin M_1 at less than 0.2 ppb. Approximately 6,000 tons of cottonseed were custom-treated at a charge of $15–20 per ton over the period March–May, 1979. Cottonseed sealed in an ammonia atmosphere did not heat or mold, nor was palatability affected when treated seed was exposed to air 24–48 hr before feeding.

Other researchers have ammoniated corn (1.5% ammonia, dry matter basis) for 12 days in a heated chamber at 49°C and reduced the corn's aflatoxin content from 180 ppb to less than 1 ppb. The carcinogenicity of the contaminated corn was reduced to a level not significantly different from that of the control diet. The nutritive value of the ammoniated corn for trout was equal to or perhaps slightly superior to that of untreated corn samples. Bagley (1979) used a large-scale experimental ammoniation procedure for detoxifying corn and reduced the aflatoxin level from 750 ppb to less than 5 ppb. Feeding trials and toxicological studies under FDA protocols have not been completed, but the corn has been fed to swine, poultry, and cattle, and no problems have been observed.

Management Practices.—Although aflatoxin probably cannot always be eliminated completely from corn, peanuts, cottonseed, and some tree nuts, good management from planting through harvest, storage, processing, transportation, and ultimate consumption can reduce aflatoxin contamination significantly. Many industry groups have issued codes and rules for guidance of growers, warehousemen, elevator operators, and processors. The U.S. peanut industry has developed and disseminated a guide entitled "Voluntary Code of Good Practices" for purchasing, handling, storing, and processing peanuts and peanut products and has promoted quality-control seminars (CAST 1979). Pecan, almond, and walnut shellers and dry millers of corn now have similar programs. An important feature of all codes is the emphasis placed on analysis for aflatoxin content at appropriate control points. The measures taken by the peanut industry could provide an excellent model for other commodity groups.

Education of food consumers, wholesalers, and retailers is essential if they are to realize the risks associated with eating and/or selling moldy food products. Processed foods, meat products, baked goods, and other prepared foods can be readily contaminated by *A. flavus* and other fungi, if they are not refrigerated or stored at low humidity. Leftover foods prepared in the home are always susceptible to mold invasion unless promptly utilized, refrigerated, frozen, or otherwise maintained in a mold-free environment.

SUMMARY

Factors influencing the growth of *A. flavus* are temperature, time, and moisture in or relative humidity around the peanut, corn, and cottonseed. Other factors contributing to preharvest invasion by the fungus and subsequent aflatoxin formation in the field are damage (insect injury) and environmental stresses such as drought, stand density, weeds, and low fertilization. At harvest time, it is essential to minimize mechanical damage to the seed and accomplish rapid drying to a safe moisture content for storage to prevent further invasion of seed by *A. flavus*. Methods for prevention and reduction of aflatoxin contamination during crop production are summarized. Chemical inactivation with ammonia was noted as the most promising method for detoxifying aflatoxin-contaminated seed of all three crops. The biological effects of aflatoxin B_1 on domesticated and experimental animals are described and correlations of epidemiological data of aflatoxin in human food and the occurrence of primary liver cancer in man in eight or ten countries is presented. As a result of aggressive research programs by universities, USDA, FDA, and industry, the aflatoxin problem in peanuts, corn, cottonseed and their products is being managed successfully by the three industries.

BIBLIOGRAPHY

ANDERSON, H.W., NEHRING, E.W., and WICHSER, W.R. 1975. Aflatoxin contamination of corn in the field. J. Agric. Food Chem. *23*, 775–782.

ASHWORTH, L.J., McMEANS, J.L., and BROWN, C.M. 1969A. Infection of cotton by *Aspergillus flavus*: Epidemiology of the disease. J. Stored Prod. Res. *5*, 193–202.

ASHWORTH, JR., L.J., McMEANS, J.L., and BROWN, C.M. 1969B. Infection of cotton by *Aspergillus flavus*: Time of infection and the influence of fiber moisture. Phytopathology *59*, 383–385.

ASHWORTH, L.J., McMEANS, J.L., and BROWN, C.M. 1969C. Infection of cotton by *Aspergillus flavus*: The influences of temperature and aeration. Phytopathology *59*, 669–673.

ASHWORTH, L.J., JR., McMEANS, J.L., HOUSTON, B.R., WHITTEN, M.E., and BROWN, C.M. 1971A. Mycoflora, aflatoxins and free fatty acids in California cottonseed during 1967–1968. J. Am. Oil Chem. Soc. *48*, 129–133.

ASHWORTH, L.J., JR., RICE, R.E., McMEANS, J.L., and BROWN, C.M. 1971B. The relationship of insects to infection of cotton bolls by *Aspergillus flavus*. Phytopathology *61*, 488–493.

AUSTWICK, P.K.C. and AYERST, G. 1963. Toxic products in groundnuts. Groundnut microflora and toxicity. Chem. Ind. (London) *2*, 55–61.

BAGLEY, E.B. 1979. Decontamination of corn containing aflatoxin by treatment with ammonia. J. Am. Oil Chem. Soc. *56*, 808–811.

BAMPTON, S.S. 1963. Growth of *Aspergillus flavus* and production of aflatoxin in groundnuts. I. Trop. Sci. *5*, 74–81.

BARTZ, J.A., NORDEN, A.J., LaPRADE, J.C., and DeMUYNK, T.J. 1978. Seed tolerance in peanuts (*Arachis hypogaea* L.) to members of the *Aspergillus flavus* group of fungi. Peanut Sci. *5*, 53–56.

BENNETT, G.A. and ANDERSON, R.A. 1978. Distribution of aflatoxin and/or zearalenone in wet-milled corn products: A review. J. Agric. Food Chem. *26*, 1055–1060.

BREKKE, O.L., PEPLINSKI, A.J., NELSON, G.E.N., and GRIFFIN, JR., E.L. 1975. Pilot-plant dry milling of corn containing aflatoxin. Cereal Chem. *52*, 205–211.

BULLERMAN, L.B. 1979. Significance of mycotoxins to food safety and human health. J. Food Prot. *42*, 65–86.

BURRELL, N.J., GRUNDEY, J.K., and HARKNESS, C. 1964. Growth of *Aspergillus flavus* and production of aflatoxin in groundnuts. V. Trop. Sci. *6*, 74–90.

CAMPBELL, T.C. and STOLOFF, L. 1974. Implications of mycotoxins for human health. J. Agric. Food Chem. *22*, 1006–1015.

CAST. 1979. Aflatoxins and other mycotoxins: An agricultural perspective. Council for Agricultural Science and Technology Report No. 80. Ames, Iowa.

CONWAY, H.F., ANDERSON, R.A., and BAGLEY, E.B. 1978. Detoxification of aflatoxin-contaminated corn by roasting. Cereal Chem. *55*, 115–117.

DICKENS, J.W. and PATTEE, H.E. 1966. The effects of time, temperature, and moisture on aflatoxin production in peanuts inoculated with a toxic strain of *Aspergillus flavus*. Trop. Sci. *8*, 11–22.

DIENER, U.L. 1960. The mycoflora of peanuts in storage. Phytopathology *50*, 220–223.

DIENER, U.L. 1973. Deterioration of peanut quality caused by fungi. *In* Peanuts—Culture and Uses. Am. Peanut Res. Educ. Assoc., Stillwater, Ok.

DIENER, U.L. and DAVIS, N.D. 1967. Limiting temperature and relative humidity for growth and production of aflatoxin and free fatty acids by *Aspergillus flavus* in sterile peanuts. J. Am. Oil Chem. Soc. *44*, 259–263.

DIENER, U.L. and DAVIS, N.D. 1968. Effect of environment on aflatoxin production in freshly dug peanuts. Trop. Sci. *10*, 22–28.

DIENER, U.L. and DAVIS, N.D. 1969. Aflatoxin formation by *Aspergillus flavus*. *In* Aflatoxin. L.A. Goldblatt (Editor). Academic Press, New York.

DIENER, U.L. and DAVIS, N.D. 1970. Limiting temperature and relative humidity for aflatoxin production by *Aspergillus flavus* in stored peanuts. J. Am. Oil Chem. Soc. *47*, 347–351.

DIENER, U.L. and DAVIS, N.D. 1976. Nature and importance of mycotoxins in grains. *In* Proc. Third International Biodegradation Symp. J.M. Sharpley and A.M. Kaplan (Editors). Applied Science Publishers Ltd., London.

DIENER, U.L., JACKSON, C.R., COOPER, W.E., STIPES, R.J., and DAVIS, N.D. 1965. Invasion of peanut pods in the soil by *Aspergillus flavus*. Plant Dis. Rep. *49*, 931–935.

FENNELL, D.I., KWOLEK, W.F., LILLEHOJ, E.B., ADAMS, G.L., BOTHAST, R.J., ZUBER, M.S., CALVERT, O.H., GUTHRIE, W.D., BOCKHOLT, A.J., MANWILLER, A., and JELLUM, M.D. 1977. *Aspergillus flavus* presence in silks and insects from developing and mature corn ears. Cereal Chem. *54*, 770–778.

FENNELL, D.I., LILLEHOJ, E.B., and KWOLEK, W.F. 1975. *Aspergillus flavus* and other fungi associated with insect-damaged field corn. Cereal Chem. *52*, 314–321.

FENNELL, D.I., LILLEHOJ, E.B., KWOLEK, W.F., GUTHRIE, W.D., SHEELEY, R., SPARKS, A.N., WIDSTROM, N.W., and ADAMS, G.L. 1978. Insect larval activity on developing corn ears and subsequent aflatoxin contamination of seed. J. Econ. Entomol. *71*, 624–628.

GOLDBLATT, L.A. 1970. Chemistry and control of aflatoxin. Pure Appl. Chem. *21*, 331–353.

GOLDBLATT, L.A. 1971. Control and removal of aflatoxin. J. Am. Oil Chem. Soc. *48*, 605–610.

GOLDBLATT, L.A. and DOLLEAR, F.G. 1977. Detoxification of contaminated crops. *In* Mycotoxins in Human and Animal Health. J.V. Rodricks, C.W. Hesseltine, and M.A. Mehlman (Editors). Pathotox Publishers, Park Forest South, Ill.

HAMSA, T.A.P. and AYRES, J.C. 1977. Factors affecting aflatoxin contamination of cottonseed. I. Contamination of cottonseed with *Aspergillus flavus* at harvest and during storage. J. Am. Oil Chem. Soc. *54*, 219–224.

HARWIG, J., PRZYBYLSKI, W., and MOODIE, C.A. 1975. A link between Reye's syndrome and aflatoxins? Can. Med. Assoc. J. *113*, 281.

HESSELTINE, C.W., SHOTWELL, O.L., KWOLEK, W.F., LILLEHOJ, E.B., JACKSON, W.K., and BOTHAST, R.J. 1976. Aflatoxin occurrence in 1973 corn at harvest. II. Mycological studies. Mycologia *68*, 341–353.

JACKSON, C.R. 1967. Some effects of harvesting methods and drying conditions on development of aflatoxins in peanut. Phytopathology *57*, 1270–1271.

JOFFE, A.Z. and BORUT, S.Y. 1966. Soil and kernel mycoflora of groundnut fields in Israel. Mycologia *58*, 629–640.

KOLTUN, S.P., RAYNER, E.T., WADSWORTH, J.I., and GARDNER, H.K. 1979. Inactivation of aflatoxin in cottonseed by ammoniation: I. Reaction studies. J. Am. Oil Chem. Soc. *56*, 803–807.

LANDERS, K.E., DAVIS, N.D., and DIENER, U.L. 1967. Influence of atmospheric gases on aflatoxin production by *Aspergillus flavus* in peanuts. Phytopathology *57*, 1086–1090.

LaPRADE, J.C. and MANWILLER, A. 1976. Aflatoxin production and fungal growth on single cross corn hybrids inoculated with *Aspergillus flavus*. Phytopathology *66*, 675–677.

LILLEHOJ, E.B., FENNELL, D.I., and KWOLEK, W.F. 1976A. *Aspergillus flavus* and aflatoxin in Iowa corn before harvest. Science *193*, 495–496.

LILLEHOJ, E.B., FENNELL, D.I., and KWOLEK, W.F. 1977. Aflatoxin and *Aspergillus flavus* occurrence in 1975 corn at harvest from a limited region of Iowa. Cereal Chem. *54*, 366–372.

LILLEHOJ, E.B., FENNELL, D.I., KWOLEK, W.F., ADAMS, G.L., ZUBER, M.S., HORNER, E.S., WIDSTROM, N.W., WARREN, H., GUTHRIE, W.D.,

FINDLEY, W.R., MANWILLER, A., JOSEPHSON, L.M., and BOCKHOLT, A.J. 1978A. Aflatoxin contamination of corn before harvest: *Aspergillus flavus* association with insects collected from developing ears. Crop Sci. *18*, 921–924.

LILLEHOJ, E.B. and HESSELTINE, C.W. 1977. Aflatoxin control during plant growth and harvest of corn. *In* Mycotoxins in Human and Animal Health. J.V. Rodricks, C.W. Hesseltine, and M.A. Mehlman (Editors). Pathotox Publishers, Park Forest South, Ill.

LILLEHOJ, E.B., KWOLEK, W.F., FENNELL, D.I., and MILBURN, M.S. 1975A. Aflatoxin incidence and association with bright greenish-yellow fluorescence and insect damage in a limited survey of freshly harvested high-moisture corn. Cereal Chem. *52*, 403–412.

LILLEHOJ, E.B., KWOLEK, W.F., MANWILLER, A., DuRANT, J.A., LaPRADE, J.C., HORNER, E.S., REID, J., and ZUBER, M.S. 1976B. Aflatoxin production in several corn hybrids grown in South Carolina and Florida. Crop Sci. *16*, 483–485.

LILLEHOJ, E.B., KWOLEK, W.F., PETERSON, R.E., SHOTWELL, O.L., and HESSELTINE, C.W. 1976C. Aflatoxin contamination, fluorescence, and insect damage in corn infected with *Aspergillus flavus* before harvest. Cereal Chem. *53*, 505–512.

LILLEHOJ, E.B., KWOLEK, W.F., SHANNON, G.M., SHOTWELL, O.L., and HESSELTINE, C.W. 1975B. Aflatoxin occurrence in 1973 corn at harvest. I. A limited survey in the southeastern U.S. Cereal Chem. *52*, 603–611.

LILLEHOJ, E.B., KWOLEK, W.F., VANDEGRAFT, E.E., ZUBER, M.S., CALVERT, O.H., WIDSTROM, N., FUTRELL, M.C., and BOCKHOLT, A.J. 1975C. Aflatoxin production in *Aspergillus flavus* inoculated ears of corn grown at diverse locations. Crop Sci. *15*, 267–270.

LILLEHOJ, E.B., KWOLEK, W.F., ZUBER, M.S., CALVERT, O.H., HORNER, E.S., WIDSTROM, N.W., GUTHRIE, W.D., SCOTT, G.E., THOMPSON, D.L., FINDLEY, W.R., and BOCKHOLT, A.J. 1978B. Aflatoxin contamination of field corn: Evaluation of regional test plots for early detection. Cereal Chem. *55*, 1007–1013.

LILLEHOJ, E.B. and ZUBER, M.S. 1975. Aflatoxin problem in corn and possible solutions: Proc. 30th Ann. Corn Sorghum Res. Conf., p. 230–250.

LOUGH, O.G., GINGG, C., and BILLOTTI, M. 1979. Detoxifying aflatoxin contaminated cottonseed. 74th Ann. Mtg. Am. Dairy Sci. Assoc., Logan, Utah, June 24–27.

MAYNE, R.Y., HARPER, G.A., FRANZ, JR., A.O., LEE, L.S., and GOLDBLATT, L.A. 1969. Retardation of the elaboration of aflatoxin in cottonseed by impermeability of the seed coat. Crop Sci. *9*, 147–150.

McDONALD, D. 1969. *Aspergillus flavus* on groundnut (*Arachis hypogaea* L.) and its control in Nigeria. J. Stored Prod. Res. *5*, 275–280.

McDONALD, D. and A'BROOK, J. 1963. Growth of *Aspergillus flavus* and production of aflatoxin in groundnuts. III. Trop. Sci. *5*, 208–214.

McDONALD, D. and HARKNESS, C. 1964. Growth of *Aspergillus flavus* and production of aflatoxin in groundnuts. IV. Trop. Sci. *6*, 12–27.

McDONALD, D. and HARKNESS, C. 1965. Growth of *Aspergillus flavus* and production of aflatoxin in groundnuts. Part VIII. Trop. Sci. *7*, 122–137.

McDONALD, D. and HARKNESS, C. 1967. Aflatoxin in the groundnut crop at harvest in northern Nigeria. Trop. Sci. *9*, 148–161.

McDONALD, D., HARKNESS, C., and STONEBRIDGE, W.C. 1964. Growth of *Aspergillus flavus* and production of aflatoxin in groundnuts. VI. Trop. Sci. *6*, 131–154.

McMILLIAN, W.W., WILSON, D.M., and WIDSTROM, N.W. 1978. Insect damage, *Aspergillus flavus* ear mold, and aflatoxin contamination in south Georgia corn fields in 1977. J. Environ. Qual. *7*, 564–566.

NOFSINGER, G.W., BOTHAST, R.J., LANCASTER, E.B., and BAGLEY, E.B. 1977. Ammonia-supplemented ambient temperature drying of high-moisture corn. Trans. ASAE. *20*, 1151–1154, 1159.

NORTON, D.C., MENON, S.K., and FLANGAS, A.L. 1956. Fungi associated with unblemished Spanish peanuts in Texas. Plant Dis. Rep. *40*, 374–376.

PAGE, J.M. 1964. The effect of plant orientation on the curing of windrowed peanuts. M.S. Thesis. North Carolina State University.

PETTIT, R.E., TABER, R.A., SCHROEDER, H.W., and HARRISON, A.L. 1971. Influence of fungicides and irrigation practice on aflatoxin in peanuts before digging. Appl. Microbiol. *22*, 629–634.

PORTER, D.M. and GARREN, K.H. 1970. Endocarpic microorganisms of two types of windrow-dried peanut fruit (*Arachis hypogaea* L.). Appl. Microbiol. *20*, 133–138.

PORTER, D.M. and WRIGHT, F.S. 1971. Proliferation of *Aspergillus flavus* in artificially infested windrow-dried peanut fruit in Virginia. Phytopathology *61*, 1194–1197.

RAMBO, G.W., TUITE, J., and CRANE, P. 1974. Preharvest inoculation and infection of dent corn ears with *Aspergillus flavus* and *A. parasiticus*. Phytopathology *64*, 797–800.

RAYNER, E.T., KOLTUN, S.P., and DOLLEAR, F.G. 1977. Solvent extraction of aflatoxins from contaminated agricultural products. J. Am. Oil Chem. Soc. *55*, 242A–244A.

RODRICKS, J.W. 1976. Mycotoxins and other fungal related food problems. Adv. Chem. Ser. 149. Am. Chem. Soc., Washington, D.C.

RODRICKS, J.V., HESSELTINE, C.W., and MEHLMAN, M.A. 1977. Mycotoxins in Human and Animal Health. Pathotox Publishers, Park Forest South, Ill.

RUSSELL, T.E., WATSON, T.F., and RYAN, G.F. 1976. Field accumulation of aflatoxin in cottonseed as influenced by irrigation termination dates and pink bollworm infestation. Appl. Environ. Microbiol. *31*, 711–713.

SANDERS, T.H., DAVIS, N.D., and DIENER, U.L. 1968. Effect of carbon dioxide, temperature, and relative humidity on production of aflatoxin in peanuts. J. Am. Oil Chem. Soc. *45*, 683–685.

SHANK, R.C. 1978. Mycotoxicoses of man: Dietary and epidemiological conditions. *In* Mycotoxic Fungi, Mycotoxins, Mycotoxicoses, Vol. 3. T.D. Wyllie and L.G. Morehouse (Editors). Marcel Dekker, New York.

SHOTWELL, O.L. 1977A. Aflatoxin in corn. J. Am. Oil Chem. Soc. *54*, 216A–224A.

SHOTWELL, O.L. 1977B. Mycotoxins—Corn-related problems. Cereal Foods World *22*, 524–527.

SHOTWELL, O.L., GOULDEN, M.L., LILLEHOJ, E.B., KWOLEK, W.F., and HESSELTINE, C.W. 1977. Aflatoxin occurrence in 1973 corn harvest. III. Aflatoxin distribution in contaminated, insect-damaged corn. Cereal Chem. *54*, 620–626.

SHOTWELL, O.L., HESSELTINE, C.W., BURMEISTER, H.R., KWOLEK, W.F., SHANNON, C.M., and HALL, H.H. 1969. Survey of cereal grains and soybeans for the presence of aflatoxin. II. Corn and soybeans. Cereal Chem. *46*, 454–463.

SHOTWELL, O.L., HESSELTINE, C.W., and GOULDEN, M.L. 1973. Incidence of aflatoxin in southern corn, 1969–1970. Cereal Sci. Today *18*, 192–195.

SHOTWELL, O.L., HESSELTINE, C.W., GOULDEN, M.L., and VANDEGRAFT, E.E. 1970. Survey of corn for aflatoxin, zearalenone, and ochratoxin. Cereal Chem. *47*, 700–707.

SHOTWELL, O.L., HESSELTINE, C.W., VANDEGRAFT, E.E., and GOULDEN, M.L. 1971. Survey of corn from different regions for aflatoxin, ochratoxin, and zearalenone. Cereal Sci. Today *16*, 226–270, 273.

STEPHENSON, L.W. and RUSSELL, T.E. 1974. The association of *Aspergillus flavus* with hemipterous and other insects infesting cotton bracts and foliage. Phytopathology *64*, 1502–1506.

STOTZKY, G. and GOOS, R.D. 1965. Effect of high CO_2 and low O_2 tensions on the soil microbiota. Can. J. Microbiol. *2*, 853–868.

TAUBENHAUS, J.J. 1920. A study of the black and yellow molds of ear corn. Texas Agric. Exp. Stn. Bull. 270.

URAGUCHI, K. and YAMAZAKI, M. 1978. Toxicology, Biochemistry, and Pathology of Mycotoxins. Halsted Press, New York.

VAN RENSBURG, S.J. 1977. Role of epidemiology in the elucidation of mycotoxin health risks. *In* Mycotoxins in Human and Animal Health. J.V. Rodricks, C.W. Hesseltine, and M.A. Mehlman (Editors). Pathotox Publishers, Park Forest South, Ill.

VAN RENSBURG, S.J., VAN DER WATT, J.J., PURCHASE, I.F.H., COUTINHO, L., and MARKHAM, R. 1974. Primary cancer rate and aflatoxin intake in high cancer area. S. Afr. Med. J. *48*, 2508a–2508d.

WATSON, S.A. and YAHL, K.R. 1971. Survey of aflatoxins in commercial supplies of corn and grain sorghum used for wet-milling. Cereal Sci. Today *16*, 153–155, 163.

WIDSTROM, N.W. 1979. The role of insects and other plant pests in aflatoxin contamination of corn, cotton, and peanuts—A review. J. Environ. Qual. *8*, 5–11.

WIDSTROM, N.W., LILLEHOJ, E.B., SPARKS, A.N., and KWOLEK, W.F. 1976. Corn earworm damage and aflatoxin B_1 on corn ears protected with insecticide. J. Econ. Entomol. *69*, 677–679.

WIDSTROM, N.W., SPARKS, A.N., LILLEHOJ, E.B., and KWOLEK, W.F. 1975. Aflatoxin production and lepidopteran insect injury on corn in Georgia. J. Econ. Entomol. *68*, 855–856.

WIDSTROM, N.W., WISEMAN, B.R., McMILLIAN, W.W., KWOLEK, W.F., LILLEHOJ, E.B., JELLUM, M.D., and MASSEY, J.H. 1978. Evaluation of commercial and experimental three-way corn hybrids for aflatoxin B_1 production potential. Agron. J. *70*, 986–988.

WILSON, B.J. 1978. Hazards of mycotoxins to public health. J. Food Prot. *41*, 375–384.

WILSON, D.M., McMILLIAN, W.W., and WIDSTROM, N.W. 1979. Field aflatoxin contamination of corn in South Georgia. J. Am. Oil Chem. Soc. *56*, 798–799.

WYLLIE, T.D. and MOREHOUSE, L.G. 1977. Mycotoxic Fungi, Mycotoxins, Mycotoxicoses, Vol. 1. Mycotoxic Fungi and Chemistry of Mycotoxins. Marcel Dekker, New York.

WYLLIE, T.D. and MOREHOUSE, L.G. 1978A. Mycotoxic Fungi, Mycotoxins, Mycotoxicoses, Vol. 2. Mycotoxicoses of Domestic and Laboratory Animals, Poultry, and Aquatic Invertebrates and Vertebrates. Marcel Dekker, New York.

WYLLIE, T.D. and MOREHOUSE, L.G. 1978B. Mycotoxic Fungi, Mycotoxins, Mycotoxicoses, Vol. 3. Mycotoxicoses of Man and Plants: Mycotoxin Control and Regulatory Aspects. Marcel Dekker, New York.

ZUBER, M.S., CALVERT, O.H., KWOLEK, W.F., LILLEHOJ, E.B., and KANG, M.S. 1978. Aflatoxin B_1 production in an eight-line diallel of *Zea mays* infected with *Aspergillus flavus*. Phytopathology *68*, 1346–1349.

ZUBER, M.S., CALVERT, O.H., LILLEHOJ, E.B., and KWOLEK, W.F. 1976. Preharvest development of aflatoxin B_1 in corn in the United States. Phytopathology *66*, 1120–1121.

ZUBER, M.S. and LILLEHOJ, E.B. 1979. Status of the aflatoxin problem in corn. J. Environ. Qual. *8*, 1–5.

9

Impact of Microorganisms and Their Toxins on Food Processing

E. M. Foster[1]

INTRODUCTION

It is generally known and widely accepted among knowledgeable people that microbiological contamination is the most important food associated health hazard in the United States. Yet, strangely enough we rarely learn about these dangers from the popular press. We hear a great deal about allegedly harmful food additives, about potentially toxic pesticide residues, and about all manner of incidental and accidental contaminants that *may* get into food and *may* cause harm. But for some reason the news media don't seem to be very interested in the agents that actually do make people sick.

This is not to say that microorganisms and their toxins have no impact on food processing. To the contrary, a major purpose of processing whether it be canning, cooking, freezing, drying, pickling, salting or refrigerating is to protect the consumer against food-borne disease. Achieving this goal often defines the nature of the process.

The impact of microorganisms and their toxins on food processing is recognized in several ways. First and foremost of these is an outbreak of disease—people get sick after they have eaten a particular food. When this happens we know that somebody has done something wrong. An outbreak of food-borne disease may signify spoiled or contaminated raw material, inadequate heating during preparation or processing, improper storage conditions, insufficient salt or other preservative, recontamina-

[1] Food Research Institute, University of Wisconsin, Madison.

tion after preparation, or any of a dozen other deviations from good manufacturing and food handling practice.

Microorganisms and their toxins also exert an impact on food processing through the actions of regulatory agencies. Whether the agency operates at a Federal, state or local level, its primary purpose is to protect the consumer from harmful food. In doing this each agency operates under a law or ordinance that provides a legal basis for its action.

As an example, the Food and Drug Administration enforces the Food, Drug and Cosmetic Act which says, in a nutshell, that it is illegal to sell adulterated food in interstate commerce. Food containing harmful microorganisms or their toxins generally is considered to be adulterated.

If such food is offered for sale the FDA may take any of several regulatory actions. It may demand that the food be recalled from the market; it may seize the food; it may petition the courts for an injunction to close the plant where the food was produced; and it may bring criminal charges against the company, including its president for violating the Food, Drug and Cosmetic Act. In some cases the FDA may even require the manufacturer to reveal details of his process for evaluation by the agency; and it may require that certain key employees such as retort operators and quality control managers receive special training in schools having approved curricula.

As another example of regulatory activity, we have long imposed formal legal microbiological standards on fluid milk and potable water supplies. Efforts now are being made to extend this approach to other foods. Only a few years ago the State of Oregon made it a crime to sell meat with a bacterial count in excess of a specific limit. This action has since been rescinded.

A third way that microorganisms and their toxins exert an impact on food processing is through the demands of various organizations for even more stringent regulation and control. One activist group, for example, petitioned the USDA to ban vacuum packaging and mechanical tenderization of meat on the grounds that these practices increase the danger of *Salmonella* contamination.

Another group has demanded that FDA reduce the amount of aflatoxin that the agency will permit in peanut products.

Still a third group sought to force the USDA to change the "inspected for wholesomeness" label on fresh poultry which, they said, implied that the product is safe. Petitioners based their objections on the high incidence of *Salmonella* contamination in poultry on the market.

Although none of these demands has been met, they did serve to focus public attention on problems relating to microorganisms and their toxins in foods.

One large consumer organization was especially effective in its campaign for bacterial limits in meats and meat products. The group performed bacteriological analyses on meats offered for sale in one metropolitan area. Publication of the results spawned a flood of "exposés" by newspapers and TV stations in several large American cities. There is little doubt that these campaigns have had an impact on the bacterial content of meat sold at retail and in fast food outlets.

What is the result of the foregoing actions? To the consumer the main effect is higher food costs. Better ingredients, better equipment, better storage facilities and better quality control measures increase the manufacturer's costs. These are passed on to the consumer in higher prices. By the same token more regulatory activity means increased cost to the government. This is passed on to the consumer in the form of higher taxes. The net result is a more costly food supply. One can hope that it is also safer.

To the food processor the impact of microorganisms and their toxins can range from devastation to a minor nuisance. Unfavorable publicity following a disease outbreak attributed to a company's product can seriously harm the product, and may even ruin the company. The impact is not necessarily limited to the individual manufacturer; it can involve an entire industry. For example, sales of canned tuna in 1963 were $50,000,000 less than they were the year before. This decline followed a widely publicized incident of botulism in March, 1963, in Detroit, Michigan. Consumption of corned beef in the United Kingdom declined sharply several years ago following an outbreak of typhoid fever attributed to canned corned beef from South America. The incident involved over 400 typhoid victims in Aberdeen, Scotland.

The cost can be high even without unfavorable publicity or an outbreak of disease. Several confectioners suffered heavy losses in the late 1960s when FDA found *Salmonella* in their products and required widespread recalls. Some companies actually went broke.

Though it may be substantial, the cost of recalling and destroying an adulterated product is not the end of the expense. Accidents involving microorganisms and their toxins in processed foods almost invariably bring stricter regulatory requirements, which usually mean more reliable process controls, more and better quality test procedures, better trained operating personnel, and the like. There is every reason to believe that a botulinum poisoning incident in 1971 attributed to canned vichyssoise soup was responsible for the adoption of FDA's low acid canned food regulations a few years ago.

With that background let us now consider the impact of individual microorganisms and their toxins on food processing.

CLOSTRIDIUM BOTULINUM

By far the deadliest of the food-borne disease agents is *Clostridium botulinum*. This organism has been a scourge of man's food supply since it was first associated with sausage poisoning over two centuries ago. It made its presence known in canned food before the turn of the century, and by World War I it was recognized as a serious threat to the American canning industry.

Using rare foresight and good sense, that industry organized the required scientific capability and developed heating procedures that would assure the destruction of botulinum spores. When applied in canning the process would yield a product that was safe to eat. This process is the so-called "botulinum cook."

Since the mid-1920s when the new, scientifically-based heat processes were first widely adopted, the American canning industry has achieved a remarkable safety record. During that half century there have been only five known incidents of botulism in which people died from eating food canned commercially in the United States. Remarkably, there were only seven fatalities in the five incidents. During that same period the industry produced an estimated one thousand billion containers of food and beverages for the American people.

Yet in spite of the relative rarity of botulinum poisoning from commercially canned foods in this country we can never let our guard down. We have to do things right *every time*. There is no margin for error. Failure to follow known effective procedures is an open invitation to disaster.

Recognition of this fact has led the industry and the FDA to adopt the low acid canned food and the acidified food regulations as a way to reduce the likelihood of another disastrous accident. I need not dwell on the impact of these regulations on individual processors both here and abroad.

Another group of food processors who have suffered from *C. botulinum* is the Great Lakes fish smokers. Prior to 1960 this was essentially a cottage industry wherein fishermen who lived on or near one of the Great Lakes smoked part of their catch and sold the product locally. Motorists driving along Lake Michigan's shore were never far from a sign, often hand lettered, offering smoked fish ahead at a roadside tavern. This delectable product was sold within hours, or at most a few days, after processing.

Then someone discovered that smoked chubs and herring kept better if they were vacuum packaged. The longer keeping time allowed wider distribution and many new markets opened up. Thus a new industry was born.

It thrived until the early 1960s, when two people died in Minneapolis after eating vacuum packed smoked herring from Lake Superior. While the authorities were still puzzling over that outbreak along came another centered in Tennessee with 17 cases and five deaths. This incident was attributed to smoked chubs from Lake Michigan.

It is not difficult to predict the impact of these experiences on the Great Lakes smoked fish industry. Most of the processors went out of business.

I should not like to leave this subject with the impression that vacuum packaging was the factor that allowed *C. botulinum* to grow in the smoked fish. Instead, vacuum packaging allowed wider distribution of the product, longer holding time, and gross temperature abuse, all of which provided opportunity for *C. botulinum* to grow and produce its deadly nerve poison. Given time and a suitable temperature, this organism will grow perfectly well in smoked fish whether vacuum packaged or not.

Aside from its importance to the smoked fish and canning industries, *C. botulinum* plays a unique role in the controversy over nitrite in cured meat, fish, and poultry. No thinking person can doubt that botulism is an ever present danger in these products. After all, the name *botulinum* is derived from the Latin word *botulus*, meaning sausage.

Banning nitrite from cured meats to reduce the risk of cancer clearly increases the risk of botulism. Thus, the prospect of cancer with nitrite vs. botulism without it has placed some of our regulatory officials on the horns of a very difficult dilemma.

Honey is another product that has suffered recently from association with *C. botulinum*. Less than four years ago a new disease called infant botulism was discovered in California. This ailment occurs only in very young babies, usually under six months of age. The causal organism actually grows and produces toxin in the baby's intestinal tract.

Astute investigators noticed that many of the early victims of infant botulism were fed honey water by their mothers. Surveys of honey by various investigators including Professor Hiroshi Sugiyama of the Food Research Institute showed that botulinum spores often can be isolated from raw or processed honey. This should come as no surprise in view of honey's origin.

Presently there is no practical way to eliminate the spores from honey. Consequently, one major processor advises mothers not to feed honey to infants under one year of age.

C. botulinum has had a major impact on the acceptance of radiation as a means of preserving food. Since its spores are among the most resistant of all microorganisms, *C. botulinum* has been used as the test agent in efforts to develop safe and practical methods of sterilizing foods with ionizing radiation. Although effective procedures have been devised they are still awaiting approval by the Food and Drug Administration.

CLOSTRIDIUM PERFRINGENS AND *BACILLUS CEREUS*

These sporeforming bacteria often are considered together. Both cause food poisoning if they multiply in a cooked product and then are consumed in large numbers. Up to now their importance has been limited to the food service industry, including institutional feeding. Their only impact on food processors thus far has been the establishment of purchase specifications which dictate the numbers of the organisms allowed in food ingredients.

STAPHYLOCOCCUS AUREUS

Some strains of *S. aureus* produce a potent enterotoxin that causes vomiting and diarrhea in man. For illness to occur the bacteria must grow and produce their toxin in the food before it is eaten. Once formed the toxin can survive most cooking and other heat treatments that foods receive.

Staphylococcal food poisoning usually is associated with errors in food service, but sometimes it causes problems with canned foods, fermented sausages, cheese and other dairy products.

S. aureus does not form spores and its vegetative cells are not unusually resistant to heat. Therefore, when staphylococcal enterotoxin appears in a canned food it is almost certain to reflect recontamination through a defective container. In 1979 extensive outbreaks of staphylococcal poisoning from canned corned beef and ox tongue occurred in several countries including the United Kingdom, France, Canada, and the United States. The outbreaks involved product canned in Brazil, Argentina, Australia, Malta, and Northern Europe. The full story has not yet emerged, but the information available to date reinforces the importance of using sound containers and proper canning procedures.

In view of its high heat resistance it is natural to wonder if pre-formed staphylococcal enterotoxin can survive the "botulinum cook" used in canning low acid foods. Extensive trials by the National Food Processors Association working with Professor Merlin Bergdoll of the Food Research Institute convinced the investigators that any pre-formed enterotoxin in a canned product will be totally inactivated by the heat process.

Even so, doubt was cast on this conclusion a few years ago when two people ate a can of lobster bisque from a commercial source and allegedly became ill with signs of staphylococcal food poisoning. FDA examined other cans from the same lot and reportedly obtained positive tests for enterotoxin in a few containers. Professor Bergdoll found evidence of a trace of enterotoxin in one of 30 cans that he examined. No viable staphylococci were present in the product.

These results leave us still wondering if staphylococcal enterotoxin is, in fact, totally inactivated during the canning process. An important factor, of course, is the amount of enterotoxin present before heating.

Several outbreaks of staphylococcal poisoning have been attributed to fermented sausages from commercial manufacturers in recent years. Appearance of enterotoxin in such a product clearly indicates failure to follow good manufacturing practice. Usually the fault lies in poor starter activity with insufficient acid development. When a toxic product is revealed in the market place by an outbreak of food poisoning the usual result is an extensive product recall with unfavorable publicity.

Cheddar, Colby and similar types of cheese have been responsible for several well known outbreaks of staphylococcal poisoning. This can happen if the starter culture fails to produce acid fast enough or in sufficient quantity. Inadequate pasteurization or recontamination with enterotoxigenic *S. aureus* will exacerbate the problem.

Staphylococcal poisoning also has been attributed to dried milk, dried whey and whipped butter from commercial sources. In every instance toxin development resulted from lapses in good manufacturing practice.

There can be no excuse for manufacturing a food product that contains staphylococcal enterotoxin. A food processor who does this is guilty of sloppy, careless and uncontrolled manufacturing practice.

SALMONELLA

Although *Salmonella* has been known as an animal pathogen for almost 100 years, it was first recognized as a problem of the food processor during the Second World War. Recognition came when people in the United Kingdom were infected by *Salmonella* serotypes that were previously unknown in Great Britain. The offending organisms were traced to dried eggs imported from North America.

Salmonella contamination continued to be a problem with egg products after World War II until finally the regulatory authorities mandated pasteurization of liquid egg before drying or freezing. The prescribed heat treatments are effective and if accomplished properly they will rid liquid egg of living *Salmonella* organisms.

During the 20 years following World War II we had a few sporadic outbreaks of salmonellosis in this country traced to processed foods, but nobody got very concerned. Most of the incidents were attributed to products containing eggs and a few to dried yeast.

Then in the mid-1960s there were several disturbing outbreaks of salmonellosis in North America and Europe involving dry food ingredients—coconut, yeast, cottonseed protein, infant cereal, thyroid extract and carmine dye. Events came to a head when brilliant detective work by the Center for Disease Control and other public health experts traced an outbreak of *Salmonella New Brunswick* infection to instant nonfat dry milk.

This incident prompted FDA in 1966 to undertake extensive surveys of processed foods for *Salmonella* contamination. As everyone knows, they found plenty. The organisms were detected in dried eggs, dried milk, cocoa, gelatin, yeast, spices, coconut, pasta, and foods containing these ingredients.

Large and costly product recalls resulted from these endeavors. Many of the recalls involved food manufacturers who had inadvertently purchased contaminated ingredients from their suppliers. The impact was obvious—manufacturers started requiring "*Salmonella*-free" guarantees from their suppliers. The suppliers had to undertake extensive testing and quality assurance programs of their own, and the manufacturers rechecked the ingredients before they used them.

Thus *Salmonella* spp. have had enormous impact on sanitation and quality control throughout the dried food industry. Some wag has said that FDA's campaign against *Salmonella* in processed foods has not done much to improve the public's health, but it has done wonders for sanitation in food processing plants.

This is not the place to consider ways to control *Salmonella* in dried food operations, but the frequent appearance of contamination has stimulated interest in ways to kill the organisms in contaminated foods and food ingredients. Ethylene oxide gas has been employed for this purpose but its use is limited to spices and seasonings. Propylene oxide also is allowed for germicidal treatment of cocoa, starch, gums, spices and all nuts except peanuts. Low intensity ionizing radiation is effective but its use has not been approved for food. This leaves heat as the only universal agent, and it is not very effective with dry products. Thus, manufacturers and users of dry food ingredients have little choice but to prevent contamination in the first place and closely monitor their operations at all stages.

The widespread incidence of *Salmonella* spp. in meat and poultry is well recognized, but that fact had little impact on food processors until the recent emergence of a new business—preparation of pre-cooked roast beef for fast food restaurants and delicatessen sales. To satisfy the American preference for rare roast beef, manufacturers tended to undercook their product. The result was a series of salmonellosis outbreaks clearly traced to rare roast beef.

To correct the problem Department of Agriculture authorities required that commercially prepared roast beef be heated to at least 145°F at the center, which meant that the meat was no longer rare. Later, USDA modified the requirements to allow less intensive yet effective conditions of cooking.

Salmonella also has had great impact on imported shrimp and frog legs.

These items fall under FDA's jurisdiction and the agency's policy has been to block the importation of shrimp and frog legs that contain salmonellae. American food processors are affected only to the extent that they depend on foreign sources of frog legs and shrimp.

OTHER GRAM NEGATIVE BACTERIA

The public first learned in the early 1970s that enteropathogenic strains of *Escherichia coli* can be a problem in processed foods. This realization came when soft cheeses imported from France were found to be responsible for several outbreaks of gastroenteritis that occurred simultaneously in various parts of the country. As it turned out, all of the contaminated cheese came from a single factory that did not follow good manufacturing practice. Eliminating the source of contamination and installing appropriate quality control tests solved the problem.

Vibrio parahaemolyticus has long been recognized as the leading cause of food-borne disease in Japan. The organism occurs in American coastal waters and is present on raw shellfish and crustaceans. Consequently, it is a potential cross contamination problem for seafood processors. *Vibrio cholera* has been found in Gulf Coast waters off Louisiana and Florida. It, too, is a hazard to processors of seafood.

Yersinia enterocolitica and *Campylobacter fetus* are two gram negative pathogens whose significance in processed foods is still to be determined. The former has been found in meat, raw milk, vegetables, shellfish, and drinking water. "Yersinia-like" organisms have been isolated repeatedly from vacuum packaged raw meat. *Y. enterocolitica* can grow at 4°C; hence it may have special significance in refrigerated food. At least one outbreak of yersiniosis has been traced to chocolate milk.

A major outbreak of gastroenteritis caused by *Campylobacter fetus* has been attributed to drinking water. Unpasteurized milk and undercooked chicken also have been implicated in disease outbreaks. Surveys of people with gastroenteritis have demonstrated *Campylobacter fetus* in the stools at least as often as they have shown *Salmonella* and *Shigella* spp. This finding suggests that *Campylobacter fetus* may be responsible for part of the heretofore unexplained incidents of gastroenteritis. It is too early to predict the impact of this organism on processed food.

VIRUSES

Workmen with an active infection of hepatitis Type A probably constitute the main viral disease hazard to food processors. Professor Dean Cliver of the Food Research Institute has been unable to find evidence of a viral hazard in food processing plants, yet we know of several food-borne hepatitis outbreaks in which a food handler was the source of the virus. Thus food processors must be concerned when a workman leaves the plant sick with a diagnosis of infectious hepatitis Type A.

Foot and Mouth Disease Virus (FMDV) has shown renewed impact on food processors in recent years. For a long time this country has maintained a strict quarantine program against animals and animal products from countries where Foot and Mouth Disease exists. Meat was admitted from those countries only if it had received a prescribed heat treatment.

Several years ago, during a period of shortage, the U.S. Government admitted substantial quantities of powdered milk from countries that are not free of Foot and Mouth Disease. This led to extensive experiments on the heat resistance of FMDV at the USDA Animal Disease Laboratory, Plum Island, New York.

Using much more sensitive recovery techniques than had been employed before, USDA scientists found evidence of infectious virus particles in milk products that had been exposed to heat treatments far more severe than were previously believed adequate to inactivate the FMDV. Other viral agents pose similar problems.

We still don't know the full impact of these findings on processed foods.

SUMMARY

Food-borne disease agents rarely pose a surprise to processors. We know what causes botulinum poisoning and how to prevent it. We know how to avoid staphylococcal poisoning. We know where salmonellae come from, how they get into food and how to protect against infection. We know how to keep food safe from all the known microbiological hazards.

Yet we still have hundreds of food poisoning outbreaks every year. Every time that happens we know that somebody did something wrong. Somebody failed to follow well established safe food handling practices.

It is true, of course, that most of the outbreaks of food-borne disease involve food handling errors in the home, in institutions and in food service establishments. Yet some of them are attributable to errors by food processors, and those are the ones that concern us today.

When I think back over events of the past quarter of a century I can find only one real surprise; that was the discovery of aflatoxin. In my opinion this and other toxic metabolites of common fungi will exert a profound and lasting impact on food processors and consumers alike.

All the other incidents that impacted unfavorably on food processors could have been avoided simply by applying the knowledge we already have. Too often, unfortunately, food processors get in a hurry and fail to ask the right question. In their zeal to gain new business they often neglect to consider the consequences of altered processes, products, and marketing methods.

Consider, for example, the botulinum poisoning problems with vacuum packaged smoked fish from the Great Lakes. The chief safety factor with this product as it was traditionally made was the short time between processing and consumption. There simply was not enough time for *C. botulinum* to develop. Vacuum packaging allowed longer holding and temperature abuse. That is all it took. At least seven people died because nobody asked if vacuum packaging would introduce a safety problem.

Consider too the canned mushroom near-miss of a few years ago. Explosive growth of the pizza business increased the demand for canned mushrooms far beyond current levels. In an effort to expand production some processors packed more mushrooms in each can. This interfered with circulation and the heat process proved to be inadequate. A lot of under-processed and potentially dangerous product was manufactured.

A similar thing happened to the market for pre-cooked rare roast beef. Processors rushed to meet the demand and gave no consideration to the *Salmonella* problem. The result was a lot of very sick people followed by more government regulation.

There are some who would require that every product along with its manufacturing process must be registered with and approved by the regulatory authorities before it can be manufactured and sold. Personally, I would hate to see this happen. The best way to avoid it is for all food processors to act responsibly and wisely. They must hire intelligent and well trained people; they must adopt adequate and effective quality control procedures; and they must use common sense in changing the composition of products, the conditions of production, and the methods of distribution.

It is not difficult to predict what will happen microbiologically under a given set of circumstances. The questions must be asked and the necessary tests must be run before, not after, the product is put on the market. It is unconscionable to use the consumer as the test animal.

10

Significance of Hypersensitivity Reactions to Chemicals in Foods

H. Tryphonas[1]

A multitude of chemical substances in the form of food additives are constantly being incorporated into foods, beverages, and drugs for the purpose of flavoring, preserving, thickening, emulsifying, coloring, and stabilizing the foods. Feingold (1968) makes reference to the use of over 2,700 food additives which have been compiled and classified by the National Research Council (Table 10.1). Most of these food additives are accepted world-wide as technologically necessary and are recognized as essential to modern food manufacturing for maintaining the nutritive value and increasing the flavor and appearance of foods.

As is the case with other chemicals that may enter the food chain, food additives undergo safety testing before they are permitted for human consumption. Safety testing of food additives in general consists of a series of *in vivo* and *in vitro* experiments which up to now at least have been primarily designed with the specific objective of determining whether a given additive is carcinogenic, mutagenic, teratogenic, or is capable of producing other toxicological effects *in vivo*. In this regard, governmental laboratories have, over the years, made a serious effort either to ban additives if testing indicates a human health hazard, or to prove safety and thus remove the stigma attached to certain additives.

In recent years, however, several case reports documented by allergists and dermatologists have given rise to suspicions that certain food ad-

[1] Toxicology Research Division, Health Protection Branch, Ottawa, Ontario, Canada.

TABLE 10.1. CLASSIFICATION OF FOOD ADDITIVES

Category	Number
Preservatives	33
Antioxidants	28
Sequestrants	45
Surface active agents	111
Stabilizers, thickeners	39
Bleaching and maturing agents	24
Buffers, acids, alkalies	60
Food colors	34
Nonnutritive and special dietary sweeteners	4
Nutritive supplement	117
Flavorings - Synthetic	1,610
Flavorings - Natural	502
Miscellaneous: yeast foods, texturizers, firming agents, binders, anticaking agents, enzymes	157
Total additives classified	2,764

Source: Feingold, B.F. (1972).

ditives may be incriminated in a variety of "allergic-like" reactions. Of these the most frequently encountered reactions were to artificial food dyes and included urticaria, contact dermatitis, asthma, and anaphylactic shock. These "allergic-like" manifestations are said to follow a non-dose response pattern and are thus considered by clinicians to have an immunological basis.

However, the term allergy or hypersensitivity as defined by Von Pisquet (1906), is a state of altered reactivity. It follows previous exposure to a given antigen and it is a consequence of the development of an immune response which involves the production of antibodies or sensitized lymphocytes able to react with the antigen.

However, a plethora of food additives are known to be of such small molecular weights that they are usually below the critical level of 500 required to elicit an antibody response. It is conceivably possible that chemicals of this magnitude can bind to larger molecular weight proteins normally present in the body to form a complex, the hapten. This hapten under favorable conditions can stimulate the immunologically competent cells to produce antibody. Such a mechanism although operable with a number of chemicals, *i.e.*, antibiotics, pesticides, etc. has not been conclusively shown to take place with any of the food additives incriminated in adverse hypersensitivity reactions.

For this reason, it would be appropriate to adopt the term hyperreactivity to denote any adverse "allergic-like" reactions to food additives for which the underlying mechanism has not been shown to be immunological, while the term allergy or hypersensitivity should be reserved for those reactions which are a result of the production of antibodies to a specific antigen and subsequent interaction with that antigen.

It is the scope of this presentation to review critically hyperreactivity reactions to artificial food additives, discuss their significance and estimate the magnitude of the human population at risk.

DIAGNOSIS

As mentioned previously, the mechanism of action of food additives resulting in hyperreactivity reactions remains largely unknown. Consequently, most of the *in vivo* and *in vitro* tests commonly employed for the diagnosis of allergy to food constituents do not find direct applicability to the identification of the particular food additives incriminated in hyperreactivity reactions. Therefore, diagnosis of these reactions has been, in the past, based on sound clinical judgement which in turn depends largely upon the results of a carefully obtained history and those of provocative tests, often preceded or followed by elimination diets.

The sublingual provocative test is simple to perform and reliable in the hands of a physician of good clinical judgement. A detailed description of this test as applied to food additives has been published by Lockey (1973). Briefly, the test involves the deposition of 1 ml of the diluted additive sublingually while the patient is blindfolded. The patient is closely observed for 20 min for hyperreactivity symptoms *i.e.* itching, swelling of the tongue, circumocular edema, edema of uvula, urticaria, bronchospasm or other signs leading to anaphylactic shock. Usually if no reaction occurs to the dilution employed the amount of the test substance is increased. Accuracy of diagnosis is enhanced by carrying out the test either in a single-blind fashion (tester knows the solution being used but the patient does not), or in a double-blind fashion (both the tester and the patient do not know what solution is being tested). Other investigators have made use of the gelatin capsule to deliver orally a known amount of the test material. A prerequisite of this method is that the substance is absorbed from the gastrointestinal tract.

A somewhat more efficient but lengthier method of diagnosing hyperreactivity to food additives is through the application of an elimination diet. Usually the patient is hospitalized for the duration of the study so as to ensure compliance to the prescribed diet and accuracy in recording symptoms. Under this regime, the patient is instructed to follow a diet devoid of the suspected substance for 1–2 wk. This is followed by oral provocative tests with foods containing the substance or an appropriate dilution of the substance itself. If the reaction is not severe usually the procedure is repeated in a double-blind study. Such elimination diets have been described and discussed at length by Feingold (1975).

The skin patch-test has also been used to demonstrate contact delayed-type hyperreactivity reactions to chemicals and has been described in detail by Rudner *et al.* (1975). It involves the application of the test solution on an untreated area of the skin, usually the inside surface of the forearm, either directly or on a small square of cloth which is held in position against the skin. Within 24–48 hr signs of vascular flushing and rash can be observed in sensitive individuals. The rash eventually develops into severe dermatitis.

HYPERREACTIVITY REACTIONS TO:

Food Colors

Colors, available for use in food, fall into three main categories: synthetic organic dyes or coal-tar colors, natural or synthetic inorganic pigments, and natural dyes of vegetables or animal origin.

Table 10.2 lists the certified synthetic food colors permitted in Canada and their corresponding terminology used in U.S. These include: Erythrosin (FD&C Red No. 3), Citrus Red #2, Sunset Yellow (FD&C Yellow No. 6), Tartrazine (FD&C Yellow No. 5), Brilliant Blue FCF (FD&C Blue No. 1), Fast Green (FD&C Green No. 3), and Indigotine (FD&C Blue No. 2). Amaranth and Ponceau Sx are allowed in Canada but prohibited in the U.S., whereas Allura Red is prohibited in Canada but accepted in the U.S. Allura Red AC (FD&C Red No. 40) was listed in U.S. in 1971. The number of synthetic food colors permitted for use in foods in other countries varies: 33 in Denmark, 25 in the U.K., 22 in Japan, and 22 in countries of the EEC (Khera and Munro, 1979).

TABLE 10.2. ARTIFICIAL FOOD COLORS PERMITTED FOR USE IN CANADA AND UNITED STATES

Canada	United States	
Erythrosin	FD&C Red	No. 3
Citrus Red #2		
Sunset Yellow	FD&C Yellow	No. 6
Tartrazine	FD&C Yellow	No. 5
Brilliant Blue FCF	FD&C Blue	No. 1
Fast Green FCF	FD&C Green	No. 3
Indigotine	FD&C Blue	No. 2
Amaranth		
Ponceau Sx		
	FD&C Red	No. 40

Clinical cases of hyperreactivity reactions to a number of synthetic food colors have been reported. Investigations by Lockey (1971–72), revealed that symptoms such as hives were vaguely associated with the ingestion of various colors contained in consumer's items such as "Crown Colony–green cake coloring" and "Handy Easter egg colors" (Table 10.3).

TABLE 10.3. HYPERREACTIVITY REACTIONS TO FOOD COLORS AND CROSS REACTIONS WITH OTHER ADDITIVES

Additive(s)	Reaction(s)	Reference
Food colors, (individual dyes were not identified)	Asthma	Speer (1958)
Tartrazine	Pruritus and urticaria	Lockey (1959)
Food colors, (individual dyes were not identified)	Asthma	Chaffee and Settipane (1967)
Tartrazine, aspirin, and sodium benzoate	Angioedema and respiratory symptoms	Samter and Beers (1968)
Tartrazine	Non-thrombocytopenic vascular purpura	Criep (1971)
"Crown Colony" green cake coloring and "Handy Easter Egg Colors"	Hives	Lockey (1971, 1972)
Tartrazine, and aspirin	Asthma, and/or urticaria	Juhlin *et al.* (1972)
Tartrazine, sunset yellow, neococcin, amaranth, aspirin, 4-OH benzoic acid, and sodium benzoate	Urticaria and/or angioedema	Michaelsson and Juhlin (1973)
Tartrazine, and sunset yellow	Nonthrombocytopenic vascular purpura	Michaelsson *et al.* (1974)
Sunset yellow, citrus red #2, indigotine, fast green FCF, Brilliant blue FCF, tartrazine, and erythrosin	Multiple symptomatology	Green (1974)
Tartrazine, amaranth, indigotine, and erythrosin	Urticaria and/or angioneurotic edema	Grambolt and Thune (1975)
Tartrazine and/or aspirin	Urticaria and acute bronchospasm	Settipane and Pudupakkam (1975)
Tartrazine, and aspirin	Chronic urticaria	Settipane *et al.* (1976)
Azo dyes, aspirin, and/or benzoates	Recurrent urticaria, and angioedema	Ros *et al.* (1976)
Food colors, (individual dyes were not identified), aspirin, and benzoates	Urticaria and angioedema	Stenius and Lemola (1976)
Aspirin. Tests with tartrazine were negative	Asthma	Pudupakkam *et al.* (1977)
Tartrazine, ponceau, erythrosine, brilliant blue, and annatto (natural color)	Urticaria and/or angioneurotic edema	Mikhelsen *et al.* (1977)
Tartrazine	Urticaria, pruritus, blurred vision, and increased naso-pharyngeal secretions	Newman *et al.* (1978)
Tartrazine	Systemic anaphylaxis	Trautlein and Mann (1978)

In a subsequent study by Green (1974), designed primarily to test for allergies to commonly ingested foods, 9% of the 506 patients tested sublingually, reacted variously to one or more of the following food dyes: Sunset yellow, citrus red #2, indigotine, Fast green FCF, brilliant blue, tartrazine, and erythrosin. Multiple symptomatology to a challenge with a specific substance was a frequent observation. It is not clear, however, from this study what symptoms would be attributable to colors alone.

Among the most common offenders of hyperreactivity reactions is tartrazine (FD&C yellow #5), a common constituent of orange drinks, various foods and pharmaceutical preparations. Smith and Slavin (1976) listed 101 pharmaceutical companies who use tartrazine in over 1000 of their products while only 45 companies do not use tartrazine in medicinal preparations. Lockey (1959) reported three patients who developed symptoms of generalized pruritus, urticaria, edema of lips, tongue, and uvula following ingestion of certain pharmaceutical preparations [10–20 mg prednisolone, 0.75 mg dexamethasone (DMS), and 0.5 mg DMS respectively] containing unspecified amounts of tartrazine. Ingestion of the drugs without the color did not produce any symptoms. Subsequently, Criep (1971), using double-blind provocative tests showed that tartrazine in butter or margarine was the causative agent of a case of nonthrombocytopenic vascular purpura in a 22-year old female. Scratch-patch tests carried out with the dye in a 1:1000 and 1:100 dilution resulted in a delayed response which consisted of erythema, induration, vesiculation, and petechiae. Passive transfer tests using the patient's serum and Ouchterlony precipitin tests were negative indicating that a biochemical mechanism other than immunologic is likely involved.

The findings of Criep were confirmed and extended by Michaelsson *et al.* (1974). These investigators reported that sunset yellow in addition to tartrazine in quantities less than 10 mg, produced nonthrombocytopenic purpura in seven patients. Provocation tests, using colorless gelatin capsules as the vehicle of the test substance and placebo, confirmed these observations. In another much larger study Newman *et al.* (1978) examined 122 patients with various allergic conditions such as urticaria, pruritus, blurred vision, and rhinitis. Twenty-six percent of these patients exhibited a variety of symptoms including general weakness, blurred vision, palpitations, pruritus, and urticaria after a single-blind challenge with tartrazine. Grambolt and Thure (1975) were able to reproduce manifestations of chronic urticaria and angioneurotic edema in 32% of patients challenged with 17 mg of tartrazine. The same symptoms but with lower frequency of incidence could be elicited by several other dyes such as amaranth, indigotin, and erythrosin (Table 10.4).

An almost fatal case of systemic anaphylaxis due to tartrazine (FD&C No. 5.) and sunset yellow (FD&C No. 6) contained in an enema was

TABLE 10.4. RESULTS OF ARTIFICIAL INDUCTION TESTS WITH DYESTUFFS

	Test dose (mg)			Number of patients	
Substance	1	2	3	urticaria/ angio- neuro- edema	Tested in all
Tartrazine	2	5	10	15	47
Para orange	2	5	10	7	46
Neococcin	2	5	10	5	29
Amaranth	2	5	10	4	27
Quinoline yellow	2	5	10	5	25
Indigotin	2	5	10	3	21
Erythrosin	2	5	10	2	19
Medium blue	2	5	10	3	31

Source: Grambolt and Thune (1975).

reported by Trautlein and Mann (1978). Quantities of the dye as minute as 1/1000 dilution produced in skin tests a marked wheal-and-flare reaction within 10 min. Other ingredients found in the enema preparations were all negative in similar tests. Attempts made by these investigators to clarify the mechanism of action of the dyes involved, failed to show that it is immunological.

An important observation of the following studies is that tartrazine hyperreactivity is found almost invariably in patients who are also intolerant to acetylsalicylic acid (ASA) commonly known as aspirin. The significance of this observation is not well understood since the two compounds bear no structural resemblance. In view of this cross reactivity however, aspirin-sensitive individuals are often advised by their clinicians to avoid taking foods that contain tartrazine in addition to foods that contain added or natural salicylates.

Cross-reactions between aspirin and tartrazine in the same individual were first observed by Samter and Beers (1968). The works of Juhlin *et al.* (1972) and Michaëlsson and Juhlin (1973) have confirmed and extended these initial findings. The frequency of cross reactivity between tartrazine and aspirin in sensitive individuals has been estimated by these authors to be from 7.5% to over 87%. Juhlin *et al.* (1972) reported that 87% of eight aspirin-sensitive patients reacted with asthma, urticaria or both following oral blind challenges with 1−2 mg of tartrazine. The study of Michaëlsson and Juhlin (1973) reported that 48% of 39 patients developed urticaria to oral provocation tests with 1−18 mg of tartrazine and 89% to aspirin. Eighty-eight percent of the 16 patients who followed up a dietary regimen without colors or preservatives were freed from urticaria completely, 6% were improved, and 12% continued to have urticaria. Other azo dyes including sunset yellow and amaranth were also tested and a certain degree of cross reactivity was evident. None of the 33 controls reacted to any of the colors tested or aspirin.

Similar cross reactivity patterns were reported by Settipane and Pudupakkan (1975). Fifteen percent of the forty aspirin-intolerant individuals reacted with generalized itchiness, urticaria or acute bronchospasm to double-blind oral provocative tests with tartrazine. Comparable challenge tests in 40 normal subjects produced negative results. An independent study of 38 patients with chronic urticaria of unknown etiology by Settipane *et al.* (1976) showed that 34% of the 38 patients improved on a diet without artificial colors. However, only 8% of these patients had an exacerbation of urticaria within 3 hr following challenge with 0.22 mg of tartrazine in a gelatin capsule. Two of the three patients who reacted to tartrazine also had known aspirin intolerance and the third patient had a questionable history of aspirin tolerance. The reported low incidence of patients reactive to a challenge with tartrazine is in contrast to results obtained by other investigators and is probably due to the low quantity of the dye used in the challenge studies.

In another study by Ros *et al.* (1976) 75 patients with recurrent urticaria and angio-edema who were positive in provocation tests to aspirin, azo dyes, and/or benzoates, were given an elimination diet and were followed-up for 6–24 months. After this time reassessment of symptoms revealed that 24% were free from urticaria and angio-edema, 57% considered themselves much better and 19% stated that they were slightly better or unchanged. Symptoms recurred as soon as they ingested foods or drugs containing the incriminated food additives.

Food additives have also in the past few years been looked upon as possible culprits of certain episodes of asthma. The clinical ailment of asthma is defined as a condition characterized by episodic or variable airways obstruction and by bronchial hyperreactivity to a variety of physical and chemical irritants (Brown 1973). Clinical observations supported by immunological data suggest that an antigen-antibody interaction may be instrumental in some cases of childhood asthma. Others believe that antigen-antibody reactions constitute but one of the many modes of stimulation of bronchial hyperreactivity in asthmatics especially in adults. It follows that several episodes of asthma have been vaguely characterized.

Speer (1958) was the first one to report that food colors were the causative agents in precipitating asthma in six children. This observation was further investigated by Pudupakkam *et al.* (1977). Fifty-four asthmatic children were subjected to randomized challenges with 25 mg of tartrazine and 600 mg of aspirin in a double-blind fashion. A decrease of more than two standard deviations from the mean population placebo response in forced expiratory volume was considered as a positive reaction. Only five children met this criterion following aspirin challenge. None of the children reacted to tartrazine provocation. In contrast to these findings, Stenius and Lemola (1976), using a fall of 20% in peak expiratory flow (PEF) as indicative of a positive reaction, showed that "slightly more than one-fifth" of the 140 asthmatic women reacted to a challenge with tartrazine, while one-quarter of the cases reacted to aspirin. Thus the negative results obtained by Pudupakkam and his group seem to suggest that tartrazine may not cause asthma in children. However, these authors pointed out that, while corticosteroid and broncho-dilator therapy was discontinued prior to challenge studies, chromolyn sodium therapy was not suspended. It is known that chromolyn sodium can inhibit hypersensitivity reactions at the cellular level, and a recent report suggests that the therapeutic agent may block aspirin-induced asthma (Delaney 1976). In view of the cross reactivity reported between aspirin and tartrazine, it is reasonable to assume that chromolyn sodium may have a similar inhibitory effect on asthma induced by tartrazine thus giving rise to falsely negative results. Another possibility is that hyperreactivity reactions to tartrazine may, as we shall see later, result in entirely different manifestations in children and in adults.

Hyperreactivity reactions are not unique to synthetic food colors but are known to occur following ingestion of naturally extracted dyes. The natural colors are derived from diverse sources and include carmine, annatto, caramel, beetroot and turmeric (Table 10.5). Mikhelson *et al.* (1977) studied 56 patients suffering from chronic urticaria and/or angioneurotic edema. In addition to reactions obtained with a number of artificial food colors 26% of the patients reacted to an oral challenge with the naturally extracted color annatto. The dosage used was the maximum allowed amount of annatto extract in 25 grammes of butter.

TABLE 10.5. FOOD COLORS EXTRACTED FROM NATURAL SOURCES

Name	Source
Carmine	Insect *Coccus cacti* L.
Annatto	Annatto seeds
Caramel	Burnt sugar
Beet root Red	Beet root juice
Turmeric	*Curcuma tinctoria*

Flavors

Flavoring substances are mostly blends of esters such as amyl acetate and ethyl butyrate. Cyclamate (sodium cyclohexyl-sulphamate) and saccharin have been used extensively as sweetening agents in many low-caloric food products and beverages. Photoallergy developing into photodermatitis is the only reported adverse hyperreactivity reaction to calcium cyclamate (Kabori and Araki 1966; Lamberg 1967), while saccharin has been reported to produce mild allergic reactions in two patients who were also sensitive to aspirin (Feingold 1968).

The flavor quinine is present in 'bitter-lemon' and 'tonic-water'. It is also added to numerous drugs. Lockey (1971, 1975) reported one case with generalized itching and urticaria and an almost fatal case of anaphylactic shock. The causative agent in both cases was shown to be quinine added to a cocktail in the form of bitter-lemon.

Other compounds reported to have caused contact dermatitis following repeated exposure include balsam of Peru (Baer *et al.* 1973; Hjorth 1961), cinnamon oil (Downing 1947), peppermint (Mazaki 1948), and bergamot oil (Campanella 1973). Baer *et al.* (1973) found that balsam of Peru accounted for 7.9% of the reactions in 340 patients tested during a 2-yr period. Balsam of Peru has been shown to cross-react with other flavoring substances including vanillin (Mitchell 1971) and poplar resins (Rothenberg 1967).

Vanillin, which appears also naturally in the spice vanilla, and ethyl vanillin, a purely synthetic flavoring agent, are known to produce dermatitis in factory workers (Rudzki 1976).

Methyl salicylate (a commercially synthesized compound formed by esterification of salicylic acid with methyl alcohol) is used to flavor various candies, cough drops, toothpastes, chewing gum, root beer and some medications. A severe case of recurrent attacks of urticaria and angioedema has been reported by Speer (1979). Cross reactivity with other commonly used salicylates *i.e.* aluminum aspirin, quinosalicylic acid, and salicylic acid, has been observed but has not been well documented.

Miscellaneous

Benzoic acid and sulfur dioxide are among the many substances used in prepared foods and beverages for the purpose of preserving the quality of foodstuffs. Several workers (Chaffee and Settipane 1967; Juhlin *et al.* 1972; Rosenhall and Zetterstrom, 1973; Freedman 1977; Kudelko 1970) have implicated sodium benzoate as the causative agent of severe cases of asthma in patients with hyperreactivity to artificial colors and aspirin. Michaëlson and Juhlin (1973) found that 59% (22/37) of patients reacted with urticaria to a single-blind challenge with sodium benzoate while 57% (21/37) reacted similarly to 4-OH benzoic acid.

Sulfur dioxide was also reported by Freedman (1977) to have caused asthma in 57% (8/14) of patients.

INCIDENCE OF REACTIONS

The incidence of hyperreactivity reactions to artificial food additives in a normal population is not known. This is largely due to the fact that allergists and dermatologists have only in recent years become aware of the potential adverse effects of artificial food additives, and to a lesser extent to the difficulties encountered by the physician in his attempt to diagnose the offending substances.

Individual well-defined case reports are few and, therefore, not conducive to making reasonable estimations of the problem. The few large studies published to-date involve well defined groups of the population such as those with asthma, allergic rhinitis, and urticaria. These studies indicate that the incidence of hyperreactivity reactions mainly to artificial food dyes ranges from 14–48%.

Somewhat more accurate estimations can be made for the incidence of tartrazine in a normal population. It has been estimated that the frequency of cross reactivity between tartrazine and aspirin in sensitive individuals is approximately 50%. Based on the incidence of hyperreactivity reactions to aspirin the FDA has estimated that 47,000–94,000 (0.023–0.047%) of the people in United States may be hyperreactive to tartrazine (H.E.W. 1977). Similar values can be obtained for the Canadian population based on the following calculations: Limited clinical observations made by an Ottawa allergist (personal communication) revealed for example that ten of 1,500 selected cases of allergic patients were diagnosed as being clinically hyperreactive to tartrazine. Also, the incidence of allergic reactions in a population has been estimated to range between 10–25% (Sherman 1965). Assuming a population of about 20,000,000 one can calculate that between 200,000 and 500,000 Canadians have the potential for developing allergies, and about 1,400–3,400 (0.007–0.017%) of these could be potentially hyperreactive to tartrazine.

SUMMARY

Hyperreactivity reactions in man can be elicited by a variety of food additives, predominantly artificial food dyes. A glance at Table 10.3 reveals that reactions to food additives vary and range from mild symptoms such as generalized weakness to more severe manifestations including asthma, generalized urticaria, angioneurotic edema and even anaphylactic shock. Contact dermatitis, and severe stomatitis also have been reported to occur following repeated exposures to cosmetics or toothpastes which contain various artificial colors, flavors or preservatives.

Cross reactivity has been observed with several artificial food colors, between tartrazine and sodium benzoate but more abundantly between tartrazine and the structurally unrelated compound aspirin. The significance of this cross reactivity is not known. However, well-defined cases of hyperreactivity reactions specifically caused by tartrazine alone have been documented and are usually of the severe anaphylactic type of reactions.

The number of cases diagnosed as hyperreactivity reactions to food additives is increasing as physicians become more and more aware of the problem. However, it is not yet possible to state what properties of these substances are responsible for the development of hyperreactivity reactions in susceptible individuals nor is it possible to predict which individuals are likely to develop it. Approximate estimations would indicate that the proportion of humans likely to suffer from this type of reaction would be very small in comparison to the large incidence of allergic reactions to foods in general.

An important observation from this review is that most of the reported cases of hyperreactivity reactions to food additives have involved adults rather than the pediatric age group. Although it is realized that the number of studies reported is very small to make accurate predictions, it is possible that food additives require a longer time of exposure for sensitization to occur. This is supported by the fact that most of the artificial food additives are of small molecular weight. Another possible explanation for the reduced incidence of hyperreactivity reactions in children could be that in children food additives may be inducing entirely different symptomatology from the "allergic-like" reactions observed in adults. In recent years, for example, Feingold (1975) and others (Conners and Goyette, 1976) have observed that artificial food colors, flavors, and other food additives may cause hyperreactivity in a small subgroup of hyperactive children. Although this hypothesis has not been fully confirmed, research in this direction indicates that there may be a small subgroup of hyperactive children who are adversely affected by artificial food additives particularly the colors. Recent information indicates that erythrosin B, one of the food colors, inhibits the uptake of neuro-transmitters by rat brain tissue *in vitro* (Logan and Swanson 1979). Whether the same chain of events occurs *in vivo* still remains to be shown.

Regardless of the mechanism, certain food additives have been shown to produce adverse hyperreactivity reactions in susceptible individuals. The incidence of these reactions may be small in comparison to the number of allergic reactions reported to an unlimited number of materials, they nevertheless must be considered carefully in terms of their potential adverse effects on health.

In particular, epidemiological studies are urgently required in order to assess the incidence of hyperreactivity reactions to food additives. Additionally, research into the mechanism(s) of reaction of these food additives would lead to either structural modification of the incriminated food additives, or their eventual elimination from the food chain.

BIBLIOGRAPHY

BAER, R.L., RAMSEY, D.I., and BIONDI, E. 1973. The most common contact allergens, 1968–70. Archs. Derm. *108*, 74–78.

BROWN, J. 1973. Asthma in childhood. Med. J. Aust. *1*, No. 13, 654–657.

CAMPANELLA, P. 1973. Photosensitivity and bergamot. Essenze Deriv. Agrum. *43*, No. 1, 32–38.

CHAFFEE, F.H. and SETTIPANE, G.A. 1967. Asthma caused by FD and C approved dyes. J. Allergy *40*, 65–67.

CONNERS, C.K., GOYETTE, C.H., SOUTHWICK, D.A., LEES, J.M., and ANDRULONIS, P.A. 1976. Food additives and hyperkinesis: A controlled double-blind experiment. Pediatrics *58*, 154–159.

CRIEP, L.H. 1971. Allergic vascular purpura. J. Allergy & Clin. Immunol. *48*, No. 1, 7–12.

DELANEY, J.C. 1976. The effect of sodium cromoglycate on analgesic-induced asthmatic reactions. Clin. Allergy *6*, 365–368.

DOWNING, J.C. 1947. Occupational dermatoses (ergodermatoses): Diagnosis, disability and treatment. New England J. Med. *237*, 755–765.

FEINGOLD, B.F. 1972. Food additives in clinical medicine. Int. J. Dermatol. *14*, No. 2, 112.

FEINGOLD, B.F. 1975. Why is Your Child Hyperactive? Random House, New York.

FEINGOLD, B.F. 1968. Recognition of food additives as a cause of symptoms of allergy. Ann. Allergy *26*, 309–313.

FOOD CHEMICAL NEWS. 1977. Food label declarations of Yellow 5 by name proposed. Food Chem. News, Feb. 7, 29.

FREEDMAN, B.J. 1977. Asthma induced by sulfur dioxide, benzoate and tartrazine contained in orange drinks. Clin. Allergy 7, 407–415.

GRAMBOLT, A. and THUNE, P.O. 1975. Urticaria and angioneuro edema induced by antiphlogistics, preservatives, and dye stuffs in foods and tablets. Tidsskrift Norske Laege Forenin *95*, 20–22 (Norwegian).

GREEN, M. 1974. Sublingual provocation testing for foods and FD and C dyes. Ann. Allergy *33*, 274–281.

HJORTH, N. 1961. Eczematous allergy to balsam, related perfume, and aromatic substance, especially Peruvian balsam. Acta Dermato-renereol. Suppl. No. *46*, 11–216.

JUHLIN, L., MICHAELSSON, G., and ZETTERSTROM, O. 1972. Uticaria and asthma induced by food-and-drug additives in patients with aspirin hypersensitivity. J. Allergy & Clin. Immunol. *50*, No. 2, 92–98.

KABORI, T. and ARAKI, H. 1966. Photoallergy in dermatology. J. Asthma Research *3*, 213.

KHERA, K.S. and MUNRO, I.C. 1979. A review of the specifications and toxicity of synthetic food colors permitted in Canada. Critical Reviews in Toxicology 6, No. 2, 81–133.

KUDELKO, N.M. 1969. Composition of commercial oleomargarines. Ann. Allergy *27*, 622.

KUDELKO, N.M. 1970. Oleomargarines. Ann. Allergy *28*, No. 4, 164–165.

LAMBERG, S.I. 1967. A new photosensitizer—The artificial sweetener cyclamate. JAMA *201*, No. 10, 747–750.

LOCKEY, S.D. 1959. Allergic reactions due to FD&C Yellow No. 5, tartrazine and aniline dye used as a coloring and identifying agent in various steroids. Ann. Allergy *17*, 719–721.

LOCKEY, S.D. 1971. Reactions to hidden agents in foods, beverages and drugs. Ann. Allergy *29*, 461–466.

LOCKEY, S.D. 1972. Sensitizing properties of food additives and other commercial products. Ann. Allergy *30*, 638–641.

LOCKEY, S.D. 1973. Drug reactions and sublingual testing with certified food colors. Ann. Allergy *31*, 423–429.

LOCKEY, S.D. 1975. Reactions to hidden agents in foods and drugs can be serious. Ann. Allergy *35*, 239–242.

LOGAN, W.J. and SWANSON, J.M. 1979. Erythrosin B inhibition of neurotransmitter accumulation of rat brain homogenate. Science *206*, 363–364.

MICHAELSSON, G. and JOHLIN, L. 1973. Urticaria induced by preservatives and dye additives in food and drugs. Brit. J. Dermatol. *88*, 525.

MICHAELSSON, G., PETTERSON, L., and JUHLIN, L. 1974. Purpura caused by food and drug additives. Arch. Dermatol. *109*, 49–52.

MIKHELSEN, G. 1977. Hypersensitivity reactions to food colours particularly annato (natural butter colour). Paper presented at the European Society of Toxicology, Copenhagen.

MITCHELL, J.C. 1971. The skin and chemical additives to foods. Arch. Dermatol. *104*, 329.

NEWMAN, I., ELIAN, R., HAHUM, H., SHAKED, P., and CRETER, D. 1978. The danger of "yellow dyes" (tartrazine) to allergic subjects. Clin. Allergy *8*, 65.

PUDUPAKKAM, K., VERDANTHAN, P.K., MOHAN, M., MENON, M.M., BELL, T.D., and BERGIN, D. 1977. Aspirin and tartrazine oral challenge: Incidence of adverse response in chronic childhood asthma. J. All. & Clin. Immunol. *60*, No. 1, 8–13.

ROS, A.R., JUHLIN, L., and MICHAELSSON, G. 1976. A follow-up study of patients with recurrent urticaria and hypersensitivity to aspirin, benzoates and azo dyes. British J. Dermatol. *95*, 19–24.

ROSENHALL, L. and ZETTERSTROM, O. 1973. Asthma provoked by analgesics, food colorants and food preservatives. Lakartidningen *70*, 1417–1421.

ROTHENBERG, H.W. and HJORTH, N. 1968. Allergy to perfumes from toilet soap and detergent in patients with dermatitis. Arch. Dermatol. *97*, 417–422.

RUDNER, E.J., CLENDENNING, W.C., EPSTEIN, E., FISHER, A.A., JILLSON, O.F., JORDAN, W.P., KANOF, N., LARSEN, W., MAIBACH, H.,

MITCHELL, J.C., O'QUINN, S.E., SCHORR, W.F., and SULZBERGER, M.B. 1975. The frequency of contact sensitivity in North America 1972–74. Contact Dermatitis *1*, 277–280.

RUDZKI, E. and GRZYWA, Z. 1976. Immediate reactions to balsam of Peru, Cassia oil and ethyl vanillin. Contact Dermatitis *2*, 360.

SAMTER, M. and BEERS, R.F., JR. 1968. Intolerance to aspirin. Clinical studies and consideration of its pathogenesis. Ann. Intern. Med. *68*, 975–983.

SETTIPANE, G.A., CHAFFEE, F.H., POSTMAN, I.M., LEVINE, M.I., SAKER, J.H., BARTICK, R.H., NICHOLAS, S.S., SCHWARTZ, H.J., HOSINGER, R.W., and KLEIN, D.E. 1976. Significance of tartrazine sensitivity in chronic urticaria of unknown etiology. J. Allergy Clin. Immunol. *57*, No. 6, 541–546.

SETTIPANE, G.A. and PUDUPAKKAM, R.K. 1975. Aspirin intolerance. III. Subtypes, familial occurrence and cross reactivity with tartrazine. J. Allergy Clin. Immunol. *56*, No. 3, 215–221.

SHERMAN, W.B. 1965. The atopic diseases. *In* Immunological Diseases, M. Samter and H.L. Alexander (Editors). Little, Brown and Co., Boston, Mass.

SMITH, L.J. and SLAVIN, R.G. 1976. Drugs containing tartrazine dye. J. Allergy Clin. Immunol. *58*, No. 4, 456–470.

SPEER, F. 1958. The Management of Childhood Asthma. Charles C. Thomas, Springfield, Ill.

SPEER, F. 1979. Allergy of methyl salicylate. Ann. Allergy *43*, 36–37.

STENIUS, B.S.M. and LEMOLA, M. 1976. Hypersensitivity to acetylsalicylic acid (ASA) and tartrazine in patients with asthma. Clin. Allergy *6*, 119.

TAKEO, M., TSUNEYOSHI, T., and NAMORU, T. 1948. The skin-irritant action of the peppermint oil. Folia Pharmacol. Japan 43, 83–84.

TRAUTLEIN, J.J. and MANN, W.J. 1978. Anaphylactic shock caused by yellow dye (FD&C No. 5 and FD&C No. 6) in an enema (case report). Ann. Allergy *41*, 28–29.

VEDANTHAN, P.K., MENON, M.M., BELL, T.D., and BERGIN, D. 1977. Aspirin and tartrazine oral challenge: Incidence of adverse response in chronic childhood asthma. J. Allergy & Clin. Immunol. *60*, 8.

VON PIRQUET, P. 1906. Cited in Immunology for Students of Medicine, J.H. Humphrey and R.G. White (Editors), third edition, p. 428. Blackwell Scientific Publications, 1970.

11

Unwanted Sugars in Processed Foods

T. O. M. Nakayama[1]

The occurrence of sugars in small but troublesome amounts presents some challenges to the food technologist. The sugars may be troublesome due to the biochemical properties of the sugar or some chemical reactions which occur during storage. Common problems include residual sugars in dry fermented wines, glucose in dried egg powder which produces browning, lactose which presents difficulties in digestion and assimilation, and certain oligosaccharides which similarly resist digestion and cause flatulence.

Methods of dealing with problems of this sort can be grouped in several ways. One is to prevent the problem's occurrence in the first place with such practices as breeding varieties which contain low levels of these troublesome compounds. Another is to eliminate them through biochemical means such as conversion to other substances (glucose to gluconic acid) or through physical removal by extraction or precipitation. This particular effort is aimed at summarizing the methods available for reducing the α-galactosidic oligosaccharides in leguminous seeds as typified by soybeans (*Glycine max* L.), but also shared by such things as cowpeas *(Vigna unguiculata)*, navy beans *(Phaseolus vulgaris)*, mung beans *(Vigna radiata)*, chick peas *(Cicer arientinum)*, pigeon peas *(Cajanus cajan)*, etc.

THE PROBLEM

Practical experience and scientific experiments have combined to establish the fact that flatulence can be experienced from the eating of

[1] Department of Food Science, University of Georgia Agricultural Experiment Station, Experiment, Georgia.

beans. Thus, it is known that about 25% of the people, in a California sampling, do not eat beans because of social awkwardness and physical discomfort (White 1971). Data implicating the oligosaccharides, particularly stachyose and raffinose, (Fig. 11.1) as the cause of diarrhea and

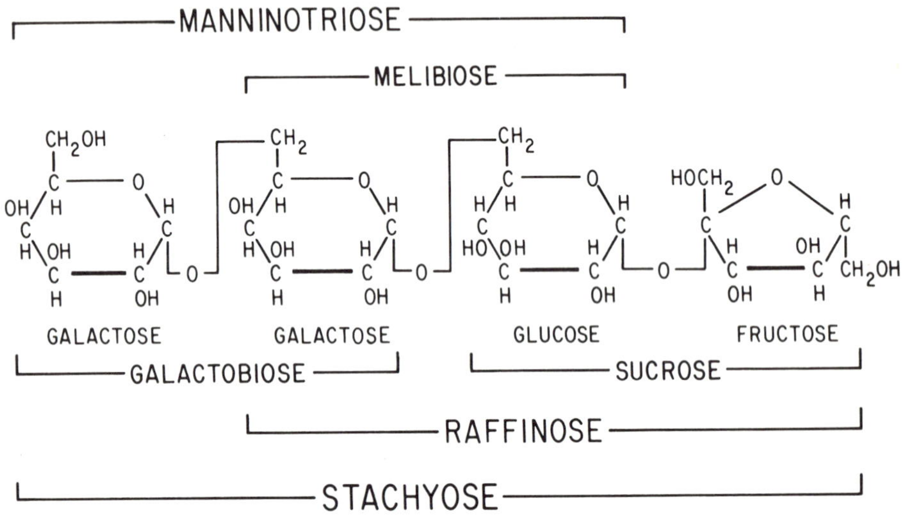

FIG. 11.1. STRUCTURAL RELATIONSHIPS OF STACHYOSE, AN α-D-GALACTOSYL SUGAR

flatulence have been reviewed many times (Calloway 1975; Rackis 1975, 1976). The causative factors are: (1) the human digestive system lacks α-galactosidase activity and thus allows raffinose and stachyose to pass into the large intestine; (2) anaerobic bacteria in the intestine are capable of fermenting the sugars to produce gas. A similar scenario is suggested for lactose (Fig. 11.2) which depends on the β-galactosidase, lactase to hydrolyze it to enable assimilation. Humans apparently vary in their complement of lactase and thus present an array of tolerances for lactose in their diet (Paige *et al.* 1975). Apparently the disappearance of lactase which occurs among the dark-skinned races with maturity is almost universal and is also present in some Caucasians. The similarity is in fact that a nonassimilable carbohydrate is fermented in the large intestine by bacteria (Hellendoorn 1973).

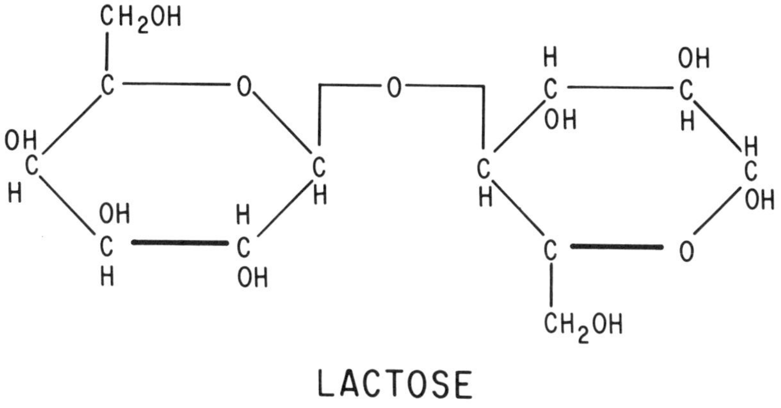

FIG. 11.2. STRUCTURE OF LACTOSE, A β-D-GALACTOSYL SUGAR

POSSIBLE SOLUTIONS

Potential solutions all involve altering the foodstuff. Suggestions for altering the human system have so far not been advocated.

Among the former are attempts to select cultivars which would contain only small amounts of the oligosaccharides. A series of studies by Hymowitz *et al.* (1972) and Hymowitz and Collins (1974) on beans, peanuts, mung beans, and cowpeas have shown that the sugar component of soybean seed is reasonably stable over several environments thus offering the possibility of selecting strains low in raffinose and stachyose content. However, strains especially low have yet to be developed and the genetic approach does not appear promising.

A variant of the foregoing would be to select a stage of development wherein the offending entities would not be as predominant. Observations of Bils and Howell (1963) indicate that a soybean at green maturity has more starch and less oligosaccharides than at later stages of development. The oligosaccharides are apparently produced at the expense of starch during the last stages of maturity resulting in virtually no starch and a build-up of oligosaccharides at harvest.

Direct removal of oligosaccharides by extraction has been shown to be effective (Ku *et al.* 1976). Eighty percent alcohol completely removed oligosaccharides from soy flour. The use of boiling water for 60 min on whole beans removed a maximum of 60%. The use of 0.5% $NaHCO_3$ which aids in tenderization of beans did not increase the removal but resulted in slightly increased loss of protein from 2.6—6.8%. A variant of extraction is to selectively precipitate constituents while leaving the oligosaccharides in the whey. Soy whey solids remaining after precipitation of the protein-lipid curd contain most of the oligosaccharides. Thus, by extrapolation, many of the protein isolation procedures involving solubilization in aqueous media with subsequent precipitation, such as in preparation of tofu, would result in less oligosaccharides in the products. The separation of oligosaccharides from a solution by ultrafiltration appears to have some promise (Omosaiye *et al.* 1978). These processes, however, are separation operations which produce products entirely different from the starting materials. Separation procedures such as dry fractionation into parts have yet to show utility in this regard.

The third alternative, conversion to less disturbing compounds, has its closest parallel with lactose in milk. The hydrolysis of lactose by β-galactosidase results in galactose and glucose which are assimilable. Similar treatment of verbascose, stachyose, and raffinose would yield galactose, glucose, and fructose. The hydrolysis reactions are readily achieved in dilute aqueous media with the aid of enzymes. These may be external enzymes supplied by microorganisms, such as molds and bacteria, extracted enzymes applied in solution or immobilized onto beds (Thanankul *et al.* 1976) or intrinsic enzymes in seeds.

The formation of β-galactosyl oligosaccharides during hydrolysis by transglycosylation appears to occur especially in concentrated solutions of lactose. These are only slowly hydrolyzed by intestinal β-galactosidase and are capable of leading to intestinal discomfort (Burvall *et al.* 1979; Asp *et al.* 1980).

The problem of lactose in milk, however, appears well poised for technological exploitation (Kilara and Shahani 1979). The case of beans is quite another matter. Although fermentation of beans for the production of various types of products such as tempeh, natto, miso, and shoyu has been practiced for centuries, it has not been primarily for reducing the flatulence-causing factors. Miso and shoyu have been shown to contain only monosaccharides as sugars (Table 11.1). Tofu on the other hand still

TABLE 11.1. ANALYSES OF SOYBEAN FOODS FOR STACHYOSE

Food	Source	Stachyose mg sugar/g of food
Shiro Miso	Japan	0.000
Aka Miso	Japan	0.000
Kikkoman Soy Sauce	Japan	0.000
La Choy Soy Sauce	U.S.A.	0.000
Curd	Univ. of Georgia, Athens, Ga.	1.087

East (1969).

retains 20–30% of the stachyose originally present (East 1969).

The use of intrinsic enzymes has been employed in at least two ways. One is to macerate the beans under controlled conditions such that enzymes and substrates are mixed. Such a process can be optimized for the particular substrates as illustrated for small white beans by Becker *et al.* (1974). An optimal pH range of 4.5–6.0 and a temperature range of 45–65°C were found for the disappearance of stachyose. This product produced less hydrogen in the rat assay. Addition of stachyose to compensate for that removed increased the gas to the original level. Interestingly, extrapolation of the curve to the value for zero oligosaccharides shows an intercept indicating that approximately 30% of the hydrogen production may be due to another component. The suggestion of Ebine (1976) that the polysaccharide arabinogalactan in soybeans has a similar role would help to explain the observations of Becker *et al.* (1974). A parallel scenario is shown for phytase which can hydrolyze 50% of the phytate in 16–20 hr at 60°C (Chang *et al.* 1977, 1979).

The use of germination likewise has a long historical precedent which obscures the original reasons for development of the process. It is not considered likely that reduction of flatulence was a factor in development, but rather that results such as taste, variety, etc. could be more easily assessed than flatulence. Even the value of ascorbic acid production was probably not causative but rather adoptive in practice. Nevertheless, it is instructive to look at the various practices and assess their potential for reducing oligosaccharides. A review of wheat and soybean germination in human nutrition is given by Finney (1978) and biochemical changes in soybeans by Rackis (1978). Germination has been carried out for as little as 10 hr to several days. Positive increases of vitamins A (carotene), B_2, and C were experienced while levels of trypsin inhibitor remained unchanged. Deleterious substances such as phytates were decreased 22% in 5 days and oligosaccharides were virtually absent after 5 days. Thus, if oligosaccharides were the causative agents of flatulence, then hydrolysis of them to monosaccharides should eliminate the problem.

A direct test of this hypothesis has been carried out by Calloway *et al.* (1971). Using soy and mung bean sprouts, they found that flatulence factors were reduced from a positive control but were higher than a negative control. Results from an enzyme treatment for comminuted soybeans showed no reduction in flatulence values except for a significant decrease in breath and flatus hydrogen. Sprouts although apparently lacking stachyose and raffinose still produced flatus. The fact that sprouts are eaten in small servings would lessen the chance that they become problem foods, and experience bears this out. Similar trials with tempeh and tofu yielded low flatus values as would be expected.

The process of germination is bidirectional in the sense that catabolism of stored material proceeds simultaneously with synthesis of new material. Thus, if one were to assay a component appearing in both metabolic pools, a composite picture would result. In the germination of barley, the stored carotenoids are catabolized while new ones are being formed, and an analysis for "carotene" would show the total (Nakayama 1962) (Fig. 11.3). It is only when the two can be separated, for instance by temperature, that the true picture can be seen (Clausen and Nakayama 1971 (Fig. 11.4, 11.5, 11.6)). The course of trypsin inhibitor in beans *(Phaseolus mungo)* during germination has been reported by

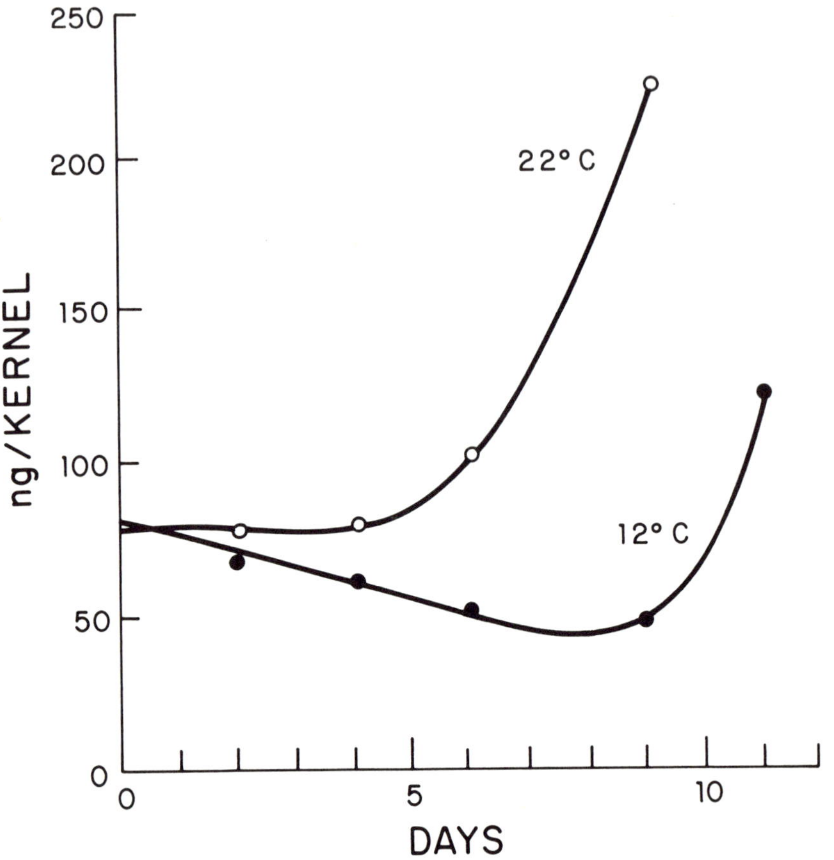

From Nakayama (1962)

FIG. 11.3. CHANGES IN CAROTENOID CONTENT OF BARLEY DURING GERMINATION AT TWO TEMPERATURES

Gupta and Wagle (1980) (Fig. 11.7). A decrease and subsequent increase in trypsin inhibitor activity illustrate the nature of the changes. An increase and decrease in sucrose content simultaneously with a decrease in levels of raffinose and stachyose in black eye peas *(Vigna sinensis)* and pink beans (*Phaseolus vulgaris* var. Gloria) has been reported by Silva and Luh (1979). Inorganic phosphorous levels show a decrease and then

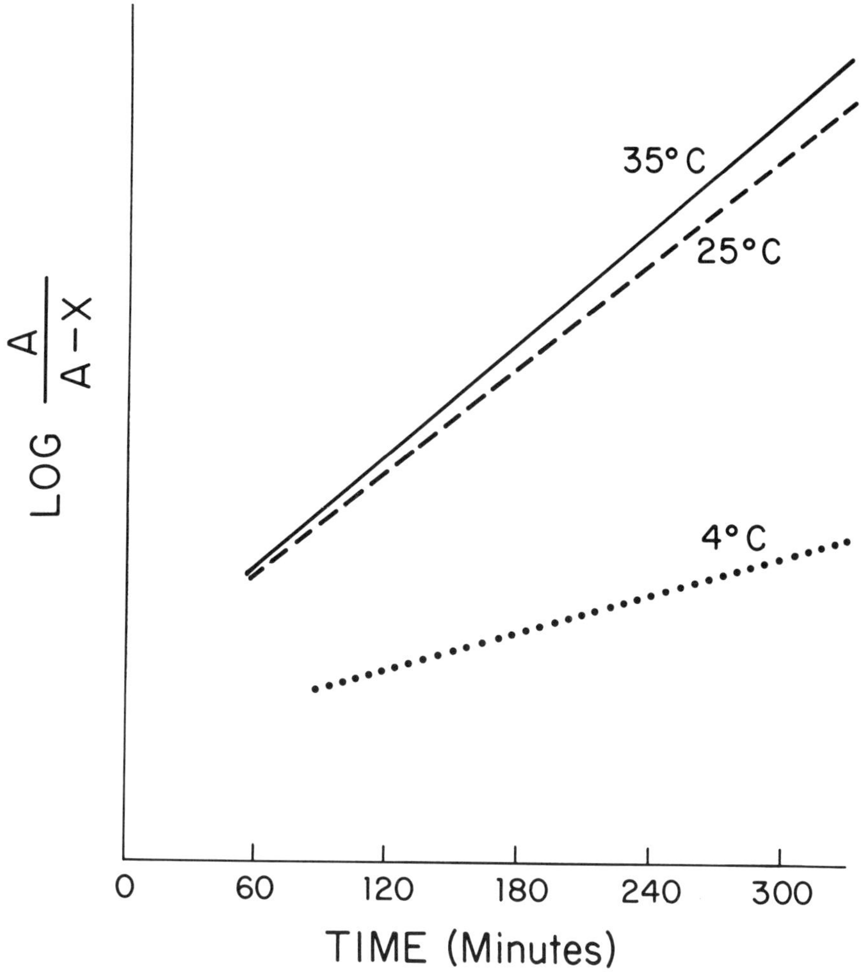

From Clausen and Nakayama (1971)

FIG. 11.4. WATER UPTAKE OF RAW BEANS WHERE A = AMOUNT AT FINAL TIME AND X = AMOUNT AT ANY PARTICULAR TIME
k at 4°C = 2.5×10^{-3}/min; k at 25°C = 7.1×10^{-3}/min; and k at 35°C = 7.7×10^{-3}/min.

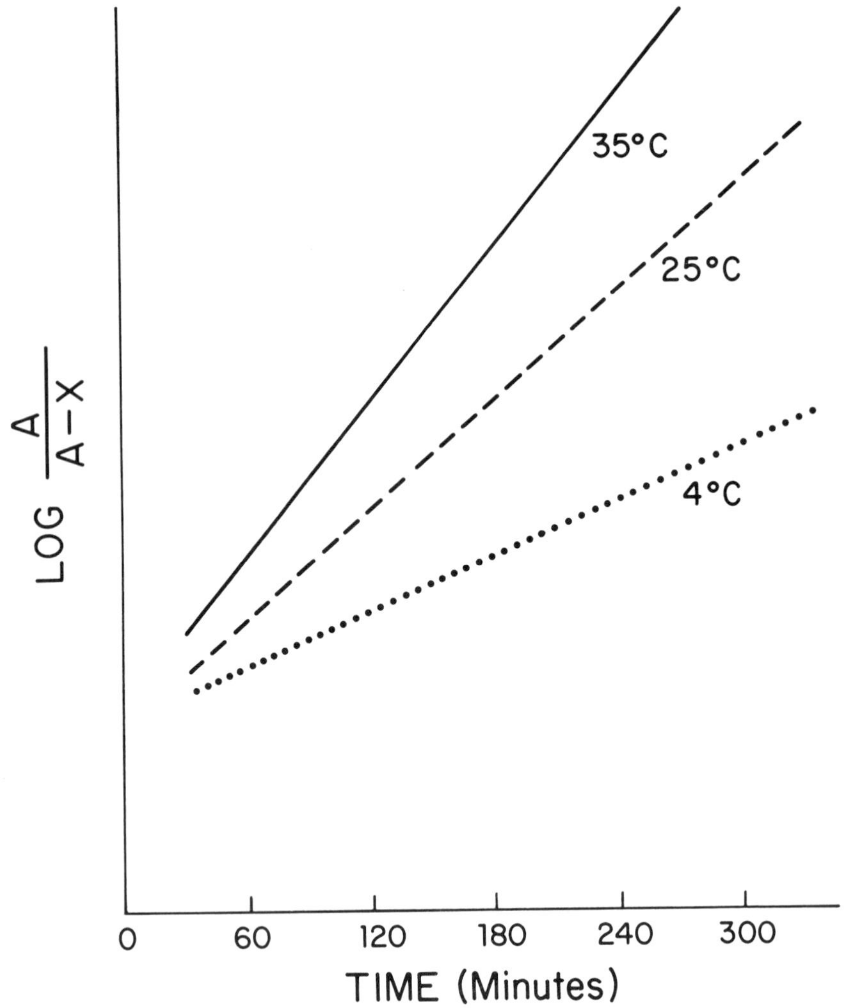

From Clausen and Nakayama (1971)

FIG. 11.5. WATER UPTAKE OF ROASTED BEANS WHERE A = AMOUNT AT FINAL TIME AND X = AMOUNT AT ANY PARTICULAR TIME
k at 4°C = 6.5 x 10^{-3}/min; k at 25°C = 9.8 x 10^{-3}/min; and k at 35°C = 15.7 x 10^{-3}/min.

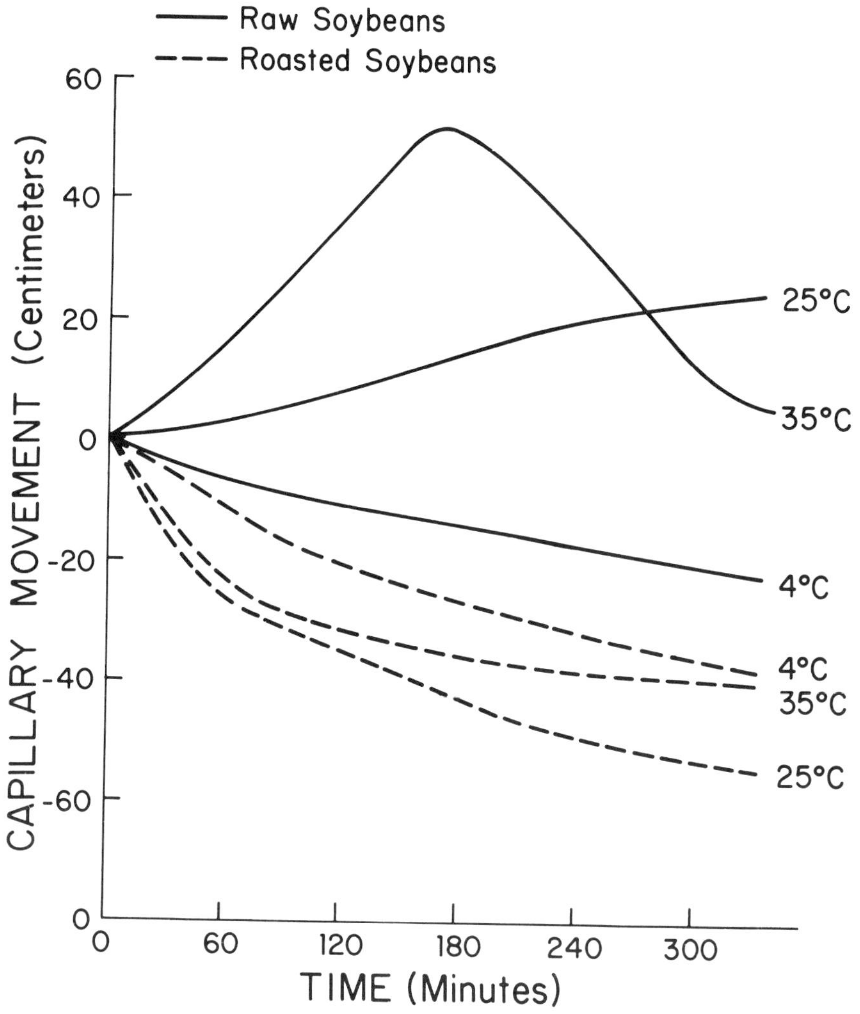

From Clausen and Nakayama (1971)

FIG. 11.6. VOLUMETRIC CHANGES DURING SOAKING

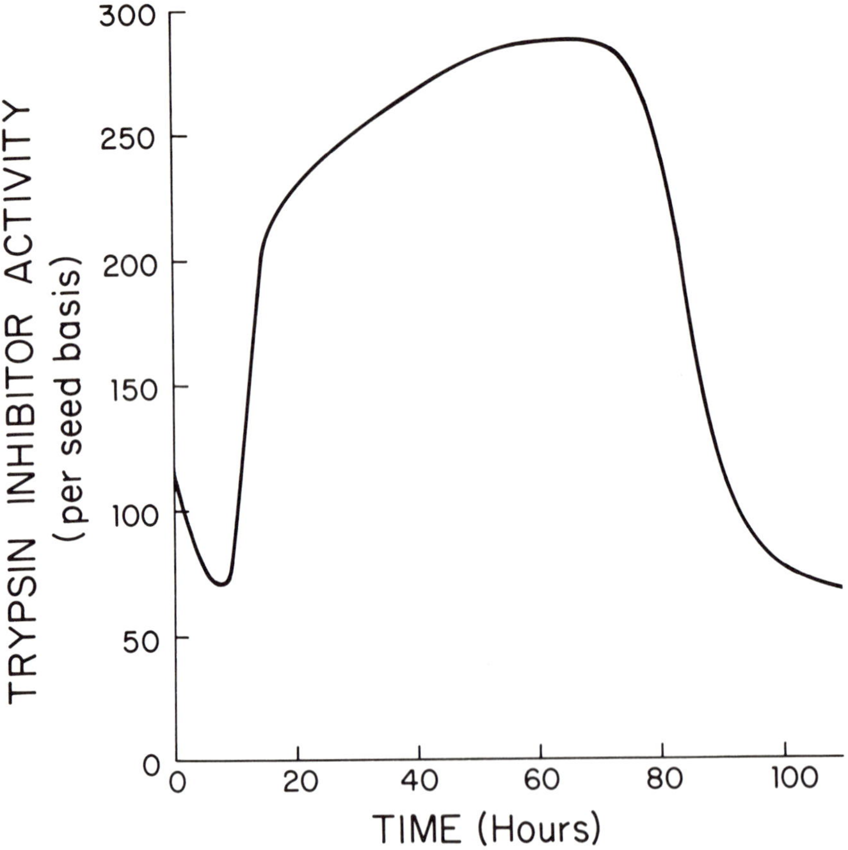

From Gupta and Wagle (1980)

FIG. 11.7. CHANGES IN TRYPSIN INHIBITOR ACTIVITY DURING GERMINATION

increase after 3 days of germination in black gram *(Phaseolus mungo)* seeds (Reddy *et al.* 1978). Similar results for other factors may be anticipated. The oligosaccharides apparently are intermediate in that they are preexisting in seeds and are also synthesized during germination (Wahab and Burris 1975A, B). Thus, the possibility of synthesis of nondigestible carbohydrates during germination is a real possibility. Such considerations were used in the studies of Kim *et al.* (1973). Studies by East *et al.* (1972) with soybeans had shown the potential of germination for hydrolysis of oligosaccharides (Fig. 11.8, 11.9, 11.10, 11.11). Hydrolysis proceeded independently of subsequent steeping which retarded rootlet growth. Thus, separation of the two processes appeared possible. It was assumed that both processes commenced upon water inbibition and that hydrolysis did not require oxygen while anaerobiosis inhibited

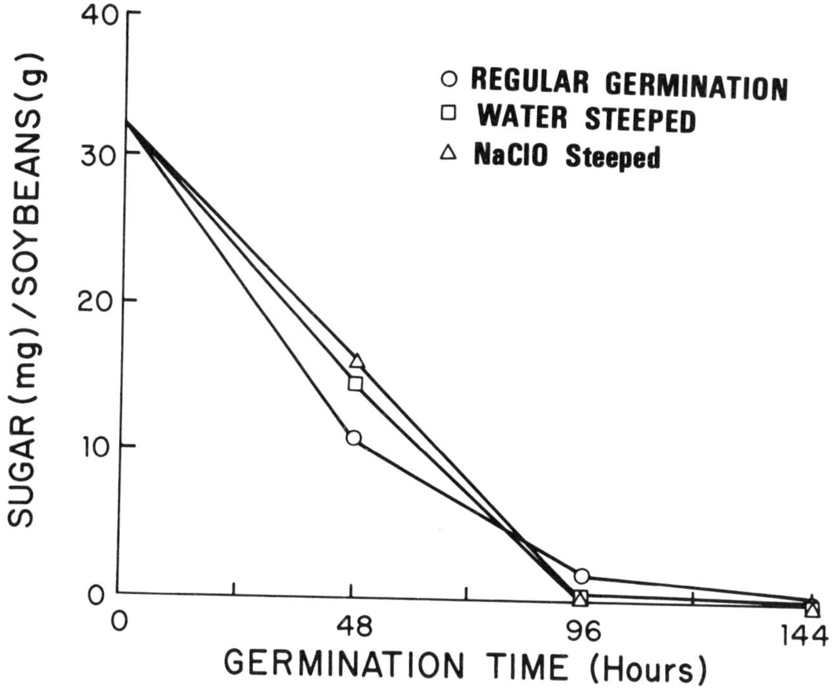

From East (1969)

FIG. 11.8. CHANGES IN STACHYOSE CONTENT DURING GERMINATION

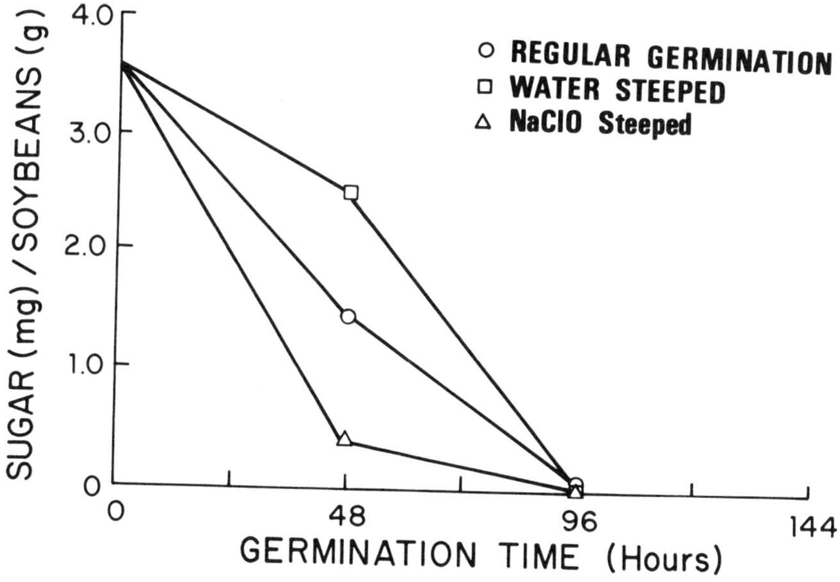

From East (1969)

FIG. 11.9. CHANGES IN RAFFINOSE CONTENT DURING GERMINATION

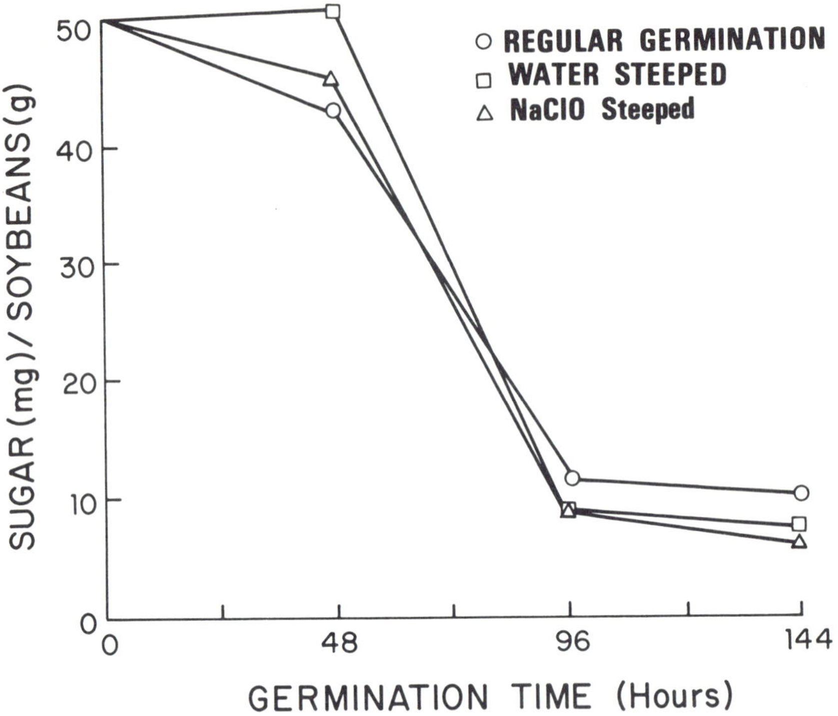

From East (1969)

FIG. 11.10. CHANGES IN SUCROSE CONTENT DURING GERMINATION

synthetic processes such as growth of roots. The process consisted of soaking soybeans for 15 hr, germinating for 24 hr, and resoaking for 24 hr. The studies revealed that more than two-thirds of the raffinose and stachyose could be removed in 63 hr with a 6.6% loss in dry matter. The malting loss is minimized by the repression of root growth. This product has not been tested for flatulence factors.

The process of growth, and thus synthesis of new carbohydrate material, could also apparently be stopped by removal of hulls and embryos from beans at an early stage. Studies (Hasegawa and Moy 1973, Snauwert and Markakis 1976) have shown that rootlet growth could be

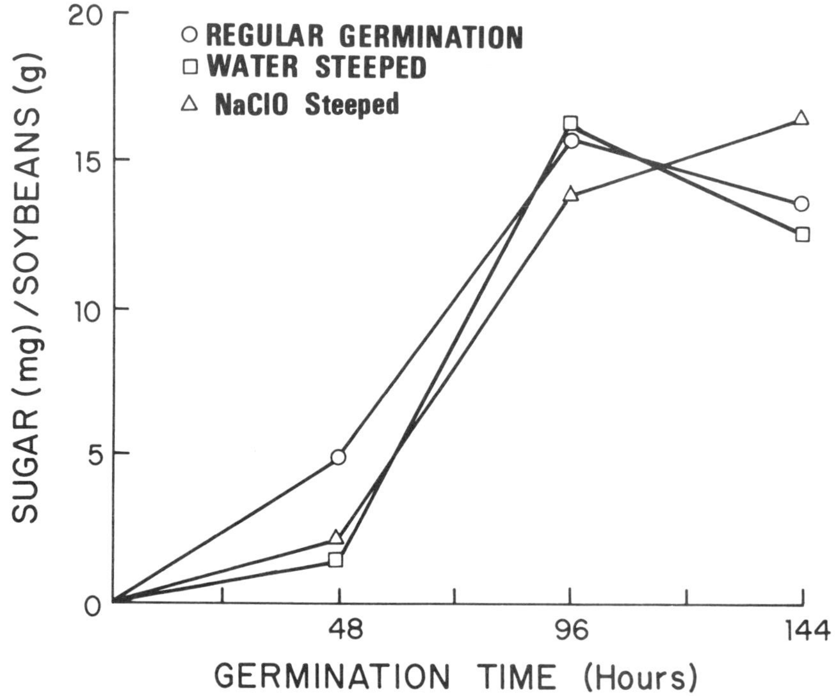

From East (1969)

FIG. 11.11. CHANGES IN MONOSACCHARIDE CONTENT DURING GERMINATION

stopped by gamma radiation while hydrolysis proceeded (Fig. 11.12).

Removal of the oligosaccharides by utilization through lactic fermentation of soy milk has potential for a relatively quick process if the utilization can be sustained (Mital and Steinkraus 1975).

In summary, it can be seen that historical processes have evolved in ways which can be utilized for improving bean products. A better understanding of the physiological and biochemical processes on a molecular level is needed to solve the problem of flatulence factors and their removal from beans. Progress has been good, and an optimistic view is warranted.

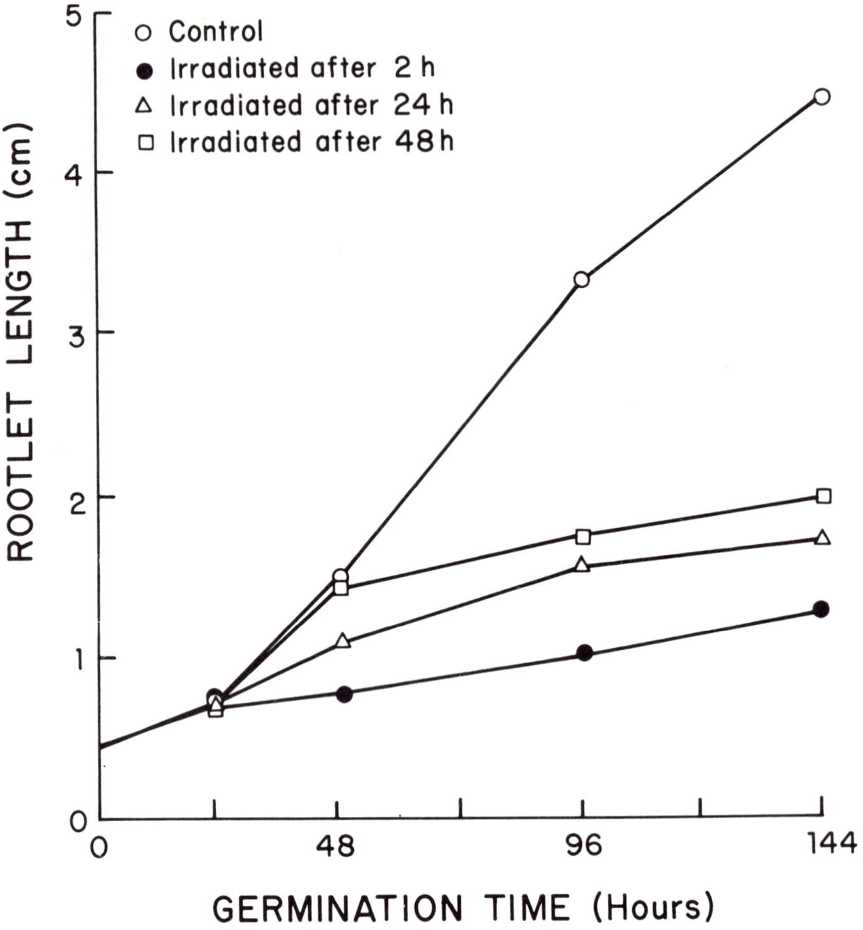

From Hasegawa and Moy (1973)

FIG. 11.12. EFFECT OF γ-RADIATION ON ROOTLET GROWTH DURING GERMINATION

BIBLIOGRAPHY

ASP, N.G., BURVALL, A., DAHLQUIST, A., HALLGREN, P., and LUNDBLAD, A. 1980. Oligosaccharide formation during hydrolysis of lactose with *Saccharomyces lactis* lactase (Maxilact®), Part 2. Food Chemistry *5*, 147–153.

BECKER, R., OLSON, A.C., FREDERICK, D.P., KON, S., GUMBMANN, M.R., and WAGNER, J.R. 1974. Conditions for the autolysis of alpha-galactosides and phytic acid in California small white beans. J. Food Sci. *39*, 766–769.

BILS, R.E. and HOWELL, R.W. 1963. Biochemical and cytological changes in developing soybean cotyledons. Crop Sci. *3*, 304–308.

BURVALL, A., ASP, N.G., and DAHLQUIST, A. 1979. Oligosaccharide formation during hydrolysis of lactose with *Saccharomyces lactis* lactase (Maxilact®), Part 1. Food Chemistry *4*(4) 243–250.

CALLOWAY, D.H. 1975. Gas-forming property of food legumes. *In* Nutritional Improvement of Food Legumes by Breeding. M. Milner (Editor). John Wiley and Sons, Inc., New York.

CALLOWAY, D.H., HICKEY, C.A., and MURPHY, E.L. 1971. The reduction in intestinal gas-forming properties of legumes by traditional and experimental food processing methods. J. Food Sci. *36*, 251–255.

CHANG, R., KENNEDY, B.M., and SCHWIMMER, S. 1979. Effects of autolysis on the nutritional qualities of beans *(Phaseolus vulgaris).* J. Food Sci. *44*, 1141–1143.

CHANG, R., SCHWIMMER, S., and BURR, H.K. 1977. Phytate: Removal from whole dry bean by enzymatic hydrolysis and diffusion. J. Food Sci. *42*, 1098–1101.

CLAUSEN, E.E. and NAKAYAMA, T.O.M. 1971. Carotenoid incorporation into soybean curd. J. Food Sci. 36, 632–634.

EAST, J.W. 1969. Changes in stachyose content of soybeans. M.S. thesis, University of Georgia.

EAST, J.W., NAKAYAMA, T.O.M., and PARKMAN, S.B. 1972. Changes in stachyose, raffinose sucrose and monosaccharides during germination of soybeans. Crop. Sci. *12*, 7–9.

EBINE, H. 1976. Fermented soybean foods. *In* Expanding the Use of Soybeans. R.M. Goodman (Editor). Proc. Conf. for Asia and Oceania. INTSOY Series *10*, Univ. of Illinois, Urbana.

FINNEY, P.L. 1978. Germinated wheat and soybeans in human nutrition. *In* Nutritional Improvement of Food and Feed Proteins. Advances in Experimental Medicine and Biology. M. Friedman (Editor). Plenum Press, New York.

GUPTA, K. and WAGLE, D.S. 1980. Changes in antinutritional factors during germination in *Phaseolus mungoreous*, a cross between *Phaseolus mungo* (M_{1-1}) and *Phaseolus aureous* (T_1). J. Food Sci *45*, 394–397.

HASEGAWA, Y. and MOY, J.H. 1973. Reducing oligosaccharides in soybeans by gamma-radiation controlled germination. *In* Radiation Preservation of Food. Int. Atomic Energy Agency, Vienna, p. 89–103.

HELLENDOORN, E.W. 1973. Carbohydrate digestibility and flatulence activity of beans. *In* Nutritional Aspects of Common Bean and Other Legume Seeds as Animal and Human Foods. W.G. Jaffe (Editor). Archivos Latin Americanos de Nutricion, Caracas, Venezuela.

HYMOWITZ, T. and COLLINS, F.I. 1974. Variability of sugar content in seed of *Glycine max* (L.) Merrill and *G. soja* Sieb. and *Zucc.* Agronomy Journal *66,* 239–240.

HYMOWITZ, T., WALKER, W.M., COLLINS, F.I., and PANCZNER, J. 1972. Stability of sugar content in soybean strains. Comm. in Soil Science and Plant Analysis *3*(5) 367–373.

KILARA, A. and SHAHANI, K.M. 1979. The use of immobilized enzymes in the food industry: A review. Crit. Rev. Food Sci. Nutr. *12*(2) 161–198.

KIM, W.J., SMIT, C.J.B., and NAKAYAMA, T.O.M. 1973. The removal of oligosaccharides from soybeans. Lebnsm-Wiss. Technol. *6,* 201–204.

KU, S., WEI, L.S., STEINBERG, M.P., NELSON, A.I., and HYMOWITZ, T. 1976. Extracting oligosaccharides during cooking of whole soybeans. J. Food Sci. *41,* 361–364.

MITAL, B.K. and STEINKRAUS, K.H. 1975. Utilization of oligosaccharides by lactic acid bacteria during fermentation of soy milk. J. Food Sci. *40,* 114–118.

NAKAYAMA, T.O.M. 1962. The carotenoids of barley and malt. Amer. Soc. Brew. Chem. Proc. 137–139.

OMOSAIYE, O., CHERYAN, M., and MATHEWS, M.E. 1978. Removal of oligosaccharides from soybean water extracts by ultrafiltration. J. Food Sci. *43,* 354–360.

PAIGE, D.M., BAYLESS, T.M., HUANG, S.S., and WEXLER, R. 1975. Lactose intolerance and lactose hydrolyzed milk. *In* Physiological Effects of Food Carbohydrates. A. Jeanes and J. Hodge (Editors). ACS Sympos. Ser. 15. Amer. Chem. Soc., Washington, D.C.

RACKIS, J.J. 1975. Oligosaccharides of food legumes: Alpha-galactosidase activity and the flatus problem. *In* Physiological Effects of Food Carbohydrates. A. Jeanes and J. Hodge (Editors). ACS Sympos. Ser. 15. Amer. Chem. Soc., Washington, D.C.

RACKIS, J.J. 1976. Flatulence problems associated with soy products. *In* World Soybean Research. Proc. of World Soybean Res. Conf. L.D. Hill (Editor). Interstate Printer and Publishers, Inc., Danville, Ill.

RACKIS, J.J. 1978. Biochemical changes in soybeans: maturation, postharvest storage and processing, and germination. *In* Postharvest Biology and Biotechnology. H.O. Hultin and M. Milner (Editors). Food and Nutrition Press. Westport, Conn.

REDDY, N.R., BALAKRISHNAN, C.V., and SALUNKHE, D.K. 1978. Phytate phosphorous and mineral changes during germination and cooking of black gram *(Phaseolus mungo)* seeds. J. Food Sci. *43,* 540–543.

SILVA, H.C. and LUH, B.S. 1979. Changes in oligosaccharides and starch granules in germinating beans. Can. Inst. Food Sci. Technol. J. *12*(3) 103–197.

SNAUWERT, F. and MARKAKIS, P. 1976. Effect of germination and gamma radiation in the oligosaccharides of navy beans (*Phaseolus vulgaris* L.). Lebnsm-Wiss. Technol. *9*(2) 93–95.

THANANKUL, D., TANAKA, M., CHICHESTER, D.O., and LEE, T.C. 1976. Degradation of raffinose and stachyose in soybean milk by α-galactosidase from *Mortierrella vinacea*. Entrapment of α-galactosidase within polyacrylamide gel. J. Food Sci. *41*, 173–175.

WAHAB, A.H. and BURRIS, J.S. 1975A. Metabolism of mono- and oligosaccharides and growth studies in germinating soybean seeds, *Glycine max* (L.) Merrill. I. Carbohydrate and growth data. Iowa State Journal of Research *50*, 29–45.

WAHAB, A.J. and BURRIS, J.S. 1975B. Metabolism of mono- and oligosaccharides and growth studies in germinating soybean seeds, *Glycine max* (L.) Merrill. II. Fate of ^{14}C-Sugars after uptake by cotyledons. Iowa State J. Res. *50*, 47–56.

WHITE, E.D. 1971. Consumer use of dry beans, peas, and lentils. Rep. 10th Dry Bean Res. Conf., Davis, Calif. USDA-ARS 74-56.

12

Impact of Toxicology on the Availability of Pesticides for Use in the Production of Food

John L. Emmerson[1]

To discuss the impact of toxicology on the availability of pesticides, it is necessary to discuss regulations. From the beginnings of modern safety evaluation work, government scientists have been consulted in matters of design or have, indeed, been responsible for some of the prototype studies done to evaluate the safety of chemicals in laboratory animals. That relationship between toxicology and regulation, which was once a natural and welcome liaison between the private sector and government, has changed dramatically over the years. Risks that were once considered to be insignificant are no longer acceptable and the role of governmental regulation in the conduct of toxicological work has become pervasive, affecting not only the type of work done and how it is conducted, but also the evaluation of the results. The degree of regulatory involvement in the development of new pesticides is so extensive that an attempt to discuss the full range of subjects to be covered would be quite impossible. It is also unnecessary because the problem can be studied by example. One area of concern, that of the evaluation of pesticides and other chemicals for carcinogenic potential, has resulted in the promulgation of more guidelines and in the stimulation of more debate than any other. We may view the general problem by studying the ability of toxicology and governmental regulatory affairs to deal with this one issue. This is the subject that I propose to cover.

[1] Director, Toxicology Studies, Lilly Research Laboratories, Greenfield, Indiana.

PERTINENT LAW AND/OR REGULATIONS

The regulation which provides the authority for the Environmental Protection Agency (EPA) to require safety evaluation data, specifically an evaluation for carcinogenic potential, in support of pesticide registrations is given in Section 162.8 of the Regulations for the Enforcement of the Federal Insecticide, Fungicide, and Rodenticide Act which became effective on August 4, 1975. The following sections are pertinent:

Section 162.8 (b) (4) (i).—Data requirements for new registration, hazard to humans and domestic animals

"(B) Subacute and chronic toxicity data will be required as specified in the Registration Guidelines and may include assessment of oncogenic, mutagenic, teratogenic . . . effects; . . ."

Section 162.8 (c) (3).—Data requirements for reregistration, subacute and chronic toxicity data

"(ii) Oncogenic evaluation of the active ingredient(s) will be required if (A) the active ingredient(s), its metabolite(s) or degradation product(s) contains a substance structurally related to a known or suspected oncogenic agent, or (B) the pesticide needs a tolerance or an exemption from the requirement to obtain a tolerance . . ."

Once the enabling legislation is in place, there is an ever-present and ultimate temptation to which a regulator may succumb. This is the attractive philosophical position that subscribes to the theory that all problems can be made manageable by the institution of guidelines. It is the hope of those who regulate that categories can be created that will cover all contingencies and will, therefore, permit decisions to be made quickly and without long and arduous debate. If the problem is difficult to resolve, if qualified scientists disagree, if administrators hesitate to act in the face of contrasting opinion, then a regulatory recourse can be provided under which no latitude is permitted on the part of either the regulator or the regulated.

The present dilemma was foretold in a speech given 27 years ago by Dr. Maurice H. Seevers of the University of Michigan. His presentation entitled "Perspective Versus Caprice in Evaluating Toxicity of Chemicals in Man" remains as one of the best commentaries available on the proper role of legislation in the regulated use of drug and nondrug chemicals (Seevers 1953). His analysis provides penetrating insight into the forces that were then shaping the Delaney Amendment. I commend it to your reading, for it is as compelling in its relevance today. Speaking of food additives, pesticides, and other nondrug chemicals, Dr. Seevers made the following remarks:

"The *a priori* determination of calculated risk is an exceedingly complicated problem. In many instances it must involve the considered judgment of a large number of fully competent specialists in a variety of fields, including nonbiological areas. This is especially true when prolonged and extensive exposure of a whole population is involved. As a result of the fact that so many persons may ultimately become involved and that so many decisions may be necessary to determine the calculated risk with accuracy, the easiest position for those in fields of great responsibility to assume is one that amounts virtually to complete prohibition based solely on absolute toxicity. This can be easily accomplished by the establishment of standards that are impossible to attain regardless of conditions of use.... Such a view is easy to assume since it is most amenable to regulation, requires the least energy to administer, and requires no effort whatsoever to muster the support of the extremists, the misinformed, and the opportunists, to mention but a few."

This prophecy we have seen come to pass. The regulations and the guidelines that have issued to prescribe the work to be done are so all-encompassing that resources that should be applied to basic experimental work are diverted to the task of satisfying the requirements posed. Attention is diverted from substance to form. These disheartening developments come at a time when the science is just beginning to develop the capabilities to study and understand the basic mechanisms of toxicity.

If you have not examined the EPA Guidelines for Hazard Evaluation which were last proposed on August 22, 1978, you may be unaware of the scope of these proposals. I am a toxicologist and the listing of studies that are presented in Table 12.1 are only concerned with safety evaluation. There are sections equally large and as detailed on product chemistry and environmental chemistry.

Before a compound can be marketed, chronic toxicity studies are prescribed. Each of these test procedures requires complex protocols and the expenditure of large sums of money to accomplish the task. With one chronic toxicity study in the rat in which three dose levels and a control are employed, 400 animals may be used. If a dietary concentration of 1% were employed for animals given the highest dose, approximately 25 kg of test compound would be needed; and, among other things, we have estimated that approximately 500,000 data points may result from the observations made in this one study. Each value must be recorded and verified. Currently the cost of each long-term rodent study is estimated to be in excess of $325,000. Costs for the conduct of a complete toxicological evaluation of a potential product easily exceed $1 million.

While the impact of guidelines on the private sector has been enormous, it has also resulted in changes in the EPA as they attempt to cope with the extensive data packages that they receive and to render the decisions they have decided to make. In addition to the normal flow of toxicological data submitted to support new product registration, submissions await review for reregistration of old products. The EPA has a perennial shortage of personnel experienced in the review of toxicological data; those few who are so qualified do not occupy positions of major authority within the agency. Given the presence of untrained, inexperienced personnel at key points, a means had to be found that would permit review

TABLE 12.1. PARTIAL LISTING OF STUDIES REQUIRED UNDER EPA GUIDELINES FOR HAZARD EVALUATION: HUMANS AND DOMESTIC ANIMALS

Acute Testing
Acute Oral Toxicity Study
Acute Dermal Toxicity Study
Acute Inhalation Toxicity Study
Primary Eye Irritation Study
Primary Dermal Irritation Study
Dermal Sensitization Study
Acute Delayed Neurotoxicity Study
Subchronic Testing
Subchronic Oral Dosing Studies
Subchronic 21-Day Dermal Toxicity Study
Subchronic 90-Day Dermal Toxicity Study
Subchronic Inhalation Toxicity Study
Subchronic Neurotoxicity Studies
Chronic Testing
Chronic Feeding Study
Oncogenicity Studies
Teratogenicity Studies
Reproduction Study
Mutagenicity Testing
Test Standards for Detecting Gene Mutations
Test Standards for Detecting Heritable Chromosomal Mutations
Test Standards for Detecting Effects on DNA Repair or Recombination
Special Testing
General Metabolism Study
Special Requirements
Domestic Animal Safety Testing

Environmental Protection Agency (1978).

to proceed and action to be taken. At the present time the agency is using the proposed guidelines as an elaborate checklist to assess the adequacy of our safety evaluation data. One may ask: Of what interest is this to the scientific community? It is because the outcome of each experiment is preconceived; data from a successful experiment fit the cells prepared for it. This system has no place for equivocal data, and such data are either discarded or transformed into something useful. The original scientist loses his prerogatives of review and interpretation, and questions that should remain open are closed, leaving in their wake academic discussions of what might have been. It is also important because the means by which data are evaluated inevitably affect the design and conduct of the experiment which yields the data.

STATEMENT OF PROBLEM

We have lost the registrations of many of the major pesticides during the last ten years as a result of regulatory action. Other products are presently under review and it is a fair assumption that a similar fate awaits many of these in use today. The basis for the denial of the use of these products is to be found primarily in the results of long-term toxicological tests in rodents from which those who regulate perceive a carcinogenic risk to man. While all agree that conclusive evidence of a carcinogenic effect in animals is a sound basis for regulatory action, experience has shown that the biological endpoint in these experiments is seldom unequivocal, and one finds eminently qualified scientists in disagreement. Confronted with this dilemma, the EPA has chosen, rather than to seek additional evidence through scientific study, to act using the data in hand, albeit equivocal. As shown in its defense of its actions in the courts, the EPA has attempted to structure the decision-making process so as to factor out scientific interpretation of the data. The scientist who should be central to the decision is, thereby, relegated to a perfunctory role in safety evaluation. This expedient, but unjust, policy will certainly result in the banning of highly beneficial compounds for which the risk to man is, at best, hypothetical.

Let us trace the development of the problem:

1. Revolutionary analytical methodology, beginning with the development of gas chromatography, made possible the accurate measurement and identification of vanishingly small residues of pesticide chemicals. Documentation of pesticide residues in water, soil, and food, as well as in human milk and body fat, was soon available.

2. The widespread distribution of residues of chemicals, many of which were used as economic poisons, was unexpected and alarming to the public and certain segments of the scientific community. Militant environmentalist and consumerist groups arose, some out of genuine concern for public safety, some to seek power and influence by fabricating a public hazard. A succession of reports of human exposure to substances potentially toxic in trace quantities (e.g., DDT, vinyl chloride, mirex, etc.) resulted in sustained news coverage which has repeatedly captured public attention. Where technical knowledge is incomplete, distinctions blur, and all chemicals acquire in the public mind a degree of risk imparted by the most frightening example. Industry has been unable to mount an effective counteroffensive, and the press has shown little interest in providing a modicum of balanced reporting of their own.

3. In parallel with the notoriety given chemical residues, congressional committees have been investigating and criticizing the practices of the EPA. Characteristically, congressional review and comment have been disparaging and have routinely insisted that the EPA is deficient in its efforts to protect the public health. The net result of these pressures has been to promote hesitation and instill a paralyzing caution into EPA regulatory affairs. The EPA has retreated into safe harbors where dif-

ficult decisions may (a) be avoided; e.g., the abandonment of the negligible residue concept, or (b) be so interpreted that the scientific (and uncertain) element becomes inconsequential; e.g., the equating of benign and malignant lesions.

4. That all aspects of hazard evaluation should be subsumed by the EPA to the question of whether or not a compound is carcinogenic is not surprising:

(a) Unlike most other toxicities that may be chemically induced, cancer is generally irreversible and a disease that medicine cannot treat effectively.
(b) Our ability to control or eliminate many life-threatening diseases in the United States has permitted longer life; in an older population, one finds cancer as a major cause of death.
(c) Publicity given chemical residues and the threat of cancer from exposure to those residues has been unstinting. To allege that a chemical causes cancer in man is easily done; to settle the question raised is a formidable task, not amenable to precise experimental solution.
(d) The spectre of "cancer-causing chemicals" is a ready-made political issue having all the essential properties: it is topical, newsworthy, and being difficult to resolve, guaranteed of a long life in the public eye. Thus, the EPA has been forced to give uncommon attention to this one facet of hazard evaluation.

The assessment of carcinogenic potential, being a complex and an imprecise procedure, involves a degree of scientific subjectivity not present in many other facets of safety evaluation work. The data to be required and the interpretation of that data are continually defined as the EPA reviews and comments on carcinogenic studies. I use as an example a United States Court of Appeals opinion (1976) which supported the EPA's action suspending most uses of Chlordane® and Heptachlor®. A portion of this opinion contains the best current summary of how the EPA interprets and acts upon data from carcinogenic studies in animals:

"In brief form the principles accept the use of animal test data to evaluate human cancer risks; consider a positive oncogenic effect in test animals as sufficient to characterize a pesticide as posing a cancer risk to man; recognize that negative results may be explained by the limited number and sensitivity of the test animals as compared to the general human population; note that there is no scientific basis for establishing a no-effect level for carcinogens; and view the finding of benign and malignant tumors as equally significant in determining cancer hazard to man given the increasing evidence that many 'benign' tumors can develop into cancers."

Chlordane® and Heptachlor® are registered trademarks of the Velsicol Corporation.

Upon the discovery of trace quantities of agricultural chemicals in our environment, the EPA was called to act and compelled to grapple with problems heretofore unknown, problems of risk that often defied solution. The problems have evoked many changes in EPA policy, not the least of which is in the manner of dealing with hazard evaluation. Risk assessment so gained the ascendency in EPA affairs that the benefit/risk concept, which was a perennial feature in EPA documents, was essentially nullified. Slowly, but certainly, the EPA moved to become the sole and final arbiter on the question of risk. The dialogue and the joint responsibility that once existed between industry and government scientists was broken. Instead of scientific discourse one found rules and concepts unilaterally imposed, a latticework that confined and divided, that sectioned and classified, according to a legal concept of what science ought to be able to do, but could not. Possible risk became probable and the probable, certain, as the data were interpreted to fit the box prepared for it. Presented with indefinable or tentative data, which will not serve as the basis for regulatory action, one can simply take the conservative view and assume a positive ill-effect. The problem then becomes manageable and the dilemma disappears (and with it the products). The practical consequences of these changes are ominous.

Lifetime feeding studies in rodents are the most practicable means we have of estimating cancer potential. While potent carcinogens can be easily classified from such experiments, chemicals of lesser potency or those without carcinogenic properties cannot. The nature of the test system is such that the practical limits fall far short of yielding the precise data one desires. Yet the EPA has reacted as if the data from every long-term study must be accepted and acted upon. The finding of benign tumors in one species is transformed into an unequivocal carcinogenic hazard to man. For the EPA to be able to accomplish what science has not, a theory of carcinogenesis was constructed to which data received must conform. Not unexpectedly, experimental data, as often as not, did not fit the theory. The solution?—enlarge the boxes, broaden the concepts, and disregard those precepts that were troublesome. Thus, benign and malignant changes were given the same administrative significance, the size of the dose was ignored, and the extrapolation of animal data to man was given an exactitude suggesting clairvoyance.

That it is scientifically difficult to evaluate a possible oncogenic response or any toxicologic effect is not a legitimate reason for a structured administrative approach. In fact, the need is for the converse; a general definition that will permit flexibility in administrative action as our understanding of the neoplastic response grows. The value of scientific research cannot, nor should be, prejudged by rigid, unrealistic concepts developed for the convenience of regulatory officials.

The problem is one of conceptual misunderstanding and the responsibility for our current dilemma also lies with those of us who conduct the studies. We have not effectively defined and communicated the limits of the test. That there is no differentiation in the regulatory eye of potent carcinogens from compounds such as safrole or saccharin is a consequence of our inaction. We design our studies cognizant individually of the shortcomings of the experiments; collectively we wring our hands two years hence when the results are forthcoming. One can list an endless number of factors other than saccharin that may have been responsible for or contributed to the positive findings in the Canadian studies (*i.e.*, the presence of carcinogenic contaminants in rat feed, impurities in the saccharin, etc.). What we are saying after the results are announced is what we knew embarking on the experiment—that the test system is imperfect, that there are innumerable factors that may result in a positive finding, that the data are, at best, an estimate of a scientific truth which may only be relevant to that one experiment and the dose given. We often appear, however, to be attempting to *discredit* our own experiments after they have been performed, and it is certain that our reservations will have no impact on regulatory action.

We have no doubt that we can clearly identify the carcinogenic properties of the nitrosamines, the aflatoxins, or other potent carcinogens in the test systems that are used. Let me suggest, however, that our current testing procedures may not permit weak or moderately active carcinogenic chemicals to be unequivocally identified. If the latter be true, then we are asking more of the test system than it can deliver. The realization that this is so is slowly coming to pass as decisions on risk are being made. Consideration of the potency of the agent is inevitable and the limitations of the test system become apparent as the results from large numbers of studies accumulate.

How does one deal with the experimental data from long-term rodent studies when the response seen does not constitute an unequivocal carcinogenic response? To this question, as I have shown in review, the EPA has in the past attempted to place the outcome of every experiment into one of two categories—positive or negative. There have been some recent developments that indicate movement toward a change in the policy by which risk is weighed. There are three recent examples that give reason for optimism.

The first involved the publication of a tolerance for the herbicide metolachlor which appeared in February of this year (Environmental Protection Agency 1980A). The sponsoring company had submitted a comprehensive package of toxicology studies but the EPA in their review concluded that certain key studies were deficient and would have to be redone. In granting a tolerance for this product in the absence of data from the additional toxicology work now in progress, the Agency has shown that it is willing to consider the overall toxicological properties of the material and act in the face of uncertainty to make a scientific decision when a large safety factor is present.

The second, which represents a more remarkable change, is the action taken on the pesticide diclofop-methyl (Environmental Protection Agency 1980B). Again, a comprehensive data package was available. The most sensitive species to the toxicity of this compound was found to be the mouse. In a two-year study a no-observable-effect-level was found to be 2 ppm, but there was an effect level at 20 ppm in male mice. In the latter animals there was a statistically significant increase in liver nodules. The questions as to whether or not these nodules represented a hyperplastic regenerative condition and were mere toxic effects or if they were hepatocellular carcinomas is still under consideration. The EPA, however, used the data to make a "worst case" assessment using mathematical models. If the response at 20 ppm were a carcinogenic response, the risk to the user/operator (which is the only significant exposure hazard) would range from 59 in one million to one in 10 million. From the no-observable-effect-level of 2 ppm an acceptable daily intake was also calculated. This, to my knowledge, is the first application of a risk analysis to this type of toxicological data (data which constitute a presumptive carcinogenic risk) that has resulted in action to propose a tolerance on a raw agricultural product.

The third example is that of nitrilotriacetic acid (NTA). NTA is a chelating agent that was developed some years ago by the detergent industry as a partial or complete replacement for phosphates in laundry detergent formulations. The primary benefits of NTA were its biodegradability and safety in the environment. Although extensive studies were done, the only significant initial finding was renal toxicity in rodents. Later, however, the compound was studied by the National Cancer Institute (1977) as a part of its bioassay program and much higher doses were employed. There were a variety of neoplastic lesions in the urinary tract of rats as a result of administration of 7500–20,000 ppm of the compound in the diet. Similar lesions were produced in mice as a result of the administration of 7500–15,000 ppm. While a carcinogenic response resulted from exposure to these massive doses, lower, but also substantial, doses did not produce the same lesions. In the conclusion of the bioassay study it is stated that "NTA and its sodium salt are eliminated rapidly through the kidneys and lesions of the urinary tract which may arise as a result of the administration of the compounds may be due to a local effect which can be brought about only by high concentrations." That this conclusion was a valid one has been substantiated by all the subsequent work done on the substance. But because of the findings in the NCI bioassay study, this material has not been permitted for use in the United States even though other countries including Canada have approved its use. In the Wall Street Journal Thursday, May 29, 1980, there was an article entitled "EPA Schedules Clearance of Laundry Use for Ingredient that May Cause Cancer" (see also Environmental Protection Agency 1980C). The phrasing of that lead sentence in itself should be cause for reflection to help us understand how we bring about our own problems. The linking of the compound with the word cancer in the headline is enough to give any agency pause in making a decision. One is tempted to digress from the general subject to discuss the pernicious effect of newspaper headlines in regulatory affairs. Be that as it may, in the article the EPA indicated it would not oppose the renewed use of NTA in U.S. detergents. That the Agency is able to make this decision is an indication of new confidence that they have developed in their risk assessment procedures which will enable them to withstand the political pressures that are ever present. Together these events constitute the most positive change that I can remember during the last decade.

The last item that I wish to discuss is a scientific development that also offers hope. There has always been tacit acknowledgment that tumors could be produced by radically different mechanisms, but data that would permit classification of chemicals based on different mechanisms of action have been lacking. Scientific data now indicate that there are two general categories into which tumor-producing agents fall—epigenetic and genotoxic. Epigenetic carcinogens merely promote tumor formation. Experimental evidence indicates that these agents show little or no interaction with genetic material, that is DNA, at low doses. If tissue injury is produced and cell death occurs, a proliferation of new tissue follows and DNA replication is stimulated. Under these conditions, damage to DNA can occur. But the important property of epigenetic agents is that the tumorigenic effects appear to be secondary to tissue damage, and the threshold dose for a positive response is at or above that producing tissue damage. Two substances considered by many to be epigenetic carcinogens are chloroform and DDT.

Genotoxic materials on the other hand initiate tumor formation. These chemicals interact directly with DNA and a tumorigenic effect can be elicited at doses that produce no evident tissue damage. For these materials, a threshold dose is extremely difficult to identify. Two examples are the nitrosamines and the aflatoxins. The scientific capabilities to distinguish these two classes of compounds are now available and the procedures can be accomplished in any well-equipped laboratory by competent personnel. I recommend to you if you wish to explore this subject in greater depth an article from the Dow Chemical Laboratories by Reitz and co-workers (1980). The compound studied in their experimental work was vinylidene chloride which is an intermediate in the synthesis of plastics. An impressive case is made that the carcinogenic activity of this material is elicited through epigenetic rather than genotoxic mechanisms. The important implications are that threshold doses can be identified and that one should be able to establish working levels to permit the use of the compound without carcinogenic hazard to those exposed.

As may be inferred from the preceding remarks, the whole process of pesticide development has been markedly slowed. What was instituted as a means to introduce uniformity of consideration and to permit speedy decisions has, in fact, complicated the evaluation process. Let us hope that we can be wise enough to recognize our past mistakes and patient enough to effect the remedies. And patience will be required. If our experience has taught us anything, it is that change does not occur quickly where government is involved.

BIBLIOGRAPHY

ENVIRONMENTAL PROTECTION AGENCY. 1978. Pesticide Programs. Proposed Rules. Proposed guidelines for registering pesticides in the U.S.; hazard evaluation: humans and domestic animals. Federal Register *43* (163) 37336–37403, Tuesday, August 22.

ENVIRONMENTAL PROTECTION AGENCY. 1980A. Pesticide Programs. Rules and Regulations. Tolerances and exemptions from tolerances for pesticide chemicals in or on raw agricultural commodities; metolachlor. Federal Register *45* (40) 12785–12786, Wednesday, February 27.

ENVIRONMENTAL PROTECTION AGENCY. 1980B. Pesticide Programs. Proposed Rules. Tolerance and exemption from tolerances for pesticide chemicals in or on raw agricultural commodities; proposed tolerance for the pesticide diclofop-methyl. Federal Register *45* (40) 12855–12856, Wednesday, February 27.

ENVIRONMENTAL PROTECTION AGENCY. 1980C. EPA makes no objection to revival of use of nitrilotriacetic acid. Pesticide & Toxic Chemical News *8* (27) 8–10, May 28.

NATIONAL CANCER INSTITUTE, U.S. DEPARTMENT OF HEALTH, EDUCATION, AND WELFARE. 1977. Bioassays of nitrilotriacetic acid (NTA) and nitrilotriacetic acid, trisodium salt, monohydrate ($Na_3NTA \cdot H_2O$) for possible carcinogenicity. Carcinogenesis, Technical Report Series No. 6, January 1977 (DHEW Publication No. (NIH) 77-806).

REITZ, R.H., WATANABE, P.G., McKENNA, M.J., QUAST, J.F., and GEHRING, P.J. 1980. Effects of vinylidene chloride on DNA synthesis and DNA repair in the rat and mouse: A comparative study with dimethylnitrosamine. Toxicol. Appl. Pharmacol. *52*, 357–370.

SEEVERS, M.H. 1953. Perspective versus caprice in evaluating toxicity of chemicals in man. JAMA *153*, 1329–1333.

UNITED STATES COURT OF APPEALS FOR THE DISTRICT OF COLUMBIA CIRCUIT. 1976. Opinion in the case of Environmental Defense Fund, Inc. *vs* Environmental Protection Agency. Federal Reporter, 2nd Series, *548*, 998–1018, November 10.

13

Antibiotics

Beverly A. Friend and Khem M. Shahani[1]

INTRODUCTION

Antibiotics have played a major role in reducing the incidence and mortality of many infectious diseases in humans and animals. Also, antibiotics are used extensively as feed additives to promote growth and improve feed efficiency. Additionally, antibiotics can be used effectively to retard spoilage and extend storage stability of food products. Their widespread application as universal prophylactics, growth stimulants, pesticides and food and feed preservatives has provided significant economic benefits for the producer as well as the consumer. However, such widespread usage may result in the incidence of small levels of these antibiotics in foods intended for human consumption. For example, antibiotic residues in dairy products have been shown to cause sensitivity reactions in certain individuals as well as technical problems because of starter culture inhibition. Moreover, the increased incidence of antibiotics in the food supply may be related to the increased emergence of antibiotic resistant microorganisms. Additional research is needed to establish and assess public health risks so that critical risk/benefit decisions regarding antibiotics can be made.

Although the incidence of antibiotics in food products is generally considered to be undesirable, there is considerable literature relative to the production of "natural" antibacterial components by lactic cultures used in the manufacture of fermented foods. While these antibiotics are inherent in cultured products like yogurt and acidophilus milk, it has not yet been established whether they are associated with the beneficial properties of these products.

[1] Department of Food Science and Technology, University of Nebraska, Lincoln.

Historically, antibiotics are defined as products from living organisms which are not toxic to the producing organisms but are capable, at low concentrations, of inhibiting the growth of one or more microorganisms. Chemically synthesized compounds are classified as chemotherapeutic agents. Today that distinction is not valid since many antibiotics, such as chloramphenicol, are chemically synthesized while some chemotherapeutic agents, notably quinine, are isolated from biological sources.

Although the term antibiosis was introduced in the late 19 century by Pasteur and Jobert, its importance was not recognized until the discovery of penicillin by Fleming in 1928 and its purification 20 years later by Florey *et al.* (1949). In the span of 20 years, world production of penicillin grew from less than 50 pounds to more than 1000 tons per year, and an intensive search was initiated for other compounds with similar antimicrobial activity (Mol 1975).

Antibiotics are relatively inexpensive and their antimicrobial action coupled with simplicity of usage has led to their application as universal prophylactics, growth stimulants, pesticides, and preservatives for both food and animal feed. One result of this massive use has been an increase in antibiotic residues in foods. While the medical use of antibiotics involves voluntary treatment for short periods of time under controlled supervision, the exposure of consumers to traces of antibiotics in the food supply is involuntary and uncontrolled and may result in a public health hazard.

This paper will review public health problems associated with antibiotic residues in food including toxic or allergic reactions in individuals and increased emergence of antibiotic resistant microorganisms. In addition, some technical and economic problems as well as benefits will be discussed.

CLASSIFICATION OF ANTIBIOTICS

Antibiotics are a chemically diverse group of drugs whose therapeutic properties can be related to structural and metabolic differences between microbial and mammalian cells. In general, antibiotics interfere with four major activities of the microbial cell: cell wall synthesis, membrane functions, protein biosynthesis and nucleic acid biosynthesis (Gottlieb and Shaw 1967). Bacitracin and penicillin are polypeptide antibiotics which interfere with the synthesis of cell wall mucopolypeptides. Membrane activity is disrupted by both the antifungal agent nystatin which binds to membrane sterols and the surface active agent polymyxin which aligns between the membrane lipid and protein films. Many antibiotics with differing chemical structures inhibit protein biosynthesis by binding to the microbial ribosomes. These include chloramphenicol, erythromycin, streptomycin, and the tetracyclines. Nucleic acid metabolism may be disrupted by streptomycin which affects DNA and griseofulvin and novobiocin which affect both DNA and RNA.

Although more than a thousand antibiotics have been isolated and evaluated, only a small percentage has been found to have application and widespread usage. Rehm (1967) has classified the more important antibiotics on the basis of their chemical structure and therapeutic properties, as shown in Table 13.1.

TABLE 13.1. CLASSIFICATION OF ANTIBIOTICS[1]

Group	Example
1. Penicillins, Cephalosporins	Ampicillin, Penicillin G
2. Oligosaccharide	Neomycin, Streptomycin
3. Chloramphenicol	Chloromycetin
4. Tetracyclines	Chlorotetracycline, Oxytetracycline
5. Macrolide antibiotics	Erythromycin, Tylosin
6. Polyene antibiotics	Nystatin, Pimaricin
7. Siderochrome antibiotics	Grisein
8. Polypeptide antibiotics	Bacitracin, Nisin, Penicillin, Polymyxin
9. Griseofulvin	Griseofulvin
10. Novobiocin	Novobiocin
11. Sulfonamides	Sulfanilamide
12. Nitrofurans	Furaspor

[1] Source: Rehm (1967)

NONMEDICAL USE OF ANTIBIOTICS

The nonmedical use of antibiotics has significantly increased during the past 25 years. As shown in Fig. 13.1, approximately 40% of the antibiotics sold in the United States are for nonmedical usage. Since 1963 the nonmedical use has averaged 1.05 million kilograms annually, of which more than 1 million kilograms are used as feed additives in animal production (Hays 1978). Table 13.2 shows some of the antibiotics currently added to animal feed for growth promotion and their recommended levels of usage. In many cases, higher levels are used for prophylactic purposes.

As the use of antibiotics increases, the possibility of residues in food also increases. According to the report by the WHO/FAO Expert Committee of Food Additives (1969), antibiotic residues may occur in foods in any of the following ways:

(a) Naturally
(b) By addition for technological reasons
(c) By contamination from the immediate environment
(d) As a feed additive for growth promotion
(e) As a feed additive for special purposes

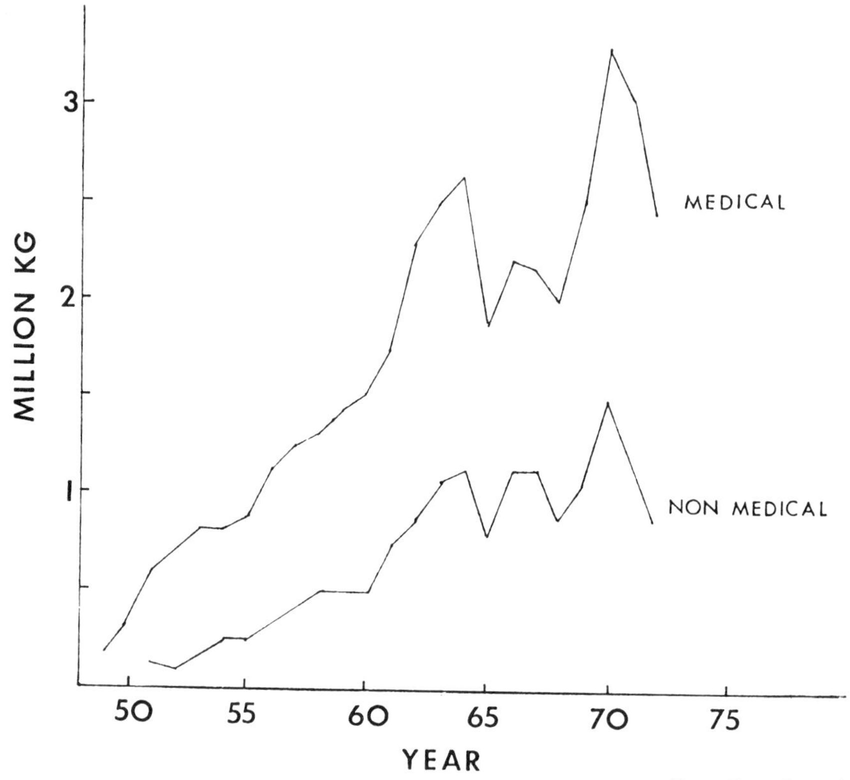

From Hays (1978)

FIG. 13.1. TOTAL MEDICAL AND NONMEDICAL USES OF ANTIBIOTICS.

(f) Through prophylactic treatment of animals
(g) Through medical treatment of animals
(h) As an unintentional feed additive
(i) By occurring naturally in feeds

PUBLIC HEALTH ASPECTS OF ANTIBIOTICS

Toxic Reactions

Antibiotics are potent drugs which are capable of producing a toxic effect depending on the dosage administered, the mode of administration (oral, injection, inhalation) and the exposure period (single dose, semi-chronic, chronic) (Mol 1975). The levels of antibiotic administered for therapy, prophylaxis or growth stimulation are considerably less than required for acute toxicity. Therefore, there appears to be little danger of acute toxic reactions occurring because of ingestion of food containing antibiotic residues. According to Mol (1975), however, it remains an open

TABLE 13.2. ANTIBIOTICS USED AS GROWTH PROMOTERS IN FEED[1]

Antibiotic	Animal	Level
Bacitracin	Poultry Swine Beef Cattle	4–50 g/ton 10–50 g/ton 35 mg/head/day
Bacitracin methylene-disalicylate	Poultry, Swine	(See Bacitracin)
Bacitracin, zinc	Poultry, Swine, Cattle	(see Bacitracin)
Bambermycins	Poultry	1–2 mg/ton
Carbadox	Swine	10–25 mg/ton
Chlorotetracycline	Poultry, Swine Beef Cattle	10–50 mg/ton 70 mg/head/day
Erythromycin	Poultry Swine Cattle	4.6–18.5 g/ton 10–70 g/ton 37 mg/head/day
Lincomycin	Poultry Swine	1–2 g/ton 5–11.25 g/ton
Oxytetracycline	Poultry Swine Calves Beef Cattle	5–7.5 g/ton 7.5–50 g/ton 25–75 mg/head/day 75 mg/head/day
Penicillin	Poultry Swine	2.4–50 g/ton 10–50 g/ton
Tylosin	Poultry Swine	4–50 g/ton 10–100 g/ton
Virginiamycin	Swine	10 g/ton

[1] Source: Aschbacher (1978)

question whether the levels of antibiotic in food are sufficient to cause long term chronic effects. Control of chronic toxicity depends on establishing safe levels of antibiotic residues in food and assuring that residues remain below the established levels. The WHO/FAO guidelines for antibiotic residues in milk, meat, and egg used for human consumption are given in Table 13.3. Chloramphenicol is highly toxic and, as shown, its use is forbidden for any purpose which might yield residues in food. Similarly, pimaricin at 15 ppm is approved in some countries outside the United States for use on the surface of cheese to prevent mold growth. In many countries, nisin has been used as a food additive with a recommended residue level of 20 units/gram.

Allergic Reactions

Certain antibiotics notably penicillin, streptomycin, chloramphenicol, and novobiocin are strongly allergenic in sensitized individuals. The

TABLE 13.3. ACCEPTABLE LEVELS OF ANTIBIOTICS IN FOOD[1]

Antibiotic	Milk (ppm)	Meat (ppm)	Egg (ppm)
1. Penicillins	0–0.006	0–0.06	0–0.18
2. Oligosaccharides			
Streptomycin	0–0.2	0–1.0	0–0.5
Neomycin	0–0.15	0–0.5	0–0.2
3. Chloramphenicol	0	0	0
4. Tetracyclines			
Tetracycline	0–0.1	0–0.5	0–0.3
Chlorotetracycline	0–0.02	0–0.05	0–0.05
Oxytetracycline	0–0.1	0–0.25	0–0.3
5. Macrolides			
Erythromycin	0–0.04	0–0.3	0–0.3
Tylosin	0	0–0.2	0
6. Polyenes			
Nystatin	0–1.1	0–7.1	0–4.3
Pimaricin[2]	0	0	0
7. Siderochromes			
8. Polypeptides			
Nisin[3]	—	—	—
Polymyxin	0–0.2	0–0.5	0–0.5
Bacitracin	0–28	0–16	0–110
9. Griseofulvin			
10. Novobiocin	0–0.15	0–0.5	0–0.1

[1] Source: WHO/FAO Report (1969).
[2] Acceptable only for cheese at a level of 15 ppm in some countries.
[3] The level of nisin recommended for use as a direct food additive is 20 units/gram.

majority of the hypersensitivity reactions, however, have occurred with penicillin and may be a reflection on its widespread usage. Sensitization occurs most often during therapeutic treatment. Once an individual is sensitized to penicillin, for example, as little as 40 IU (0.024 mg) administered orally may elicit allergic reactions (WHO/FAO 1969). The only food-related episodes of hypersensitivity reported in the literature have occurred in penicillin-sensitive individuals after consumption of milk containing penicillin (Vickers *et al.* 1958; Erskine 1958; Zimmerman 1959; Borrie and Barret 1961). It is possible, however, that other allergic reactions caused by antibiotic residues in food have gone unrecognized.

In the 1966 Symposium on Antibiotics in Agriculture, Malten (1968) noted that as the use of antibiotics increases, the number of antibiotic sensitive persons will also increase. Since any trace of antibiotic could cause a harmful allergic reaction, he recommended that all antibiotic residues should be eliminated in food products. At the same symposium, Frazer (1968) noted that limiting the antibiotic residues in food for the sole purpose of controlling allergic reactions was an unsound proposition since these reactions represent an individual response. A more realistic approach, according to Frazer, would be to label foods appropriately so that sensitive individuals would be able to avoid certain antibiotic-containing products. The WHO/FAO Committee on Food Additives (1969) also notes that it is not feasible to control allergic reactions directly by regulation. They do recommend, however, that if a certain form of sensitization is known to be relatively common in a given community, contamination of important foods such as milk with the allergen should be avoided. They also note that special consideration should always be given to the possibility of antibiotic residues, particularly penicillin, in staple foods which are extensively consumed by children.

Antibiotic Resistant Microorganisms

As early as 1957, Smith and Crabb (1957) showed that the use of tetracycline in animal feeds increased the number of tetracycline-resistant *E. coli* in swine and poultry. A later study by Watanabe (1963) revealed that the resistance was transferable. Microbial resistance to antibiotics is not harmful *per se*, but may create a public health hazard if the resistance interferes with the control of a given microorganism, especially a pathogen, in animals or humans. For this reason the Food and Drug Administration required antibiotic sponsors to submit the evidence by April 1975, that showed conclusively that the addition of antibiotics to animal feeds did not pose hazards to animal or human health (Gardner 1973). The government guidelines for establishing a human health hazard were as follows:

1. If administration of antibiotics to animals significantly increased the animal reservoir of pathogenic gram-negative bacilli which could be transferred to humans via the food chain, the antibiotics were hazardous to health.
2. If antibiotic use significantly increased gram-negative bacilli in animals resistant to antibiotics used in human medicine, a potential hazard existed.
3. If antibiotics enhanced the pathogenicity of gram-negative bacilli in animals by increasing the development and linkage of certain genetic elements with R factors, and if these organisms could be transmitted to humans through the food chain, the antibiotics would not be permitted as a feed supplement.
4. If ingestion of antibiotic residues in foods led to an increase of antibiotic-resistant pathogenic organisms in human flora, the antibiotics could not be used in animal feeds.

One important aspect of the Guidelines is the effect of feed antibiotics on the *Salmonella* reservoir in animals. These gram-negative bacilli may contaminate food products and cause illness and death in humans. Moreover, a large proportion of the *S. typhimurium* isolated from humans carry R factors. These R factors are DNA containing plasmids which reside and replicate in the cellular protoplasm, independently of the chromosome, and are responsible for the transfer of antibiotic resistance.

The effect of feeding antibiotics to animals infected with *Salmonella* varies with the antibiotic susceptibility of the organisms. The *Salmonella* reservoir decreased when animals were infected with an antibiotic-sensitive organism (Evangelisti *et al.* 1975; Gutzmann *et al.* 1976; Jarolmen *et al.* 1976), but increased when infected with an organism resistant to the antibiotic used (Silver and Mercer 1978). Neu and coworkers (Winshell *et al.* 1969; Neu *et al.* 1975) have confirmed that antibiotic resistance is increasing in *Salmonella* isolated from both humans and animals (Table 13.4). Resistance of *S. typhimurium* to ampicillin increased from 23.4% in 1969 to 36.9% in 1974, resistance to streptomycin from 27.3% to 45.6%, and resistance to tetracycline from 12.5% to 44.8%.

It has also been well documented that antibiotics in animal feeds lead to a high level of antibiotic resistant coliforms (Smith and Crabb 1957; Smith 1967; Loken *et al.* 1971; Mercer *et al.* 1971; Siegel *et al.* 1974). As illustrated in Table 13.5, Siegel *et al.* (1974) found that Illinois farm animals which were continuously fed rations containing antibiotics had considerably more antibiotic-resistant *E. coli* than Montana range cattle which were minimally exposed to antibiotics.

A recent study by Hankin *et al.* (1979) showed that raw milk contains substantial numbers of antibiotic resistant microorganisms and that organisms resistant to streptomycin, tetracycline, and polymyxin can survive pasteurization. Several gram-negative isolates were also capable of transferring their resistance to *E. coli.*

Humans in contact with animals receiving antibiotic supplemented feeds have been shown to carry a larger population of antibiotic resistant

TABLE 13.4. ANTIBIOTIC RESISTANCE OF *SALMONELLA* IN HUMANS[1]

Serotype	% Resistant 1965	1969	1974
S. typhimurium	18.5	36.7	57.6
S. enteritidis	4.2	4.9	5.8
S. heidelberg	28.6	10.5	30.0
S. saint paul	12.5	21	15.9
S. newport	16.7	20	36.3

[1] Source: Winshell *et al.* (1969) and Neu *et al.* (1975).

TABLE 13.5. EFFECT OF ANTIBIOTIC SUPPLEMENTATION OF ANIMAL FEEDS ON THE INCIDENCE OF RESISTANT *E. COLI*[1]

	% Resistant			
Antibacterial drugs	Illinois Swine	Illinois Poultry	Illinois Beef	Montana Range Cattle
Oxytetracycline	89.8	59	49.1	0
Dihydrostreptomycin	93.2	72	50.0	0.6
Ampicillin	52.5	17	13.2	1.3
Neomycin	20.5	0	12.3	0
Sulfamerazine	82.9	21	29.2	0.6

[1] Source: Siegel *et al.* (1974).

coliforms than do control populations (Linton *et al.* 1972; Fein *et al.* 1974; Siegel *et al.* 1975; Levy *et al.* 1976A). It also appears that antibiotic-resistant coliforms can be spread from animal to animal and from animal to man (Levy *et al.* 1976B). The question remains, however, whether the large domestic animal reservoir of antibiotic-resistant *E. coli* is the source of resistant strains commonly isolated from humans. The origin of *E. coli* is difficult to determine since it normally inhabits the intestinal tract of both humans and animals and methods for its identification and serotyping have not as yet been refined (Silver and Mercer 1978).

Although plasma mediated transfer of resistance has been recognized for a number of years, it has been shown only recently that resistant genes may migrate from one plasmid to another or from a plasmid to the bacterial chromosome. Genes specifying resistance to ampicillin, kanamycin, chloramphenicol, trimethoprim, and streptomycin reside on DNA sequences which can translocate as discrete units (Hedges and Jacob 1974; Kopecko and Cohen 1975; Berg *et al.* 1975; Gottesman and Rosner 1975; Foster *et al.* 1975; Kleckner *et al.* 1975; Barth *et al.* 1976; Heffron *et al.* 1977). In addition, plasmids also appear to contribute to the pathogenicity and survival ability of an organism (Heffron *et al.* 1977).

According to Silver and Mercer (1978), the increase in antibiotic resistance in *Salmonella* will not lead to a widespread epidemic in this country, since poor sanitation and lack of health care facilities contribute to the occurrence of epidemics. A greater human health hazard, in their opinion, is the large reservoir of R factors in the normal flora of animals, which can transfer resistance from nonpathogenic to pathogenic organisms. According to these authors, the emergence of widespread resistance to penicillin in Group A streptococci or pneumococcus would have far greater impact than resistance in *Salmonella* or *E. coli*.

TECHNICAL PROBLEMS ASSOCIATED WITH ANTIBIOTICS IN MILK

The primary cause of antibiotic residues in milk and milk products is the failure of producers to withhold milk from the market for a sufficient time period following veterinary therapy for mastitis or other diseases in dairy cattle. Consumption of antibiotic-supplemented feed may also lead to residues in the milk. Antibiotics are quite stable and remain in the milk even after manufacturing processes including pasteurization, drying, or freezing. Marth and Ellickson (1959), Marth (1966), and Mol (1975) have extensively reviewed problems in the dairy industry associated with antibiotic residues in the fluid milk supply.

Inhibition of Starter Cultures

According to Marth (1966), the major problem associated with antibiotic residues has been partial or complete inhibition of acid production by bacterial starter cultures used in the manufacture of dairy products such as cheese, buttermilk, sour cream or yogurt. Shahani and Harper (1958) determined the minimum amount of penicillin and aureomycin needed to inhibit satisfactory growth of 19 stock cheese cultures, and the results are summarized in Table 13.6. Whitehead and Lane (1956) also noted that during cheese manufacture, as little as 0.05 IU of penicillin per milliliter of milk considerably delayed acid production, while 0.5 IU/ml completely inhibited acid production. Low levels of antibiotic will also affect the flavor and texture of the final product (Hunter 1949B; Mol 1975), as well as increase the probability of growth of undesirable antibiotic resistant coliforms (Kastli 1948; Mol 1975).

Effect on Milk Quality Tests

Several workers (Hunter 1949A; Johns and Desmaris 1953) reported an increase in the methylene blue reduction time when 0.05–0.5 IU penicillin were present per milliliter of milk.

Similarly, Manokidis *et al.* (1971) noted that penicillin and oxytetracycline were responsible for a false positive phosphatase test in pasteurized or partially pasteurized milk while streptomycin, erythromycin, and neomycin inhibited the phosphatase test to some extent in partially pasteurized milk, but not in raw milk. In no case was raw milk containing antibiotic residues ever mistakenly identified as pasteurized. These authors suggest, however, that as a "precaution" antibiotic assays be run in conjunction with the phosphatase test.

TABLE 13.6. MINIMUM LEVELS OF PENICILLIN AND AUREOMYCIN REQUIRED TO INHIBIT GROWTH OF STARTER CULTURES[1]

Cultures	Penicillin U/ml	Aureomycin μg/ml
Lactobacillus lactis A	0.05	1.0
Lactobacillus lactis B	0.05	1.0
Lactobacillus lactis VI04	0.05	3.0
Lactobacillus lactis 431	0.30	0.5
Lactobacillus lactis kw	0.30	1.0
Lactobacillus lactis V109	0.05	0.3
Lactobacillus lactis, myc	0.05	1.0
Lactobacillus bulgaricus 488	0.10	3.0
Lactobacillus bulgaricus 444	0.10	5.0
Lactobacillus bulgaricus R	0.30	3.0
Lactobacillus bulgaricus V71	0.20	2.0
Lactobacillus bulgaricus V12	0.05	0.3
S and R[2]	1.00	10.0
Streptococcus thermophilus H	0.05	0.3
Streptococcus thermophilus T	0.05	0.3
Streptococcus lactis 9	0.05	0.05
Lactobacillus casei	0.05	0.05
Streptococcus durans	0.10	0.2
Micrococcus 8406	0.05	0.05

[1] Source: Shahani and Harper (1958).
[2] Commercial Mixed Culture Containing *L. lactis* and *L. bulgaricus*.

BENEFITS OF ANTIBIOTICS

Use of Antibiotics for Food Preservation

Several antibiotics including tetracyclines, penicillin, streptomycin, bacitracin, neomycin and subtilin inhibit food spoilage microorganisms (Marth 1966). Until 1967, chlorotetracycline and oxytetracycline were approved by the FDA for limited use in poultry and fish chill water. The purpose was to extend the shelf life of these raw products and it was assumed that all residues were destroyed during the normal cooking process. The FDA subsequently rescinded approval primarily because antibiotics were used to cover up poor sanitary practice. In the United States, antibiotics may not be directly added to food for human consumption but may be added to animal feeds.

Use of Antibiotics for Growth Promotion

For more than 25 years, antibiotic feed supplements have been routinely and successfully used for efficient livestock production. According to Hays (1978), the growth promoting activity may be due to: (a) a metabolic effect which directly alters the rate of metabolism; (b) a nutrient sparing effect in which dietary nutrient requirements are reduced through stimulation of beneficial microorganisms which synthesize vitamins and amino acids, by inhibition of microorganisms which compete for nutrients through increased nutrient availability, or by improvement in nutrient absorption in the intestinal tract; and (c) a disease control effect by which disease or toxin producing microorganisms are inhibited.

Table 13.7 summarizes the effect of feeding a combination of 100g of chlorotetracycline, 100g sulfamethazine, and 50g of penicillin per ton of feed to swine over a 5-yr period. Although growth responses have been observed to increase up to a limit of approximately 250 g/ton, high level usage is not economically feasible. The level selected in practice is usually a compromise based on the cost-benefit ratio (see Table 13.2).

It is interesting to note that the recommended level of broad spectrum antibiotic has increased from 10–20 g/ton in the early 1950s to 40–50 g/ton in 1975. Hays (1978) reported that improved methods of antibiotic production and increased competition have decreased the cost of feed-grade penicillin and streptomycin to 15–20% of their cost in 1950 and suggests that economics rather than loss in effectiveness is responsible for higher use levels.

Economic Advantage of Antibiotics in Feeds

Antibiotic supplementation of feeds results in a significant savings to the producer and, ultimately, the consumer. In a report to the FDA Task Force on Antibiotics in Feeds, Butz (1970) noted that the value of antibiotics in swine feed totaled $1.04 per pig or $89 million dollars annually for the U.S. Swine Industry. Recently, the annual saving of U.S. pork consumers has been estimated as $200 million (CAST 1980). Henry (1970) also reported annual savings of $241 million for broilers and $73 million for market turkeys when antibiotic supplementation was used.

Inherent Biosynthesis of Antibiotics in Foods

Several lactic organisms have been shown to produce natural antibiotics in milk and milk products. For example, *Streptococcus lactis* produces nisin (Mattick and Hirsch 1944), *Lactobacillus bulgaricus* produces bulgarican (Reddy and Shahani 1971), *L. brevis* produces lactobacillin (Kavasnikov and Sodenko 1967), *L. acidophilus* produces acidophilin (Shahani *et al.* 1976, 1977), acidolin (Hamdan and Makolajcik 1974), lactobacillin (Wheater *et al.* 1951), lactocidin (Vincent *et al.* 1959), and *L. plantarum* produces lactolin (Kodama 1952).

In many countries outside the United States, nisin is permitted as a direct food additive. Nisin is inhibitory against several gram-positive streptococci, lactobacilli, clostridia, staphylocci, and bacilli (Hawley 1957; Shahani 1962), but has no effect on gram-negative organisms

TABLE 13.7. EFFECT OF ANTIBIOTICS ON WEIGHT GAINS OF SWINE DURING THE PERIOD, 1960–1965[1]

	Average Daily Gain			Feed Efficiency		
Experiment	Control (g)	Antibiotic (g)	Improvement (%)	Control (g)	Antibiotic (g)	Improvement (%)
1	263	413	57	2.13	2.11	1.0
2	222	395	78	2.08	1.85	11.1
3	186	359	93	2.15	1.81	15.8
4	191	336	76	2.99	2.18	27.1
5	200	322	61	2.71	2.36	12.9
6	250	331	62	2.77	2.28	17.7

[1] Source: Hays (1978).

(Mattick and Hirsch 1947). Its major use has been to prevent the growth and subsequent gas production by clostridia in cheese and processed cheese products. In France, for example, nisin-producing streptococci have been employed in the manufacture of processed cheese. Nisin can also be added to canned foods provided the pH is less than 4.5, or sufficient heat treatment has been provided to destroy *Clostridium botulinum*.

Nisin is digested in the upper GI tract and has shown to be relatively nontoxic and nonallergenic. Moreover, there appears to be no cross resistance between nisin and other antibiotics (WHO/FAO 1969).

Shahani and coworkers (Reddy and Shahani 1971; Shahani *et al.* 1976, 1977) have studied the lactobacilli antibiotics acidophilin and bulgarican. These low molecular weight compounds possess a wide spectrum of activity *in vitro*. As shown in Table 13.8, acidophilin inhibited a variety of gram-negative and gram-positive organisms which included nonpathogens as well as pathogens. Milk was essential for the production of the antibiotic. Although these antibiotics have been elaborated in cultured milk, their benefits to humans ingesting such products have not as yet been conclusively demonstrated.

SUMMARY

Antibiotics have played a major role in reducing the incidence and mortality of many infectious diseases in humans and animals. Supplementation of animal feed with antibiotics has increased the efficiency of livestock production and provided significant economic benefits for both the producer and the consumer. As the world population increases, the use of antibiotics to control disease and improve food production becomes more essential. Nevertheless, there are risks associated with wanton use of antibiotics as a panacea for worldwide disease and famine.

Sensitivity reactions and technical problems have occurred with antibiotic residues in dairy products. In addition, feed supplementation has

TABLE 13.8. *IN VITRO* ANTIBACTERIAL ACTIVITY OF ACIDOPHILIN[1]

No.	Test Organism	Strain	IC_{50}[2] ($\mu g/ml$)
1	*Bacillus subtilis*	ATCC 6633	30
2	*Bacillus cereus*	Difco 902072	29
3	*Bacillus stearothermophilus*	ATCC 7954	43
4	*Streptococcus faecalis*	ATCC 8043	45
5	*Streptococcus faecalis var. liquefaciens*	ATCC 4532	42
6	*Streptococcus lactis*	NU C_{10}	30
7	*Lactobacillus lactis*	LY-3 France	40
8	*Lactobacillus casei*	ATCC 7469	42
9	*Lactobacillus plantarum*	ATCC 8014	60
10	*Lactobacillus leichmannii*	ATCC 7830	59
11	*Sarcina lutea*	ATCC 9341	30
12	*Serratia marcescens*	NU	29
13	*Proteus vulgaris*	NU	32
14	*Escherchia coli*	NU	32
15	*Salmonella typhosa*	ATCC 167	30
16	*Salmonella schottmulleri*	ATCC 417	30
17	*Shigella dysenteriae*	ATCC 934	30
18	*Staphylococcus aureus*	NU (coagulase + ve)	50
19	*Staphylococcus aureus*	Phage 80/81	60
20	*Klebsiella pneumoniae*	ATCC 9997	60
21	*Vibrio comma*	ATCC 9459	30

[1] Source: Kilara and Shahani (1978).
[2] IC_{50} = concentration inhibiting 50% of growth.

been implicated in the emergence of potentially dangerous antibiotic resistant microorganisms. For this reason, it has been suggested that antibiotics which are commonly used in humans or are cross-resistant with important antibiotics used in humans be eliminated from animal use. Additional research is required to make assessment of the public health risks involved. Only then can critical risk/benefit decisions be made for antibiotics.

BIBLIOGRAPHY

ASCHBACHER, P.W. 1978. Distribution and fate of growth-promoting drugs. *In* Nutrition and Drug Interrelations. J.N. Hathcock and J. Coon (Editors). Academic Press, New York.

BARTH, P.T., DATTA, N., HEDGES, R.W., and GRINTER, N.J. 1976. Transposition of a deoxyribonucleic acid sequence encoding trimethoprim and streptomycin resistances from R483 to other replicons. J. Bacteriol. *125*, 800–810.

BERG, D.E., DAVIES, J., ALLET, B., and ROCHAIX, J.D. 1975. Transposition of R-Factor genes to bacteriophage λ. Proc. Natl. Acad. Sci. U.S.A. *72*, 3628–3632.

BORRIE, P. and BARRET, J. 1961. Dermatitis caused by penicillin in bulk milk supplies. Brit. Med. J. *11*, 1267.

BUTZ, E.L. 1970. Statement before FDA Task Force on antibiotics in feeds. *In* Proceedings of the Antibiotic Presentations to the U.S. Food and Drug Administration Task Force on the Use of Antibiotics in Feeds. Washington, D.C.

COUNCIL FOR AGRICULTURAL SCIENCE AND TECHNOLOGY (CAST). 1980. Feed Additives in Food from Animals: Quantity, Quality and Safety. No. 82.

ERSKINE, D. 1958. Dermatitis caused by penicillin in milk. Lancet *1*, 431–432.

EVANGELISTI, D.G., ENGLISH, A.R., GIRARD, A.E., LYNCH, J.E., and SOLOMONS, I.A. 1975. Influence of subtherapeutic levels of oxytetracycline on *Salmonella typhimurium* in swine, calves, and chickens. Antimicrob. Agents and Chemother. *8*, 664–672.

FEIN, D., BURTON, G., TSUTAKAWA, R., and BLENDEN, D. 1974. Matching of antibiotic resistance patterns of *Escherichia coli* of farm families to their animals. J. Infect. Dis. *130*, 274–279.

FLOREY, H.W., CHAIN, E., HEATLEY, N.G., JENNINGS, M.A., SANDERS, A.G., ABRAHAM, E.P., and FLOREY, M.E. 1949. Antibiotics. Oxford University Press, London.

FOSTER, T.J., HOWE, T.G.B., and RICHMOND, M.H. 1975. Translocation of the tetracycline resistant determinant from R100-1 to the *Escherichia coli* K-12 chromosome. J. Bacteriol. *124*, 1153–1158.

FRAZER, A.C. 1968. Toxicological aspects of antibiotics. *In* Antibiotics in Agriculture. J.C. Somogyi and A.C. Francois (Editors). Proc. 5th Symp. Group Eur. Nutr., S. Karger, Basel.

GARDNER, S. 1973. Statements of policy and interpretation regarding animal drugs and medicated feeds. Fed. Regis. *38*, 9811–9814.

GOTTESMAN, M.M. and ROSNER, J.L. 1975. Acquisition of a determinant for chloramphenicol resistance by coliphage lambda. Proc. Natl. Acad. Sci. USA *72*, 5041–5045.

GOTTLIEB, D. and SHAW, P.D. 1967. Antibiotics. I. Mechanism of Action. Springer-Verlag, New York.

GUTZMANN, F., LAYTON, H., SIMKINS, K., and JAROLMEN, H. 1976. Influence of antibiotic-supplemented feed on occurrence and persistence of *Salmonella typhimurium* in experimentally infected swine. Am. J. Vet. Res. *37*, 649–655.

HAMDAN, I.Y. and MAKOLAJCIK, E.M. 1974. Acidolin: an antibiotic produced by *Lactobacillus acidophilus*. J. Antibiotics. *27*, 631–636.

HANKIN, L., LACY, G.H., STEPHENS, G.R., and DILLMAN, W.F. 1979. Antibiotic-resistant bacteria in raw milk and ability of some to transfer antibiotic resistance to *Escherichia coli*. J. Food Protect. *42*, 950–953.

HAWLEY, H.B. 1957. Nisin in food technology. Food Manuf. *32*, 370–376.

HAYS, V.W. 1978. The role of antibiotics in efficient livestock production. *In* Nutrition and Drug Interrelations, J.N. Hathcock and J. Coon (Editors). Academic Press, New York.

HEDGES, R.W. and JACOB, A.E. 1974. Transposition of ampicillin resistance from RP4 to other replicons. Mol. Gen. Genet. *132*, 31–40.

HEFFRON, F., RUBENS, C., and FALKOW, S. 1977. Transposition of a plasmid deoxyribonucleic acid sequence that mediates ampicillin resistance: identity of laboratory constructed plasmids and clinical isolates. J. Bacteriol. *129*, 530–533.

HENRY, W.R. 1970. Economic improvements in poultry production. *In* Proceedings of the Antibiotic Presentations to the U.S. Food and Drug Administration Task Force on the Use of Antibiotics in Feeds.

HUNTER, G.J.E. 1949A. A note on the effect of penicillin in the reductase test for milk quality. J. Dairy Res. *16*, 149–151.

HUNTER, G.J.E. 1949B. The effect of penicillin in milk on the manufacture of cheddar cheese. J. Dairy Res. *16*, 235–241.

JAROLMEN, H., SAIRK, R.J., and LANGWORTH, B.F. 1976. Effect of chlorotetracycline feeding on the *Salmonella* reservoir in chickens. J. Appl. Bacteriol. *40*, 153–161.

JOHNS, C.K. and DESMARIS, J.G. 1953. The effect of residual penicillin in milk on the dye reduction tests for quality. Can. J. Agr. Sci. *33*, 91–97.

KASTLI, P. 1948. Defects of milk products through mastitis treated with penicillin. Schweiz. Arch. Tierheilk. *90*, 685–695. (German).

KAVASNIKOV, E.I. and SODENKO, V.I. 1967. Antibiotic properties of *Lactobacillus brevis*. Mikrobiol. Zh. Kyviv. *29*, 146 (Dairy Sci. Abstr. *29*, 3972)

KILARA, A. and SHAHANI, K.M. 1978. Lactic fermentations of dairy foods and their biological significance. J. Dairy Sci. *61*, 1793–1800.

KLECKNER, N., CHAN, R.K., TYE, B.K., and BOTSTEIN, D. 1975. Mutagenesis by insertion of a drug resistance element carrying an inverted repetition. J. Mol. Biol. *97*, 561–575.

KODAMA, R. 1952. Studies on lactic acid bacteria. II. Lactolin, a new antibiotic substance, produced by lactic acid bacteria. J. Antibiotics *5*, 72–74.

KOPECKO, D.J. and COHEN, S.N. 1975. Site-specific RecA independent recombination between bacterial plasmids: Involvement of palinodromes at the recombination loci. Proc. Natl. Acad. Sci. USA *72*, 1373–1377.

LEVY, S.B., FITZGERALD, G.B., and MACONE, A.B. 1976A. Changes in intestinal flora of farm personnel after introduction of a tetracycline-supplemented feed on a farm. N. Engl. J. Med. *295*, 583–588.

LEVY, S.B., FITZGERALD, G.B., and MACONE, A.B. 1976B. Spread of antibiotic resistant plasmids from chicken to chicken and from chicken to man. Nature (London) *260*, 40–42.

LINTON, K.B., LEE, P.A., RICHMOND, M.H., GILLESPIE, W.A., ROWLAND, A.J., and BAKER, V.N. 1972. Antibiotic resistance and transmissible R-factors in the intestinal coliform flora of healthy adults and children in an urban and rural community. J. Hyg. *70*, 99–104.

LOKEN, K.I., WAGNER, L.W., and HENKE, C.L. 1971. Transmissible drug resistance in Enterobacteriaceae isolated from calves given antibiotics. Am. J. Vet. Res. *32*, 1207–1212.

MALTEN, K.E. 1968. Allergy to antibiotics in minute amounts in foods. *In* Antibiotics in Agriculture. J.C. Somogyi and A.C. Francois (Editors). Proc. 5th Symp. Group Eur. Nutr., S. Karger, Basel.

MANOKIDIS, K.S., ALICHANIDIS, E.S., and VARVOGLIS, A.G. 1971. Effects of some antibiotics on the milk phosphatase pasteurization test. J. Dairy Sci. *54*, 335–338.

MARTH, E.H. and ELLICKSON, B.E. 1959. Problems created by the presence of antibiotics in milk and milk products—A review. J. Milk Food Technol. *22*, 266–272.

MARTH, E.H. 1966. Antibiotics in foods—naturally occurring, developed and added. Residue Revs. *12*, 65–161.

MATTICK, A.T.R. and HIRSCH, A. 1944. A powerful inhibitory substance produced by group N streptococci. Nature *154*, 551–554.

MATTICK, A.T.R. and HIRSCH A. 1947. Further observations on an inhibitory substance (nisin) from lactic streptococci. Lancet *253*, 5–8.

MERCER, H.D., POCURULL, D., GAINES, S., WILSON, S., and BENNETT, J.V. 1971. Characteristics of microbial resistance of *Escherichia coli* from animals: Relationship to veterinary and management uses of antimicrobial agents. Appl. Microbiol. *22*, 700–705.

MOL, H. 1975. Antibiotics and Milk. A.A. Balkema, Rotterdam.

NEU, H.C., CHERUBIN, C.E., LONGO, E.D., FLOUTON, B., and WINTER, J. 1975. Antimicrobial resistance and R-factor transfer among isolates of *Salmonella* in the northeastern United States: A comparison of human and animal isolates. J. Infec. Dis. *132*, 617–622.

REDDY, G.V. and SHAHANI, K.M. 1971. Isolation of antibiotic from *Lactobacillus bulgaricus.* J. Dairy Sci. *54*, 748 (Abstr).

REHM, L. 1967. Industrielle Mikrobiologie. Springer-Verlag, Berlin.

SHAHANI, K.M. and HARPER, W.J. 1958. The development of antibiotic resistance in cheese starter cultures. Milk Prod. J. *49*, 15–16, 53–54.

SHAHANI, K.M. 1962. Inhibitory effect of nisin upon various organisms. J. Dairy Sci. *45*, 827–832.

SHAHANI, K.M., VAKIL, J.R., and KILARA, A. 1976. Natural antibiotic activity of *Lactobacillus acidophilus* and *bulgaricus.* I. Culture conditions for the production of antibiosis. Cult. Dairy Prod. J. *11*(4) 14–17.

SHAHANI, K.M., VAKIL, J.R., and KILARA, A. 1977. Natural antibiotic activity of *Lactobacillus acidophilus* and *bulgaricus.* II. Isolation of Acidophilin from *L. acidophilus.* Cult. Dairy Prod. J. *12*(2) 8–11.

SIEGEL, D., HUBER, W.G., and ENLOE, F. 1974. Continuous nontherapeutic use of antibacterial drugs in feed and drug resistance of gram-negative enteric flora of food-producing animals. Antimicrob. Agents and Chemother. *6*, 697–701.

SIEGEL, D., HUBER, W.G., and DRYSDALE, S. 1975. Human therapeutic and agriculture uses of antibacterial drugs and resistance of the enteric flora of humans. Antimicrob. Agents and Chemother. *8*, 538–543.

SILVER, R.P. and MERCER, H.D. 1978. Antibiotics in animal feeds: An assessment of the animal and public health aspects. *In* Nutrition and Drug Interrelations. J.N. Hathcock and J. Coon (Editors). Acad. Press, New York.

SMITH, H.W. and CRABB, W.E. 1957. The effect of the continuous administration of diets containing low levels of tetracyclines on the incidence of drug-resistant *Bacterium coli* in the feces of pigs and chickens: The sensitivity of *Bact. coli* to other chemotherapeutic agents. Vet. Rec. *69*, 24–30.

SMITH, H.W. 1967. The effect of the use of antibacterial drugs, particularly as food additives, on the emergence of drug resistant strains of bacteria in animals. N. Z. Vet. J. *15*, 153–166.

VICKERS, H.R., BAGRATUNI, L., and ALEXANDER, S. 1958. Dermatitis caused by penicillin in milk. Lancet *1*, 351–352.

VINCENT, J.G., VEOMETT, R.C., and RILEY, R.I. 1959. Antibacterical activity associated with *Lactobacillus acidophilus.* J. Bacteriol. *78*, 477–484.

WATANABE, T. 1963. Infective heredity of multiple drug resistance in bacteria. Bacteriol. Rev. *27*, 87–115.

WHEATER, D.M., HIRSCH, A., and MATTICK, A.T.R. 1951. "Lactobacillin," an antibiotic from Lactobacilli. Nature *168*, 659.

WHITEHEAD, H.R. and LANE, D.J. 1956. The influence of penicillin on the manufacture and ripening of cheddar cheese. J. Dairy Res. *23*, 355–360.

WHO/FAO EXPERT COMMITTEE ON FOOD ADDITIVES. 1969. Specifications for the identity and purity of food additives and their toxicological evaluation: Some antibiotics. 12th report. WHO Technical Report Series No. 430, Geneva.

WINSHELL, E.B., CHERUBIN, C., WINTER, J., and NEU, H.C. 1969. Antibiotic resistance of *Salmonella* in the Eastern United States. *In* Antimicrob. Agents and Chemother, p. 86–89.

ZIMMERMAN, M.C. 1959. Chronic penicillin urticaria from dairy products, proved by penicillin cures. Arch. Dermatol. (N.Y.) *79*, 1.

14

The Safety of Antioxidants—Fact or Fallacy

J. W. Daniel[1]

INTRODUCTION

Antioxidants are used by food manufacturers to prevent those changes in flavor quality and nutritive value that result from the oxidative deterioration of unsaturated fats. They are probably the most ubiquitous of food additives being present in animal fats, vegetable oils, milk powder, cured meats, fruit juices, and breakfast cereals at concentrations of between 5 and 2000 ppm. The Code of Federal Regulations, Chapter 21, lists as direct additives to human foods the compounds shown in Table 14.1, the most effective being BHA, BHT, and PG which may be used either alone or in various combinations providing that the total antioxidant content does not exceed 200 ppm, a value which is based on the fat content of the product.

It is difficult to estimate with any precision the daily intake of these additives but it has been suggested that it is unlikely to exceed 5 mg, equivalent to 0.1–0.3 mg/kg bodyweight for adults and juveniles, respectively. Although BHT is also used in the manufacture of food contact materials the amount of migration into packaged foods will not make a significant contribution to the total daily intake.

The toxicity of BHA, PG and, in particular, BHT has been extensively investigated using a variety of experimental conditions whereas, in contrast, there are few published reports of studies with the remaining compounds. The information used to assess the safety of these three additives has been reviewed on several occasions (Joint FAO/WHO Expert Committee on Food Additives 1976; Daniel 1975; Hathway

[1] Life Science Research, Stock, Essex, United Kingdom.

TABLE 14.1. ANTIOXIDANTS PERMITTED FOR USE IN HUMAN FOODS

Ascorbic acid	Erythorbic acid
Ascorbyl palmitate	Ethoxyquin
Butylated hydroxyanisole (BHA)	Propyl gallate
Butylated hydroxytoluene (BHT)	Tocopherols
tert-Butyl hydroquinone (TBHQ)	Thiodipropionic acid
tert-Butyl hydroxymethyl phenol (Ionox 100)	2,4,5-Trihydroxypropiophenone (THBP)
Dilauryl dithiopropionic acid	

1966) and although the design and conduct of many of the earlier studies may be considered inadequate the data provide little evidence to suggest that the compounds will be hazardous at the permitted levels of use.

Decisions relating to the safety of food additives are rarely absolute for they depend upon several variable factors including the reliability of the data and the validity of the interpretation of any response. If confidence is to be retained in the use of these materials the basis for such decisions should be examined periodically, particularly when new information becomes available. This is an opportune moment to reconsider the safety of synthetic antioxidants for there are several issues, the significance of which has yet to be resolved.

SUB-ACUTE AND CHRONIC TOXICITY

Conventional toxicological studies in dogs and rodents with BHA, BHT, PG and TBHQ indicate the absence of any deleterious effects on either organ structure or function when administered in the diet at concentrations that are equivalent to a daily intake of between 250 and 500 mg/kg bodyweight. Ethoxyquin is appreciably more toxic, producing renal necrosis and tubular atrophy in rats at dosages greater than 3 mg /kg bodyweight (Wilson and DeEds 1959).

BHT has no effect on reproduction; neither is there any evidence that it is a teratogen. Studies in *Salmonella typhimurium* (Strains 1535, 1537, 1538, 98 and 100) with BHT, BHA, and ethoxyquin both in the absence and presence of hepatic microsomes showed the compounds to be nonmutagenic (Joner 1977) a conclusion supported by a report claiming that BHT did not induce dominant lethal mutations in mice or chromosomal abnormalities in rats or mice when administered in the diet for 9 months at a concentration of 15,000 ppm.

ALLERGENIC ACTIVITY

PG has been reported to induce delayed contact hypersensitivity in guinea-pigs and in a small number of human subjects (Kahn *et al.* 1974).

A similar effect has been obtained with BHT and BHA although at a frequency which suggests that sensitization is likely to occur only rarely.

MORPHOLOGICAL AND BIOCHEMICAL CHANGES

There is evidence from several sources to suggest that some of the effects induced by BHA and BHT, both *in vivo* and *in vitro*, are the result of changes in the structure and functional capacity of cell membranes. Metcalfe (1971) showed that the inhibitory effect of BHT on cell division and on the rate of synthesis of DNA, RNA, and protein in primary cultures of monkey kidney cells was probably due to decreased permeability of the cells to essential nutrients. The cells were histologically normal and as they were capable of dividing once the antioxidant was removed from the culture medium it was inferred that the effects were unlikely to be of toxicological significance. Similar changes were obtained with a variety of lipid-soluble compounds and would appear to be due to physical rather than chemical factors. In contrast, the addition of BHT (0–50 μg/ml culture medium) to phytohaemagglutinin-stimulated human leucocytes produced extensive damage to the cell membrane and uncoiling of the chromosomes (Sciorra *et al.* 1974). Increased permeability of the cell membrane has also been observed in hepatic lysosomes and mitochondria incubated with BHT or BHA at concentrations (0.5 mM) that suppressed lipid peroxidation. (Sgaragli and Rizzotti-Conti, 1971). Such *in vitro* studies are difficult to interpret and it is uncertain to what extent they can be used to predict *in vivo* toxicity.

Altered cell permeability may also account for the inhibitory effect of BHA and BHT on the accumulation of p-aminohippurate, and of BHA on that of N-methylnicotinamide by rat kidney slices *in vitro* (Ford *et al.* 1980). A similar depression of the transport of p-aminohippurate was observed within 24 hr of the administration to rats of either antioxidant at a dose of 500 mg/kg bodyweight but despite continued treatment the capacity of the kidney to transport the organic anion was unaffected after six days. This could be due to enhanced metabolism of the individual antioxidants suggesting that they are effective without metabolic activation. Whether the effects are specific to BHT and BHA do not appear to have been investigated.

A further example of the influence of BHT upon cell structure was provided by Marino and Mitchell (1972) who reported that the antioxidant, when administered to mice by intraperitoneal injection at dosages in excess of 40 mg/kg bodyweight, produced marked histological changes in the lungs. This phenomenon has been investigated in detail by Witschi and his colleagues and has been observed to occur in several strains of mice (Swiss-Webster, DBA, BALB/c, C3H, C57, BDF) following both oral and parenteral dosing. Morphological changes affecting the lungs, including perivascular edema and necrosis of type I alveolar cells were apparent within 24 hr of treatment and were followed after an interval of between 24 and 72 hr by extensive proliferation of type II cells. Proliferation of capillary endothelial cells, interstitial cells and some interstitial fibrosis occurred at a later stage. These events are associated with an increase in lung weight and in the rate of synthesis of DNA and RNA (Saheb and Witschi 1975). They are freely reversible and can be prevented by exposure of the animals to terpenes in cedar wood (Malkinson 1979) or by the administration of piperonyl butoxide or SKF 525A, both of which inhibit cytochrome P_{450} dependent microsomal enzymes (Kehrer and Witschi 1980) suggesting that there is a requirement for metabolic activation. Although it is possible that these changes are themselves of toxicological significance, the fact that they may potentiate the activity of other respiratory toxins is of equal if not greater significance.

HEPATOMEGALY

The ability of BHA, BHT, TBHQ and ethoxyquin to stimulate liver growth in rats is a response that is a characteristic of many lipid-soluble compounds (Schulte-Hermann 1974). The histological appearance of the enlarged liver is essentially normal and apart from an increase in the amount of smooth endoplasmic reticulum there is little of note in the ultrastructure of individual cells. The increase in mass is attributed principally to enlargement of the hepatocytes although there is evidence that this is preceded by a stage during which the synthesis of DNA is stimulated, resulting in an increase in the mitotic index and cell ploidy. Biochemical investigations have shown that in most, but not all, instances the enlarged liver is associated with an increase in the activity of those hepatic microsomal enzymes that catalyze the oxidation of drugs, pesticides, and other exogenous chemicals. The morphological and biochemical changes are freely reversible once treatment is discontinued and using evidence from acute and short-term studies Golberg (1966) concluded that liver enlargement when accompanied by an increase in microsomal enzyme activity represents an adaptive rather than a toxic response.

The relationship between liver enlargement, enzyme induction and certain forms of liver damage has been compared in female rats following treatment with BHT (4000 ppm), phenobarbitone (2500 ppm), safrole (2500 ppm), or the azodyestuff, Ponceau MX (10,000 ppm) for periods of 80 or 85 wk. Although induced enzyme activity was observed in all groups after 7 days of treatment, it was relatively short-lived in animals treated with the two hepatotoxins, safrole and Ponceau MX, and it was

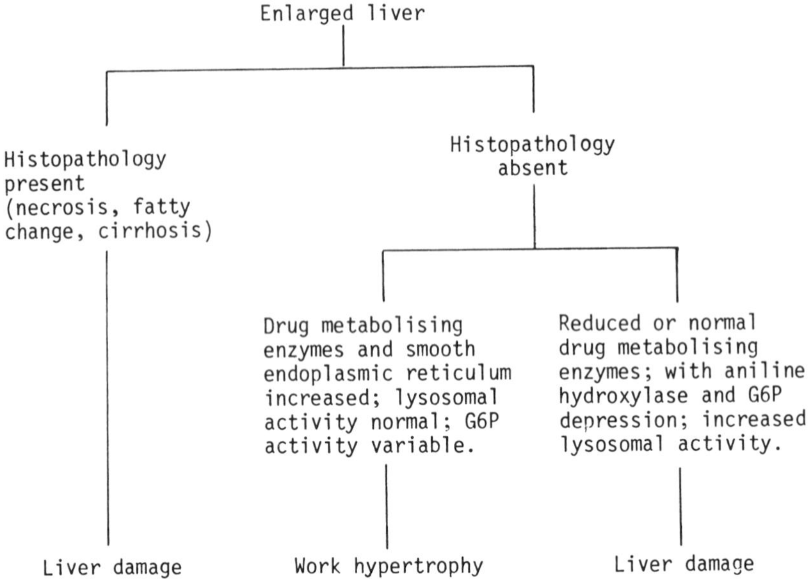

From Golberg (1966)

FIG. 14.1. TYPES OF ENLARGED LIVER IN THE RAT

suggested that liver enlargement in the absence of a sustained effect on microsomal enzyme activity may provide an index of hepatotoxicity (Crampton *et al.* 1977A, B).

Although there is general acceptance of this interpretation of the data and which is summarized in Fig. 14.1, there is some doubt concerning the significance of the hypertrophy induced in rats by BHA in the absence of any tissue injury or of a demonstrable effect on microsomal enzyme activity. BHA has a more pronounced effect than BHT on liver weight and enzyme activity in young primates and although the reasons for this difference in sensitivity have not been investigated it is possible that it is due to variation in the rate of hepatic metabolism of the antioxidant (Allan and Engblom 1972).

METABOLIC CONSIDERATIONS

Despite the importance of comparative metabolic studies in assessing the safety of drugs and food additives, controlled experiments in human volunteers have been reported for only BHA and BHT. The metabolic profile of BHA in man is similar to that of rat and rabbit and there is no evidence that the compound accumulates in the tissues. The transformation of BHT is, in contrast, more complex due to the influence of the *tert*-butyl substituents on the reactivity of the phenolic group. The major urinary metabolites in man, rat, and rabbit have been identified and the results are presented in Fig. 14.2.

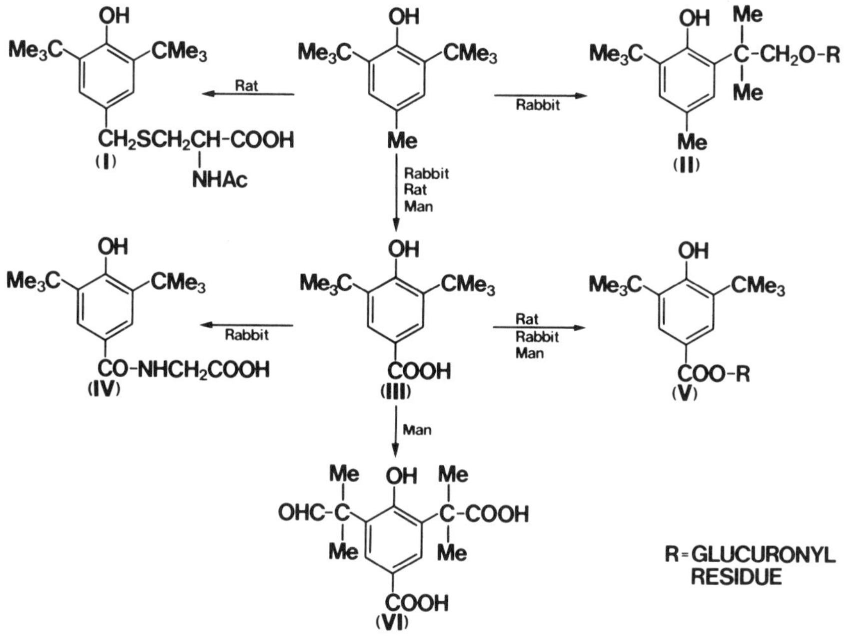

FIG. 14.2. COMPARATIVE METABOLISM OF BHT IN MAN, RAT, AND RABBIT

Metabolite III is derived from the corresponding alcohol that is produced when BHT is incubated *in vitro* with rat liver microsomes, while the precursor of I is probably the free radical VII (R = *tert*-butyl) which then reacts with reduced glutathione.

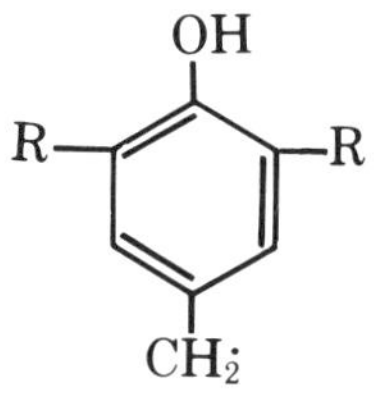

VII

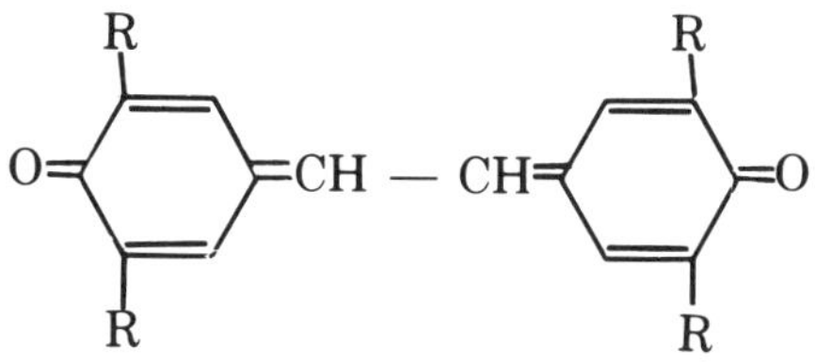

VIII

This radical is also implicated in the formation of the substituted stilbenequinone, VIII, the presence of which has been reported in cereals and snack foods. Takahashi and Hiraga (1979) reported the isolation of 2,6-di-*tert*-butyl-4-methylene-2,5-cyclohexadienone (IX) from the livers of rats that had been fed BHT (12,000 ppm) for 2 wk, while 4-hydroxy-4-methyl-2,6-di-*tert*-butyl cyclohexa-2,5-dienone (X) and the corresponding hydroperoxy compound have been detected in hepatic microsomes.

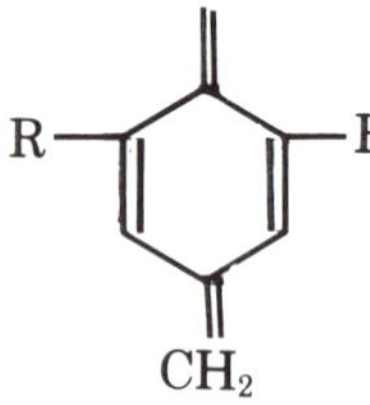

IX

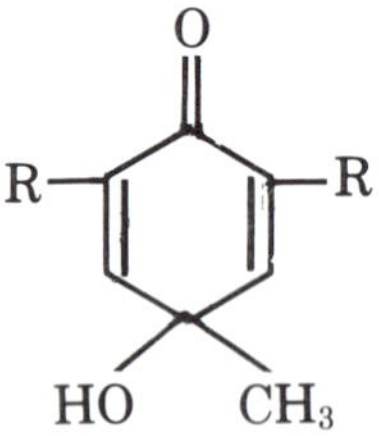

X

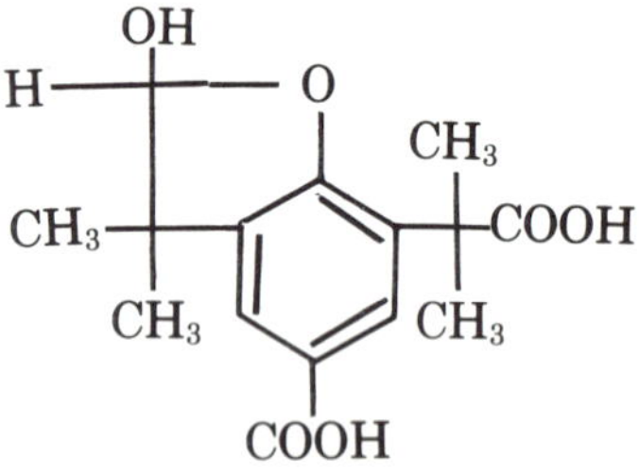

XI

An alternative structure, XI, has been proposed for the major metabolite in human urine (Wiebe *et al.* 1978), the formation of which involves the simultaneous oxidation of all three alkyl substituents. No evidence has been obtained for metabolite VI in any species other than man and nothing is known of its intrinsic toxicity. Despite these differences the biological half-life of BHT in man is similar to that in the rat.

It is becoming increasingly evident that many toxic chemicals, including carcinogens, mutagens and those that produce necrosis and hypersensitivity reactions, are converted in the target organs to intermediates that become covalently bound to tissue macromolecules. Nakagawa *et al.* (1979) showed that covalently bound radioactivity was present in all the major organs, including brain, lung, liver, spleen, and kidney following the administration of BHT labelled with carbon-14 to rats and that binding to hepatic microsomes *in vitro* only occurred in the presence of $NADPH_2$, oxygen, and functional cytochrome P_{450}. Kehrer and Witschi (1980) compared the binding of radioactivity in the lung, liver, and kidney of male BALB/c mice and SD rats at intervals after the administration of BHT by intraperitoneal injection and found that although bound radioactivity was present within 2 hr in all tissues examined, the highest concentration was in mouse lung. It was also reported that binding was a linear function of the dose of BHT in the range examined (50–600 mg/kg bodyweight) and could be reduced, although not abolished, by the simultaneous administration of SKF 525A, whereas binding to all other tissues was not affected. This suggests that the lung damage observed in mice is due to a reactive metabolite and, in addition, that some of the bound radioactivity is the result of an interaction with free radicals.

CARCINOGENICITY

Although the evidence of chronic toxicity studies indicates the absence of neoplastic change, few studies have been designed specifically to assess the carcinogenic potential of the individual compounds. A report from the National Cancer Institute (1979) in which Fischer rats and B6C3F1 mice were fed BHT at dietary concentrations of 3000 and 6000 ppm for 2 yr concluded that treatment had no effect on tumor incidence in either species. Although the number of tumors in the lungs of female mice in the low dose group (16/46) was significantly higher than in the corresponding control group (1/20), it was considered not to be treatment-related as the incidence of similar tumors in the top-dose group (7/50) was not dose-related. The only criterion used for the selection of the Maximum Tolerated Dose was a 10% reduction in bodyweight and the possibility of enhanced metabolism at the higher dose resulting from enzyme induction appears to have been ignored. A previous study in which BHT was fed to CF1 mice at concentrations of 1000, 2500, and 5000 ppm for 100 wk reported an incidence of lung tumors (adenomas and carcinomas) of 47, 53, 74, and 75% for the control and treated groups, respectively. However, there were no morphological features to distinguish between the tumors in the control and treated animals and it is possible that BHT merely enhanced the rate of tumor development (Brooks *et al.* 1976).

There is now evidence to suggest that BHT may, under some circumstances, act as a promoter of chemical carcinogenesis. Witschi *et al.* (1977) reported that the repeated administration of BHT (250 mg/kg) to male Swiss-Webster and strain A/J mice commencing 7 days after the administration of urethan (1 mg/g) significantly increased the yield of lung tumors in both strains, whereas the incidence in control and treated mice was similar if the antioxidant was administered prior to the carcinogen. Subsequent studies in those strains of mice with a low spontaneous incidence of lung adenoma failed to demonstrate any effect of BHT on urethan-induced tumorigenesis (Table 14.2) despite the fact that the antioxidant produced proliferative changes in the lungs of all the strains examined (Witschi and Lock 1979).

Among the criteria used to characterize a promoting agent is the ability to be effective when applied several months after the initiator and to stimulate tumor formation when low doses of the initiator are administered (Boutwell 1974). Although BHT has been shown to be effective in

TABLE 14.2. INFLUENCE OF BHT ON THE TUMOR INCIDENCE IN MICE FOLLOWING TREATMENT WITH URETHAN (1000 mg/kg)

Strain	Treatment	No. of mice with tumors (%)	No. of tumors/mouse
C57BL	BHT[a]	41	0.55
	Corn oil	22	0.43
C3H	BHT	27	0.27
	Corn oil	21	0.26
BALB/C	BHT	77	1.50
	Corn oil	56	0.96
Swiss-Webster	BHT	100	19.1
	Corn oil	100	12.5

[a] Witschi and Lock (1979).

susceptible strains when applied 19 wk after urethan, no effect was observed when a low dose (50 μg/g) of the initiator was used (Witschi 1980).

Promoting agents usually stimulate cell division in target tissues and BHT is known to increase DNA-synthesis in the lungs of treated mice although not in rats (Larsen and Tarding 1978). The ability of BHT to increase tumor incidence in mice treated with urethan, however, is not dependent upon cell proliferation for Witschi (1980) found that the administration of SKF 525A which prevents both the increase of thymidine uptake into pulmonary DNA and the associated proliferation of Type II alveolar cells failed to influence the response to BHT. Moreover the antioxidant was found to be effective at a dose (50 mg/kg bodyweight) which does not produce any morphological or biochemical changes in the lung. The possible role of BHT as a promoter of hepatic carcinogenesis emerges from studies in which male rats were fed 2-acetylaminofluorene (200 ppm) for 18 days and were then maintained for 58 wk on a diet containing 5000 ppm of the antioxidant (Peraino *et al.* 1977). The incidence of hepatic tumors was 7% in control rats and 26% in those treated with BHT. The response was considerably less than that observed in rats treated with phenobarbitone and there was no increase in the rate of DNA-synthesis in animals receiving BHT.

The temporal sequence between BHT treatment and exposure to chemical carcinogens is clearly of importance for it has been shown that the prior administration of BHA, BHT, and ethoxyquin can protect against the effects produced by benzo-(a)pyrene, 2-acetylaminofluorene, p-dimethylaminoazobenzene, 7,12-dimethylbenzanthracene and other carcinogens (Wattenberg 1978). This is probably a nonspecific action resulting from enhanced microsomal metabolism of the individual carcinogens with a corresponding reduction in the amount of proximate carcinogen that is covalently bound to DNA and protein.

APPRAISAL

Although reference is made frequently to the greater toxicity of BHT, comparison with the other antioxidants is precluded by the lack of equivalent data for all apart from BHA, PG, and TBHQ. Threshold values have been obtained for all of the effects obtained *in vivo* and it would appear that there is an adequate margin of safety between these levels and the estimated human exposure.

There is presumptive evidence that the proliferative lesions in the lungs of mice following oral or parenteral administration of BHT is due to the formation of a reactive metabolite which becomes bound to components within the cell. Such binding also occurs in rats, although at a reduced level, and it is possible that the susceptibility of the mouse is due either to differences in the rate of formation of the reactive intermediate or of enhanced sensitivity of the cells to the initiator rather than to the production of a specific metabolite. The characterization of such toxic intermediates in target cells is technically demanding and few have been identified unequivocally. It is unlikely therefore that conventional metabolic studies in mice as stipulated by the Food and Drug Administration for BHT will serve to elucidate the mechanism whereby BHT enhances urethan-induced tumorigenesis in susceptible strains of mice. Although these strains have been used for screening chemicals for carcinogenic activity whether they are appropriate for safety evaluation is questionable. The tumors have no direct counterpart in human pathology and it would be unwise to take precipitate action on the basis of such studies without corroboration from other sources. Moreover, the reported ability of BHT to enhance tumor formation even when proliferation of Type II alveolar cells is prevented indicates that the action of the antioxidant is atypical of other promoting agents.

Further studies, including the use of different strains of rats and mice, of carcinogens that affect tissues other than the lungs and dose levels that correspond more closely to human intake, are necessary before an informed judgement of the possible significance of this phenomenon can be made. Moreover, the issue may not be resolved until action of urethan, rather than that of BHT, is further elaborated.

The extrapolation to man of experimental observations in laboratory animals is a complex process and it is customary to use a 'safety factor' to compensate for any possible differences in sensitivity between the species. It is probable that some of the effects observed with BHT can be attributed either to the compound itself or to free radicals produced *in situ* and that metabolism results in reduced toxicity. Whether this is true for man is conjectural and in the absence of any information from an "appropriate" species there is no alternative but to rely on the use of an adequate safety factor.

BIBLIOGRAPHY

ALLEN, J.R. and ENGBLOM, J.F. 1972. Ultrastructural and biochemical changes in the liver of monkeys given butylated hydroxytoluene and butylated hydroxyanisole. Fd. Cosmet. Toxicol. *10*, 769–779.

BOUTWELL, R.K. 1974. The function and mechanisms of promoters of carcinogenesis. Crit. Revs. Toxicol. *2*, 419–443.

BROOKS, T.M., HUNT, P.F., THORPE, E., and WALKER, A.I.T. 1976. Personal communication. Shell Chemical Co., Sittingbourne, Kent, U.K.

CRAMPTON, R.F., GRAY, T.J.B., GRASSO, P., and PARKE, D.V. 1977A. Long term studies on chemically induced liver enlargement in the rat. I. Sustained induction of microsomal enzymes with absence of liver damage on feeding phenobarbitone or butylated hydroxytoluene. Toxicology 7, 289–306.

CRAMPTON, R.F., GRAY, T.J.B., GRASSO, P., and PARKE, D.V. 1977B. Long term studies on chemically induced liver enlargement in the rat. II. Transient induction of microsomal enzymes leading to liver damage and nodular hyperplasia produced by safrole and Ponceau MX. Toxicology *7*, 307–326.

DANIEL, J.W. 1975. Synthetic antioxidants: A re-appraisal of safety. Proc. 6th Inter. Cong. Pharmacol. (Helsinki), 137–146.

FORD, S.M., HOOK, J.B., and BOND, J.T. 1980. The effects of butylated hydroxyanisole and butylated hydroxytoluene on renal function in the rat. II. Effects on organic acid and base transport. Fd. Cosmet. Toxicol. *15*, 21–26.

GOLBERG, L. 1966. Liver enlargement produced by drugs; its significance. Proc. Eur. Soc. Drug Toxicity, *VII*, 171–184.

HATHWAY, D.E. 1966. Metabolic fate in animals of hindered phenolic antioxidants in relation to their safety evaluation and antioxidant function. Adv. Food Res *15*, 1–56.

JOINT FAO/WHO EXPERT COMMITTEE ON FOOD ADDITIVES. 1976. Toxicological evaluation of certain food additives. WHO Fd. Additive Series No. 10.

JONER, P.E. 1977. Butylhydroxyanisol (BHA), butylhydroxytoluene (BHT) and ethoxyquin (EMQ) tested for mutagenicity. Acta Vet. Scand. *18*, 187–193.

KAHN, G., PHANUPHAK, P., and CLAMAN, H.N. 1974. Propyl gallate contact sensitization and orally induced tolerance. Arch. Dermatol. *109*, 506–509.

KEHRER, J.P. and WITSCHI, H-P. 1980. Effects of drug metabolism inhibitors on butylated hydroxytolune-induced pulmonary toxicity in mice. Toxicol. Appl. Pharmacol. *53*, 333–342.

LARSEN, J.C. and TARDING, F. 1978. Stimulation of DNA synthesis in mouse and rat lung following administration of butylated hydroxytoluene. Arch. Toxicol. Suppl. 1., 147–150.

MALKINSON, A.M. 1979. Prevention of butylated hydroxytoluene lung damage in mice by cedar-terpene administration. Toxicol. Appl. Pharmacol. *49*, 551–560.

MARINO, A.A. and MITCHELL, J.J. 1972. Lung damage in mice following intraperitoneal injection of butylated hydroxytoluene. Proc. Soc. Exp. Biol. Med. *140*, 122–125.

METCALFE, S.M. 1971. Cell culture as a test-system for toxicity. J. Pharm. Pharmac. *23*, 817–823.

NAKAGAWA, Y., HVAGE, K., and SINGA, T. 1979. Biological fate of butylated hydroxytoluene(BHT); binding *in vivo* of BHT to macromolecules in rat liver. Chem. Pharm. Bull. *27*, 442–446.

NATIONAL CANCER INSTITUTE. 1979. Bioassay of butylated hydroxytoluene (BHT) for possible carcinogenicity. CAS No. 128-37-0. Tech. Rep. Ser. No. 150.

PERAINO, C., FRY, R.J.M., STAFFEDT, E., and CHRISTOPHER, P. 1977. Enhancing effects of phenobarbital and butylated hydroxytoluene in 2-acetylaminofluorene-induced hepatic tumorigenesis in the rat. Fd. Cosmet. Toxicol. *15*, 93–96.

SAHEB, W. and WITSCHI, H-P. 1975. Lung growth in mice after a single dose of butylated hydroxytoluene. Toxicol. Appl. Pharmacol. *33*, 309–319.

SCHULTE-HERMANN, R. 1974. Induction of liver growth by xenobiotic compounds and other stimuli. Crit. Revs. Toxicol. *3*, 97–158.

SCIORRA, L.J., KAUFMANN, B.N., and MAIER, R. 1974. The effects of butylated hydroxytoluene on the cell-cycle and chromosome morphology of phytohaemagglutinin-stimulated lymphocyte cultures. Food Cosmet. Toxicol. *12*, 33–44.

SGARAGLI, G. and RIZZOTTI-CONTI, M. 1971. Effects of lipid peroxidation inhibitors (BHA, BHT) on the membrane of rat liver lysosomes and mitochondria. Pharmacol. Res. Commun. *3*, 315–325.

TAKAHASHI, O. and HIRAGA, K. 1979. 2,6-Di-tert-butyl-4-methylene-2,5-cyclohexadienone: a hepatic metabolite of butylated hydroxytoluene in rats. Fd. Cosmet. Toxicol. *17*, 451–454.

WATTENBERG, L.W. 1978. Inhibition of chemical carcinogenesis. J. Nat. Cancer Inst. *60*, 11–18.

WIEBE, L.E., MERCER, J.R., and RYAN, A.J. 1978. Urinary metabolites of 3,5-di-(1-[^{13}C]methyl-1-methylethyl)-4-hydroxytoluene (BHT-^{13}C) in man. Drug. Metab. Dispos. *6*, 296–302.

WILSON, R.H. and DeEDS, F.J. 1959. Toxicity studies on the antioxidant 6-ethoxy-1,2-dihydro-2,2,4-trimethylquinoline. J. Agr. Food Chem., 7, 203–206.

WITSCHI, H-P. 1980. Personal communication. Oak Ridge National Lab., Tennessee.

WITSCHI, H-P. and LOCK, S. 1979. Enhancement of adenoma in mouse lung by butylated hydroxytoluene. Toxicol. Appl. Pharmacol. *50*, 391–400.

WITSCHI, H-P., WILLIAMSON, D., and LOCK, S. 1977. Enhancement of urethan tumorigenesis in mouse lung by butylated hydroxytoleune. J. Natl. Cancer Inst. *58*, 301–305.

15

Condiments, Spices, and Flavors

Richard L. Hall[1]

Flavors, including spices, include more than three-quarters of the "intentional additives" in our food supply, and it is appropriate that they be considered in this Symposium (Table 15.1). However, "unwanted chemical substances in foods," the phrase used in the title of this section, will, in this paper, exclude contaminants, both naturally occurring and man-made. Mycotoxins and bacterial toxins have been discussed separately and, in any event, spices have not historically been major carriers of these unwelcome materials.

Except for fumigants, pesticides are probably less used on spices than on other, more intensively grown crops. Environmental contaminants affect the natural sources of flavor no more, and perhaps somewhat less, than they do other components of our food supply. The major substances of toxicological interest in condiments, spices, and flavors, almost without exception, are the naturally occurring constituents themselves—often the valuable characterizing constituents.

Of the large number of flavoring substances, and the even larger number of constituents of the complex natural flavors, only a few—twelve more or less, depending on one's criteria—have so far been identified as posing serious or unusual toxic risks. These few cover a considerable spectrum of toxic effects (Fig. 15.1) (NAS 1973; Drinkwater *et al.* 1976).

This is enough to suggest that flavors, whether natural, nature-identical, or synthetic, should not automatically be exempt from safety evaluation, but it says little about the possible extent of the risks involved in their use.

[1] McCormick & Company, Inc., Hunt Valley, Maryland.

Substances Added to Foods for Specific Technical Effects

GRAS & REGULATED SUBSTANCES

	GRAS	REGULATED
DIRECT		
Flavors	1650	860
Other 21CFR172	200	120
PRIOR SANCTION	100 (?)	
Color		30
INDIRECT		
Packaging	110	2900
Pesticides	—	60
	2060	3850
		2060
		5910
FLAVORING DUPLICATED GRAS & REGULATED		- 860
		5050

(List generally accurate as of early 1979)

Prepared 5/2/80

Conflicting considerations apply. Flavoring materials and their constituents have been evaluated for safety, but most have not received extensive toxicological testing. Structural analogy between the substances in Table 15.1 and other flavor constituents suggests the high probability that others could be shown to possess similar toxicity. Conversely, the low levels either of use, or of occurrence in food of most flavoring substances, suggest that the actual toxic *risk* is small.

It is an established fact that most flavoring substances are self-limiting in use; i.e., over-flavoring renders a food unpalatable at a multiple of normal use far smaller than the safety factors commonly employed in safety evaluation. But not all flavors are self-limiting.

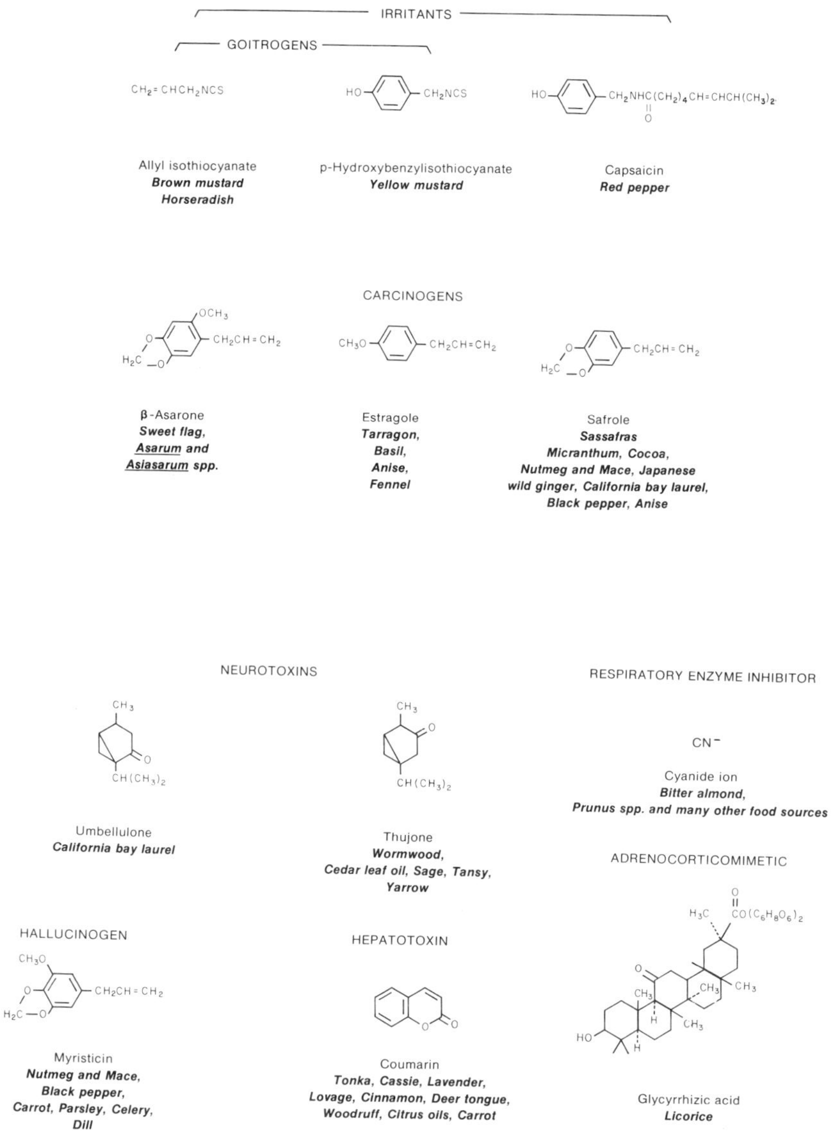

FIG. 15.1. FLAVORING SUBSTANCES AND/OR CONSTITUENTS OF COMPLEX NATURAL FLAVORS, IDENTIFIED AS POSING UNUSUAL TOXIC RISKS

Underlying this discussion is an economic problem. Three-quarters of all flavors are used at less than 500 kilograms per year in the United States, and half are used at less than 100 kilos. This is an impossibly small quantity on which to base a major testing program. Put differently, for more than half the flavors in use, the total amount of each used annually in the United States is not enough to run a chronic study in rats.

Thus, more than any other group of food ingredients, flavors raise compellingly the need to apply the principle of commensurate effort—to devote effort to each risk only in proportion to the size of the risk.

This is easier said than done. As we have had several occasions to observe, knowledge of risk is never either complete or certain, and even relative completeness and certainty are achievable only in retrospect. But the impossibility of pursuing every risk equally and the immorality of misallocating scarce effort in the face of significant risks force us to make a strenuous attempt to apply the principle of commensurate effort.

RISK ESTIMATION

In the last few years, there have been a number of proposals for pencil and paper—or computer—toxicology (Arthur D. Little, Inc. 1977; Enslein 1980). The publication that attempts to reach furthest in risk estimation is that of Cramer *et al.* (1978). It uses a series of questions in the form of a decision tree, shown in schematic form in Figure 15.2, to classify any ingested organic or metallo-organic substance of known structure into one of three classes of probable toxicity. This classification, and knowledge of intake can be combined to place each such substance into one of the boxes in a "presumable risk" matrix (Figure 15.3). Each box has associated with it a "Protection Index" (P.I.), the reciprocal of a very conservative estimate of risk, calculated, as shown in the figure, from the lowest "no effect level" for each class, and the upper limit of each intake bracket.

Accompanying the P.I. for each box is a letter, ranging from A for high P.I.s, to D for the lowest P.I.s, which designates the approximate quantity and kind of data needed for safety evaluation. To this point, no serious flaw in the function of the tree has been noted, and it appears of real value in arriving at (1) priorities for further study, and (2) a preliminary estimate of the data that should be available for comfortable evaluation of the safety of each compound in view of this preliminary, but conservative estimate of risk.

Toxicology is far from the point, however, when any of us can feel satisfied with a completely pencil-and-paper approach. At least for higher priority categories, appropriate animal data are needed. Here we find flavors present another dilemma. For the reasons already dis-

Decision tree prediction of toxic risk

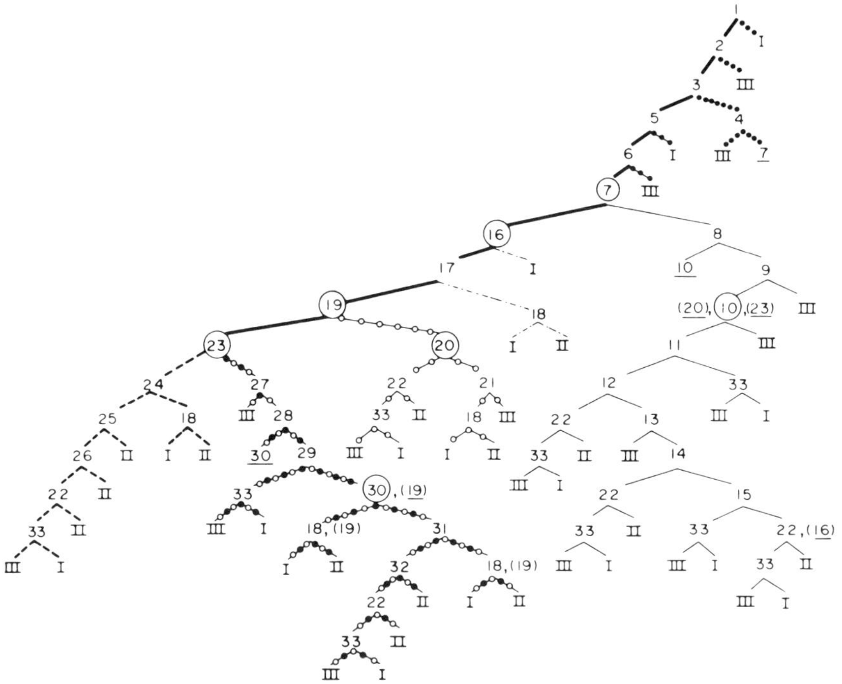

FIG. 15.2. SCHEMATIC DIAGRAM OF DECISION TREE FOR ESTIMATING PROBABLE TOXICITY

Assessors should (a) start with question 1, (b) proceed by "no" ↙ or ↘ "yes," (c) move from any underscored number encountered to same circled number, and (d) proceed to final classes I, II or III. Parenthesized questions are those which may be called into use, depending upon the substance, by the previous question in the tree. Working downwards through the tree, the symbols designate the following groupings: biological normality (● ● ●), high and low toxicity (●—●—●); heterocyclics (————); terpenoids (— · — · —); aliphatics (—O—O—O); aromatics (O—●—O); alicyclics (— — — — — —)

cussed—the large number of exceedingly small-volume substances—no industry stands in greater need of reproducible, inexpensive, short-term tests which correlate well with animal studies in predicting human risk. And no industry can less afford false positives and conflicting results. The currently available short-term tests include at least those shown in Table 15.2 compiled from the Report of the Scientific Committee of the Food Safety Council (FSC) (Food Safety Council 1980). Of all these tests, the salmonella assay (Ames Test) is by far the most frequently used.

Such test systems have an understandable appeal for the regulator who must show that he has paid some attention to the thousands of substances for which he is responsible. He thinks globally—statistically—without interest in a particular substance.

CLASS	Per capita Intake in Milligrams							
	$<10^{-5}$ (s)	10^{-5} to 10^{-4} (t)	10^{-4} to 10^{-3} (u)	10^{-3} to 10^{-2} (v)	10^{-2} to 10^{-1} (w)	0.1 to 1.0 (x)	1.0 to 10. (y)	>10 (z)
I	$>2.5\times10^{8}$ A	$>2.5\times10^{7}$ A	$>2.5\times10^{6}$ A	$>2.5\times10^{5}$ A	$>2.5\times10^{4}$ B	$>2.5\times10^{3}$ C	>250 C	<250 D
II	$>2.5\times10^{7}$ A	$>2.5\times10^{6}$ A	$>2.5\times10^{5}$ A	$>2.5\times10^{4}$ B	$>2.5\times10^{3}$ C	>250 C	>25 D	<25 D
III	(5.0×10^{5}) A	(5.0×10^{4}) B	(5.0×10^{3}) C	(500) C	(50) D	(?) D	(?) D	(?) D

$$\text{"Protection Index" (P.I.)} = \frac{\text{Lowest NEL for Class (mg/kg bwt.)} \times 50 \text{ kg bwt.}}{\text{Maximum of intake range (mg) in column}}$$

FIG. 15.3. TABULATION OF CLASSIFICATION BY PRESUMABLE RISK SHOWING "PROTECTION INDEX" AND CATEGORIES OF SAFETY CRITERIA

For the person interested in a particular substance, the quality of data, the relevance of the test, the reproducibility of the system, and its cost, loom much larger, and in this respect, the short-term tests still are seriously lacking.

While each test has at least potential merit for the detection of some type of genetic damage, and thus may have implications for possible carcinogenic activity as well, all, including the salmonella assay, suffer from a number of problems. Reproducibility between laboratories, or even within the same laboratory, is often poor. Correlation with the results of chronic feeding studies in higher animals is good for some categories of chemical structure, but only fair, poor, or unknown for others. Both activating and protective mechanisms—metabolic or immunological—which may operate in higher animals are partly or completely absent. DNA repair processes may differ sharply in the test organism, in conventional animal models, and in humans. Dose/response relationships are difficult to translate to higher animals. The standard of comparison—the multilevel, three-generation study in a rodent species—is itself a bit of a rubber ruler. Finally, we need the perspective that results from applying these tests to a multitude of the normal components of our environment, including our diet, before we can interpret wisely the results from work on substances under question.

The Safety Evaluation Coordination Committee of the Flavor and Extract Manufacturers' Association (FEMA), the Expert Panel (a panel

TABLE 15.2. OPERATIONAL CHARACTERISTICS OF SOME CURRENT TESTS FOR MUTAGENIC ACTIVITY

Test system	Time to run test	Relative ease of detection	
		Gene Mutations	Chromosome Aberrations
Microorganisms with metabolic activation:			
Salmonella typhimurium	2 to 3 days	Excellent	
Escherichia coli	2 to 3 days	Excellent	
Yeasts	3 to 5 days	Good	Unknown
Neurospora crassa	1 to 3 weeks	Very good	Good
Cultured mammalian cells with metabolic activation	2 to 5 weeks	Excellent to fair	Unknown
Host-mediated assay with:			
Microorganisms	2 to 7 days	Good	
Mammalian cells	2 to 5 weeks	Unknown	Good
Body fluid analysis	2 days	Excellent	
Plants:			
Vicia faba	3 to 8 days		Relevance unclear
Tradescantia paludosa	2 to 5 weeks	Potentially excellent	
Insects:			
Drosophila melanogaster:			
Gene mutations	2 to 7 weeks	Good to excellent	
Chromosome abberations	2 to 7 weeks		Good to excellent
Mammals:			
Dominant lethal mutations	2 to 4 months		Unknown
Translocations	5 to 7 months		Potentially very good
Blood or bone marrow cytogenetics	1 to 5 weeks		Potentially good
Specific locus mutations	2 to 3 months	Unknown	

Source: Food Safety Council (1980).

of nonindustry toxicologists), and consulting specialists on the subject recently reviewed the current state of the short-term tests.

FEMA has not now adopted a formal position on these tests. However, it seems clear that the following statements are likely to summarize the Association's use of these tests, subject to continued rethinking of the subject, and to the continuing evolution of (i) basic understanding of the significance of what each of the tests measures, (ii) the technology of running the tests in a replicable way, and (iii) interpretive value particularly in terms of dose/response and interspecies differences.

1. If used at all, a battery of tests should be employed, following one of the groupings or hierarchies such as that recommended by the Food Safety Council.

2. Among flavoring substances, the tests should at present be used primarily as a research tool, and not routinely in safety evaluation.
    a. As a research tool, they may be useful in selecting substances for further development which are less likely to raise later problems, or in choosing a process which avoids mutagenic impurities.
    b. In safety evaluation, they should be employed only as a supplement or preliminary to extensive, conventional animal testing.

As the tests improve in replicability, interpretability, and one vainly hopes, relative cost, we may see wider use in the area of their greatest promise—as replacements for expensive, lengthy, complex, and less than perfect chronic studies.

For those compounds on which substantial animal data now exist, we are beginning the process of attempting to correlate the Protection Index derived from applying the decision tree to each compound, with risk estimates derived from various methods of extrapolating animal data. In part, this will serve either to confirm further, to alter, or to disprove the utility of the decision tree. But it may have another value as well. In our debates on food safety, we are groping our way toward more consistent and graduated, if not quite semi-quantitative, handling of risk. In this process, some effort at risk comparison seems inevitable. It is possible that naturally occurring toxicants in our food supply can provide us with relevant benchmarks for acceptable risks of various kinds. At the very least, they will provide us with the background level of risk in food beyond which the pointless pursuit of ever smaller risks will obviously be unproductive.

FOOD ADDITIVES

It is customary to define an additive broadly, as any minor ingredient added to food to produce a specific technical effect. We then categorize additives by these technical effects. Most such categories contain at least some substances which also occur naturally.

The nutrients, by definition, consist essentially entirely of "nature-identical" materials. Again, flavors include by far the most such nature-identical substances. Indeed, there is very little possibility that a chemical will be a useful flavoring ingredient unless it is identical or closely similar in chemical structure to naturally occurring ingredients responsible for a desirable flavor. Only a handful—less than a dozen—possess structures such as to suggest there is virtually no possibility of finding them naturally in food. Toxicological considerations reinforce this tendency to imitate nature.

Where an ingredient appears in the diet only as a result of intentional addition, the basic principles for evaluation and regulation are relatively clear—not necessarily indisputable—but clear. The Food and Drug Act, and the regulations issued under it, outline the current regulatory requirements. Sources such as *Risk Assessment/Safety Evaluation of Food Chemicals* (National Academy of Sciences-National Research Council 1980), and the Report of the Scientific Committee of the Food Safety Council (1980) lay out the scientific basis for risk evaluation; the Report of the Committee on Saccharin and Food Safety (NAS 1979) and the Report of the Social and Economic Committee of the Food Safety Council (1979) propose general principles relating to the acceptability of risk, and contribute usefully to the developing debate on statutory change.

Different and more strict regulation of an intentionally added substance is often based on the proposition "let's control what we can." This has a certain logic, but that logic begins to erode as more and more of our intake comes from uncontrolled natural sources. This poses an anomaly. In our current debate over nitrite, for example, it seems clear that the United States Department of Agriculture could much more effectively reduce our total nitrite exposure if it could regulate nitrogen fertilizer applications to green leafy vegetables rather than by banning nitrite in cured meats.

Again, flavors present the widest range of possibilities. Of the very few exclusively synthetic flavors, such as ethyl methyl phenylglycidate, methyl 2-octynoate, or musk ambrette (Fig. 15.4), we obviously derive all of our intake from intentional use. Regulation of such use, therefore, regulates our exposure. In the broad middle of the range are substances such as vanillin or cinnamaldehyde, most of our intake of which is from intentional use as synthetically produced material. But others, like citral, come mostly from natural food sources. Still others, such as spice components, may come principally from natural sources, but intentionally used for their flavor rather than for nutritional purposes. But as Dr. Jan Stofberg (Stofberg 1979, 1980) has recently pointed out, at the extreme are a large number of flavoring substances of which typical examples are shown in Fig. 15.5. Note that for the combined pyrazines, the intake from a single popular "natural" source, coffee, is about 3,000 times the total intake from intentional use in all foods. For decadienal, the intake from potato chips alone is approximately 100 times greater than the intentional use in all foods. Unless safety questions so urgent as to result in the regulation of coffee or potato chips arise, it seems difficult to develop a reasonable rationale for regulating these relatively trace increments. More generally, it seems clear that where serious risk is not implied, and where the overwhelming preponderance of present or probable exposure

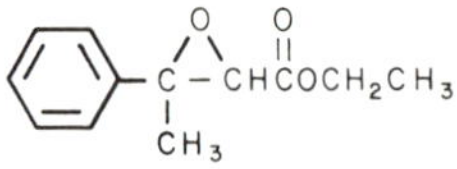

ETHYL 3-METHYL-3-PHENYLGLYCIDATE ("EMPG")

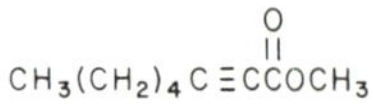

METHYL 2-OCTYNOATE

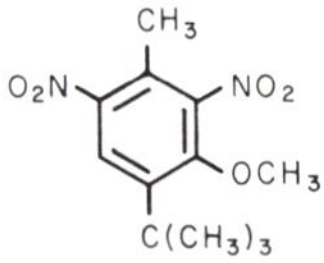

2,6-DINITRO-3-METHOXY-1-METHYL-4-tert-BUTYLBENZENE
("MUSK AMBRETTE")

FIG. 15.4. FLAVORING MATERIALS UNLIKELY TO OCCUR NATURALLY IN FOOD

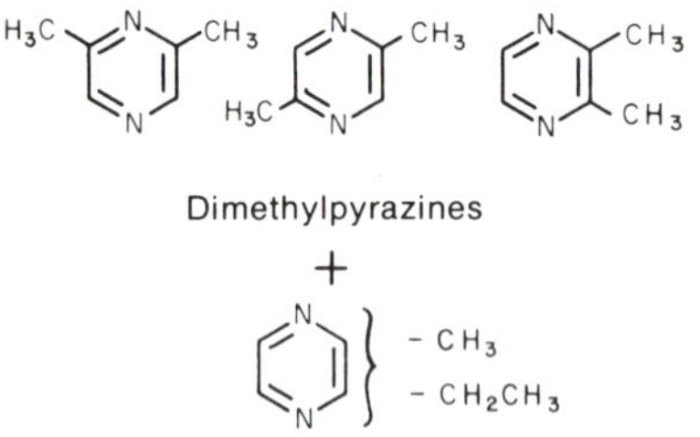

Dimethylpyrazines
+
Methylethylpyrazine

TOTAL ANNUAL "DISAPPEARANCE" IN U.S. FOOD USE FROM--

OCCURRENCE IN COFFEE	INTENTIONAL FLAVOR USE
~ 100,000 lbs.	~ 33 lbs.

$CH_3(CH_2)_2CH=CHCH=CHCHO$

2-trans-4-trans-Decadienal

OCCURRENCE IN POTATO CHIPS	INTENTIONAL FLAVOR USE
~ 1,350 lbs.	~ 15 lbs.

FIG. 15.5. COMPARISON OF INTAKES FROM NATURAL OCCURRENCE IN ONE FOOD VS. INTENTIONAL USE IN ALL FOODS

comes from uncontrolled naturally occurring sources, there is little reason to regulate intentional addition, although there is every reason to recognize and monitor it.

This last point is reinforced by a dawning realization explored more fully elsewhere (Hall 1980). Once we believed that the essential oils and related natural constituents of plants were highly characteristic of each plant, although certain few components, such as α-pinene, were widely distributed. That was before the days of sensitive gas chromatography, high-pressure liquid chromatography, and computerized mass spectrometry.

In the past two decades, the emphasis has subtly shifted. Many plants do contain one or a few substances highly characteristic of the genus or family; e.g., piperine or capsaicin. But we have increasingly begun to realize that most of the components of essential oils, including many that are characterizing in some oils, occur widely throughout the plant kingdom. Thus, eugenol, the major constituent of oil of cloves, occurs also in cinnamon, basil, nutmeg, pepper, and vanilla, quite unrelated botanical families. Linaloöl, the major component of basil, occurs in most spices and herbs which have been carefully examined. Thus, it often is not the singular occurrence of components which distinguishes essential oils but rather the proportions—the pattern—of their common constituents. This makes even less appropriate a yes-or-no, ban-or-permit, natural versus synthetic approach to safety evaluation and regulation.

As mentioned earlier, we are moving toward some form of risk comparison—possibly anchored to benchmarks representing widely acceptable level of food-related risks. No food or ingredient is wholly without risk, however rare, small, or hypothetical. Thus, we do not avoid risk by avoiding a particular food or additive; we simply exchange the risk of the food we avoid for the risks of the food we do eat. Risk comparison where the data exist or can be found, has a necessary place.

We have too often in the past reacted piecemeal to adverse results, peremptorily replacing a newly suspect substance with another which only appears safer because it has not been as adequately studied. Thus, we have replaced Red No. 2 with Red No. 40 (or beet juice!), DDT with organic phosphates, and triclorethylene with methylene chloride. It is not clear that any of these actions has advanced human health. Risk comparison, rather than piecemealing, is clearly more rational.

RISK/BENEFIT ANALYSIS

Beyond risk comparison, however, we now find ourselves discussing the possibility of some form of risk/benefit analysis—a prospect that makes almost everyone very nervous—but the discussion goes on anyway. The ultimate resolution of this may not be as difficult as now appears. Health (or vital) risks and health (or vital) benefits are commensurable concepts measured in the same currencies. In fact, health benefits are almost always simply the reduction of certain health risks. Thus, if we compare health risks and health benefits, we really are engaging in a form of risk comparison restricted to health risks.

It is when we come to the consideration of nonhealth benefits, the benefits of economy, convenience, aesthetics, or supply, benefits measured in the marketplace in dollars and not in lives, that we run into problems of commensuration and exchange. It seems unlikely that we will be willing routinely to pursue administrative determinations that accept even small vital or health risks for nonhealth or nonvital health benefits, even though we have done exactly that with aflatoxin residues on grain and peanuts. By and large, people are willing to make such decisions for themselves as individuals, but it appears that most administrators are properly reluctant to make them, and many consumers unwilling to have them made for them.

But there may be a pragmatic solution. We may make risk/benefit decisions on substances as classes rather than as individual, unrelated substances, providing that these decisions are anchored to widely accepted benchmarks. For example, traditional foods and their major useful components, nutritional, functional, or aesthetic, are widely accepted as conferring "benefit," and people are not usually willing to do without them without persuasive evidence of probable harm. This is, in effect, a not very explicit, but widely accepted risk/benefit decision involving a fairly high standard of risk to continue to receive a long-accepted and valued benefit.

A distinction to which we have already alluded would need to be made. Functionally useful natural constituents of traditional foods, and their chemically identical counterparts would deserve the highest benefit, highest tolerable risk category if their intentional use involved substantially less potential for exposure than their natural occurrence.

If intake from intentional use may exceed intake from uncontrolled natural sources, then only a lower category of risk would be acceptable.

Where there is no known risk from a natural or nature-identical component, and the estimate of probable risk lies far below the background risk in food, then functionality alone should be a sufficient demonstration of benefit.

For natural or man-made contaminants difficult or impossible to avoid without loss of valued foods, a substantially lower but still significant level of risk is probably acceptable with continuing pressure to reduce it.

For nontraditional, but familiar substances which confer nonhealth benefits not otherwise obtainable, a similarly low level of health risk may be generally acceptable with labeling that leaves the ultimate decision to the consumer.

Unfamiliar (i.e., new) substances should have no known risk or should contribute to overall reduction of health risks, perhaps by diffusing the risk, or by avoiding overuse and metabolic overload. And they should also confer other nonhealth benefits. This is a still lower level of acceptable net risk.

This scheme rather closely approximates recent proposals of Dr. Thomas Grumbly of USDA (1979) and Gardner and Larkin (1980). But it recognizes explicitly the risk and benefit comparisons implied in their comments.

So far as condiments, spices, and flavors are concerned, some such approach seems necessary. With these food ingredients, the benefits are real—flavor largely determines what food we eat. But such judgments are wholly subjective. Our basis of hard objective data on the physiological and psychological benefits of flavors is sketchy indeed, although a major effort is now beginning to enlarge it. Here we should note a point that deserves more attention in the context of this symposium than it has yet received. Spice consumption is characteristically higher in many tropical areas, and in general, spice use is roughly proportional to temperature. This fact is consistent with the possible role of spices as food preservatives and antioxidants, masking agents, or gastrointestinal antiseptics. These are benefits Americans value less, or obtain in other ways. We should avoid the arrogant but common assumption that the benefits and risks of spices—or of any food or environmental factor—are necessarily the same in other countries as in the United States. Too often we seek to export our priorities—sometimes out of thoughtlessness, other times for regulatory convenience or commercial advantage.

While the demonstrated benefits of flavors—for us in the United States—are subjective, the risks, with few exceptions, are small, remote, and largely hypothetical. Furthermore, in flavors, usually both risks and benefits revolve around the same substances and factors. Paraphrasing Paracelsus—"Only the dose makes the poison;" but also, only the dose makes the functionality.

It would be foolish to hope that this complex situation, applying to so many hundreds of substances used in such small quantity, would ever lend itself to detailed risk/benefit analysis. If we cannot comfortably do risk/benefit analysis with something as much studied as saccharin, we are unlikely to do it with 2,4-decadienal. A more pragmatic, but still rational and scientifically defensible approach is needed. This paper attempts to point toward some steps in that direction.

BIBLIOGRAPHY

ARTHUR D. LITTLE, INC. 1977. Pre-screening for Environmental Hazards—A System for Selecting and Prioritizing Chemicals. Prepared for Environmental Protection Agency, Office of Toxic Substances, Washington, D.C. PB-267 093. U.S. Dept. of Commerce, National Technical Information Service, Springfield, Va.

CRAMER, G.M., FORD, R.A., and HALL, R.L. 1978. Estimation of toxic hazard—a decision tree approach. Fd. Cosmet. Toxicol. *16*, 255–76.

DRINKWATER, N.R., MILLER, E.C., MILLER, J.A., and PITOT, H.C. 1976. The hepatocarcinogenicity of estragole (1-allyl-4-methoxybenzene) and 1′-hydroxyestragole in the mouse and the mutagenicity of 1′-acetoxyestragole in bacteria. J. Nat. Cancer Inst. *57* (6) 1323–31.

ENSLEIN, K. 1980. Personal communication. Genesee Computer Center, Inc., Rochester, New York.

FOOD SAFETY COUNCIL. 1979. Principles and Processes for Making Food Safety Decisions. Report of the Social and Economic Committee. December.

FOOD SAFETY COUNCIL. 1980. Proposed System for Food Safety Assessment. Report of the Scientific Committee. June.

GARDNER, S. and LARKIN, T. 1980. Food safety policy: Problems, perspectives, and possibilities. J. Legis. *7*, 26.

GRUMBLY, T.P. 1979. New directions in food safety policy. Given at Food Animal Industry Conference, American Farm Bureau Federation, Chicago, Ill. September 18.

HALL, R.L. 1980. The history, use, and pharmacology of spices. Perfumer & Flavorist. In press.

NATIONAL ACADEMY OF SCIENCES. 1973. Toxicants Occurring Naturally in Foods, Second Edition. National Academy of Sciences, Washington, D.C.

NATIONAL ACADEMY OF SCIENCES. 1979. Food Safety Policy: Scientific and Societal Considerations. Part 2 of a 2-Part Study of the Committee for a Study on Saccharin and Food Safety Policy. National Academy of Sciences, Washington, D.C.

NATIONAL ACADEMY OF SCIENCES. 1980. Risk Assessment/Safety Evaluation of Food Chemicals. National Academy of Sciences, Washington, D.C.

STOFBERG, J. 1979. FEMA Food Additives Committee Report. Perfumer & Flavorist *3*, Dec./Jan., 62–64.

STOFBERG, J. 1980. Report of the FEMA Food Additives Committee. Perfumer & Flavorist (In press).

16

Vitamins in Food: Implications for Quality and Toxicity

K. C. Hayes[1]

One measure of food quality relates to the variety and amount of vitamins present in a particular foodstuff. Generally speaking, the more vitamins present, the better; and the more balanced the vitamin profile in the food, the greater its marketability. We have only to inspect the advertisements for modern breakfast cereals to appreciate the impact of that statement.

On the other hand, there are certain practical considerations related to vitamin-nutrient interactions in foods that have important biological and nutritional implications. For instance, the high level of vitamin E normally found in polyunsaturated vegetable oils is both desirable and necessary since polyunsaturated fat is apt to undergo lipid peroxidation unless it contains adequate antioxidant protection. In vivo, similar peroxidation is associated with disruption of cell membranes and concomitant development of vitamin E deficiency in growing mammals. In the same vein, it is useful to know that ascorbic acid can serve as a strong reducing agent to aid in the absorption of iron. However, these finer points tend to be overshadowed by the more practical consideration for the food processor that vitamin loss is apt to result from denaturing induced by heat or oxidation (Table 16.1). One response is to supplement the food product in an attempt to restore its appeal and "nutritional value." Over-supplementation by this means is unlikely, but it is probable that some individuals receive more than the RDA for certain vitamins by consuming numerous fortified products.

[1] Department of Nutrition, Harvard School of Public Health, Boston, Massachusetts.

TABLE 16.1. EFFECTS OF FOOD PROCESSING ON VITAMIN STABILITY

Vitamin and Source	Percent Loss	Cause of Destruction
Vitamin C		
citrus juices	30–70	oxidation in 24 hr
Thiamin	50–80	sulfite processing
vegetables	20–65	blanching
meat	60–65	cooking
milk	3–4	pasteurization
Riboflavin		
milk	20–80	light, heat, oxidation
milk	10	pasteurization
meat	10–30	cooking
vegetables	10–25	blanching
Niacin	most stable to heat and processing	
vegetables	may be leached out during cooking	
meat	enzymes can degrade with aging	
Vitamin B_6	pyridoxine	heat stable, light sensitive
milk and meat	pyridoxal, 20–55	heat, sunlight (pasteurization stable)
vegetables	pyridoxal, 20–30	cooking, canning
wheat	pyridoxal, 70–90	milling removed
Folacin	ascorbate stablizes, copper catalyzes oxidation	
vegetables	unconjugated (mono-glutamate)	heat stable
vegetables	conjugated (tri- and hepta-glutamate)	heat labile
milk	40–90	boiling
meat	>75	cooking
Vitamin B_{12}	destroyed by ferrous ion	
meat	relatively stable to low heat, pasteurization rapid loss with high heat, light	
Pantothenic acid		
vegetables	25–35	blanching
meat	5–10	roasting
Biotin	relatively stable (few data)	
Vitamin A		
vegetables (carotene)	relatively stable	except dehydration, oxidation
vegetables	15–35	excessive cooking
vegetables	increased availability	cooking high fiber (carrots)
meat (retinyl palmitate)	10–20	cooking
milk	>50	sunlight
Vitamin D		
milk	extensive loss	oxidation, light

TABLE 16.1. *(Continued)*

Vitamin and Source	Percent Loss	Cause of Destruction
Vitamin K		
green plants	extensive loss	light
Vitamin E		
vegetable oils	extensive loss	oxidation, heat, light

An attitude of nonchalance concerning vitamin overdosing on the part of the consumer is partially attributable to the concept of megavitamin therapy that derives from the pseudoscientific commercial literature which thrives on bits and pieces of half-truths extracted from reports on vitamin research. The classical example is vitamin E, which has been cited for its broad application to a variety of specific diseases and several lessor maladies without substantial evidence to support the claims.

The obvious extension of this concept is the possibility that toxicity may result from an unrestricted intake of vitamins. It is essentially true that the vitamin content of normally consumed foodstuffs will never induce toxicity, and that the more realistic concern is that vitamins may be lost during processing or storage. However, the potential public reaction to "poisoning by industrial manipulation" is a real possiblity in today's ultra-sensitized society. The key is to exercise prudence based on good sense and information relevant to vitamin toxicity.

This review is not intended as an exhaustive compilation of the literature concerning the relationship between vitamins and food or the toxicity of the vitamins, but strives to highlight the significance of this relationship and points out the potential damage from vitamin excess.

VITAMIN EXCESS

In light of these comments, it is important to appreciate the limits of vitamin intake (Table 16.2) and the physiology of vitamin toxicity. The two vitamins that are potentially most dangerous are vitamin A and vitamin D, both of which are fat-soluble and both of which can be stored in substantial quantities in the body. As an example of the considerations involved in the pathophysiology of vitamin deficiency and excess, the range for normal intake of vitamin A as well as limits for deficiency and toxicity in man, are summarized in Figure 16.1. This figure demonstrates that essentially a 100-fold range exists between an intake of vitamin A that leads to deficiency and one that results in toxicity. The slopes in the response at either end of the scale also indicate that stages of deficiency or toxicity are progressive (night blindness, hyperkeratosis, inanition, and death on the deficient side and erythema, cerebrospinal fluid pressure increase, hepatic necrosis, and death on the toxic side).

TABLE 16.2. RELATIONSHIP BETWEEN RDA AND TOXIC INTAKE OF VARIOUS VITAMINS

Vitamins	RDA	Toxic Dose Range
Major concern		
Vitamin D	400 IU	2,000 IU+ (infants) 50,000–100,000 IU (adults)
Vitamin A	5000 IU	25,000–100,000 IU
Minor concern		
Vitamin C	60 mg	>500 mg (1–10 gr)
Vitamin E	15 mg	>1 gr
Thiamin	1 mg	>1 gr
Niacin	15 mg	>150–3,000 mg
Folacin	400 μg	>1 mg (not toxic, *per se*)

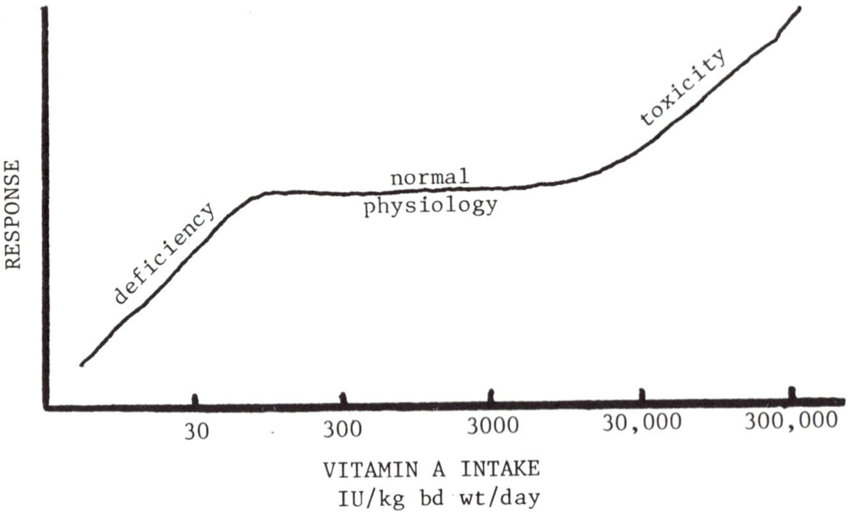

FIG. 16.1. PATHOPHYSIOLOGY OF THE RESPONSE TO VITAMIN A

Vitamin A

Vitamin A was the first in the long series of vitamin discoveries that began early in this century. We now know that this fat-soluble vitamin is ingested in two basic forms, the most prevalent of which is pro-vitamin A, or β-carotene, found in pigmented plants. This, in turn, is hydrolyzed and converted to retinol by the body and stored as retinyl ester, the form which is ingested when meat and other animal products are consumed (Smith and Goodman 1979).

β-Carotene generally is not considered toxic and is the safest way to supply vitamin A in foodstuffs, although its relative lack of potency and potential for discoloration of products may detract from its usefulness. In addition, it requires hydrolysis for conversion to vitamin A. Because of these drawbacks commercial retinyl esters (acetate and palmitate) are generally used to supplement the food supply. Excessive intake of carotene is typically observed in persons consuming abnormal quantities of carrot juice, or in infants fed pureed, colored vegetables, resulting in yellowing of skin. The condition does not represent a toxic state (Hayes and Hegsted 1973).

Vitamin A toxicity is seldom reported as a result of ingesting natural foodstuffs. Exceptions are examples of acute toxicity following the consumption of either polar bear liver by Arctic explorers or fish liver by fishermen eating generous portions obtained from large fishes (halibut, cod) which tend to store extraoridinary amounts of this vitamin (Hayes and Hegsted 1973). Liver historically has served as an excellent source of vitamin A since biblical times when night blindness and xerophthalmia were known to respond to liver ingestion, and in the recent past, codliver oil was widely utilized for its vitamin A and D content. Today the usual cause of vitamin A toxicity is chronic consumption of prescribed or self-medicated vitamin supplements. Acute toxicity also has occurred in a small percentage of 2–4 year old children following a massive dose (300,000 IU) during field trials in India and Indonesia designed to establish the maximum safe dose which would alleviate the devastation of chronic vitamin A deficiency. This dose of vitamin A has proved effective for reducing the prevalence of severe deficiency (Swaminathan *et al.* 1970).

Toxicity of vitamin A is expressed by many symptoms including dizziness, headache, anorexia, vomiting, weight loss, alopecia, erythema, dryness and cracking of skin with peeling of palms and soles of the feet in acute toxicity. Increased cerebrospinal fluid pressure (CSFP) is common in infants as in the occurrence of subperiosteal exostosis associated with hypercalcemia (Hayes and Hegsted 1973). Hypercalcemia is not dependent on a concomitant increase in vitamin D consumption (Katz and Tzagournis 1972). Many of these symptoms represent a pharmacologic or hyperphysiologic response of an organ system to high concentrations of vitamin A prior to actual toxicity and cellular dysfunction.

Vitamin D

Vitamin D is not actually a vitamin, but a hormone, because it can be synthesized by the skin from 7-dehydrocholesterol via the ultraviolet irradiation in sunlight. Furthermore, during its metabolism the active metabolite is synthesized by the kidney and transported to the gut and bone where it participates in the absorption or mobilization of calcium (DeLuca 1979). Nonetheless, because of the restricted exposure to sunlight of a large segment of the human population in northern latitudes, it has become customary to fortify certain foods, particularly milk and cereals, with vitamin D.

There are two basic reasons why this fortification is pursued. The first is to assure the health of a population against rickets in children and osteomalacia in older subjects, and the second is to be commercially competitive with a vitamin-balanced product. In essence, these are acceptable reasons or goals and should not cause concern, but it is our responsibility as health councilors and/or processors of the nation's food supply to be aware that there may be a potential hazard in this fortification process.

Excessive vitamin D can be toxic by exaggeration of its physiologic role in raising the serum calcium level, and the threshold of toxicity apparently varies with different individuals (Hayes and Hegsted 1973). Furthermore, there is growing evidence that the oxidation products of certain sterols, including cholesterol and vitamin D, may themselves be cytotoxic, particularly to vascular smooth muscle cells where it tends to accentuate the atherosclerotic process. These possible mechanisms of toxicity are outlined in Figure 16.2. Generally, feedback regulation of vitamin D metabolism occurs in both liver and kidney conversions, but these can be distorted by excessive consumption and absorption of vitamin D.

The minimal level of vitamin D that represents an excess has not been carefully documented at the present time, but the available information suggests that age makes a difference. Children develop toxic effects when ingesting 10,000 IU/day for 4 months or 200,000 IU/day for 2 weeks with most reported cases ranging from 25,000 to 60,000 IU/day for 1–4 months (Hayes and Hegsted 1973; Seelig 1970). Obviously, normal food fortification would not contribute appreciably to the problem if this high level of intake were required for all toxicity effects. However, it has been reported that as little as 1,800 IU/day of D_2 impaired linear skeletal growth of infants, and a modest increase in vitamin D consumption in England in the 1950s was associated with an increased incidence of idiopathic hypercalcemia of infancy (Seelig 1969). On the other hand, many infants undoubtedly consume 2,000 IU/day without apparent effect. The Committee on Nutrition of the American Academy of Pediatrics described a maximum dose of 1,000–3,000 IU/kg body wt/day as dangerous for the typical child. Until recently rheumatoid arthritis was treated with large doses of vitamin D (50,000 IU/day), but the occurrence of calcinosis has largely eliminated that therapy (DiPalma 1978).

As indicated in Figure 16.2 different aspects of toxicity from vitamin D may occur via at least three possible routes. The most widely accepted means is related to its physiological role of elevating serum calcium levels

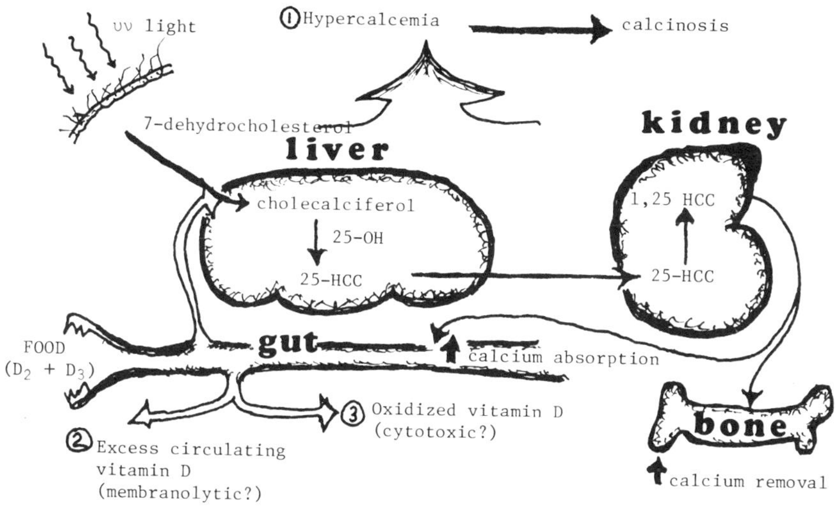

FIG. 16.2. PROPOSED MECHANISMS FOR VITAMIN D TOXICITY

leading to widespread calcification of tissues. This occurs especially in the arterial wall, kidney tubules, and lung interstitium which can have fatal consequences. It is also likely that a high serum concentration of lipid-soluble vitamin D is in itself membranolytic. This can result in cell death and may be relevant to the cardiac myopathy in this syndrome. A third possibility recently described is that oxidized products of vitamin D are cytotoxic. Evidence is available that indicates these products may exacerbate the development of atherosclerosis when accompanied by hyperlipemia. It is unlikely, however, that our normal daily exposure to vitamin D would result in appreciable atherosclerosis.

Other Vitamins

Although the vitamins ordinarily are obtained in sufficient quantity by eating a variety of foods, there are those who would have you believe that particularly generous amounts of certain vitamins are beneficial and even required. Most attention in the lay literature has been given to ascorbic acid and vitamin E (tocopherol).

Vitamin C

It has been argued that man historically has been removed from a natural diet high in vitamin C and that many chronic disease problems which now confront us are related to altered biochemical/physiological functions resulting from the relative lack of this vitamin. The biggest impetus for its supplementation came from the suggestion that 1–10 gr of ascorbic acid/day would prevent or cure the common cold. The rationale was only partially supported by the fact that ascorbate can act as an antihistamine to assuage secondary symptoms. Ascorbate may also influence hydroxylation reactions for steroid production by the adrenal glands, a process which is depressed by severe physical stress such as surgery, exaggerated exercise, or exposure to severe cold. Controlled studies have rather disproved definite beneficial effects of vitamin C on the common cold. As might be anticipated from such controversy, many have tried the treatment and usually have been disappointed.

Large doses of vitamin C may cause diarrhea, intestinal cramps, and acidification of urine leading to cystine or oxalate stones in the kidneys or urinary tract. Exaggerated supplementation during pregnancy can elevate the fetal requirement and precipitate scurvy in the newborn fed an otherwise normal intake of the vitmain. Ascorbate interferes with dicoumarol anticoagulant therapy, normalizing clotting time (prothrombin time) and has been accused of destroying vitamin B_{12} in food during digestion, but this issue is not resolved. It seems likely that the analytical procedure for assessment of vitamin B_{12} was inadequate (Barness 1975; Hogenkamp 1980).

Vitamin E

Since its original discovery in the prevention of abortion and sterility in rats, tocopherol has been widely touted as therapy for threatened abortion and male sterility in humans. It has also been prescribed for heart disease, atherosclerosis, muscular dystrophy, retrolental fibroplasia, hemolytic disease of the newborn, and various other ailments. Such widespread use has resulted in megadose consumption of vitamin E. Fortunately, there have been few reports of vitamin E toxicity (Hayes and Hegsted 1973; Farrell and Bieri 1975).

Thiamin

Thiamin was once a problem when used for megadose parenteral therapy, causing hypersensitivity reactions with rapid pulse, vasodilation, edema, and cardiac arrhythmia.

Niacin

Niacin was used unsuccessfully in megadose form as a treatment for schizophrenia. It induced flushing, itching, skin rash, heartburn, nausea, vomiting, diarrhea, gastric and duodenal ulcers, low blood pressure, rapid heart rate and hyperglycemia. Liver dysfunction and jaundice were reported occasionally before this therapy was discontinued. Niacin also was used in the Coronary Drug Project to lower cholesterol without appreciable improvement, but did cause an increase in cardiac arrhythmias (DiPalma 1978).

Pyridoxine

Convulsive disorders in infants result from an excess or deficiency of vitamin B_6. It is believed to act by interfering with other drugs, such as increasing the catabolism of L-Dopa used for Parkinson's Disease.

Folic Acid

Excess folate causes convulsions in patients treated with the anticonvulsant, phenytoin, for unknown reasons. But phenytoin is thought to work by altering folate metabolism in the brain. Excess folate has also caused renal tubular hypertrophy and tubular necrosis in animals.

A summary of these effects is included in Table 16.3.

TABLE 16.3. SUMMARY VITAMIN TOXICITY

Vitamin	Signs, symptoms, pathologic consequence
Major concern	
Vitamin D	hypercalcemia, weakness, vomiting, azotemia, polyuria, dehydration, generalized calcinosis, aortic stenosis, nephrocalcinosis
Vitamin A	headache, vomiting, increased CSFP, alopecia, hypercalcemia, bony exostoses, dry, cracking, peeling skin, liver necrosis and fibrosis
Minor concern	
Vitamin C	gastrointestinal upset, hyperoxaluria, increased uric acid excretion, renal stones in susceptible persons, false positive glucosuria (ascorbate is reducing agent), super-elevates fetal requirement, interferes with dicoumarol therapy (corrects prothrombin time)
Vitamin E	muscle weakness, nausea, headache, depressed prothrombin level
Thiamin	hypersensitivity reaction
Niacin	skin rash, GI disturbance, cardiac arrhythmias
Folacin	may mask vitamin B_{12} deficiency (leads to neurologic damage)

CONCLUSION

It should be apparent from the above discussion that vitamins in foodstuffs are not apt to be a threat to the public health and that the food processor should be more concerned with loss of vitamins during food preparation. The only vitamins of major concern in terms of toxicity are vitamins A and D. Since we do not fully appreciate the lower limits of vitamins D toxicity the overconsumption of vitamin D in fortified foods may be a problem for a few hypersensitive children. Further research is needed to estimate the levels required and mechanisms involved in vitamin D toxicity as well as many of the more subtle toxicities.

BIBLIOGRAPHY

BARNESS, L.A. 1975. Safety considerations with high ascorbic acid dosage. Ann. N.Y. Acad. Sci. *258*, 523.

DeLUCA, H.F. 1979. The vitamin D system in the regulation of calcium and phosphorus metabolism. Nutr. Revs. *37*, 161.

DiPALMA, J.R. 1978. Vitamin toxicity. Amer. Fam. Phys. *18*, 106.

FARRELL, P.M. and BIERI, J.G. 1975. Megavitamin E supplementation in man. Am. J. Clin. Nutr. *28*, 1381.

HAYES, K.C. and HEGSTED, D.M. 1973. Toxicity of the vitamins. *In* Toxicants Occurring Naturally in Foods, p. 235. NAS, Washington, D.C.

HOGENKAMP, H.P.C. 1980. The interaction between vitamin B_{12} and vitamin C. Am. J. Clin. Nutr. *33*, 1.

KATZ, C.M. and TZAGOURNIS, M. 1972. Chronic adult hypervitaminosis A with hypercalcemia. Metabolism *21*, 1171.

SEELIG, M.S. 1969. A Vitamin D and cardiovascular, renal, and brain damage in infancy and childhood. Ann. N.Y. Acad. Sci. *147*, 537.

SEELIG, M.S. 1970. Are American children still getting an excess of vitamin D? Clin. Ped. *9*, 380.

SMITH, J.E. and GOODMAN, D.S. 1979. Retinol-binding protein and the regulation of vitamin A transport. Fed. Proc. *38*, 2504.

SWAMINATHAN, M.C., SUSHEELA, T.P., and THIMMAYAMMA, B.V.S. 1970. Field prophylactic trial with a single annual oral dose of vitamin A. Am. J. Clin. Nutr. *23*, 119.

17

Toxicity and Safety Requirements of Colors

John C. Kirschman[1]

COLOR USE

The 1964 World Health Organization document (FAO 1966) entitled, "Specifications for Identity and Purity and Toxicological Evaluation of Food Colors", although in much need of updating still serves as a handy reference. It lists the specifications of over 40 synthetic organic colors. Table 17.1 shows the number of synthetic as well as natural colors permitted in various countries today. The synthetics range from a low of

TABLE 17.1. NUMBERS OF COLORS USED INTERNATIONALLY

Country	Number of Colors Permitted		
	Synthetic		Natural
	Present No.	Change Since '77	
Australia	22		6
Austria	21		10
Belgium	11	−7	22
Canada	8		21
Denmark	13	−3	19
Finland	10		11
France	11	−7	22
West Germany	18		22
Italy	11	−7	21
Japan	9	+1	16
Netherlands	18		21
Norway	9		10
South Africa	13		10
Sweden	10		10
Switzerland	13		20
United Kingdom	21	−1	23
U.S.A.	7	−2	12

[1] General Foods Corporation, White Plains, New York.

seven in the United States to 22 in Australia. The disturbing fact emerging from this table is the decrease in the number of permitted colors in various countries. In Belgium, in France, and in Italy as well there were seven colors delisted, and, of course, two were lost in the U.S. in the last two years. Obviously unless some forceful action is undertaken to defend the use of colors by the industry, where the science does not support regulatory action, this trend will continue. More on this a little later.

The common names of most of these colors appear in Table 17.2, and represent nine chemical classes. Structural formulas representing each of these classes of color are shown in Fig. 17.1. Complicated aren't they?

TABLE 17.2. FOOD COLORS IN USE WORLDWIDE

Synthetic		Natural	
Allura Red	Oil Yellow XP	Alkanet	Canthaxanthin
Ponceau 4R	Fast Yellow	Annatto	Lactoflavin (Riboflavin)
Carmoisine	Quinoline Yellow	Anthocyanins	
Amaranth	Chrysoin S	Beetroot	Orchil
Red 10B	Green S	Caramel	Saffron
Erythrosine	Fast Green FCF	Carmine	Sandalwood
Red 2G	Blue VRS	Carbon Black, Vegetable	Xanthophylls
Red 6B	Indigo Carmine		β-APO-8′-Carotenal
Red FB	Indanthrene Blue	Carbon Black, Channel	Iron Oxides
Fast Red E	Patent Blue V		Titanium Dioxide
Ponceau 6R	Brilliant Blue FCF	Chlorophyll	Ag, Au, Al
Scarlet GN	Brown FK	Cu-Chlorophyll	$CaCO_3$
Ponceau SX	Chocolate Brown FB	Curcumin	
Orange G	Chocolate Brown HT	Carotene	
Orange RN	Black PN	Carotenoids	
Orange GGN	Black 7984		
Oil Yellow GG			
Tartrazine			
Yellow 2G			
Sunset Yellow FCF			

Based on 1967 data (NAS 1971), it has been estimated that the concentration of certified colors in the total food supply of the United States is about nine parts per million, with the average value for total color ingested per capita per day being approximately 15 milligrams.

Table 17.3 lists major food categories and color concentrations. You will notice that the range is from 200–600 ppm, with the highest intake of 15 mg/day coming from baked goods. This, of course, is old data and is in the process of being up-dated for FDA via the GRAS 3 survey by the National Academy of Sciences.

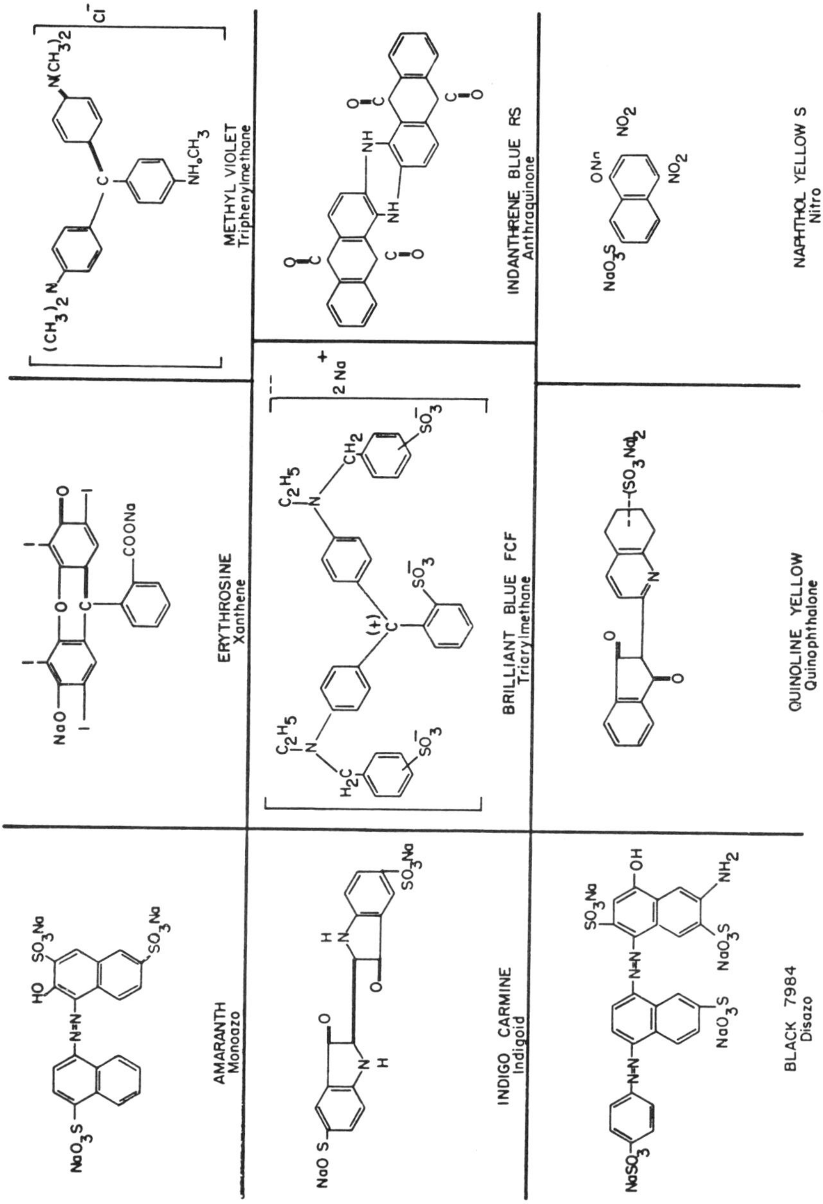

FIG. 17.1. CHEMICAL CLASSES OF FOOD COLORS

TABLE 17.3.[1] ESTIMATED TOTAL COLOR THAT MIGHT BE INGESTED PER CAPITA PER DAY BASED ON MAXIMUM COLOR CONCENTRATION AND CALCULATED FROM TOTAL PRODUCTION[2] FOR EACH FOOD CATEGORY

Category	Total Average Consumption per Capita (lb)	Equivalent (g)	Daily Consumption per Capita (g)	Color Concentration Maximum (ppm)	Maximum Color Ingested per Capita per Day (mg)
Candy, Confections	10.0	4,536	17	400	7.0
Beverages	38.0	17,238	64	200	12.8
Dessert Powders	6.7	3,039	11	600	6.6
Cereals	1.5	680	3	500	1.5
Maraschino Cherries	0.85	386	1	400	0.4
Bakery Goods	17.8	8,074	30	500	15.0
Ice Cream, Sherbet, Dairy Products	15.0	6,806	25	200	5.0
Sausage	6.6	2,994	11	250	3.0
Snack Foods	0.87	395	2	500	1.0
Miscellaneous	1.85	839	3	400	1.2
Total					53.5

[1] Data presented in "Food Colors", National Academy of Sciences (1971).
[2] During first 9 months of 1967.

COLOR REGULATION

In 1970 there were 10 synthetic FD&C colors permitted for use in the United States, and now there are only seven certifiables left . . . What has happened?

Let's look at the cases: First of all, in 1971 a report from Russia, based on studies done on an unknown material of questionable origin and purity, which was called Amaranth, implicated FD&C Red #2 as being embryotoxic. While Red #2 was saved from this challenge, through inter-industry testing efforts, it was subsequently banned following the completion of a chronic study in FDA's own laboratories. Although documented as having been competely "fouled up," the Commissioner held that Red #2 had not been proven to be safe and should be banned—which he proceeded to do. Requiring proof of absolute safety is a dangerous precedent since it is not only impossible for Red #2 but for any other food or chemical.

The Certified Color Manufacturers fought this case through the Hearing Procedure only to lose within the last several months when the Commissioner of FDA agreed with the findings of the Hearing Judge who upheld the former Commissioner's original ban on Red #2. The Association is planning to pursue this case through the courts, and I personally think wisely and with full justification.

The second case relates to a 1973 Japanese report finding mammary tumors in rats fed Acid Violet 6B, which when analyzed was found to be not as pure as the FD&C Violet 1 used in the U.S. Although an adequate chronic study done by FDA was negative for material which actually passed the U.S. Certification Procedure, the FDA banned this color some time in 1973.

Case number three might be referred to as the case of increasing analytical sensitivity. Over the decades, the analytical chemists continue to improve the sensitivity of their methods which result effectively in the reduction of zero. Ten years ago zero was considered in relationship to parts per million. Today, parts per trillion quantities are becoming almost routine while research chemists are actually able to analyze some materials down to the range of 10 to the −15th or femptogram range. The analytical prowess and the Delaney Amendment relative to food additives have been on a collision course for some time. Now they have reached the collision point and again the colors have been prime suspects in the case and Orange B specifically is the prime example. FDA proposed banning Orange B following notification by the Stange Corporation that they had found the carcinogen betanaphthylamine in parts per billion in their Orange B. The FDA, however, has not put this ban into effect, primarily because of the problems it would raise. Were FDA to proceed in a consistent manner in banning all food additives for which somewhere in their manufacturing process there was a detectable amount of a material presumed to be a carcinogen in man, virtually all food additives would have to be banned. This has put extreme pressure on FDA to establish a policy that can be uniformly applied to the regulation and control of contaminants that get into food additives and foods in trivial amounts. They expect to have their draft of this in proposal form for public dissemination by the end of this year. All of us involved with food additive safety are very anxiously awaiting this proposal. The timing is especially important to colors since the color files are open and under review awaiting completion of the chronic feeding tests. Most studies will be completed within the next two years at which time the full review of all of their safety dossiers will be undertaken by the FDA and other governments around the world.

The next case and one that resulted in the recent actual ban of color in the U.S. was that of FD&C Red #4 which had been permitted solely for the use in coloring maraschino cherries.

Another case on the docket involves FDA plans to require labeling of FD&C Yellow 5 because of hypersensitivity it reportedly induces in some people.

Of course, the one FD&C color that is presently approved but now shown on the list of those under test is FD&C Red #40, or Allura Red, which just apparently weathered a rather severe storm of challenge to its safety. I think this is the most stable of our colors, regulatorywise for the next five years. The most likely next challenge to this color might be expected in the course of the cyclic review of food additives.

TOXICITY TESTING

Table 17.4 shows the colors that are presently under long term chronic testing in the U.S. and Europe. These are all being tested with essentially the same protocol where all the animals were exposed in utero which involved dosing female rats before and during pregnancy and then dosing the offspring for their lifetime. From these studies there is going to be a formidable and massive set of reports to evaluate.

It's going to be an exciting, stimulating and precarious several years until we bring these studies home. Approximately 45 chronic feeding study reports will hit the FDA and other regulators around the world within a very short period of time. Nothing like it has ever been accomplished before. Table 17.5 shows the postponement dates requested by U.S. industries for filing their chronic study reports with the FDA. These associations have also requested postponement by FDA of the present 1/31/81 closing date on the colors to 12 months after full report submissions.

TABLE 17.4. IN UTERO CHRONIC FEEDING STUDIES UNDERWAY ON SYNTHETIC COLORS

United States		Europe
FD&C Blue 1	D&C Red 27	Quinolene Yellow[2]
FD&C Blue 2	D&C Red 30	Patent Blue V[2]
FD&C Green 3	D&C Red 33	Carmoisine[1]
FD&C Red 3	D&C Red 36	Ponceau 4R[1]
FD&C Yellow 5	D&C Orange 5	Amaranth[1]
FD&C Yellow 6	D&C Orange 17	Green 5[2]
	D&C Green 5	Carmine[2]
	D&C Green 6	
	D&C Yellow 10	
	D&C Red 6	
	D&C Red 9	
	D&C Red 19	
	D&C Red 21	

[1] Rats only, otherwise both rats and mice.
[2] Mice only, otherwise both rats and mice.

TABLE 17.5. CERTIFIED COLOR PETITION DUE DATES

Petitioner	Color	Requested Report Submission Date
CCMA	FD&C Blue 1	10/30/81
	FD&C Blue 2	10/30/81
	FD&C Green 3	11/16/81
	FD&C Red 3	10/2/82
	FD&C Yellow 5	10/7/82
	FD&C Yellow 6	2/28/83
PMA	D&C Yellow 10	4/30/82
	D&C Red 33	3/31/82
CTFA	D&C Red 30	5/30/81
	D&C Green 5	5/30/81
	D&C Red 27 (28)	10/30/81
	D&C Orange 5	10/30/81
	D&C Red 21 (22)	11/30/81
	D&C Red 6 (7)	12/31/81
	D&C Red 19 (33)	2/28/82
	D&C Orange 17	3/31/82
	D&C Red 9 (8)	9/30/82
	D&C Red 36	9/30/83

In addition to these chronic studies there are a variety of other types of investigations underway on colors, especially within the European program. This research includes metabolic studies, teratology, and multigeneration reproduction tests on certain colors which will also be completed in the next several years.

Well, where do we go from here? Do we just sit and wait for the natural course of events to take place, for the present studies to be finished and reviewed by FDA and other governments and we the users await the final results? Definitely not. There are things that can be done and must be done. Some of them are underway.

NATURAL COLORS

Do we run from the synthetic colors because of all the pressure upon them and the whims of bureaucracies and rely on natural colors for the use in our products? I think not. The challenge to our industry is to the use of colors to artificially color foods rather than the use of synthetic colors in foods. While I am sure that most of us have some higher level of comfort in relying on "natural material," I have to caution you that there are already enough regulatory and toxicological storm warnings to indicate that our course for natural colors will be through just as stormy a sea for us as the synthetic colors have encountered. During FDA's Cyclic Review the natural colors can be expected to be looked at as any other color additive regardless of their source. From what has been published and discussions I have already had with regulatory scientists both here and abroad, one can anticipate that the requirements for toxicological evaluation of natural colors will fall into a number of categories as follows:

1. A color that is isolated in a chemically unmodified form from the recognized foodstuff and is used in the foodstuff from which it is extracted in levels normally found in that food will not require toxicological testing.
2. A color isolated in a chemically unmodified manner, but used in levels in excess of those normally found in the food or used in a food other than that from which it is extracted, might require some toxicological testing similar to that usually required for synthetic colors.
3. The isolation of a natural color from its food source that is chemically modified during its production will require toxicological testing similar to that for synthetic colors.

A very serious consideration with the natural colors is the lack of uniformity in their composition. Because of this, if toxicological studies are required, the testing of one color would not provide assurance of safety of similar colors differing in composition.

At the European Society of Toxicology several years ago, Drs. Mikhelsen, Larsen and Tarding of Denmark reported (Mikhelsen *et al.* 1977) that they had found 14 of 56 patients suffering from chronic urticaria and/or angioneurotic oedema were sensitive to annatto extract, a natural color often used to color butter. When the subjects were tested with synthetic dyes similar symptoms were observed at the following incidences: Tartrazine 9%, Ponceau 4R 15%, Erythrosine 12%, and Brilliant Blue 14%. These data indicate that the natural color annato caused twice the incidence of allergenic responses than did any of the four synthetic colors tested. It should be noted, however, that it was hypersensitivity work in Sweden that brought attention and pressure to tartrazine which has resulted in demands in the U.S. for its labeling on food and drug products.

NEW DEVELOPMENTS

From the foregoing it is apparent that both the natural and synthetic food colors will be under the gun for a number of years and we need not only pay particular attention to these concerns but should also look to new developments. Of course, a new development that all color users are interested in is the polymeric color additives developed by Dynapol. Dynapol has submitted to the Food and Drug Administration the first Food Additive Petition for an additive tied "to polymer backbones" which prevents the additive from being absorbed in the body. Later this year color additive petitions will be filed for a red color to replace FD&C Red 40 and FD&C Red 3, and for a yellow color to replace FD&C Yellow 5 and FD&C Yellow 6.

Dynapol has asked that the food and color additives be handled under FDA's new "Fast Track" system. If these colors are approved and work as planned, they will undoubtedly find a significant place in the food system.

There is a specific reason for my having included the tables on the FD&C colors, and on the testing underway in Europe. We would like not only to save those FD&C colors presently available to us in the U.S., but would also like to have some additional colors made available. The greatest potential for these lies in those colors currently being used in other parts of the world. We are keenly interested in the red colors Carmoisine, Ponceau 4R, and Amaranth. Should the contaminant issue we discussed with relationship to Orange B be resolved such that Orange B is, in fact, not delisted and if the studies underway in Europe on these three colors show them not to be carcinogenic, then consideration will be given to petitioning the Food and Drug Administration for the addition of these colors to the FD&C list. Quinoline Yellow being tested in Europe is the same color as the D&C Yellow #10 being tested in the United States by the pharmaceutical manufacturers. Here again, if this color proves to be satisfactory after toxicological assessment we should petition for its approval for food use in the U.S.

The burden of testing the FD&C colors has been assumed totally by the Certified Color Manufacturers Association. However, within the past year the concerns over the colors have finally prompted a number of food manufacturers, users of the food colors, to convene themselves into a working industry committee under the auspices of the International Life

Sciences Institute, (ILSI). Having worked since 1971 on behalf of the Grocery Manufacturers of America as a toxicologist on the color program with CCMA, I am gratified to finally see more direct involvement of the color user companies in the food industry bringing more direct supportive attention to present and future food color issues. It is my privilege to be serving presently as Chairman of this ILSI Color Committee.

I would like now to briefly outline for you the structure of that Committee, the program that it has just approved and the plans that will be undertaken in the next year or two. We presently have 14 member food companies and continue to receive expressions of interest from others.

The Committee has structured itself into five major permanent subcommittees. These are:

1. Color Safety Evaluation Committee (COSEC)
2. Certifiable Colors Committee
3. Color Information Committee
4. Non-Certifiable Colors Committee
5. Functional Attributes of Colors Committee.

Dr. Harold Grice, formerly head of the Chemical Safety Division of the Health Protection Branch in Canada, is the Committee's Scientific Coordinator and Chief Toxicologist. As such he chairs the COSEC Committee which becomes involved on all toxicological questions of interest to the Committee.

The COSEC is in the process of reviewing data generated on Textile Grade Carmoisine and Yellow #6 by the NCI Bioassay Program.

Of course, the Certifiable Colors Committee presently has many items warranting its attention. Liaison and collaboration are underway or planned with the major testing and research programs around the world including that of CCMA (Certified Color Manufacturers Association), CTFA (Cosmetic, Toiletry & Fragrance Association), and PMA (Pharmaceutical Manufacturers Association) in the U.S. and the European industry.

Examples of collaboration include: Dr. Grice is working directly with Dr. Borzelleca, the toxicology consultant to the CCMA and the COSEC Committee is available for added support when needed for CCMA's testing program.

The question of potential contribution of iodine to our foods via use of FD&C Red #3 prompted the ILSI Committee and CCMA jointly to grant financial support to Dr. Ingbar of Harvard Medical School for his studies into possible effect of Erythrosine (FD&C Red No. 3) on thyroid function in man. This work is still in process.

Of course, the key to all these activities is sound and complete scientific information. Therefore, an Information Sub-Committee was established, to develop and maintain a central file activity. This sub-committee will shortly be publishing a catalogue on colors that will also be available for purchase outside of the committee. The catalogue will include monographs on all food colors, both natural and synthetic, including the specifications and toxicological data.

Another role of the Information Center is to keep abreast of and advise membership on all matters relating to colors. For example, the committee was made privy to the recently released report of the National Advisory Committee on Hyperkinesis and Food Additives, sponsored by the Nutrition Foundation. I think it appropriate to include in its brief entirety the Committee's recommendations.

"The studies reported here represent the efforts of dozens of investigators over more than a four year period at a cost which has probably exceeded the million dollar level. It is our opinion that the studies already completed provide sufficient evidence to refute the claim that artificial food colorings, artificial flavorings, and salicylates produce hyperactivity and/or learning disability. We see no indication based on this evidence for the continuation of high priority, specially funded programs for further investigation in this area. We also see no need for changes in public policy with regard to the use of artificial food colorings in the food industry based upon the putative relationship between artificial colorings and behavior problems in children. There is insufficient evidence to suggest a ban of foods containing artificial food colorings in the federally supported school lunch program. The general need to remain vigilant regarding the safety of food colors should stand on its own merits and bears no relationship to the specific disorders of hyperactivity and/or learning disability. There is no scientific need, in our opinion, for a symbol on food labels indicating the absence of food additives for the purpose of treating hyperactivity and learning disability. The question of what does constitute an appropriate food label is an issue that lies outside the scope of this committee's deliberations."

The Sub-Committee on Non-Certifiable Colors of course will be working with suppliers and others interested in natural colors to generate the information needed for assuring that such candidates can be made available for use in foods.

The Sub-Committee on functional attributes has approved the expenditure of funds to do some testing for the evaluation for the perceived attributes of colors. Indeed, a year ago, the EEC requested European industry to provide them with documentation of the benefits of colors. Industry's showing was quite inadequate. It is urgent that some good data are collected on the attributes of colors.

What do we see as the next step following the completion of chronic testing? The new areas in toxicology are the behavioral toxicology and neuro-behavioral effects as well as hypersensitivity and allergy. Therefore, even if we weather the storm through the completion and evaluation of the present testing programs, we probably haven't heard the last call for financial and scientific as well as moral support for research programs on food colors.

BIBLIOGRAPHY

FOOD AND AGRICULTURE ORGANIZATION OF THE UNITED NATIONS, World Health Organization. 1966. Specifications for Identity and Purity and Toxicological Evaluation of Food Colours, Geneva, 8-17 December, 1964.

MIKHELSEN, M., LARSEN, J.G., AND TARDING, F. 1978. Hypersensitivity reactions to food colours particularly annatto (natural butter colour). Arch. Toxicol. (Supp.) IS 1:141−143.

NATIONAL ACADEMY OF SCIENCES, Committee on Food Protection, Food and Nutrition Board, Division of Biology and Agriculture. 1971. Food Colors. N.R.C., Washington, D.C.

18

Bulking Agents and Fillers

John J. Beereboom[1]

INTRODUCTION

The design of tests required and the factors to be considered in safety assessment are frequently quite different for bulking agents and fillers than for other classes of food additives. The purpose of this presentation is to contrast the two situations and to discuss some of the approaches that are necessary in evaluating the safety of bulking agents and fillers.

Food additives, as the name implies, are added to food to enhance a particular property of the food. Most food additives such as acidulants, antioxidants, and preservatives are actually used in food in small quantities. This factor is taken into account in the design of the toxicological tests that are needed for their safety assessment. Table 18.1 lists the tests likely to be needed for such additives.

Generally, performing these tests is relatively straightforward, requiring only time, money and careful application of accepted methodology. The most common problem usually encountered is the interpretation of the significance of the results. Mutagenicity studies are known to give conflicting results and, carcinogenicity studies at high dosages are prone to a variety of problems. With the latter tests we seem to have reached the point where the statistician plays as large a role in counting tumors as the pathologist does in observing and judging significance of tumors—a situation aptly described by Dr. Kirschman as "the exact use of an inexact science" (Kirschman 1976).

[1] Central Research, Pfizer Inc., Groton, Connecticut.

TABLE 18.1. SAFETY ASSESSMENT PROTOCOLS FOR FOOD ADDITIVES

1. *In vitro* mutagenicity tests
2. 90-day study in rats
   (three dose levels, 10 animals/sex/level)
3. 90-day study in dogs
   (three dose levels, 4 animals/sex/level)
4. Reproduction and teratology studies
   Rabbit teratology test (three dose levels, 10 animals/level)
   Three-generation rat study (three dose levels, 45 animals/level)
5. 18-month mouse carcinogenicity study
   (three dose levels, 50 animals/sex/level)
6. 30-month chronic rat study
   (three dose levels, 50 animals/sex/level)
7. 12-month chronic dog study
   (three dose levels, 6 animals/sex/level)

STATISTICAL CONSIDERATIONS

Several years ago, Dr. David Salsburg, our senior statistician, published a paper (Salsburg 1977) in which he pointed out that the use of standard tests of hypothesis as they are widely applied to these chronic studies can lead to false positives as often as 20–50% of the time, as shown in Table 18.2, depending upon the test species, the duration of the test and an assumption that a variety of tests of hypothesis are applied to the observed lesions. The implication of this paper is that a number of potentially valuable food additives may have been lost because a study was not designed to evaluate such a range of parameters.

TABLE 18.2. MONTE CARLO ESTIMATES OF PROBABILITY OF A FALSE POSITIVE

Species	Study length (months)	No. organs/ tumor types	% false positives
Male rats	24	5	51.2
Female rats	24	4	19.6
Male mice	18	5	21.5
Female mice	18	5	13.6
Male hamsters	19	3	12.1
Female hamsters	19	4	12.5
Male mice	20	5	57.3
Female mice	20	5	50.2

Source: Salsburg (1977).

More recently, Salsburg (1980) has published a statistical treatment of the chronic studies done with xylitol, sucrose, and sorbitol by the Huntingdon Laboratories. In essence, his processing locates clusters of different types of lesions, relates these to the dose response and tests the hypothesis of whether the treatment induces a shift of animals from one cluster of lesions to another. Table 18.3 presents the statistical results of

TABLE 18.3. RAT STUDY: "SIGNIFICANT" DOSE RESPONSES FOR XYLITOL USING MARGINAL TABULATION OF LESIONS

Sex	Organ	Pathology	Significance Level
Males	Heart	Myocardial fibroses	0.006
	Liver	Hepatocyte vacuolation	0.998
	Liver	Fatty change	0.986
	Liver	Venous congestion	0.995
	Kidney	Glomerulonephrosis	0.985
	Parathyroid	Hyperplasia	0.999
	Adrenal	Hyperplasia in medulla	<0.001
	Lymph Nodes	Histocytes	0.977
	Adrenal	Pheochromocytoma	0.027
Females	Heart	Myocardial degeneration	0.017
	Lung	Inflam. cell infiltration	0.967
	Lung	Congestion	0.975
	Liver	Hepatocyte vacuolation	0.980
	Liver	Fatty change	0.999
	Liver	Congestion	0.981
	Liver	Granulocyte infiltration	0.038
	Kidney	Nephrocalcinosis	0.016
	Kidney	Epithelial hyperplasia	<0.001
	Kidney	Mineralization	<0.001
	Adrenal	Cystic degeneration	0.001
	Adrenal	Hemorrhage in cortex	0.026
	Adrenal	Hyperplasia in medulla	0.001
	Lymph	Histocyte-like cells	0.998
	Stomach	Epithelial hyperplasia	0.984
	Cutaneous	Inflam. cell infiltration	0.002
	Subcutaneous	Fibrosarcoma	0.987

Source: Salsburg (1980).

this analysis in the rat study with xylitol. In his treatment a significance close to zero implies that increasing the dosage increased the number of animals with a particular lesion, while a significance approaching one would imply that increasing the dosage tended to protect the animals from developing that particular type of lesion. What the entire table shows is that while there were dose-related increases in 12 pathological lesions there were also significant dose-related decreases in another 14 lesions. In other words, what Dr. Salsburg is trying to point out is that the chronic study in rodents as customarily practiced today produces shifts in the incidence of senile lesions that have little or no bearing on determining whether the test ingredient is a true carcinogen. I highly recommend Salsburg's papers for some specific recommendations on what could be done to alleviate this dilemma.

ACCEPTABLE DAILY INTAKES

With the results of the chronic feeding studies available and analyzed by both the statistician and the toxicologist, what happens next? Usually, the regulatory toxicologist would take the highest "no effect" dose level used in the most sensitive species in the lifetime studies and simply apply a 100-fold safety factor; a tenfold factor for differences between the test species and man and a tenfold factor to account for individual differences. This level is considered to be the dose which can be safely consumed by man daily for a lifetime. Internationally it is referred to as the acceptable daily intake (ADI). For example, if the highest "no effect" level was found to be 500 mg/kg/day, the ADI is calculated to be 350 mg/day for a 70 kg adult and is usually expressed as 0−5 mg/kg/day. It is then a simple matter to compare probable daily intake of the additive based upon its intended use in foods with the ADI. As long as the proposed average usage of the additive is less than the ADI, the additive would be considered safe.

Many typical food additives have some sort of biological or pharmacological activity, and this activity generally will cause toxic effects at some relatively low and finite dosage so the upper limit dosage for chronic studies can be relatively low. Bulking agents and fillers on the other hand are substances used at high levels. Properly selected they will have a very low order of toxicity. Since the highest dose used is usually the so called maximum tolerated dose where some evidence of toxicity is observed, bulking agents are tested at very high levels indeed, which can create a further set of problems. In fact bulking agents and fillers from both the use and toxicity standpoints should be considered as food ingredients rather than as food additives.

How does the ADI situation work out with bulking agents and fillers? These materials are used to replace a food ingredient which normally is present in significant quantities in the food, and frequently they can be used in a variety of foods. Many of these are carbohydrate or carbohydrate derived and are expected to be innocuous by their very composition. These substances include the modified celluloses and starches, the polyols and a variety of carbohydrates such as corn syrups, dextrins and lactose. Since the ingestion level of a bulking agent could easily exceed 1% of the diet, it obviously cannot be tested in animals at 100 times this intake level. The Joint FAO/WHO Expert Committee on Food Additives (JECFA) which has been responsible for much of the work on the concept of acceptable daily intakes recognized this problem and addressed it in their 17th Report (Anon. 1974). JECFA concluded that it would be unreasonable to apply the 100-fold safety factor in the following situations:

(1) Substances that are normal constituents of the human diet or are normal intermediary metabolites.

(2) Substances that are not absorbed from the gastrointestinal tract.
(3) Evidence that a substrate in the human body is converted by digestion or metabolism to a normal constituent of the diet.
(4) Other experimental data obtained from tests directly in man.

The report further states that an ADI would not be applicable for bulking agents and fillers such as the modified cellulose products that are added to food to reduce the energy content of the food for special dietary purposes. The overall message of this report is that in the case of bulking agents which are intended to replace normal food ingredients, there is an increased need to study the metabolism of the material and to do clinical trials in man to provide the basis for a sound safety judgement without using a finite 100-fold safety factor.

Human clinical trials, however, can also present problems for the investigators. Frequently, complications of an ethical or legal nature will occur and in many instances require radioactive samples of the test ingredient if studies on absorption or metabolic turnover are to be done. Nevertheless, these studies in man can be very important. This was well illustrated by the situation that developed a few years ago with single-cell protein. These new ingredients were shown to be very innocuous in the diets of a variety of species of animals but several groups of investigators (Waslien *et al.* 1970; Scrimshaw 1975) found that even at quite modest doses side effects occurred in man.

Even with the recognition that an ADI based on a 100-fold safety factor cannot be set for certain food ingredients such as bulking agents, there is a natural tendency to push the dosage in chronic feeding studies to very high levels in an attempt to provide as large a safety factor as possible. In the xylitol studies alluded to earlier, this was done by adapting the animals to high dosages at the start of the study. The interpretation of the results of these studies has been such that this potentially useful noncariogenic replacement for sugar cannot be used in the U.S., despite the fact that it is a normal human metabolite with a turnover of 5–15 g/day.

Recently we ran into a situation that also illustrates the dangers of exceptionally high dosing. Our toxicologists had some dogs under study where the normal laboratory chow was supplemented with ordinary lactose. At the level of 50% lactose in the diet, the food was readily consumed by the animals. However, the high level of lactose caused a watery diarrhea to occur on a daily basis. During these experiments the most remarkable finding was a very significant decrease in urinary sodium output as shown in Figure 18.1. For example this dog had quite severe diarrhea throughout the study. His urinary sodium excretion consistently was only a fifth of what it was during pretreatment phase.

The dog also showed gradual elevations in serum calcium values so that by day 156 he was hypercalcemic, and marked elevations in both BUN and creatinine values were also observed. The other animals under test showed similar but less pronounced effects. After 370 days on test the animals were sacrificed. This particular animal was found to have severe, grossly evident calcium nephropathy.

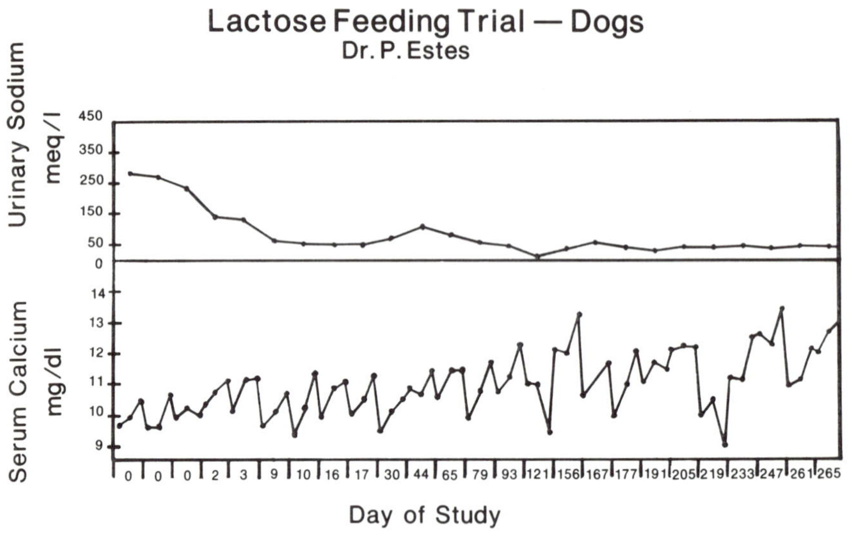

From P. Estes, Pfizer Inc.

FIG. 18.1. LACTOSE FEEDING TRIAL—DOGS

Figure 18.2 describes what our pathologist, Dr. Paul Estes, believes to be the mechanism by which this lesion is brought about. The high dietary levels of lactose produce an osmotically induced diarrhea in the animals which in turn leads to fluctuating intravascular fluid volumes by wasting water and electrolytes, particularly sodium.

This sodium wastage stimulates renal tubular reabsorption of this ion. The renal handling of calcium is closely interrelated with that of sodium. While this obligatory calcium reabsorption by the renal tubules is going on, the lactose in the diet is also enhancing the gastrointestinal absorption of calcium. These factors together eventually cause sufficient build-up of calcium levels so toxic effects occur. This is first manifested in the kidney where the levels are undoubtedly higher, and where the lesion is produced; first in the subacute form observed in several of the dogs or if conditions are sufficiently severe, in a gross, acute form.

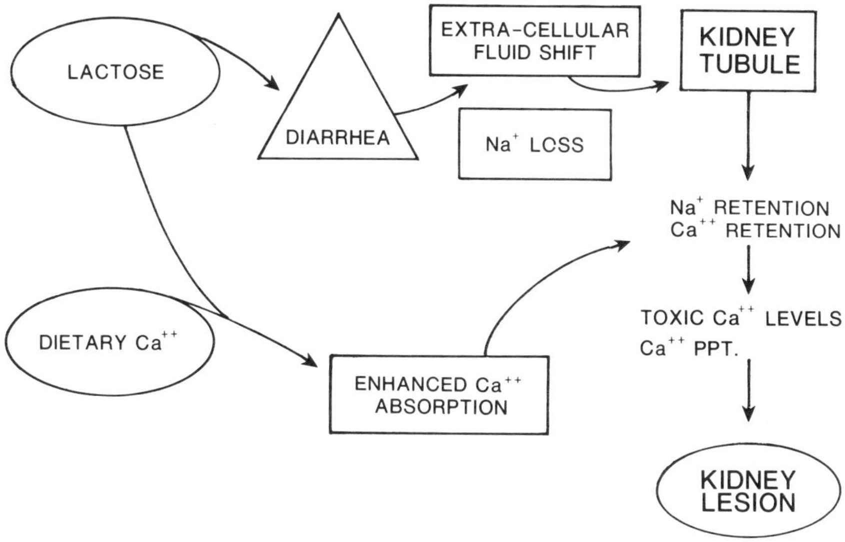

From P. Estes, Pfizer Inc.

FIG. 18.2. MECHANISM OF DIARRHEA-INDUCED CALCIUM NEPHROPATHY

To summarize this situation within the context of the subject at hand—simple administration of a perfectly normal food ingredient, lactose, at a level sufficiently high to produce a chronic diarrhea state can lead to calcium nephropathy that, in itself, if found during a chronic study with a new food ingredient could be regarded as a significant toxicological finding and if the mechanism for the formation of the lesions was not understood.

It is interesting to note that JECFA in their 17th report (Anon. 1974) mentions that no toxicological significance should be placed upon laxative effects due to bulk or osmotic load or even to cecal enlargement in the rodent. Overconsumption of certain food ingredients such as the polyols can cause a laxative effect in humans as well. This situation is usually controlled by appropriate labeling of the food products.

SAFETY EVALUATION OF BULKING AGENTS-POLYDEXTROSE

Since it is not possible to conduct feeding trials at levels sufficiently high to allow the application of a large safety factor for bulking agents, what studies should be done for the safety assessment of new materials of this type? Clearly some special studies are called for, that address any potential problems with new substitute food ingredients. Perhaps a discussion of the various studies that we have done with a low caloric bulking agent called polydextrose can illustrate the approach that we feel is reasonable. Polydextrose, structurally described in Figure 18.3, was originally discovered at Pfizer by Dr. H. Rennhard who prepared a series of polysaccharides that might have potential as noncaloric or low-calorie replacements for sugar or flour in foods (Rennhard 1973). He prepared polydextrose by the melt polycondensation of glucose with small amounts of sorbitol and citric acid, all common food ingredients.

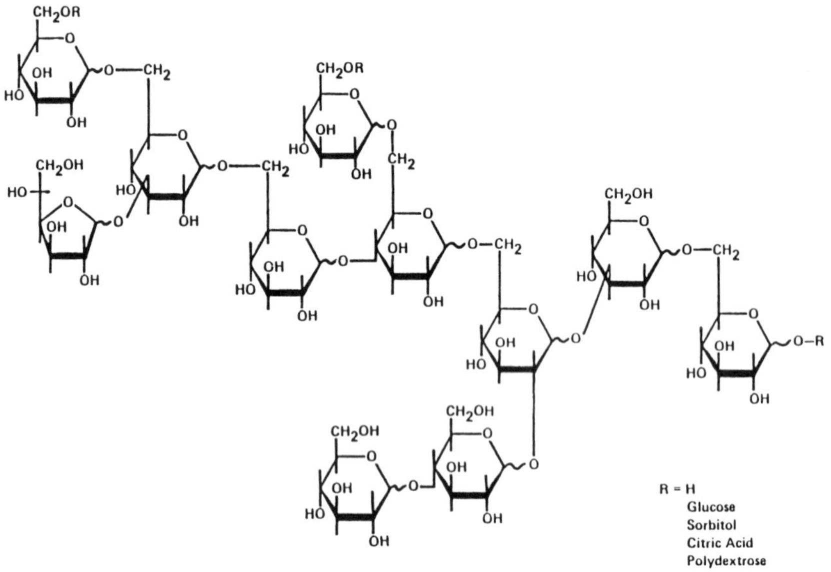

From H.H. Rennhard, Pfizer Inc.

FIG. 18.3. POLYDEXTROSE CHEMICAL BONDING

Polydextrose is not sweet, but it does possess physicochemical properties that allow it to function as a replacement for sugar and occasionally as a partial replacement for fat. Hard candy and ice cream are two examples of polydextrose use in foods. Our senior food scientist, Annibal Torres, has made hard candy in which polydextrose serves as a complete replacement for the bulk and texture of sugar so that a clear melt product is produced. An artificial sweetener is required to provide sweetness for a "sugar-free" hard candy. By only replacing a portion of the sugar in hard candy with polydextrose a caloric reduction of one-third can be obtained providing candies with excellent taste qualities and sweetness adequate for most individuals.

In certain food systems polydextrose can serve as a partial replacement for fat while acting as a total or partial replacement for sugar. An ice cream-like frozen dessert product is the best illustration of this effect. Using sugar or high fructose corn syrups as the sweetening source, in combination with polydextrose, it is possible to produce a good quality ice cream-type frozen dessert with an 80% reduction in fat content compared to normal ice cream—the total caloric reduction exceeds one-third.

In terms of the safety assessment of polydextrose, we recognized at the outset that because of its structure it would likely be a very innocuous material. However, considering the proposed use of the product, special studies would be needed to provide a complete safety assessment. In addition to the conventional toxicology studies that are listed on Table 18.1 and which supported the position that polydextrose was innocuous, we also undertook a series of special studies.

We felt it was very important to understand in detail the metabolic fate of polydextrose. This work in the rat, dog, and man was undertaken by Dr. Hans Rennhard and Dr. Sandford Figdor of our laboratories. The pathway is depicted in Figure 18.4. It was found in the rat that the polymer passes through the upper G.I. tract unchanged. In fact, much of the polymer is simply excreted in the feces. However, like many ingested polysaccharides which are not easily metabolized by digestive enzymes, and the polyols, polydextrose can serve as a substrate for the bacterial flora resident in the lower gut. These microorganisms elaborate two kinds of products: carbon dioxide, which is of no nutritional value; most of it is expelled as flatus, but some is absorbed into the bloodstream, transported to the lung, and exhaled. The other class of microbial metabolite, is the volatile fatty acids (VFA), which are absorbed, in part, by the host and utilized as a source of energy. Since the animal converts most of these molecules to CO_2, the caloric utilization can be estimated by measuring exhaled $^{14}CO_2$ after ingestion of ^{14}C-polydextrose. A series of additional studies including tests in prestressed animals and measuring serum half-lives in both the rat and dog were done, and finally, studies in man were undertaken after obtaining FDA agreement that such studies should be conducted.

In man, as in animals, much of the administered polydextrose is recovered in the feces as shown in Table 18.4 with only a trace amount absorbed and excreted in the urine. By direct measurement of exhaled $^{14}CO_2$ the maximum caloric utilization has been determined to be about 25%, so the actual caloric value of polydextrose is about 1 calorie/gram

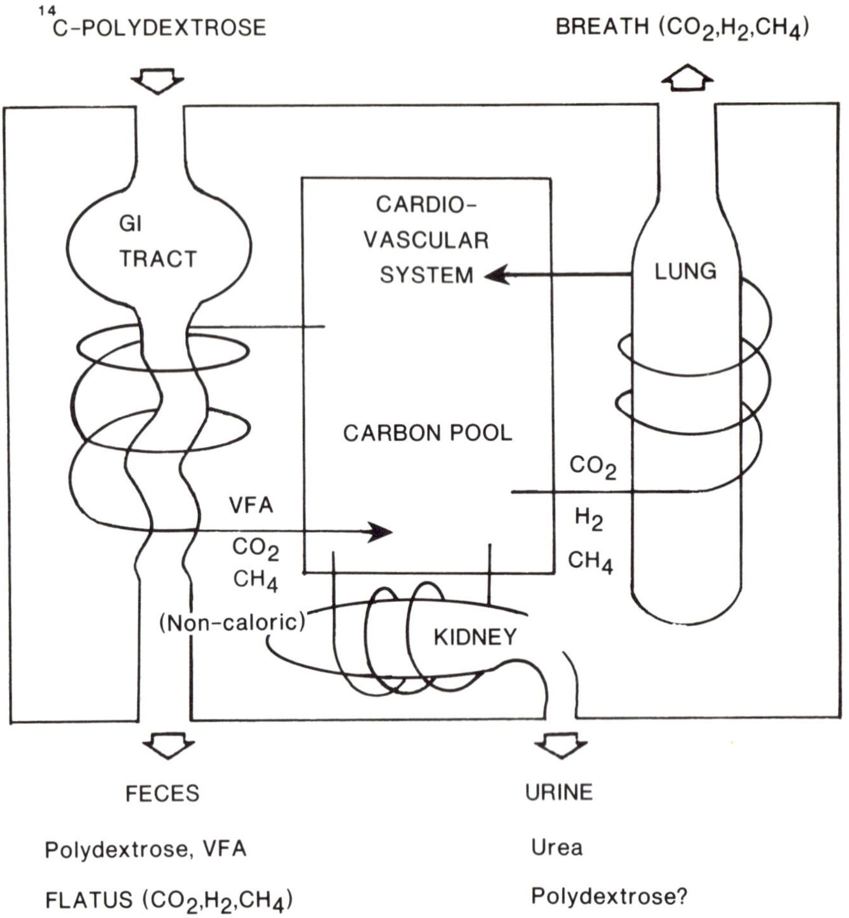

From S. Figdor, Pfizer Inc.

FIG. 18.4. POLYDEXTROSE METABOLISM PATHWAYS

compared to the 4 calories/gram for most dietary carbohydrates. In addition to establishing the caloric utilization value, these studies have demonstrated that the human would handle polydextrose in exactly the same fashion as many poorly digestible natural polysaccharides including some of the components of dietary fiber. The metabolic products of polydextrose are exactly the same as those normally encountered from the utilization of other food ingredients. The studies also establish that polydextrose is metabolized by man and animals in a similar fashion providing a basis for direct correlation of other animal studies to man.

TABLE 18.4. ORAL ADMINISTRATION OF ^{14}C-POLYDEXTROSE TO MAN. Percent recovery of administered dose (average of 4 subjects)

	Mean ± Std. Dev.
$^{14}CO_2$	16.0 ± 4.2
Caloric utilization	26.6 ± 7.0
Total urine, 0–7 days	1.41 ± 0.04
Total feces, 0–7 days	50.1 ± 7.5
Total, urine and feces plus caloric utilization	78.1 ± 2.5

Source: S. Figdor, Pfizer Inc.

Because we knew that polydextrose is not absorbed but is utilized in part by the gut microflora, the question of toleration to large doses had to be explored. A series of studies involving over 300 subjects was conducted by Dr. Anthony Knirsch and Dr. Harvey Raphan. In one study the average laxative threshold dosage in adults was found to be 90g of polydextrose a day. In this particular study, sorbitol was used as a control, and its average laxative threshold dosage was found to be 70g/day, a value consistent with that reported by other investigators. Adults on a 20–60g intake of polydextrose each day over a 3-month period showed no significant change in clinical or laboratory parameters except for an average weight loss of 0.1 lb/person/week. Children on dosages up to 1 g/kg/day, the maximum dose used, experienced only transient effects such as flatulence. In maturity-onset diabetics, a 50g slug dose of polydextrose produced no gastrointestinal effects except infrequent flatus under the standard conditions of the glucose toleration test with no significant effect on plasma glucose or insulin levels.

Another point that we felt deserved careful investigation was the effect polydextrose might have on the absorption and utilization of essential dietary ingredients. A study was conducted by Professor Nevin Scrimshaw and Professor Vernon Young at MIT under metabolic ward conditions. The amount of essential nutrients was controlled and the amounts excreted in feces and urine were measured daily. The volunteers were on a strict standardized diet for an 8-week period with a control and a treatment group. There was a 2-week period to determine baseline values. Among the various parameters measured during the study were: for electrolytes, the balances for sodium, potassium, calcium, iron and zinc were determined, and for vitamins, measurement of thiamin and riboflavin blood levels were made. In addition, nitrogen balance, fecal fat and serum cholesterol, vitamin A, carotene, vitamin E, vitamin C, folic acid, and the usual hematological factors were determined. The subjects were under daily clinical observation as well. Over a 6-week test period during which the volunteers consumed graduated doses of 30–50g of polydextrose each day, there was no significant change in any of the clinical parameters nor was there any evidence of significant change in the absorption and utilization of the essential nutrients.

It is our opinion that all of these special studies taken together substantiate the supposition we made about the product at the very beginning; namely, that the material is innocuous and entirely suited for its intended uses as a low caloric bulking agent to serve as a substitute for sucrose.

SUMMARY

Safety assessment of bulking agents and fillers that will constitute a significant level in the diet presents special problems and requires innovative approaches. The substances are frequently innocuous and because of this, animal studies are sometimes conducted at heroic dosage levels. This can lead to situations such as chronic diarrhea, which, while not of toxicological significance can cause toxic effects that confound the safety assessment. In such cases it is important to determine the mechanism and establish that the abnormal findings in animals do not apply to man. In addition, special clinical studies in man should be performed to address any specific issues raised by a particular bulking agent. In general these materials from both the use and toxicity standpoints should be considered as food ingredients rather than as food additives. As substitute food ingredients which are shown to be as safe as the ingredients they replace, they need not be limited in their use other than by good manufacturing practice; in other words that amount needed to achieve their intended purposes.

BIBLIOGRAPHY

ANON. 1974. Toxicological Evaluation of Certain Food Additives with a Review of General Principles and of Specifications. Seventeenth Report of the Joint FAO/WHO Expert Committee on Food Additives, Tech. Rep. Ser. World Health Org. 539, Food and Agricultural Organization of the United Nations.

KIRSCHMAN, J.C. 1976. Toxicology—The exact use of an inexact science. Food Product Dev. *10*, 85–90.

RENNHARD, H.H. 1973. Polysaccharides and Their Preparation, U.S. Patent 3,766,165, October 16.

SALSBURG, D.S. 1977. Use of statistics when examining lifetime studies in rodents to detect carcinogenicity. J. Toxicol. Environ. Health *3*, 611–628.

SALSBURG, D.S. 1980. The effects of lifetime feeding studies on patterns of senile lesions in mice and rats. Drug and Chem. Toxicol. *3*, 1–33.

SCRIMSHAW, N.S. 1975. Single-cell protein for human consumption—An overview. *In* Single-Cell Protein II, S.R. Tannenbaum and D.I.C. Wang (Editors). M.I.T. Press, Cambridge, Mass.

WASLIEN, C.I., CALLOWAY, D.H., MARGEN, S., AND COSTA, F. 1970. Uric acid levels in men fed algae and yeast as protein sources. J. Food Sci. *35*, 294–298.

19

Irradiated Foods—Are They Safe?

J. F. Diehl[1]

BENEFITS OF FOOD IRRADIATION

Some 30 years have passed since the first research reports on food irradiation were published, 18 years since the Food and Drug Administration cleared wheat irradiation, 17 years since it cleared potato irradiation, and still no irradiated food has reached the market in the United States. Is this not proof enough that this new process is without interest to the food industry? Are we not wasting our time when we debate the wisdom of granting clearance for other irradiated foods? Such questions are often heard, and they require a few words about the potential benefits of food irradiation before we discuss its possible risks.

The two clearances granted by the FDA have turned out to be the wrong ones for the American food industry. Long-term storage of potatoes is not necessary in the United States. By the time Idaho potatoes begin to sprout, a new crop is available from California or Florida. There is no need for sprout inhibition by irradiation. Disinfestation of wheat can be achieved by fumigation, and both industry and FDA seem to be satisfied with available fumigants. There is no incentive for investing large sums in facilities for irradiation of wheat. The promise of the new process is in other applications, such as:

[1] Federal Research Center for Nutrition, Karlsruhe, West Germany.

Hygienization of Spices and Other Dry Condiments Presently Treated With Ethylene Oxide

There is mounting evidence of ethylene oxide being mutagenic (Embree *et al.* 1977) and carcinogenic (Hogstedt *et al.* 1979). Ethylene chlorohydrin, a reaction product of ethylene oxide with chlorides present in food, is similarly under suspicion (Brem *et al.* 1974; Rosenkranz *et al.* 1974; Pfeiffer and Dunkelberg 1980). As a consequence, the use of ethylene oxide has been restricted and a complete ban is considered in some countries. Radiation is the only remaining alternative. Its effectiveness for this purpose has been demonstrated by Proctor *et al.* (1950) and numerous other studies have provided additional evidence (*e.g.* Tjaberg *et al.* 1972; Vajdi and Pereira 1973; Farkas *et al.* 1973; Silberstein *et al.* 1979).

Elimination of Salmonellae

The frequency of salmonellosis has increased almost explosively—a public health problem world-wide. The effectiveness of radiation for the elimination of salmonellae has been demonstrated long ago and many experts in this field (*e.g.* Mossel 1977) have supported the use of radiation for this purpose. For heat-sensitive products, such as frozen chicken, irradiation is the only treatment that can guarantee freedom of salmonellae.

Irradiation of Tropical and Subtropical Fruits

Quarantine restrictions inhibit international trade with fruits in many areas. In cases where fumigation is ineffective (*e.g.* against the mango seed weevil) irradiation offers itself as an alternative (IAEA 1971). In addition, radiation, especially when used in combination with hot-water dipping, greatly prolongs storage life of many fruits (Brodrick and Thomas 1978). Some tropical fruits presently transported to European countries by plane and sold at exorbitant prices could be shipped by surface after irradiation, thus opening export markets for producers and providing consumers with tropical fruits at reasonable prices.

Hygienization of Shrimps

European brown shrimps *(Crangon vulgaris)*, much smaller than the shrimps consumed in the United States, still cannot be satisfactorily peeled by machine. Hand-peeling as presently practiced can introduce pathogens and requires heavy use of chemical preservatives. Radiation effectively reduces the contamination and improves shelf life (Ehlermann and Münzner 1976; Ehlermann and Diehl 1977).

Sterilization of Meat

The process of producing high-quality shelfstable meat products by a combination of (a) mild heat treatment for enzyme inactivation, (b) freezing, and (c) irradiation at subfreezing temperatures, as developed at the U.S. Army Natick Laboratories (Josephson *et al.* 1973) has been considered by some as being too expensive for the civilian market. However, interest in the process has been strengthened by the recognition that its energy requirement, with subsequent storage at ambient temperature, is lower than that for canning or that for freezing with storage at freezing temperature (Brynjolfsson 1978). The demonstration that irradiation can greatly reduce the need for nitrite in cured meats (Wierbicki 1979) has given further impetus to these studies.

RISKS OF FOOD IRRADIATION

Although "radiation" and "radioactivity" are easily confused by the layman, fears of induced radioactivity are not the reason for restrictive legislation. The energy of radiations used for the treatment of foods (1.3 MeV from cobalt-60, 0.66 MeV from cesium-137, up to 10 MeV from electron accelerators) *will not* produce radioactivity in food constituents. Concerns over the microbiological safety of foods irradiated with nonsterilizing doses have been discussed and have led to many experimental investigations. The consensus of informed scientists is that, in principle, irradiation does not create different microbiological problems than other preservation processes such as heat pasteurization (Idziak 1973; Ingram and Farkas 1977). Irradiation at high doses can cause considerable losses of some vitamins, especially if air is not excluded from the food package. The same is true of heating, and such losses need not cause more concern in irradiated foods than in heated foods.

The only remaining concern has to do with the chemical changes produced in foods as a consequence of radiation energy input. Irradiated foods contain substances which they did not contain or which they contained at lower concentration before irradiation. It is therefore not illogical that legislation introduced in the United States in 1958 classified irradiated foods as food additives—each type of irradiated food being a different additive, requiring separate proof of safety before it could be "cleared." (The logic is missing, however, when foods treated by other new methods which also cause chemical changes are not controlled in the same way: microwave heating, sonication, freeze drying, extrusion processing, etc.). This thinking has been adopted by other countries and by international agencies. When the wholesomeness of irradiated foods was assessed by an FAO/IAEA/WHO Joint Expert Committee for the first time (WHO 1965), this committee found: "The tests which must be applied to an irradiated food to establish its safety for consumption are broadly similar to those generally applied to ensure the safety of food additives." This referred to long-term feeding studies on several species of animals. The committee added: "It is of utmost importance that the material tested shall have the same characteristics and properties as that to be produced commercially so that food subjected to safety testing must, insofar as may reasonably be required, be closely comparable with irradiated food as it will be consumed by man." This concept had disastrous consequences for the further development of food irradiation. It meant in effect that a long-term feeding study with irradiated wheat had no relevance for clearing irradiated rice, a feeding study with irradiated whole fish could not be used to clear irradiated packaged fish filets, a clearance for irradiated haddock was not valid for cod. Feeding studies were required ad infinitum.

The linking of irradiated foods with food additives created another problem. Risk estimations based on animal feeding tests require administering a dose level high enough to produce an unfavorable effect. It is normal practice to regulate intake of the test substance to no more than 1% of the threshold dose, or more precisely of the maximum dose at which no unfavorable effect is observed. However, with foods irradiated in the normal dose range of up to 5 Mrad[1], it has never been possible to produce significant toxic effects attributable to irradiation. When unfavorable effects were found, they were shown to be due to nutritional inadequacies, especially due to feeding too high a level of the test food (Elias 1980). It is not surprising to see rats get sick when their diet contains 30% onions—regardless of whether the onions were irradiated or not.

If a clear-cut, radiation-related effect cannot be found even at the highest level of feeding, the experimenter does not know what the target organs might be or what systems require particularly careful examination. It is not very satisfactory for the evaluating toxicologist having to conclude after a 3-year feeding study that "nothing" has been found in any of the groups. Perhaps the level of irradiated food was just below the threshold or "effect level?" If man would consume such food in quantity,

[1] The better known dose unit rad (= 100 erg/g; 1000 rad = 1 krad; 1000 krad = 1 Mrad) is used in this paper. The SI unit of radiation dose, now being introduced, is the gray, where 1 Gy = 1 J/kg (= 100 rad).

would the safety factor perhaps be only five, rather than the usually demanded 100?

This problem is not unique to irradiated foods—it applies to the testing of foods in general, and arises from the impossibility of testing foods by the same methods as food additives, drugs or pesticides. Golberg recognized this when he stated ten years ago that "the solution attempted for the problem of irradiated food has proved a colossal and costly failure; feeding irradiated fruit salad to dogs has not established safety, nor has the whole vast exercise provided an advance in fundamental knowledge to serve as a springboard for further work" (Golberg 1970).

CHEMICAL STUDIES

The desired advance in fundamental knowledge has come from chemical investigations. "Many early studies by chemists recognized that elucidation of the chemical changes produced in food by irradiation would have a favorable impact on the evaluation of the safety of irradiated food" (Merritt 1978). Symposia on the chemistry of food irradiation were held in Atlantic City in 1965 (ACS 1967), in Los Angeles in 1971 (Josephson and Merritt 1972) and in Mexico City in 1975 (Merritt 1978). A book on *Radiation Chemistry of Major Food Components* has been published (Elias and Cohen, 1977). It was shown that an approximate estimate of maximal chemical changes in an irradiated food is possible on the basis of existing information, and it was suggested that further evaluations of the safety of irradiated foods should take such estimates into account (Diehl and Scherz 1975; Taub *et al.* 1976).

When the Joint Expert Committee on Food Irradiation (JECFI) was convened in 1976, it largely accepted the new thinking: "The analyses of radiolytic products that have been carried out so far have removed much of the previous uncertainty about the validity of extrapolating from one food to another in arriving at an evaluation of the consequences of irradiation . . . The general principle of radiation chemical reactions, as revealed by analytical studies, will reduce considerably the extent to which toxicological testing is needed and will simplify the testing procedures" (WHO 1977). The term "chemiclearance" was soon invented (Basson 1977) and the concept was applied in evaluating the wholesomeness of irradiated fruits (Basson *et al.* 1979).

This general approach is also the basis of reports prepared by the Select Committee on Health Aspects of Irradiated Beef, a committee created by the Life Science Research Office of the Federation of American Societies for Experimental Biology. By gas chromatography/mass spectrometry Merritt *et al.* (1978) had identified over 100 compounds in beef radiation-sterilized by the Natick procedure, at concentrations of 1–700 μg/kg, with a total yield of 9 mg/kg. Aliphatic hydrocarbons constituted 90% of the total, the rest being aldehydes, ketones, alcohols and traces of sulfur- and nitrogen-compounds. The Select Committee concluded that there were no grounds to suspect that these radiolysis products, at these low concentrations, would constitute any hazard to the consumer (FASEB 1977, 1979).

One criticism directed against this approach points out that even the most sophisticated analytical technique cannot discover everything. However, after so many years of research it is unlikely that unidentified compounds are produced in high yield; the uncertainties are probably in the concentration range of below 100 μg/kg. As the diet of animals in long-term experiments cannot consist of 100% meat, an experimental diet would contain such unidentified compounds at concentrations of 30 μg/kg or less. Obviously, such compounds would have to have the biological effectiveness of aflatoxins or similar extremely toxic substances to be detectable in a feeding study. Aflatoxins, botulinus toxin and other compounds having biological activity at such low levels have rather complicated structures and it is inconceivable that they are formed by irradiation—a process which primarily breaks molecules down to smaller fractions; CO_2, H_2, CH_4 usually being the main products.

Through cross-linking reactions irradiation can also cause the formation of very large molecules, such as protein aggregates and lipid polymers. Due to their insolubility and lack of volatility such aggregates are more difficult to study than smaller molecules and it must be admitted that much less is known about the nature of radiation-induced polymers in foods than about the volatiles. On the other hand, insolubility also impairs absorption in the gastro-intestinal tract and it is unlikely that very small amounts of such polymers are of physiological significance. The scores of lifetime and multigeneration feeding studies which have been carried out with diets irradiated with a sterilizing dose should have given some indications of physiological effects if they exist.

Nevertheless, these considerations indicate that chemical studies alone could not have established the safety of irradiated foods. As explained above, animal feeding studies alone were not satisfactory either. Only the intelligent use of information offered by biological and chemical studies together can provide the necessary confidence in judging the wholesomeness of irradiated foods.

The identification and quantification of radiolytic products in foods and food components has been developed into a high art in many laboratories, of which only a few "centers of excellence" can be mentioned here: Natick Laboratories on irradiated meat (Merritt *et al.* 1978; Taub *et al.* 1979B), Nawar's group at the University of Massachusetts on irradiated lipids (Nawar 1977), von Sonntag's group at the Mulheim Max-Planck-Institute on irradiated carbohydrates (von Sonntag 1980), Namiki's Laboratory, University of Nagoya, also on irradiated carbohydrates (Kito *et al.* 1979). Other radiation chemical studies have helped to provide a basis of knowledge upon which extrapolations can be made from one food to another and from one set of radiation conditions to another (role of water content, packaging under air or vacuum, dose-rate, radiation temperature etc.).

There is a voluminous literature on the radiation chemistry of pure compounds and of dilute solutions of pure compounds. A direct application of this information to the situation in foods can lead to very wrong conclusions. For example, amino acids in dilute solutions are extensively decomposed when irradiated in the kilorad range, while the same amino acids are stable to megarad doses when present as a protein constituent in foods. Ascorbic acid in orange juice is much more resistant to radiation than in pure aqueous solution (Proctor and Goldblith 1951). A more recent example is given in Fig. 19.1: While α-tocopherol in isooctane is completely destroyed by a dose of 5 Mrad, increasing concentrations of

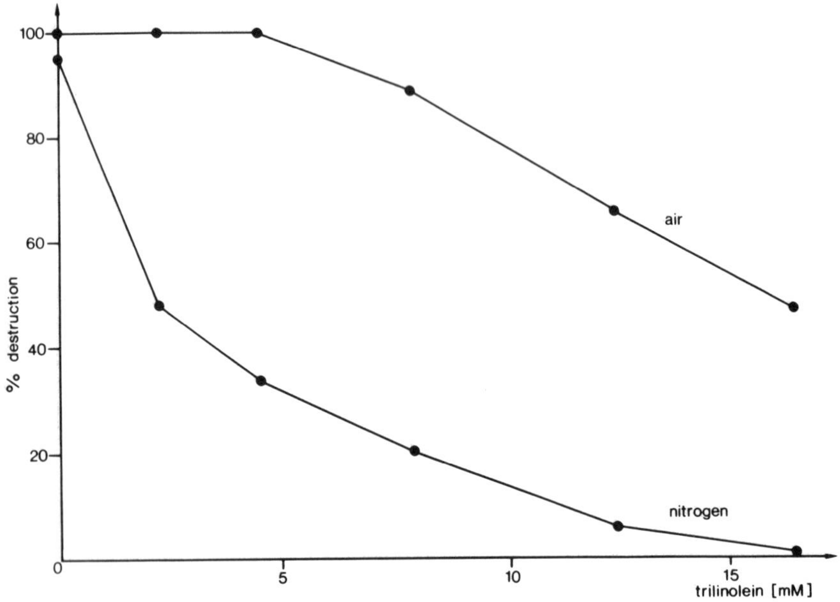

From Diehl (1979)

FIG. 19.1. EFFECT OF INCREASING CONCENTRATIONS OF TRILINOLEIN ON DESTRUCTION OF α-TOCOPHEROL (0.5 mM IN ISOOCTANE) BY ELECTRON IRRADIATION IN AIR OR NITROGEN trilinolein provide increasing protection. The protective effect increases in the series trilinolein < triolein < tristearin < tributyrin (Diehl 1979).

Based on earlier studies by Fujimaki's group (Tajima *et al.* 1969) on the protective effect of cysteine on glucose, we have systematically investigated the radiation protection of carbohydrates by various amino acids. The example of trehalose is shown in Fig. 19.2. In a similar way we have studied radiation effects on proteins, lipids and carbohydrates irradiated separately and together (Diehl *et al.* 1978). Other investigations have been devoted to the radiation chemistry of polysaccharides as

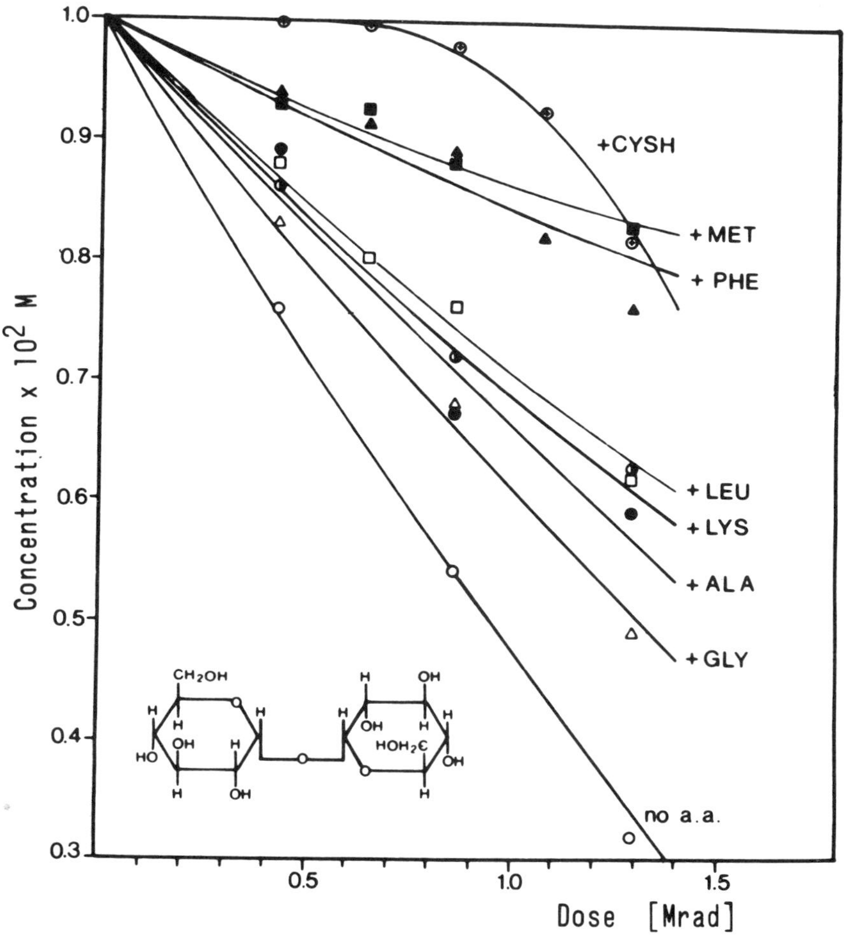

FIG. 19.2. EFFECT OF ADDED AMINO ACIDS (10^{-2}M) ON THE DECOMPOSITION BY γ-IRRADIATION OF TREHALOSE IN AIR SATURATED AQUEOUS SOLUTION (10^{-2}M).

influenced by water activity (a_w). Expanding on studies by Saint-Lèbe's group on starch containing up to 20% water (Berger *et al.* 1977) we have taken dextran as a model polysaccharide and have determined product formation over the full range of water activities (Fig. 19.3). While the overall yield of monomer products was practically independent of a_w, the formation of 5-deoxy-xylo-hexodialdose decreased and the formation of threo-tetrodialdose and threonic acid lactone increased with increasing a_w.

Efforts to find methods that would permit identification of irradiated foods and that would permit regulatory agencies to recognize food items which have been illegally irradiated, have not been particularly successful—but they have greatly contributed to our knowledge of what happens (or does not happen) in irradiated foods (Commission of the European Communities 1974). Chemical changes caused by irradiation are quantitatively very small and with few exceptions they are qualitatively nonspecific. An extensive investigation by Hamm's group, carried out with the aim of finding a method for identifying irradiated meats, led to the conclusion that beef and pork irradiated at a dose of 5 Mrad resembled in all investigated parameters meat heated to not more than 70°C (Roessler and Hamm 1979). In our institute irradiation of meat from beef, pork, and chicken has produced a new ninhydrin-positive peak (called "Y" in Fig. 19.4) which appears between histidine and lysine in the chromatogram of the meat extract. The same substance is produced when carnosine is irradiated (Partmann and Schlaszus 1980). The amount of Y produced depends on radiation dose and on the carnosine content of the irradiated meat.

Another study showing that radiation-induced product formation is much the same in meats from different mammalian species has come from Natick Laboratories. Aliphatic hydrocarbons were determined in irradiated beef, pork, chicken, and ham and the yields were found to depend only on radiation dose and on fat content (Taub *et al.* 1979A). As an example, octene formation is shown in Fig. 19.5, but similar curves were obtained for other hydrocarbons. The results indicate that the differences in product formation from irradiated beef and irradiated chicken, both having 11% fat, are smaller than in product formation from two cuts of beef, one having 10%, the other having 15% fat. Such information should not be without consequence in further deliberations on wholesomeness and clearances.

NATICK FEEDING STUDIES

The Natick food irradiation program has involved very extensive and costly feeding studies with irradiated meats—none of the results giving

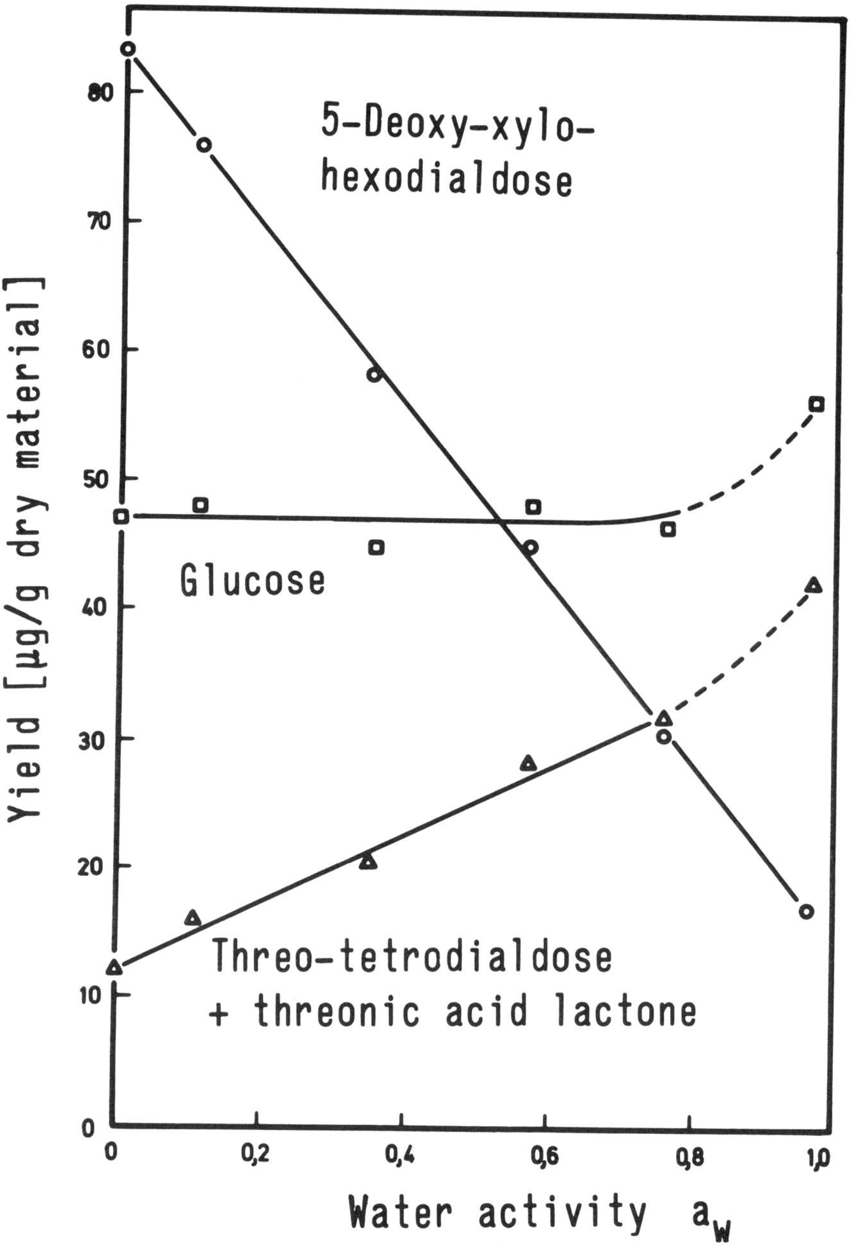

From Adam et al. (1979)

FIG. 19.3. INFLUENCE OF WATER ACTIVITY ON YIELDS OF MONOMERIC PRODUCTS FROM ELECTRON-IRRADIATED DEXTRAN.

The analytical method used—gas chromatography after $NaBH_4$=reduction and trimethylsilylation—does not allow separation of threo-tetrodialdose and threonic acid lactone.

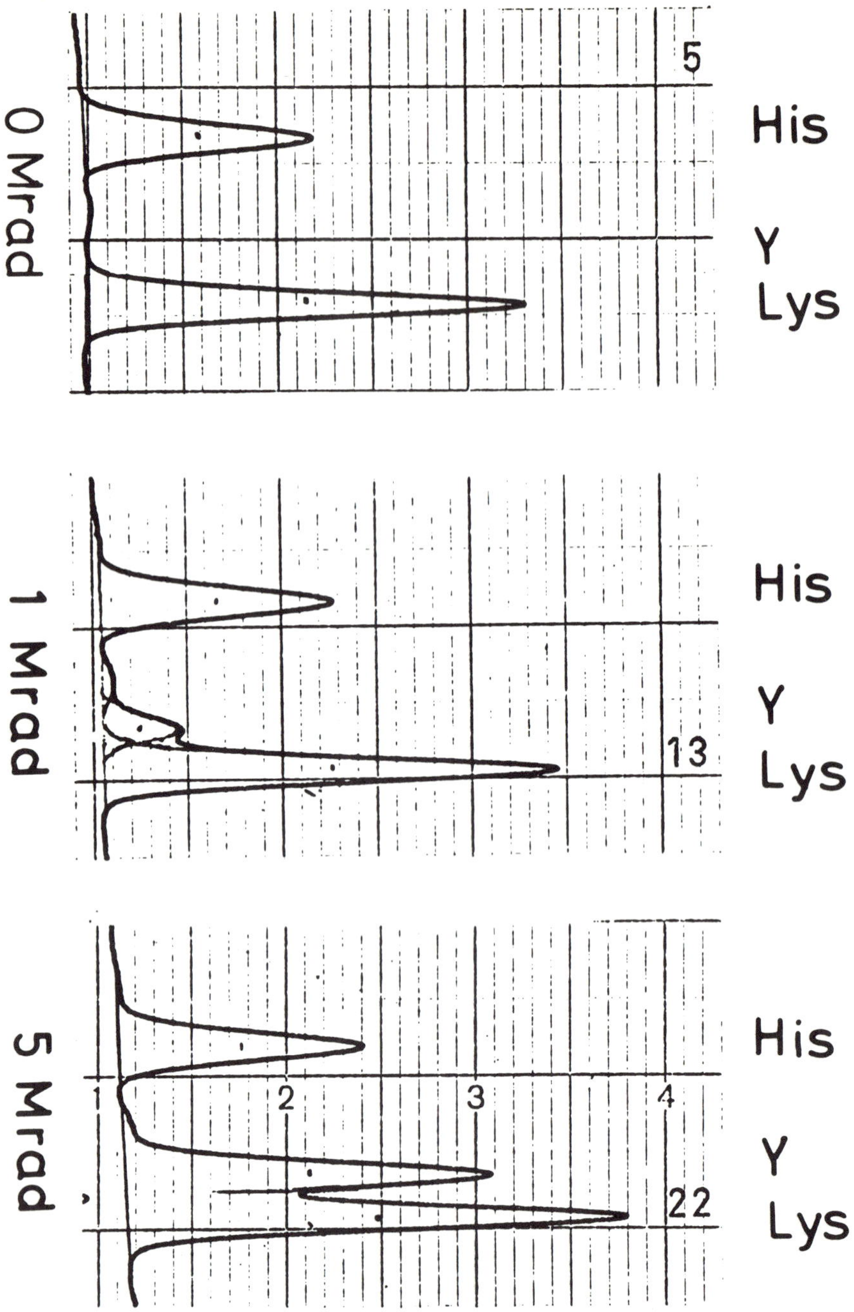

From Partmann and Keskin (1979)

FIG. 19.4. IDENTICAL SECTIONS OF 3 CHROMATOGRAMS OF NINHYDRIN-REACTIVE SUBSTANCES IN EXTRACTS OF MINCED BEEF, UNIRRADIATED AND ELECTRON-IRRADIATED AT DOSES OF 1 AND 5 MRAD.

Irradiation at room temperature in presence of air.

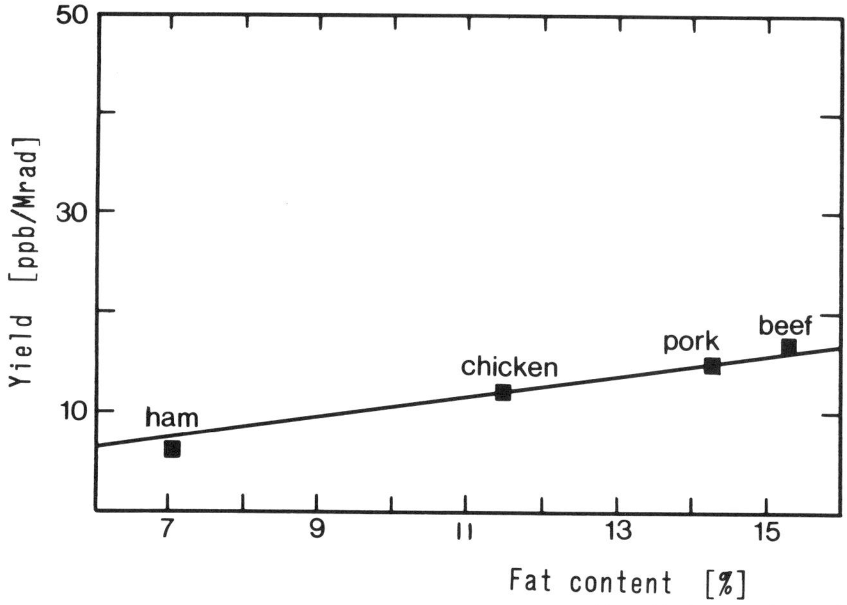

FIG. 19.5. YIELD OF OCTENE AS A FUNCTION OF FAT CONTENT IN MEATS IRRADIATED AT −40°C, IN ABSENCE OF AIR.

Yields were determined from the linear increase in the amount of octene formed in each sample with increasing dose.

indications of adverse effects. At present a study of irradiated chicken meat is nearing completion. To be more specific, three species of animals (rats, mice, dogs) were fed five diets (frozen, heat-sterilized, electron-irradiated and gamma-irradiated chicken, and a control group receiving pelleted laboratory feed). In addition to these long-term feeding studies, a teratology study was carried out with hamsters. Mutagenicity was studied by the sex-linked recessive lethals test in drosophila, the heritable translocation test in mice, the dominant lethal test in mice, and the Ames salmonella assay. Not all of these studies have been completed and evaluated. Assuming that the final evaluation continues to show no adverse effect of irradiation, and considering the chemical studies which show so little species-related difference in product formation, it is my firm conviction that further animal feeding studies on irradiated beef, pork, lamb etc. would be a waste of the taxpayer's money.

MUTAGENICITY TESTING

What has just been said about mutagenicity testing of irradiated chicken meat requires some additional comments, because the question of mutagenicity has long played such a prominent role in discussions of the safety of irradiated food. Early studies had demonstrated cytotoxic (Molin and Ehrenberg 1964) and mutagenic effects of certain irradiated substrates, especially sugar solutions, when tested under *in vitro* conditions (Moutschen and Matagne 1965; Shaw and Hayes 1966). Some of these effects where shown to be due to pH changes (Schubert 1967; Bradley *et al.* 1968); formation of carbonyls also seems to be involved (Wilmer *et al.* 1980). Because of the observed *in vitro* mutagenicity it was essential to test for mutagenicity under *in vivo* conditions, and close to 40 such studies have been carried out, mostly with negative effects. Observations of chromosome aberrations (Vijayalaxmi and Sadasivan 1975) and of dominant lethal mutations (Vijayalaxmi and Rao 1976) were attributed to the feeding of freshly irradiated wheat. Two other groups of authors could not confirm these observations (Chauhan *et al.* 1977; Reddi *et al.* 1977). An extensive collaborative study, sponsored by the International Project in the Field of Food Irradiation, gave no indication of mutagenic effects of irradiated wheat or rather of a diet prepared from irradiated wheat, irrespective of the time of storage (Tesh *et al.* 1977).

The fact that irradiation causes the formation of free radicals and that these are quite stable in dry foods (Diehl and Hofmann 1968) has often been mentioned as a reason for special caution with irradiated dry foods. It should be pointed out, however, that free radical formation is not limited to irradiated foods. Electron spin resonance measurements have shown that the milling of grain (Redman *et al.* 1966) and the heating of proteins having a low water content (Uchiyama and Uchiyama 1979) also produce long-lived free radicals. A long-term feeding study especially designed to look for possible effects of an irradiated diet containing a high free radical concentration has been negative with regard to tumor formation (Renner and Reichelt 1973) and to mutagenic effects in a dominant lethal assay (Renner *et al.* 1973). Another study in our institute was designed to test for a possible comutagenic effect of an irradiated diet fed together with a known chemical mutagen. The result was again negative (Renner 1975).

INTERNATIONAL PROJECT IN THE FIELD OF FOOD IRRADIATION (IFIP)

Animal feeding studies like Natick Laboratories' above-mentioned project for evaluating the wholesomeness of irradiated chicken, are so expensive that only a few countries can afford them. This fact and the realization that progress in the field of food irradiation depended upon finally getting the question of wholesomeness answered, led to the creation of IFIP in 1970. Under the sponsorship of the International Atomic

Energy Agency (IAEA) in Vienna and the Organization for Economic Cooperation and Development (OECD) in Paris, 19 countries joined their resources. In the meantime the number has grown to 24. The World Health Organization is associated with the work of the Project in an advisory capacity. The Project Director has his headquarters at the Federal Research Center for Nutrition, Karlsruhe, Germany. Toxicologists of international standing have directed the Project: J.R. Hickman (1971–1973) and D.J. Clegg (1974–1975) were on leave of absence from the Canadian Department of Health and Welfare during their association with the Project. The present director, Dr. P.S. Elias, was Principal Medical Officer at the Department of Health and Social Security in London before joining the Project.

Feeding studies contracted by IFIP with various laboratories, mostly in the USA, UK, and France, involved irradiated wheat flour, potatoes, rice, several species of iced fish, mangoes, spices, dried dates, cocoa beans, and legumes. The research program also includes *in vitro* screening tests (Phillips and Elias 1979) and the evaluation of chemical investigations (Elias and Cohen 1977). All studies are documented in publicly available Technical Reports, Activity Reports and a periodical, Food Irradiation Information.

The work of the Project has contributed much to the positive attitude shown by the Joint Expert Committee at its last meeting (WHO 1977). The "unconditional acceptance" granted by JECFI to irradiated wheat (maximum dose 100 krad), potatoes (15 krad), papaya (100 krad), strawberries (300 krad) and chicken (700 krad) and the "provisional acceptance" for irradiated fresh cod and redfish (220 krad), onions (15 krad) and rice (100 krad) have led to a Codex Alimentarius General Standard on Irradiated Foods, thus providing the basis for legislation at the international level. In October 1980 JECFI will meet again, to consider the results of studies carried out since its last meeting. The outcome of the Committee's deliberations will have a decisive influence on future developments in this field.

IRRADIATED DIETS FOR LABORATORY ANIMALS

In feeding studies designed to test individual food items such as irradiated meat or potatoes or onions, the physiological demands of the animals must be considered and the food to be tested constitutes only a certain percentage of the total diet. The results of such studies are greatly strengthened by observations on animals receiving radiation-sterilized stock diets. In this case 100% of the feed intake is irradiated.

With regard to palatability, nutrient value and microbiological safety irradiated feeds have clear-cut advantages over heat-treated or ethylene oxide-fumigated feeds. Consequently, radiation processing for the hygienization of laboratory animal diets is practiced worldwide and on a growing scale (IAEA 1979). In the United Kingdom alone 1200 tons of laboratory animal diets are irradiated annually (Ley 1979). If we take the average daily feed consumption of rats as 20g and their average lifetime in the laboratory as 6 months, we may assume that each year some 300,000 rats are maintained on irradiated feed, in the UK alone. (Mice consume less, dogs consume more—a calculation based on the daily consumption of rats cannot be too far off the actual figure). The purpose for which these animals are kept requires close observation of their health status and breeding performance. In some laboratories records on animal colonies maintained on irradiated diets have been kept for 15 years. If adverse effects were produced by irradiated diets they should have been noticed by now. Sterilization requires a dose of 2–3 Mrad. If no effects are observed with 100% irradiated diets processed at this high dose level, it really does not make much sense to go on testing individual food items irradiated with a lower dose and fed as 30% (or less) of the diet.

IRRADIATED FOODS ARE SAFE

When the Surgeon General evaluated 10 years of wholesomeness research carried out under the U.S. Army program at a cost of $6.1 million, he came to the conclusion: "Food Irradiation up to absorbed doses of 5.6 megarads with a cobalt-60 source of gamma radiation or with electrons with energies up to 10 million electron volts have been found to be wholesome; i.e. safe, and nutritionally adequate" (Congress of the United States 1965).

The immense amount of information gathered worldwide in the 15 years since then has greatly strengthened this conclusion. The degree of confidence with which we can say that irradiated foods *are* safe, is at least as good as that reached in judging the safety of new food additives or of foods processed in other ways.

BIBLIOGRAPHY

ADAM, S., BLANKENHORN, R., and DIEHL, J.F. 1979. Effect of water activity upon electron-radiolysis of dextran. Starch *31*, 423.

ACS. 1967. Radiation Preservation of Food. Advances in Chemistry Series No. 65. American Chemical Society, Washington, D.C.

BASSON, R.A. 1977. Chemiclearance. Nuclear Active *17*, 3.

BASSON, R.A., BEYERS, M., and THOMAS, A.C. 1979. A radiation-chemical approach to the evaluation of the possible toxicity of irradiated fruits. 1. The effect of protection by carbohydrates. Food Chem. *4*, 131.

BERGER, G., DAUPHIN, J.F., MICHEL, J.P., ENRICO, G., AGNEL, J.P., SEGUIN, F., and SAINT-LEBE, L. 1977. Studies of the formation processes of some identified radiolysis products after gamma irradiation of maize starch. *Starch 29*, 80.

BRADLEY, M.V., HALL, L.L., and TREBICOCK, S.J. 1968. Low pH of irradiated sucrose in induction of chromosome aberrations. Nature *127*, 1182.

BREM, H., STEIN, A.B., and ROSENKRANZ, H.S. 1974. The mutagenicity and DNA-modifying effect of haloalkanes. Cancer Res. *34*, 2576.

BRODERICK, H.T. and THOMAS, A.C. 1978. Radiation preservation of subtropical fruits in South Africa. *In* Food Preservation by Irradiation, Vol. 1, p. 167. Internat. Atomic Energy Agency STI/PUB/470, Vienna.

BRYNJOLFSSON, A. 1978. Energy and food irradiation. *In* Food Preservation by Irradiation, Vol. 2, p. 285. Internat. Atomic Energy Agency, STI/PUB/470, Vienna.

CHAUHAN, P.S., ARAVINDAKSHAN, M., KUMAR, N.S., RAO, V.S., AYAR, A.S., and SUNDARAM, K. 1977. Evaluations of freshly irradiated wheat for dominant lethal mutations in Wistar rats. Toxicology *7*, 85.

COMMISSION OF THE EUROPEAN COMMUNITIES. 1974. International Colloquium on the Identification of Irradiated Foodstuffs. EUR 5126, Luxembourg.

CONGRESS OF THE UNITED STATES. 1965. Radiation Processing of Foods. Hearings before the Subcommittee on Research, Development and Radiation of the Joint Committee on Atomic Energy, June 9 and 10, p. 105.

DIEHL, J.F. and HOFMANN, S. 1968. Electronspinresonance studies on radiation-preserved foods. 1. Influence of radiation dose on spin concentration. Lebensm. Wiss. Technol. *1*, 19 (German).

DIEHL, J.F., ADAM, S., DELINCEE, H., and JAKUBICK, V. 1978. Radiolysis of carbohydrates and of carbohydrate-containing foodstuffs. J. Agr. Food Chem. *26*, 15.

DIEHL, J.F. 1979. Influence of irradiation conditions and of storage on radiation-induced vitamin E losses in foods. Chem. Mikrobiol. Technol. Lebensm. *6*, 65. (German).

DIEHL, J.F. and SCHERZ, H. 1975. Estimation of radiolytic products as a basis for evaluating the wholesomeness of irradiated foods. Int. J. Appl. Rad. Isotopes *26*, 499.

EHLERMANN, D. and DIEHL, J.F. 1977. Economic aspects of the introduction of radiation preservation of brown shrimps in the Federal Republic of Germany. Radiat. Phys. Chem. *9*, 875.

EHLERMANN, D. and MÜNZNER, R. 1976. Radurization of brown shrimps. Arch. Lebensmittelhyg. *27*, 41. (German).

ELIAS, P.S. and COHEN, A.J. 1977. Radiation Chemistry of Major Food Components. Elsevier, New York.

ELIAS, P.S. 1980. The wholesomeness of irradiated food. Ecotoxicol. Environm. Safety *4*, 172.

EMBREE, J.W., LYON, J.P., and HINE, C.H. 1977. The mutagenic potential of ethylene oxide using the dominant-lethal assay in rats. Tox. Appl. Pharmacol. *40*, 261.

FARKAS, J., BECZNER, J. and INCZE, K. 1973. Feasibility of irradiation of spices with special reference to paprika. *In* Radiation Preservation of Food. Internat. Atomic Energy Agency, STI/PUB/317, Vienna.

FASEB. 1977. Evaluation of the Health Aspects of Certain Compounds Found in Irradiated Beef. Life Sciences Research Office, Federation of American Societies for Experimental Biology, Bethesda, Md.

FASEB. 1979. Evaluation of the Health Aspects of Certain Compounds Found in Irradiated Beef. Supplements I and II. Life Sciences Research Office, Federation of American Societies for Experimental Biology, Bethesda, Md.

GOLBERG, L. 1970. Chemical and biochemical implications of human and animal exposure to toxic substances in food. Pure Appl. Chem. *21*, 309.

HOGSTEDT, C., MALMQUIST, C.N., and VADMAN, B. 1979. Leukemia in workers exposed to ethylene oxide. JAMA *241*, 1132.

IAEA. 1971. Disinfestation of Fruit by Irradiation. Internat. Atomic Energy Agency, STI/PUB/299, Vienna.

IAEA. 1979. Decontamination of Animal Feeds by Irradiation. Internat. Atomic Energy Agency, STI/PUB/508, Vienna.

IDZIAK, E. 1973. Effect of radiations on microorganisms. Int. J. Rad. Sterilization *1*, 45.

INGRAM, M. and FARKAS, J. 1977. Microbiology of foods pasteurized by ionizing radiation. Acta Aliment. *6*, 123.

JOSEPHSON, E.S. and MERRITT, C. JR. 1972. Recent advances in the chemistry of food irradiation. Radiation Res. Rev. *3*, 283.

JOSEPHSON, E.S., BRYNJOLFSSON, A., WIERBICKI, E., ROWLEY, D.B., MERRITT, C. JR., BAKER, R.W., KILLORAN, J.J., and THOMAS, M.H. 1973. Radappertization of meat, meat products and poultry. *In* Radiation Preservation of Food, p. 471, Internat. Atomic Energy Agency, STI/PUB/317, Vienna.

KITO, Y., KAWAKISHI, S., and NAMIKI, M. 1979. Radiation-induced degradation of D-fructose in anaerobic condition. Agric. Biol. Chem. (Tokyo) *43*, 713.

LEY, F.J. 1979. Radiation processing of laboratory animal diet. Radiat. Phys. Chem. *14*, 677.

MERRITT, C. JR., ANGELINI, P., and GRAHAM, R.A. 1978. Effect of radiation parameters on the formation of radiolysis products in meat and meat substances. J. Ag. Food Chem. *26*, 29.

MERRITT, C. JR. 1978. Symposium on current studies on the chemistry of food irradiation. J. Ag. Food Chem. *26*, 1.

MOLIN, N. and EHRENBERG, L. 1964. Anti-bacterial action of irradiated glucose. Int. J. Rad. Biol. *8*, 223.

MOSSEL, D.A.A. 1977. The elimination of enteric bacterial pathogens from food and feed of animal origin by gamma irradiation with particular reference to Salmonella radicidation. J. Food Quality *1*, 85.

MOUTSCHEN, J. and MATAGNE, R. 1965. Cytological effects of irradiated glucose. Radiat. Bot. *3*, 1.

NAWAR, W.W. 1977. Radiation Chemistry of Lipids. *In* Radiation Chemistry of Major Food Components, P.S. Elias and A.J. Cohen (Editors). Elsevier, New York.

PARTMANN, W. and SCHLASZUS, H. 1980. Investigations on the origin of two radiation-induced compounds in irradiated meat. Z. Lebensm. Unters. Forsch. *171*, 1.

PFEIFFER, E.H. and DUNKELBERG, H. 1980. Mutagenicity of ethylene oxide and propylene oxide and of the glycols and halohydrins formed from them during the fumigation of foodstuffs. Fd. Cosmet. Toxicol. *18*, 115.

PHILLIPS, B.J. and ELIAS, P.S. 1979. A new approach to investigating the genetic toxicity of processed foods. Fd. Cosmet. Toxicol. *16*, 509.

PROCTOR, B.E. and GOLDBLITH, S.A. 1951. Electromagnetic radiation fundamentals and their application in food technology. Adv. Food Res. *3*, 119.

PROCTOR, B.E., GOLDBLITH, S.A., and FRAM, H. 1950. Effect of supervoltage cathode rays on bacterial flora of spices and other dry food materials. Food Res. *15*, 490.

REDDI, O.S., REDDY, P.P., EBENEZER, D.N., and NAIDU, N.V. 1977. Lack of genetic and cytogenetic effects in mice fed on irradiated wheat. Int. J. Rad. Biol. *31*, 589.

REDMAN, D.G., AXFORD, D.W.E., ELTON, G.A.H., and BRIVATI, J.A. 1966. Mechanically produced radicals in flour. Chem. Ind. (London), 1298.

RENNER, H.W. 1975. Search for a combined effect of a chemical mutagen and radiation-sterilized feed by mutagenicity test and reproduction study in mice. Fd. Cosmet. Toxicol. *13*, 427. (German)

RENNER, H.W., GRÜNEWALD, T., and EHRENBERG-KIECKEBUSCH, W. 1973. Mutagenicity test of irradiated foods by dominant-lethal assay. Humangenetik *18*, 155. (German)

RENNER, H.W. and REICHELT, D. 1973. On the wholesomeness of high concentrations of free radicals in irradiated foods. Zentralbl. Vet. Med. B. *20*, 648. (German)

ROESSLER, I. and HAMM, R. 1979. Changes in muscle proteins due to treating beef and pork with electron rays. Fleischwirtschaft *59*, 1325. (German)

ROSENKRANZ, S., CARR, H.S., and ROSENKRANZ, H.S. 1974. 2-Haloethanols: Mutagenicity and reactivity with DNA. Mutation Res. *26*, 367.

SCHUBERT, J. 1967. Inadequacies in radiobiological experiments on medium effects. Int. J. Radiat. Biol. *13*, 297.

SHAW, M.W. and HAYES, E. 1966. Effects of irradiated sucrose on the chromosomes of human lymphocytes *in vitro*. Nature *211*, 1254.

SILBERSTEIN, O., GALETTO, W., and HENZI, W. 1979. Irradiation of onion powder; effect on microbiology. J. Food Sci. *44*, 975.

TAJIMA, M., MORITA, M., and FUJIMAKI, M. 1969. Radiation chemistry of foods. 3. Radiolysis of sulfur-containing amino acids in aqueous glucose solution. Agr. Biol. Chem. (Tokyo) *33*, 1277.

TAUB, I.A., ANGELINI, P., and MERRITT, C. JR. 1976. Irradiated food: validity of extrapolating wholesomeness data. J. Food Sci. *41*, 942.

TAUB, I.A., KAPRIELIAN, R.A., HALLIDAY, J.W., WALKER, J.E., ANGELINI, P., and MERRITT, C. JR. 1979A. Factors affecting radiolytic effects in food. Radiat. Phys. Chem. *14*, 639.

TAUB, I.A., ROBBINS, F.M., SIMIC, M.C., WALKER, J.E., and WIERBICKI, E. 1979B. Effect of irradiation on meat proteins. Food Technol. *33* (5) 184.

TESH, J.M., DAVIDSON, E.S., WALKER, S., PALMER, A.K., COZENS, D.D., and RICHARDSON, J.C. 1977. Studies in rats fed a diet incorporating irradiated wheat. International Project in the Field of Food Irradiation. Technical Report Series IFIP-R 45. Karlsruhe, W. Germany.

TJABERG, T.B., UNDERDAL, B., and LUNDE, G. 1972. The effect of ionizing radiation on the microbiological content and volatile constituents of spices. J. Appl. Bact. *35*, 473.

UCHIYAMA, S. and UCHIYAMA, M. 1979. Free radical production in protein-rich foods. J. Food Sci. *44*, 1217.

VAJDI, M. and PEREIRA, R.R. 1973. Comparative effects of ethylene oxide, gamma irradiation and microwave treatments on selected spices. J. Food Sci. *38*, 893.

VIJAYALAXMI and SADASIVAN, G. 1975. Chromosomal aberrations in rats fed irradiated wheat. Int. J. Rad. Biol. *27*, 135.

VIJAYALAXMI and RAO, K.V. 1976. Dominant lethal mutation in rats fed on irradiated wheat. Int. J. Rad. Biol. *29*, 93.

VON SONNTAG, C. 1980. Free radical reactions of carbohydrates as studied by radiation techniques. Adv. Carbohydr. Chem. Biochem. *37*, 7.

WHO. 1965. The Technical Basis for Legislation on Irradiated Food. World Health Organization Technical Report Series No. 316, Geneva.

WHO. 1977. Wholesomeness of Irradiated Food. World Health Organization Technical Report Series No. 604, Geneva.

WIERBICKI, E. 1979. The importance and feasibility of irradiated low nitrite meat products. Activity Reports (Natick) *31* (2) 70.

WILMER, J., LEVELING, H. and SCHUBERT, J. 1980. Mutagenicity of irradiated solutions of 2-deoxy-D-ribose. Mutation Res. *78*, 85.

20

Food Packaging: An Overview of Regulatory and Safety Assessments

Robert M. Miller[1]

There is a popular Virginia Slims cigarettes advertisement indicating that "You've come a long way, baby." It seems that this slogan adequately describes developments in food packaging and food packaging regulations over the last several years. Even though the package is not usually eaten, there can be some wanted and unwanted substances present in it too, some of which might transfer to the food. That is why we have regulations and safety evaluations for food packages, as well as for food.

We have gone from the cracker barrel or very little packaging to complex, convenient, functional, and fancy packaging made up of myriads of materials; we have progressed in analytical chemistry accomplishments from the detection of as little as one part per million to the capability of detecting one part per billion or even a few parts per trillion; we have gone from relatively simple, short laws and regulations to more expanded laws and complex, restrictive regulations which many do not understand; and, finally, we have been pushed from little or no concern about food additives and food packaging to widespread public concern about such things. Indeed, we have come a long way, baby, but has it been entirely for the best?

In the beginning, packages probably were developed as a convenient means of holding food and getting it to the consumer, as well as offering some protection from the environment. Later it became evident that the package not only could perform these functions but also could act as a sales or marketing aid for the product packaged. This fostered the development of fancier, more functional, more convenient packages

[1] Hercules Inc., Wilmington, Delaware.

which blazed forth trade names of products and their manufacturers to bring them into the public's eye. How is the safety of these packages evaluated?

FEDERAL REGULATIONS

Since the Food Additives Amendment of 1958, amending the U.S. Federal Food, Drug, and Cosmetic Act, all food additives, including those migrating to food from food packaging materials and equipment, must have clearance from the U.S. Food and Drug Administration (FDA) prior to use unless they are exempt under one of the provisions of the law. A "food additive," according to the Act, is defined as any substance "the intended use of which results or may reasonably be expected to result" in its becoming a component of food, unless the substance is "generally recognized as safe" (GRAS) or has prior approval. The significance of meeting this definition is that no food additive can be used unless it has received the prior approval of the FDA. The burden of establishing safety rests squarely on the person seeking approval. On the other hand, if a substance is not a food additive, its use in food or food packaging is not prohibited unless it is a "deleterious substance which may render the food injurious to health." In this instance, the burden is on the government to establish a reasonable potential for harm.

Prior to 1958, food packaging was not specifically regulated under the food and drug law; it was covered indirectly by the fact that no poisonous or deleterious substance could be added to food, including transfer from packaging. At that time, a compound was considered to be nonmigrating if it extracted into food-simulating solvents at a level of less than one part per *million*. Many substances were tested at this level and found not to migrate, becoming prior sanctioned and exempt from the 1958 law. Most still remain exempt. Some materials also were tested for toxicity, and if they were extremely low in toxicity, were permitted to be used in contact with food after referral to the FDA. There were no regulations listing substances that could be safely used in contact with food, as there are today. It was a fairly simple procedure.

The U.S. Department of Agriculture, which has jurisdiction over the packaging of meat and poultry food products in federally inspected packing establishments, had a procedure similar to that of the FDA prior to 1958. They still do not have regulations listing materials which may be used, as does the FDA, but they do approve packages and contact articles for meat and poultry products. Approval may be obtained by means of private communications, after supplying information on composition, toxicity, and safety of use. Clearance by the FDA usually is required as a condition for approval. The USDA approval is not published.

Over the 20-plus years since the advent of the Food Additives Amendment and its specific coverage of food-contact materials, numerous new packaging materials have been developed, some based on newly created polymers, additives, and combinations of a variety of substances. In addition, new types of foods have been developed, as well as methods of preparation. Thus we have gone from the simple cracker barrel era to standard types of packages (glass jars, cans, paper and paperboard, plastic), to more sophisticated forms and combinations of these standard packages (laminates, new coatings, coextrusions, molded metal, paperboard and plastic containers, retort pouches, etc.). Some foods are cooked or reheated in the container, under normal cooking or baking conditions or in microwave ovens, thus creating somewhat different processing circumstances than were formerly considered usual. Of course, the packaging material used must be safe for its intended use and must be in compliance with appropriate FDA (or USDA) food additive regulations.

ANALYSIS AND DETECTION

Another change during this time period is the current ability to detect miniscule quantities of substances in food or food-simulating solvents with the development of sophisticated analytical equipment and techniques. Whereas a few years ago it was considered an accomplishment to be able to detect a compound at a level of one part per million, facilities are available today for the detection of these substances at levels of parts per billion or even parts per trillion. Therefore, compounds previously thought to be absent at one part per million or even at tenths of a part per million and not detected may now be found and confirmed present at these much lower levels. It is obvious that this can affect the conclusion that a substance is not present or does not migrate to food. This can be important, since if a component of food packaging does not migrate ("no migrations") to food under use conditions, it is not a food additive and is exempt from formal clearance. However, there is no definition for "no migration," and as analytical sensitivity improves, the "no migration" level, if there is one, creeps lower and lower. We do not know where this will lead us, but let us hope that the various government agencies recognize the problem and are reasonable in their interpretation of what is significant.

DETERMINATION OF SAFETY LEVELS

With the introduction of new and improved food packaging materials, new food types and methods of preparation, and the ability to detect these miniscule quantities, how does one establish the safety of new or modified packaging compounds for use with all these types of foods under various conditions of preparation and storage? The answers are basic, except where one is attempting to demonstrate that a material does not migrate to food, since in this latter instance the analytical detection limits come into play. For the usual situation, it is necessary to determine what may migrate to food, how much may migrate under normal and exaggerated conditions of use, and whether this amount is safe. This requires analytical data to determine what migrates, migration studies to ascertain how much may migrate, and toxicological studies to determine if the amount that may enter the diet from contact with food is safe. These toxicological studies, usually feeding tests, are the same type used for direct food additives. With these data in hand, a safety evaluation may be made. If the results are promising and the product is of commercial interest, a food additive petition would be prepared and submitted to the FDA, requesting a regulation permitting the use of the product in food packaging. If the FDA agrees with the results and is satisfied that the proposed use is safe, a regulation will be prepared and published in the *Federal Register*. After publication, the product then may be marketed and used for the purpose described in the regulation.

The above sounds simple; it is not. It is much more complicated in real life than in theory and may encompass a total of a few to several years and many thousands of dollars from start to finish in obtaining a regulation. Usually the product must be defined chemically with appropriate specifications and methods of analysis. Problems may be encountered in migration studies, requiring difficult method development in the presence of other compounds, with validation of the procedure. Sometimes radioactive labeling must be resorted to in order to establish migration level. Depending upon the amount of migration to food or the results of short-term feeding studies, more detailed and costly longer-term toxicological studies may be required. An environmental impact analysis report may be necessary to indicate the effect on the environment. There may be additional questions from the FDA which must be answered in order to establish fully the safety of the product in use.

This demonstrates how complicated it can be to obtain FDA clearance for a new food packaging material. Of course, some clearances are much more complex, costly, and time-consuming than others, depending upon the product, use, migration level, toxicity, and other circumstances. A case history, in summary form, will serve as one example. This is the FDA clearance of polypropylene for broad, general use in contact with food. The major steps, not necessarily in chronological order, are listed below:

FDA Clearance of Polypropylene

1. Commercial product defined.
2. Potential uses evaluated, including food packaging.
3. New product—need for FDA petition determined.
4. Migration to food—does it migrate, what migrates, how much, how to find out?
5. No good analytical handle—decision to use radioactive labeling.
6. Tagged sample prepared—demonstrated to be typical of commercial material.
7. Migration studies showed no significant migration to aqueous foods; only migrates to fatty foods.
8. Substance migrating is low molecular weight polypropylene and noncrystalline polypropylene.
9. Decision made not to feed whole polymer—best to feed material that could migrate.
10. Tagged sample extracted with hot vegetable oil—extract fed rats to determine if any absorbed from gastrointestinal tract. None was absorbed, thus product was safe for ingestion.
11. Petition written, defining polymer found to be safe, and submitted to FDA.
12. Regulation published, permitting use.
13. Epilogue—with new uses like retort pouches, extraction tests at these higher temperatures conducted to demonstrate safety.

This example demonstrates how some packaging materials receive FDA clearance for food contact use. How do the food companies and food packagers assure the safety of the packaging they use? First of all, they demand certification of FDA compliance from the package supplier. In turn, the package supplier requires certification of compliance from his supplier, usually the furnisher of the raw materials. The raw material supplier can certify compliance, since he usually is the manufacturer, although he may find it necessary to obtain guarantees for compliance of minor additives or other materials he purchases and uses. At any rate, the burden of providing compliance certification usually falls on the raw materials supplier.

How can the raw material supplier furnish this certification? It is general practice to conduct sufficient tests on a manufacturer's product to assure compliance with the appropriate regulation. These investigations may comprise analytical tests, solubility determinations or toxicological studies if indicated. The customary industry policy is to run enough tests on a product of their manufacture to assure themselves, and government agencies if necessary, that their product is safe for its intended use. Suppliers also usually have a quality assurance or good manufacturing practices program to ensure compliance and uniformity of product.

Yes, things have changed, as they should, and yes, we have come a long way, baby, sometimes for the better and sometimes perhaps not. Life has become more complicated with these changes, regulations, and increased requirements, but remember: there is no known instance where there has been human injury caused by a food packaging material. Government regulation of food contact items may become more unbearable and restrictive in the 1980s in many respects, but there is light at the end of the tunnel which may indicate a more reasonable realistic attitude before this decade ends. The slogan for the decade will be "Risk Assessments;" let us hope it works and that we continue to have government-industry cooperation to produce safe and useful food packaging materials.

Index

Other AVI Books

ALCOHOL AND THE DIET
Roe
BASIC FOOD MICROBIOLOGY
Banwart
EVALUATION OF PROTEINS FOR HUMANS
Bodwell
EXPERIMENTAL FOOD CHEMISTRY
Mondy
FOOD ANALYSIS: THEORY AND PRACTICE
Revised Edition *Pomeranz and Meloan*
FOOD LAW HANDBOOK
Schultz
FOOD MICROBIOLOGY: PUBLIC HEALTH AND SPOILAGE ASPECTS
deFigueiredo and Splittstoesser
FOOD QUALITY ASSURANCE
Gould
FOOD SANITATION
Second Edition *Guthrie*
FOOD SCIENCE
Third Edition *Potter*
FOODBORNE AND WATERBORNE DISEASES: THEIR EPIDEMIOLOGIC CHARACTERISTICS
Tartakow and Vorperian
FUNDAMENTALS OF FOOD MICROBIOLOGY
Fields
IMMUNOLOGICAL ASPECTS OF FOODS
Catsimpoolas
NUTRITION AND FOOD PROCESSING
Muller and Tobin
PRINCIPLES OF FOOD CHEMISTRY
Revised Edition *deMan*
PROTEIN RESOURCES AND TECHNOLOGY
Milner, Scrimshaw and Wang
SAFETY OF FOODS
Second Edition *Graham*
SELENIUM IN BIOLOGY AND MEDICINE
Spallholz, Martin and Ganther
SOURCE BOOK OF FLAVORS
Heath
SOURCE BOOK OF FOOD ENZYMOLOGY
Schwimmer